*crimson
angel*

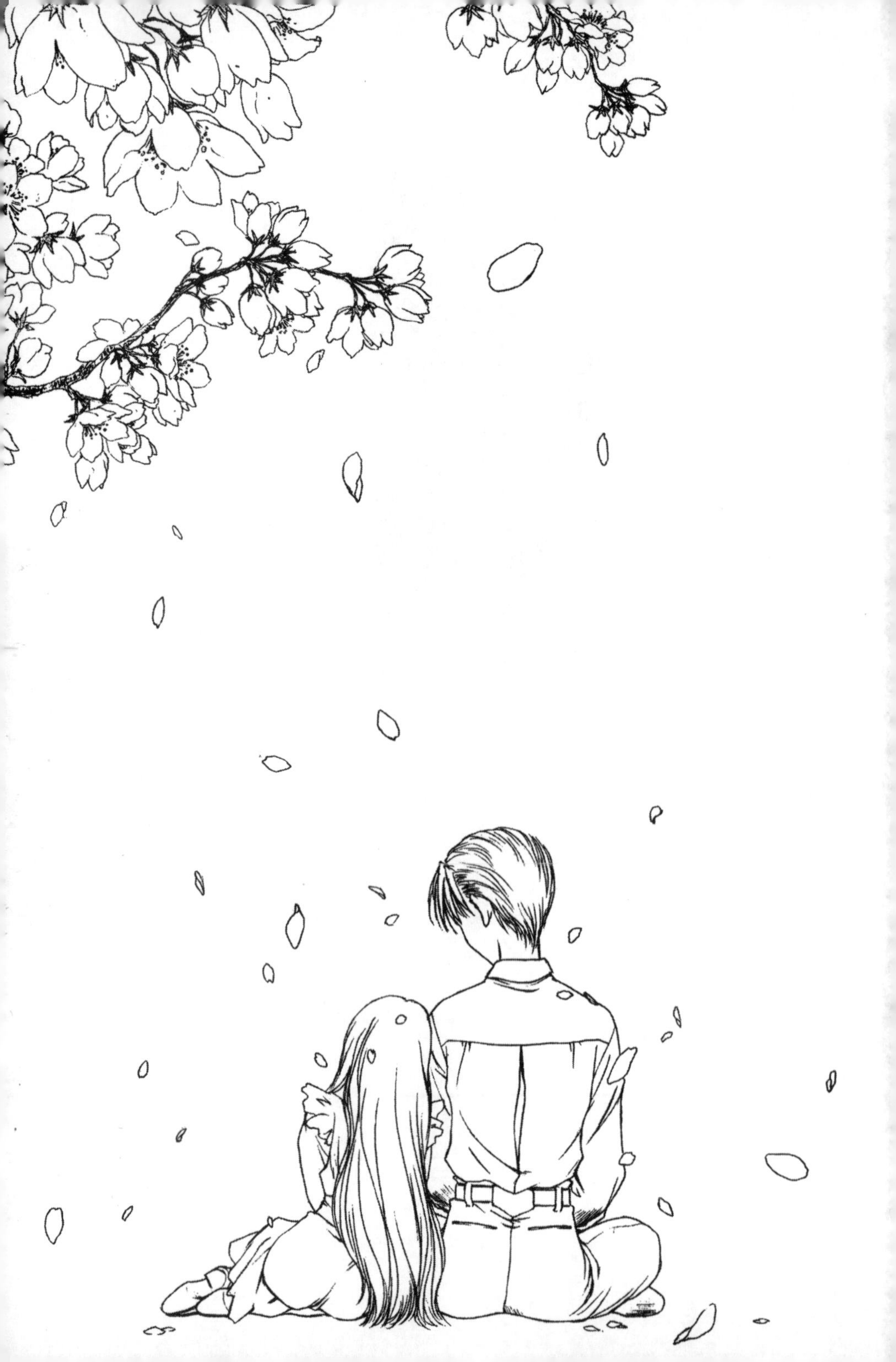

SERAPHIC FEATHER

Crimson Angel

art
HIROYUKI UTATANE

story
YO MORIMOTO

translation
DANA LEWIS and ADAM WARREN

lettering and touch-up
PAT DUKE & RADIO COMIX,
DAN JACKSON

DARK HORSE COMICS®

publisher
MIKE RICHARDSON

series editor
MIKE HANSEN

series executive editor
TOREN SMITH *for* STUDIO PROTEUS

collection editor
CHRIS WARNER

collection designer
DARIN FABRICK

art director
MARK COX

English-language version produced by STUDIO PROTEUS, RADIO COMIX,
and DARK HORSE COMICS, INC.

SERAPHIC FEATHER VOL. I: CRIMSON ANGEL

THIS VOLUME COLLECTS SERAPHIC FEATHER STORIES FROM ISSUES ONE, TWO, AND FOUR THROUGH NINE OF THE DARK HORSE COMIC-BOOK SERIES SUPER MANGA BLAST!

PUBLISHED BY
DARK HORSE COMICS, INC.
10956 SE MAIN STREET
MILWAUKIE, OR 97222

WWW.DARKHORSE.COM

TO FIND A COMICS SHOP IN YOUR AREA, CALL THE COMIC SHOP LOCATOR SERVICE TOLL-FREE AT 1-888-266-4226

FIRST EDITION: NOVEMBER 2001
ISBN: 1-56971-555-6

1 3 5 7 9 10 8 6 4 2

PRINTED IN CANADA

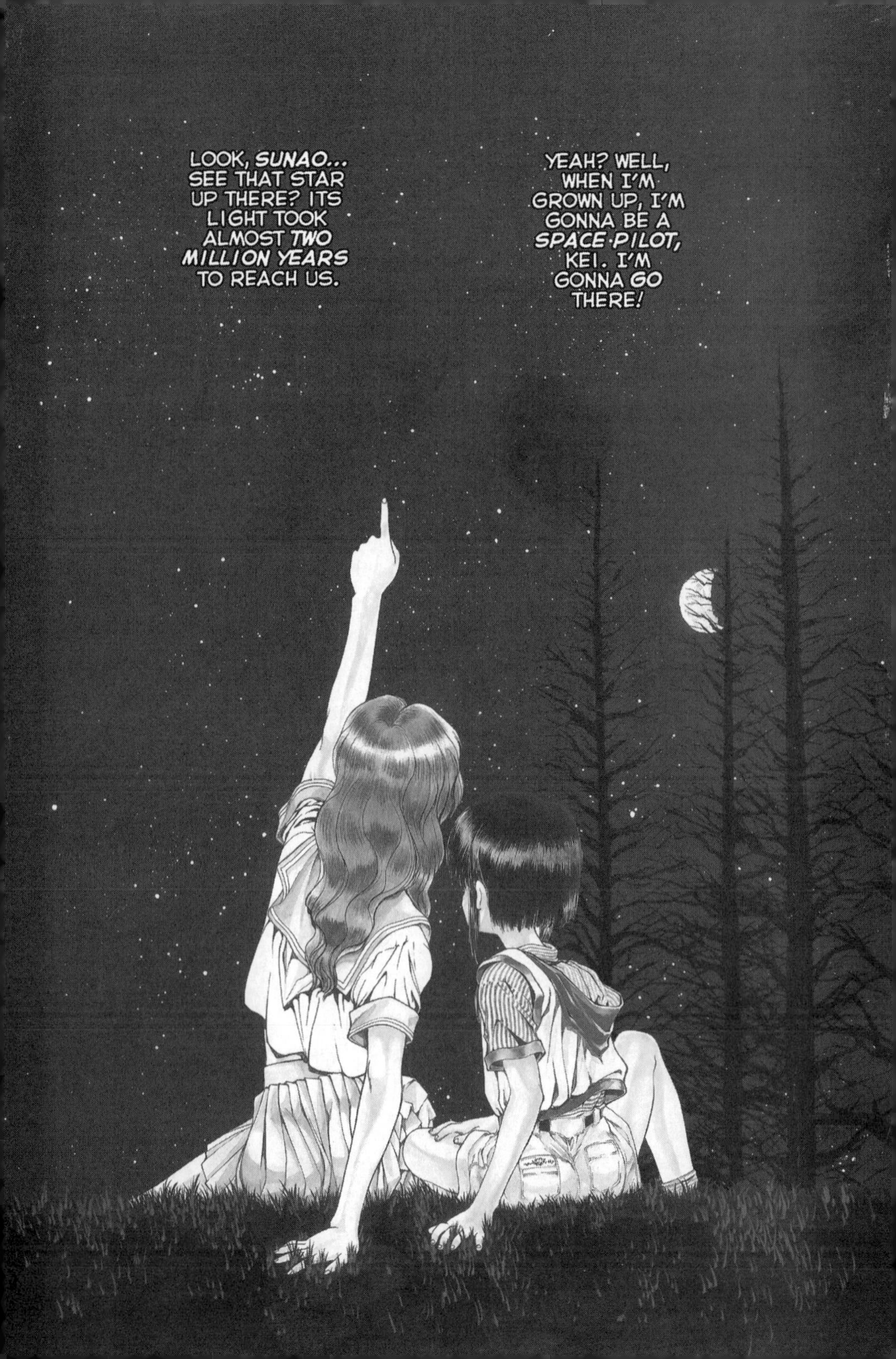
LOOK, SUNAO... SEE THAT STAR UP THERE? ITS LIGHT TOOK ALMOST TWO MILLION YEARS TO REACH US.
YEAH? WELL, WHEN I'M GROWN UP, I'M GONNA BE A SPACE-PILOT, KEI. I'M GONNA GO THERE!

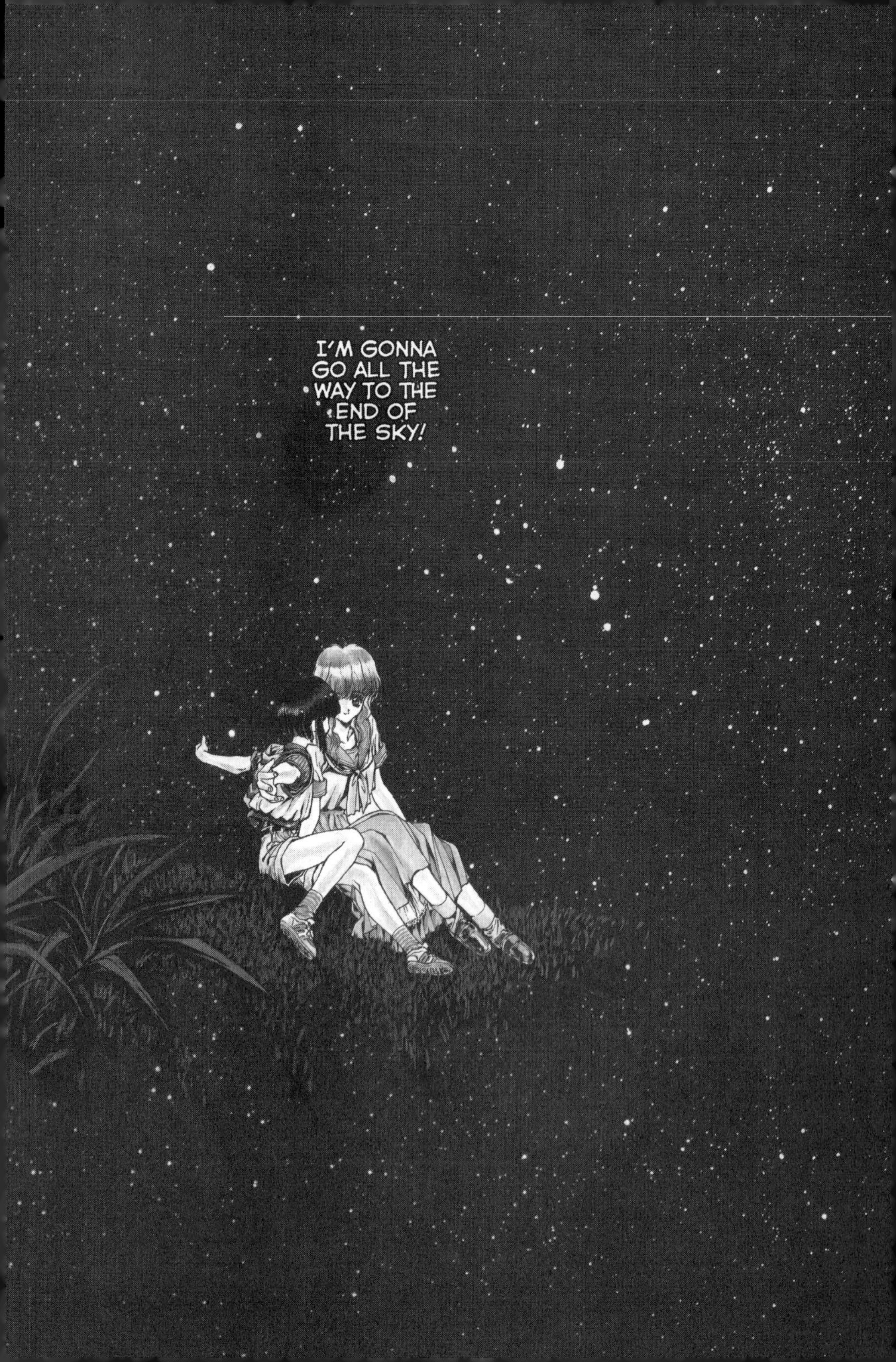
I'M GONNA GO ALL THE WAY TO THE END OF THE SKY!

SERAPHIC FEATHER

ACT 1

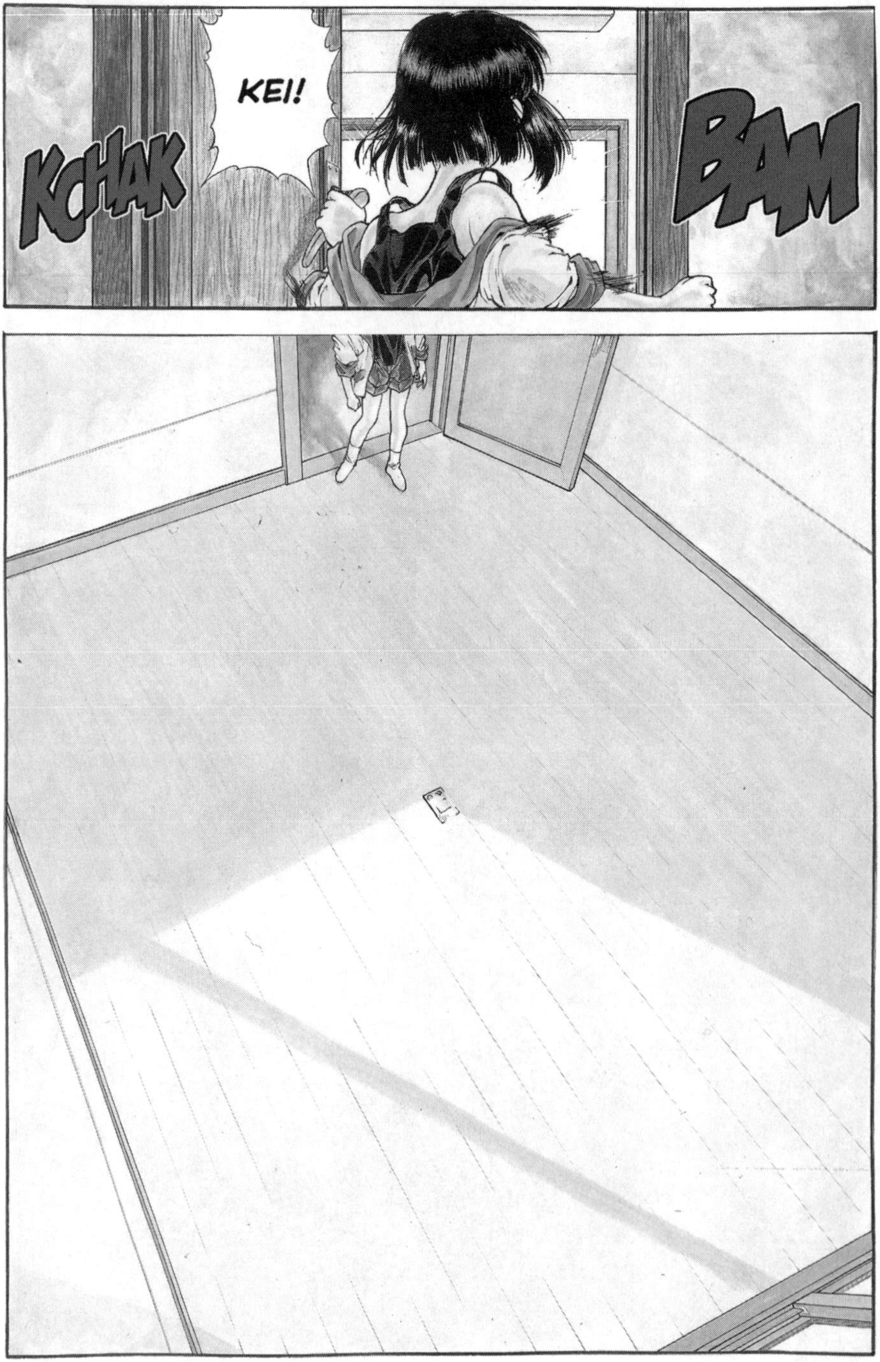
KCHAK
KEI!
BAM

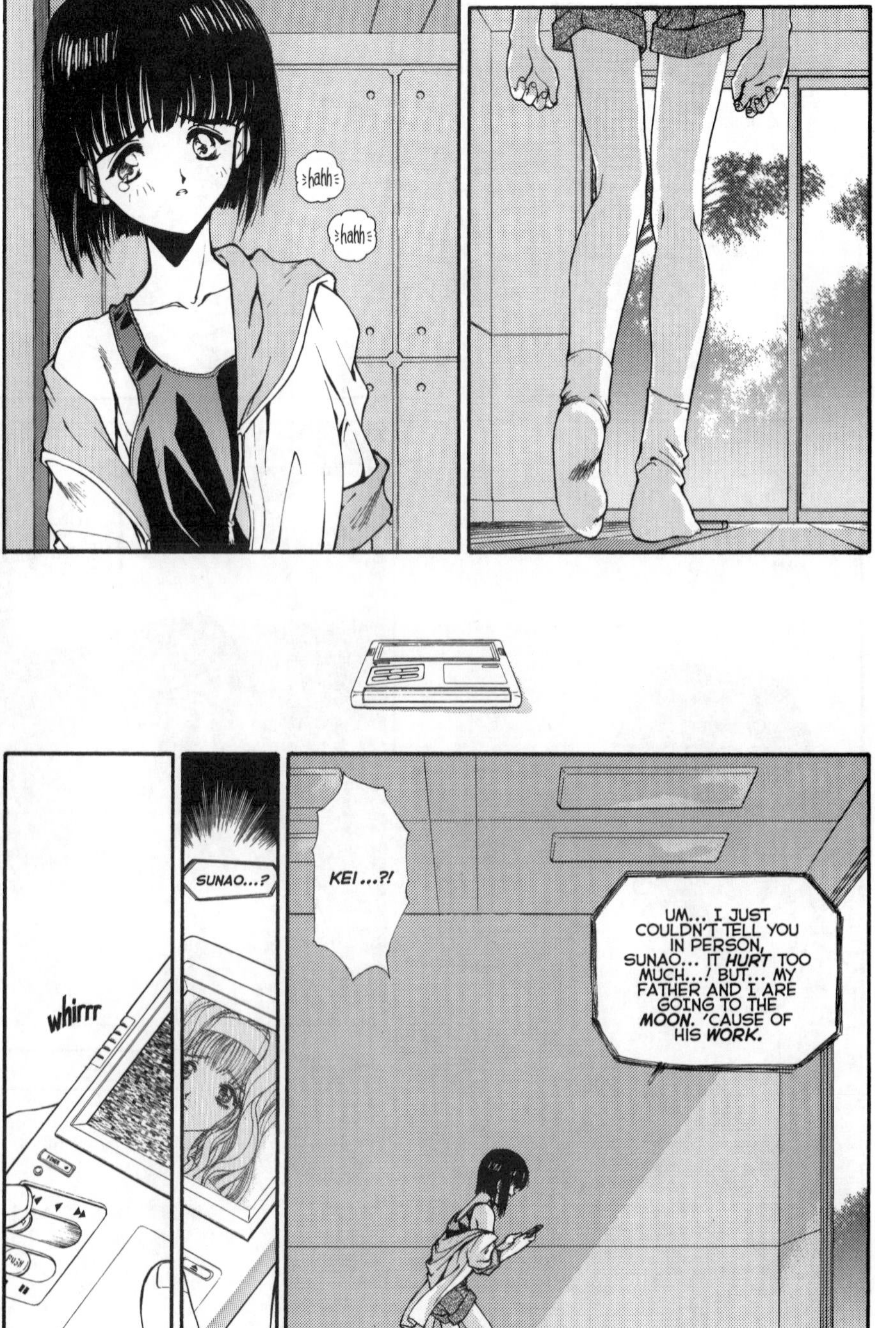
hahh
hahh
whirrr
SUNAO...?
KEI...?!
UM... I JUST COULDN'T TELL YOU IN PERSON, SUNAO... IT HURT TOO MUCH...! BUT... MY FATHER AND I ARE GOING TO THE MOON. 'CAUSE OF HIS WORK.

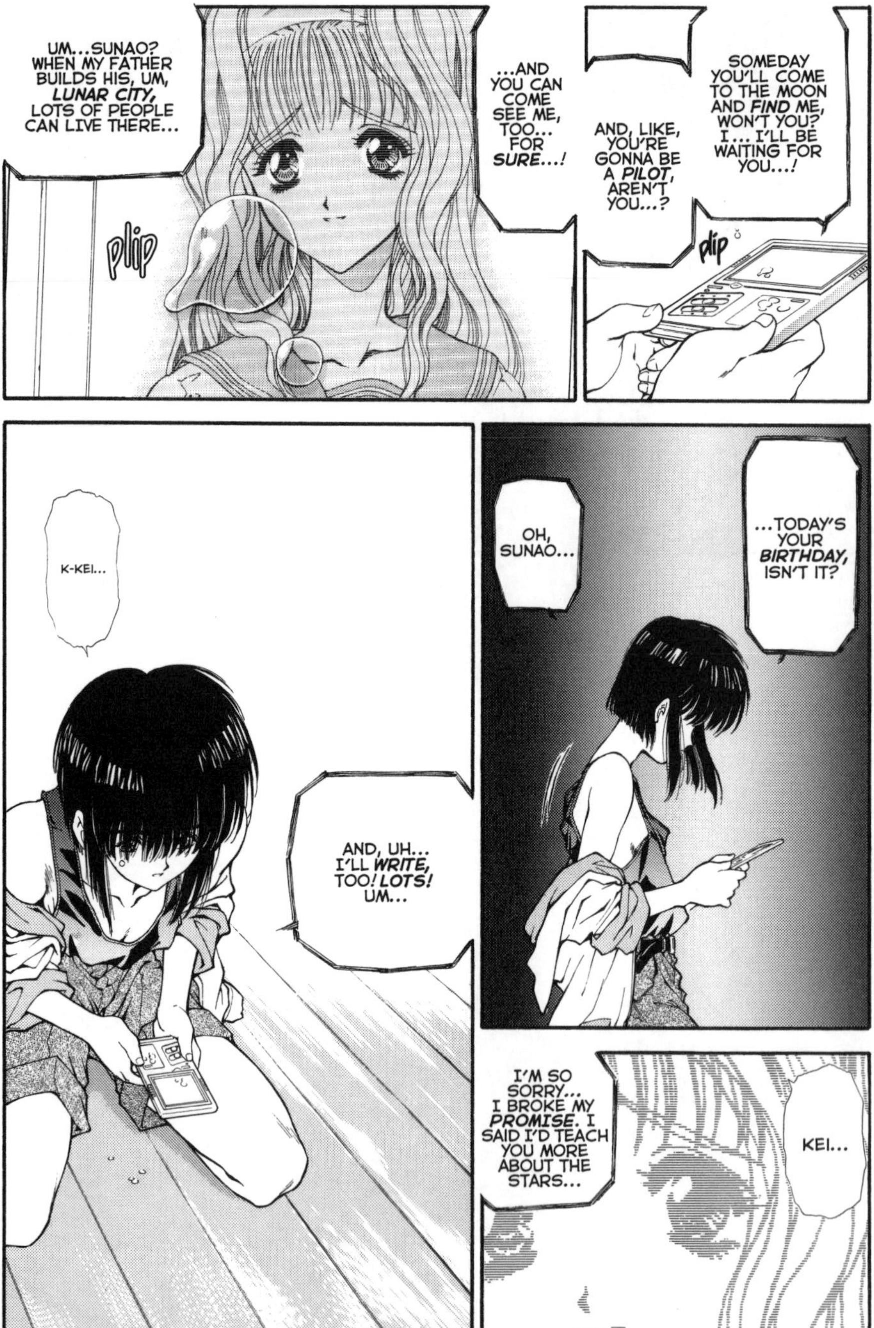

UM...SUNAO? WHEN MY FATHER BUILDS HIS, UM, LUNAR CITY, LOTS OF PEOPLE CAN LIVE THERE...
...AND YOU CAN COME SEE ME, TOO... FOR SURE...!
plip
AND, LIKE, YOU'RE GONNA BE A PILOT, AREN'T YOU...?
SOMEDAY YOU'LL COME TO THE MOON AND FIND ME, WON'T YOU? I... I'LL BE WAITING FOR YOU...!
plip
K-KEI...
AND, UH... I'LL WRITE, TOO! LOTS! UM...
OH, SUNAO...
...TODAY'S YOUR BIRTHDAY, ISN'T IT?
I'M SO SORRY... I BROKE MY PROMISE. I SAID I'D TEACH YOU MORE ABOUT THE STARS...
KEI...

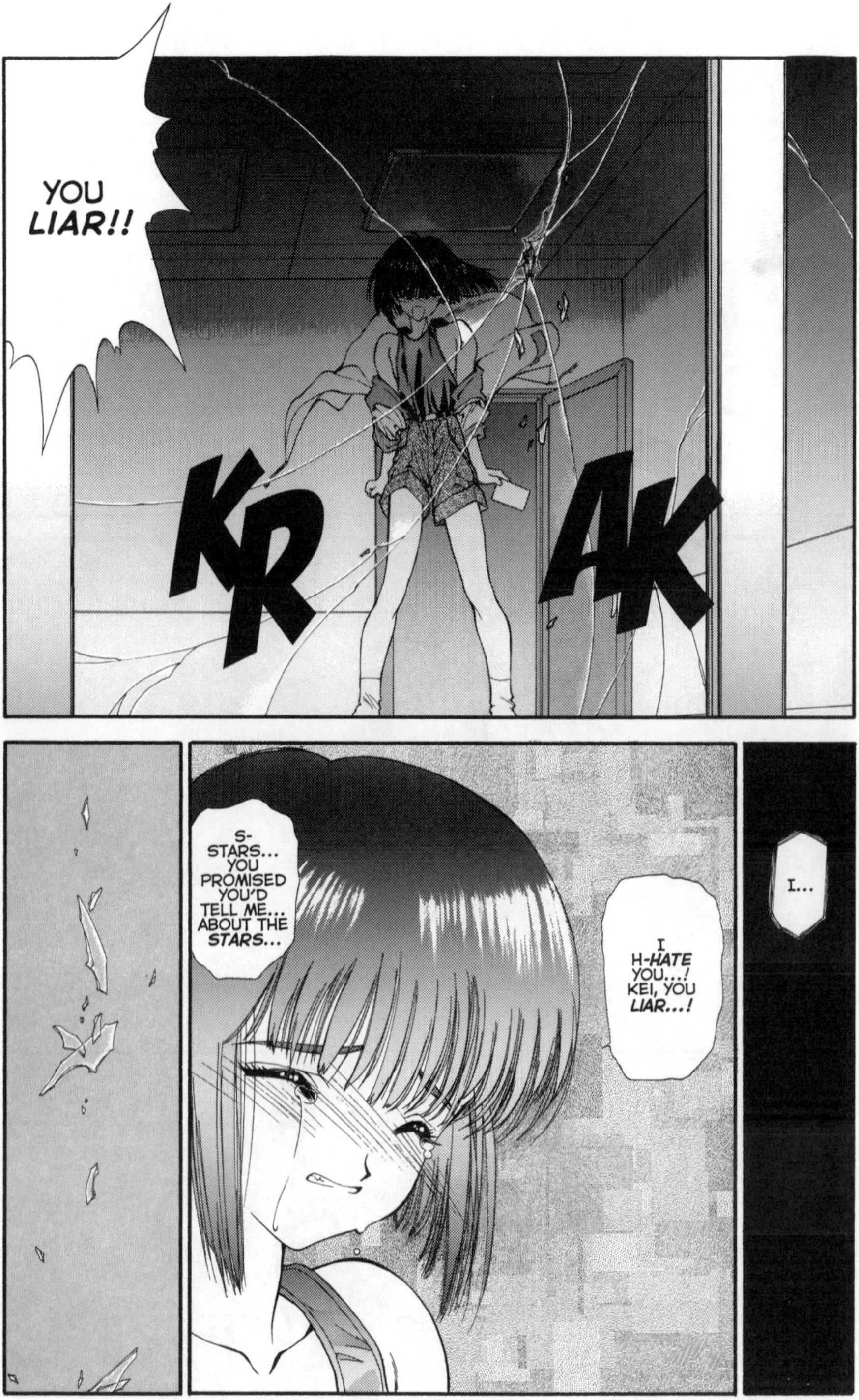
YOU *LIAR!!*
KRAK
S-STARS... YOU PROMISED YOU'D TELL ME... ABOUT THE *STARS...*
I H-*HATE* YOU...! KEI, YOU *LIAR...!*
I...

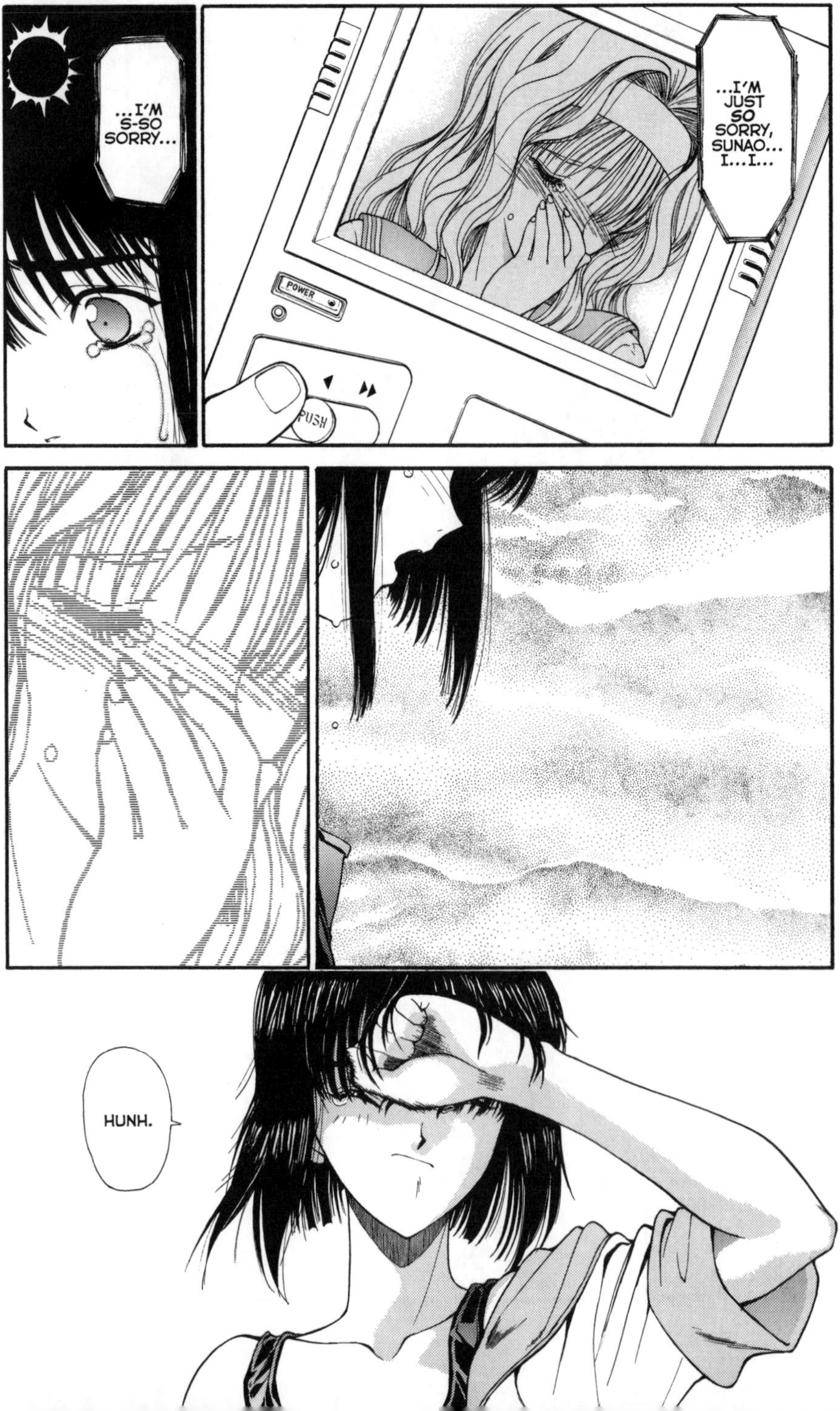
...I'M S-SO SORRY...
...I'M JUST SO SORRY, SUNAO... I...I...
POWER
PUSH
HUNH.

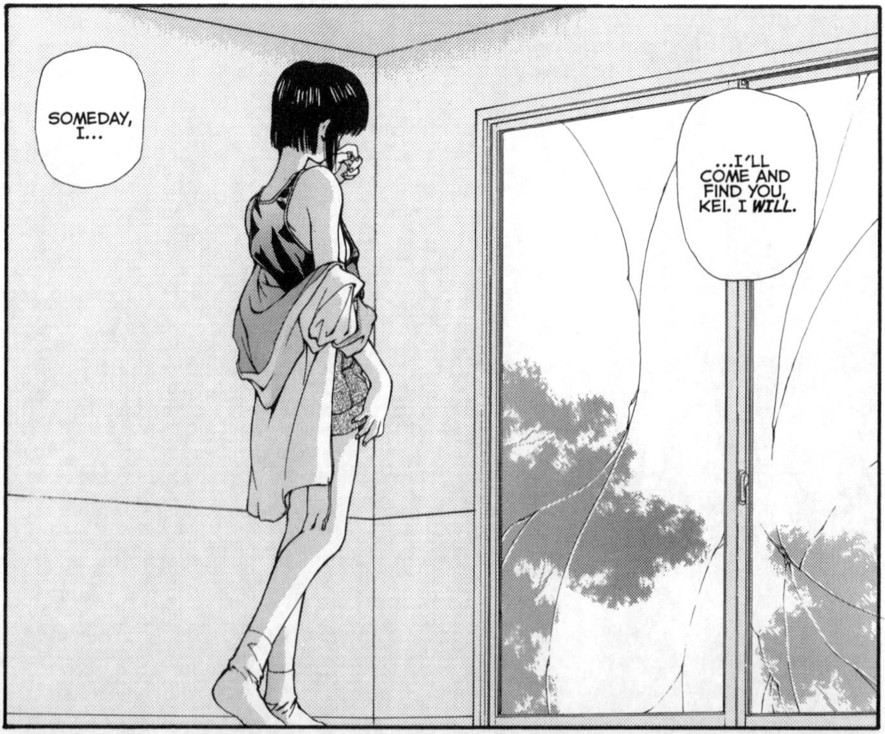
SOMEDAY, I...
...I'LL COME AND FIND YOU, KEI. I *WILL*.

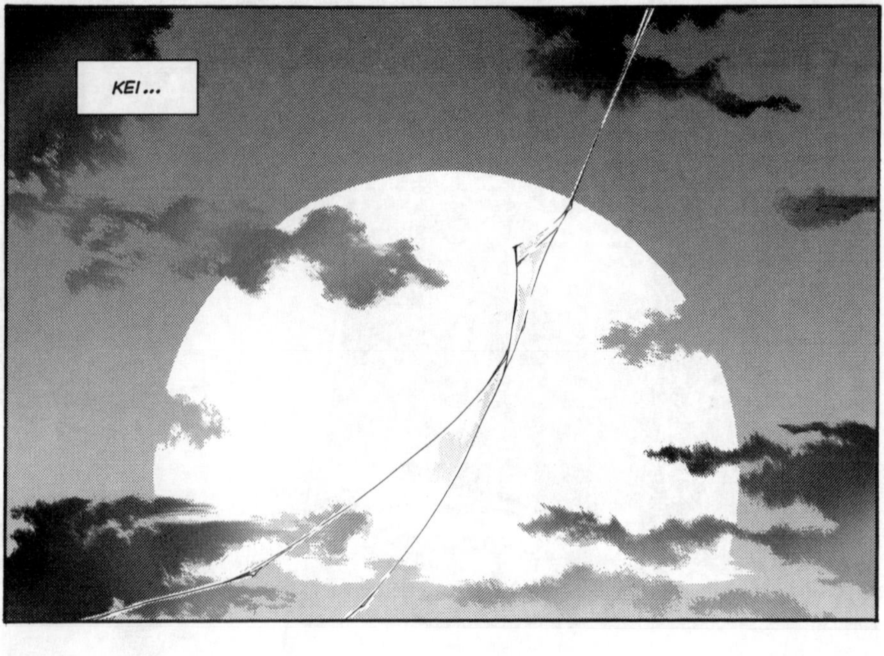
KEI...

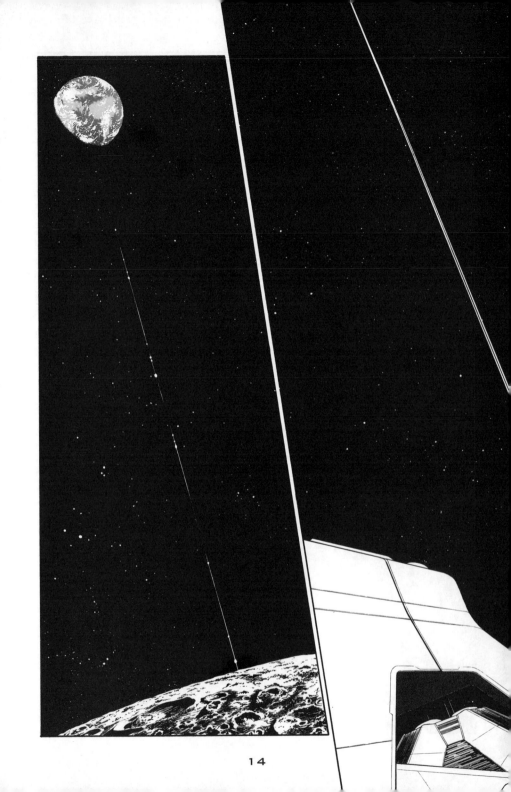

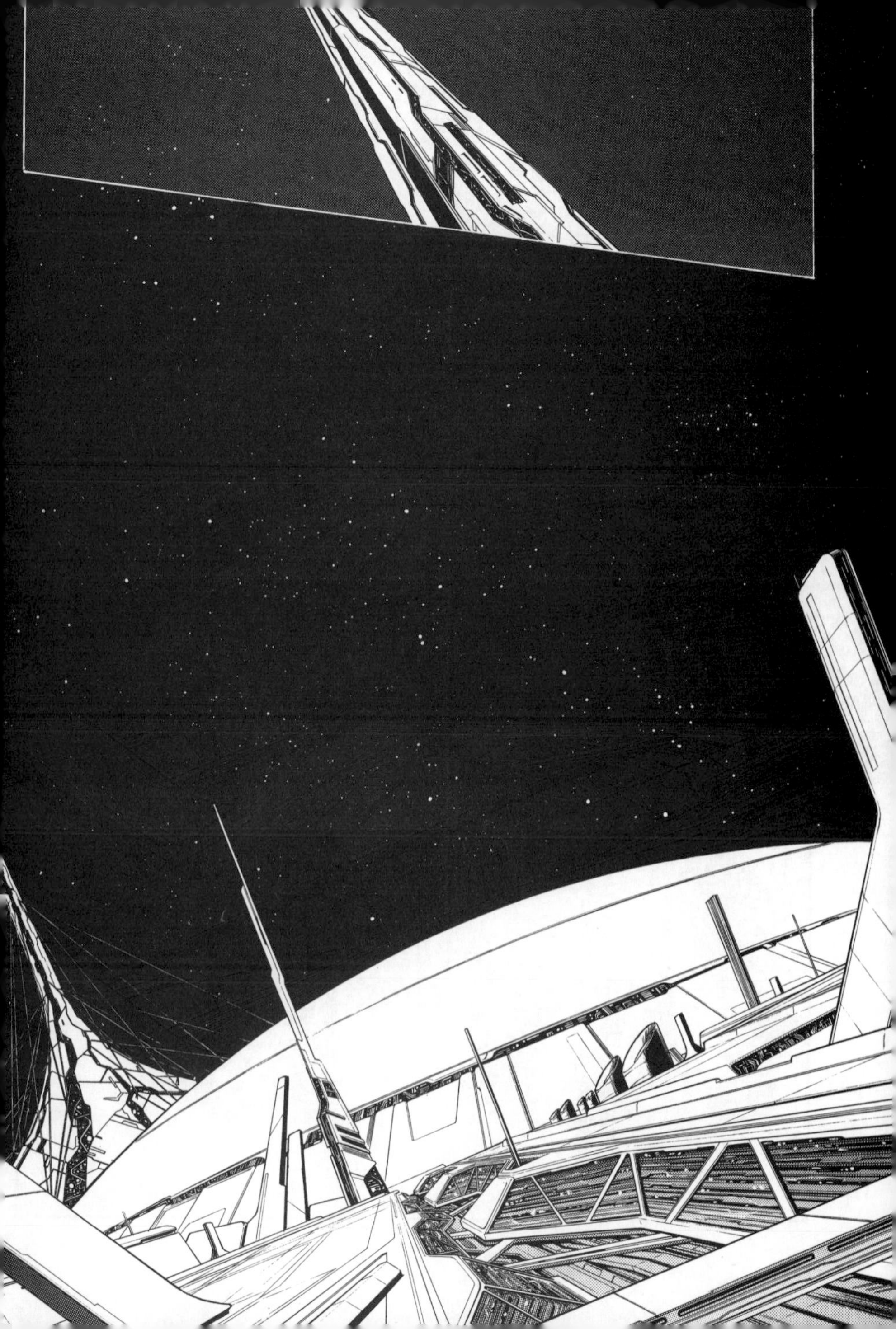

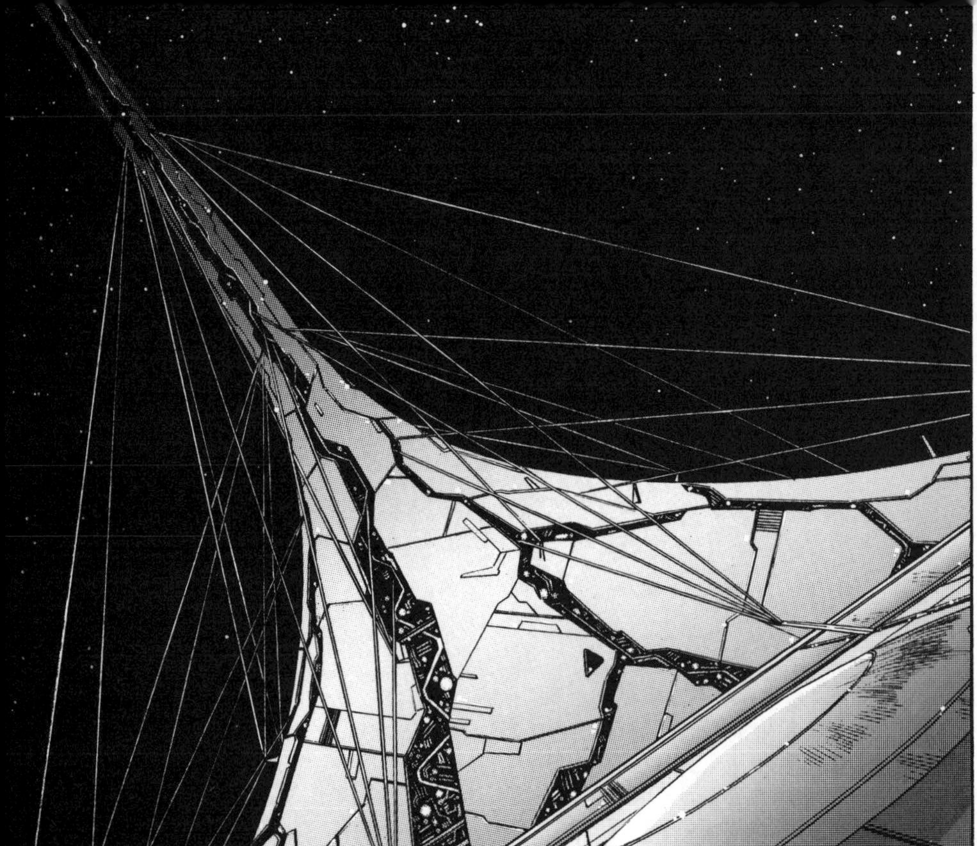

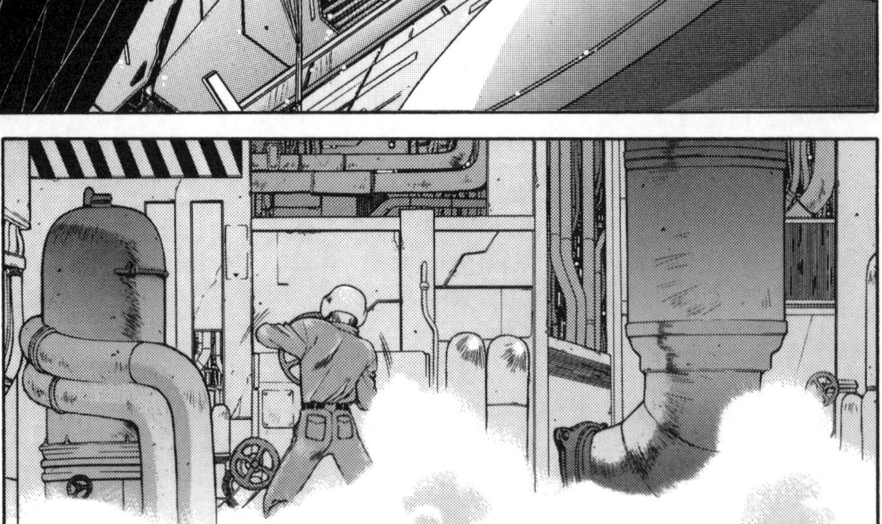

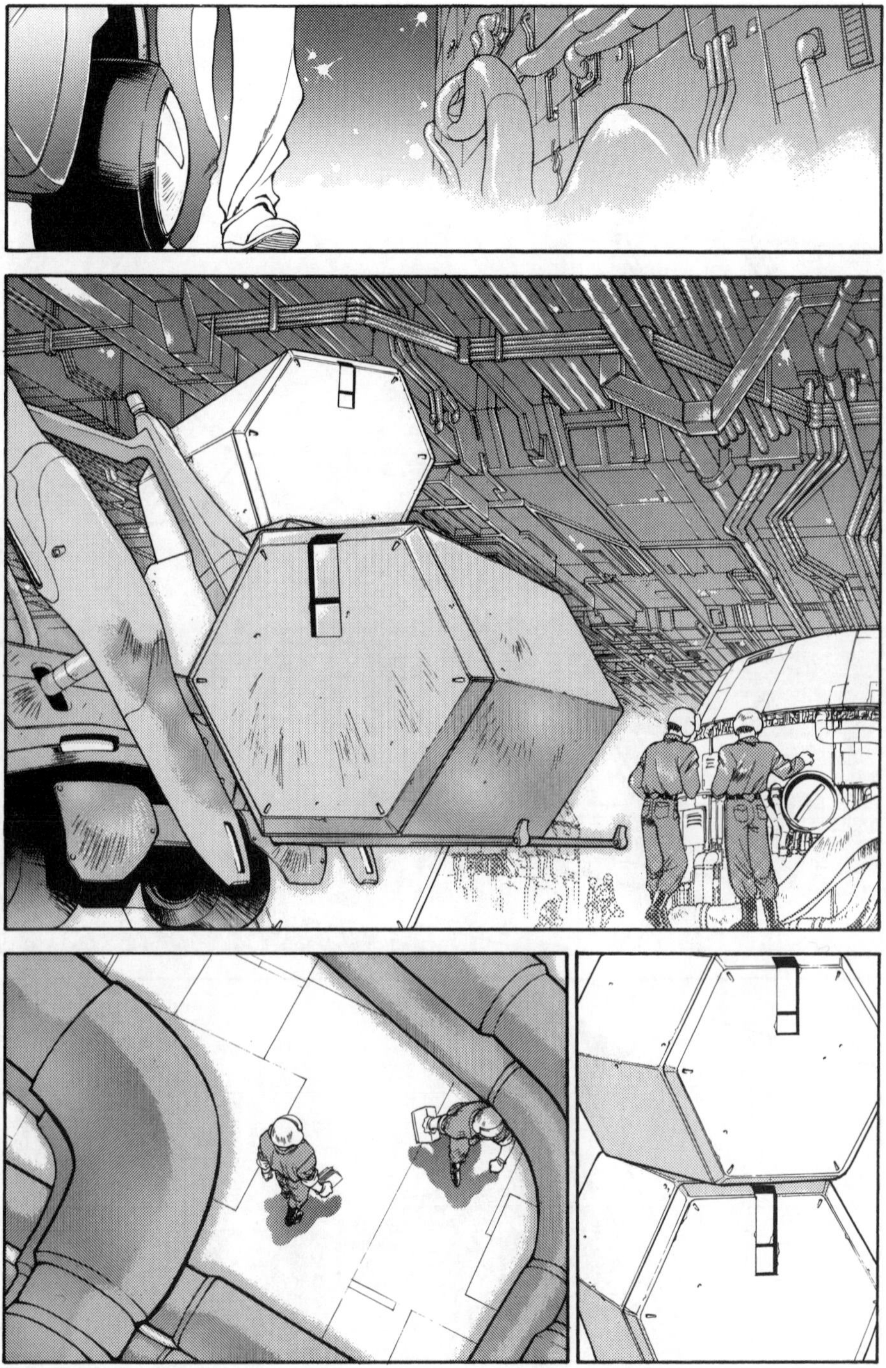

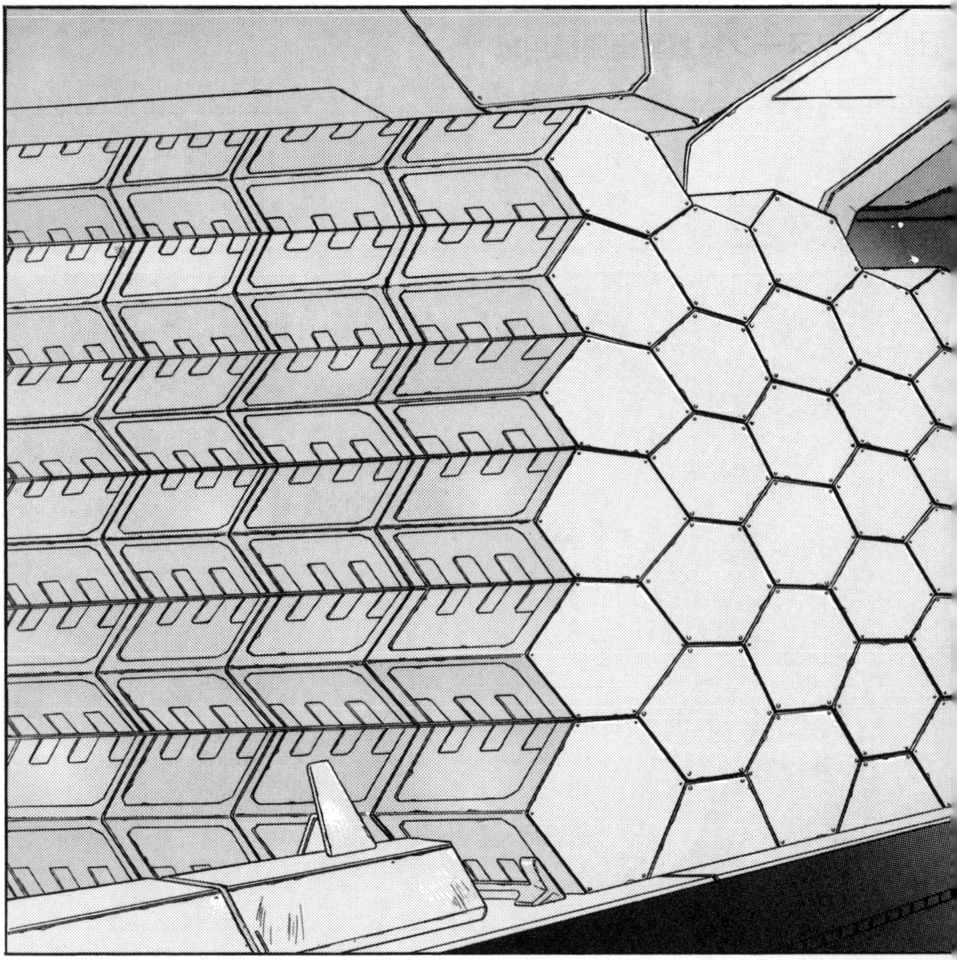

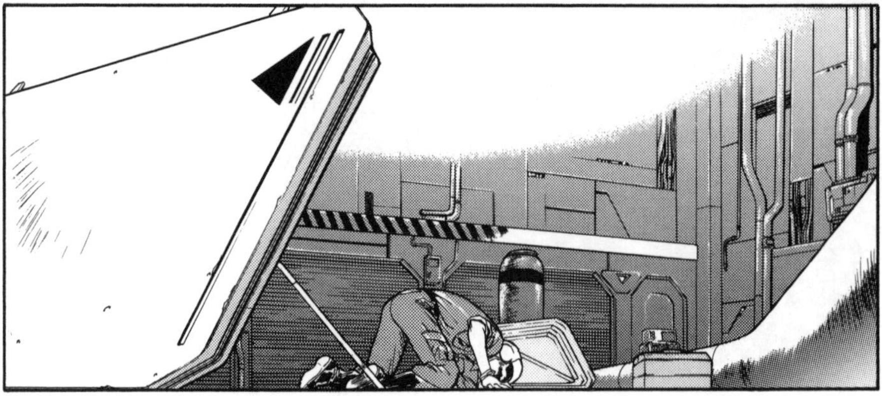

GAHH --!
Ting
Ktang

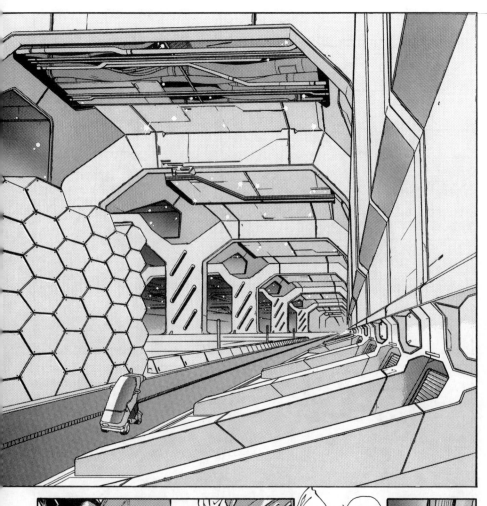

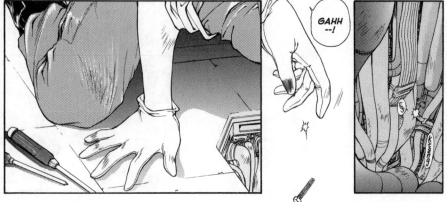

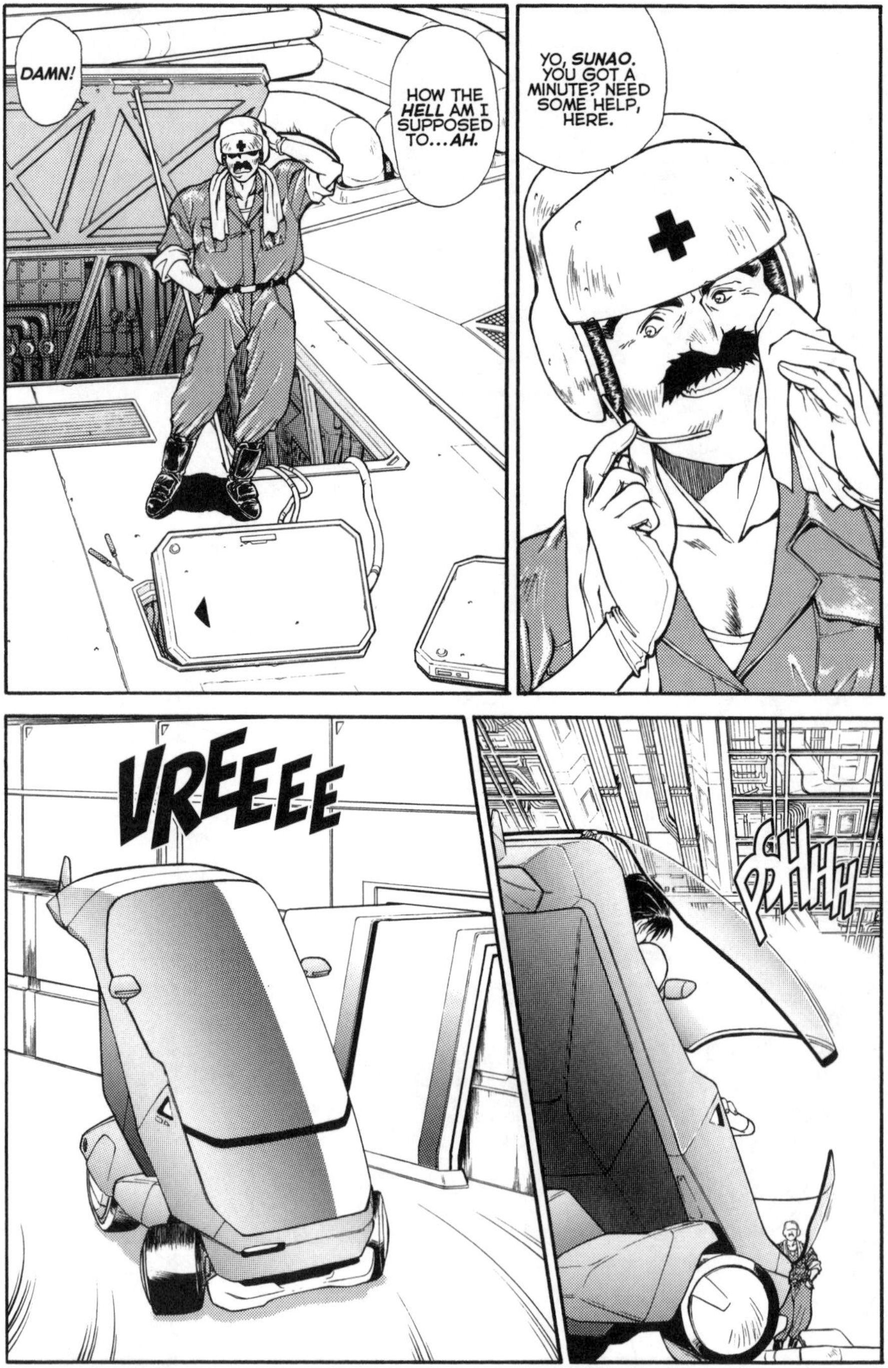

DAMN!
HOW THE HELL AM I SUPPOSED TO... AH.
YO, SUNAO. YOU GOT A MINUTE? NEED SOME HELP, HERE.
VREEEEE
PSHHH

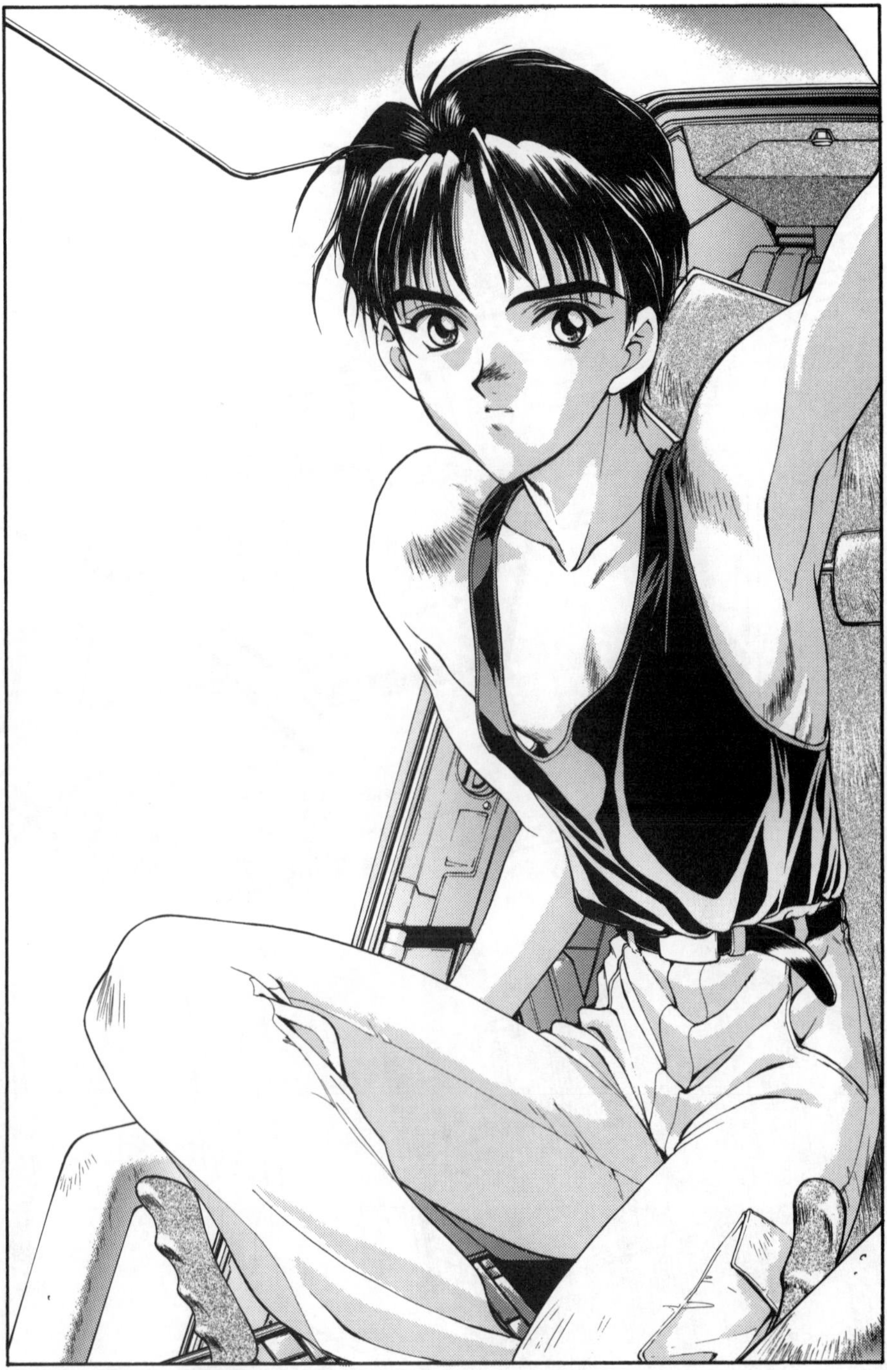

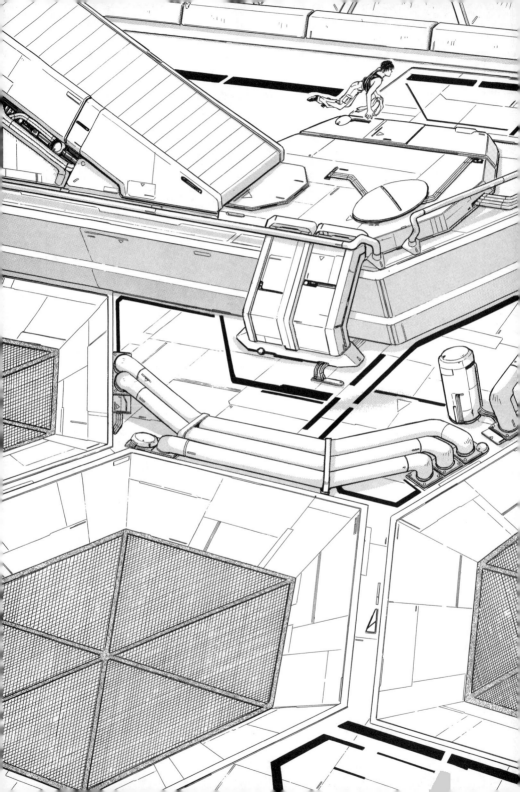

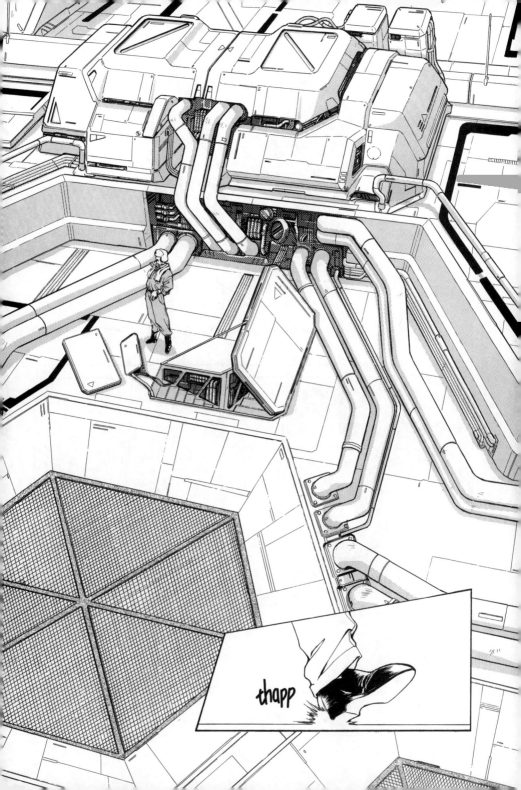

thapp

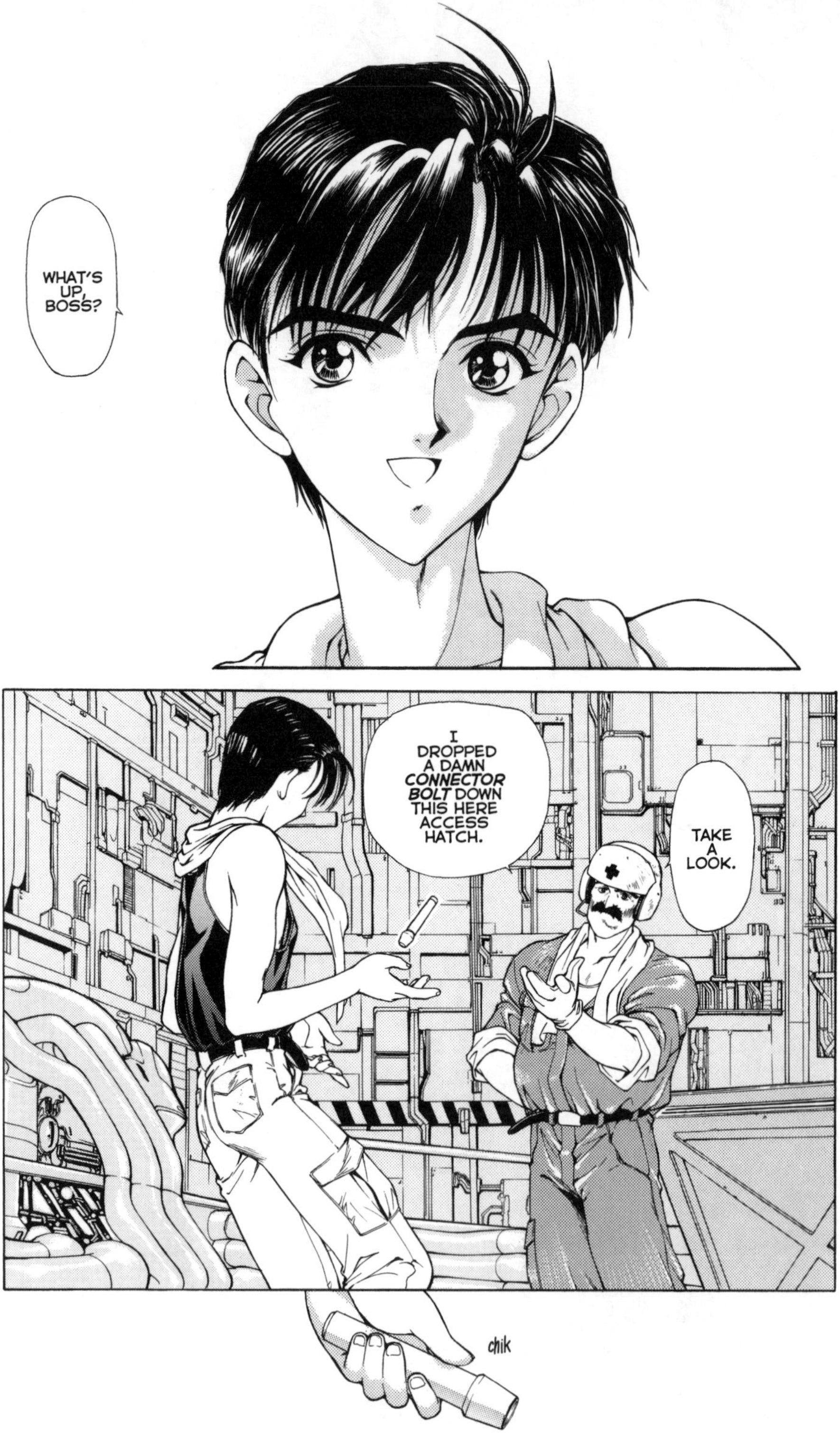
WHAT'S UP, BOSS?
I DROPPED A DAMN CONNECTOR BOLT DOWN THIS HERE ACCESS HATCH.
TAKE A LOOK.
chik

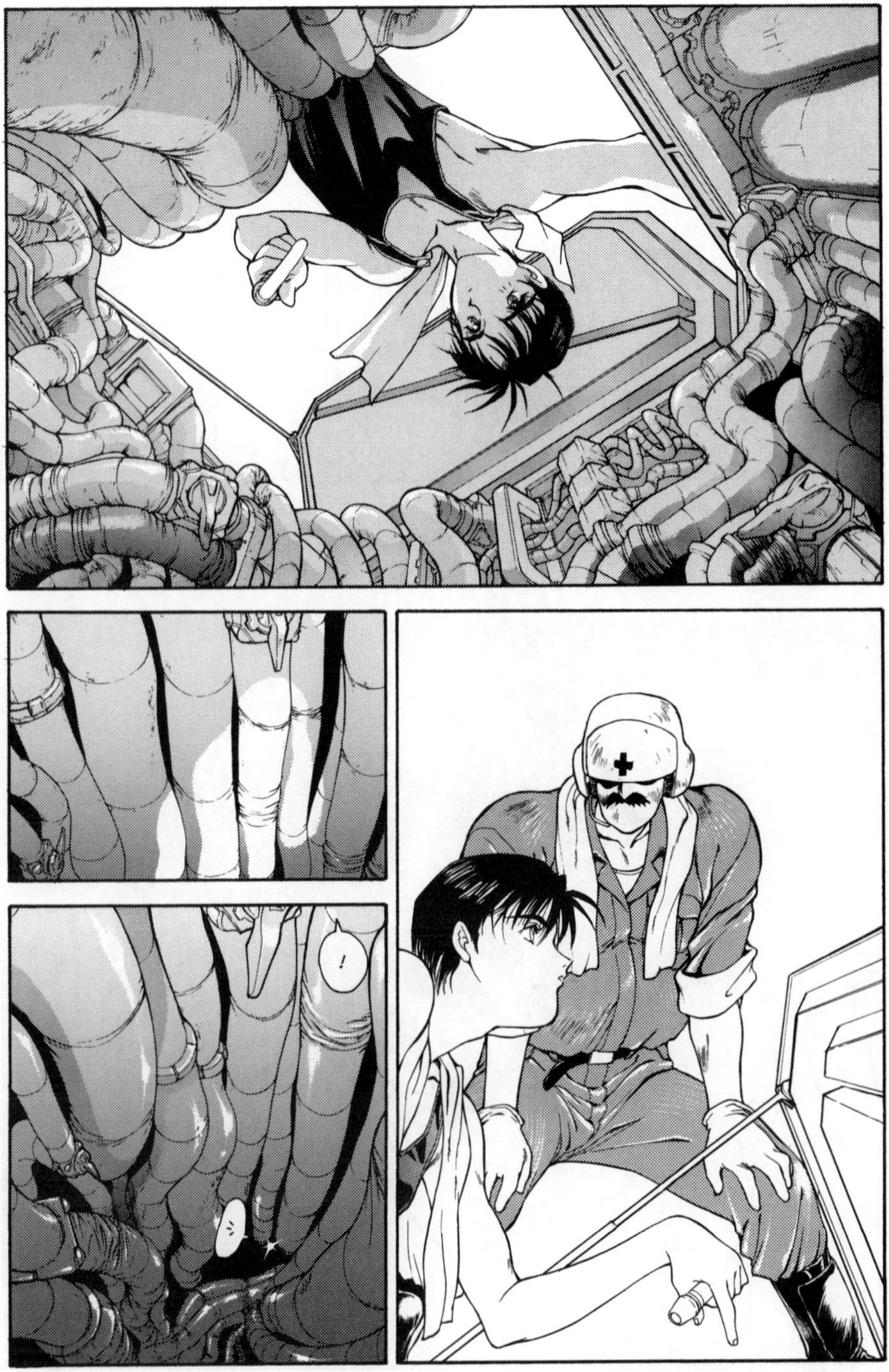
!

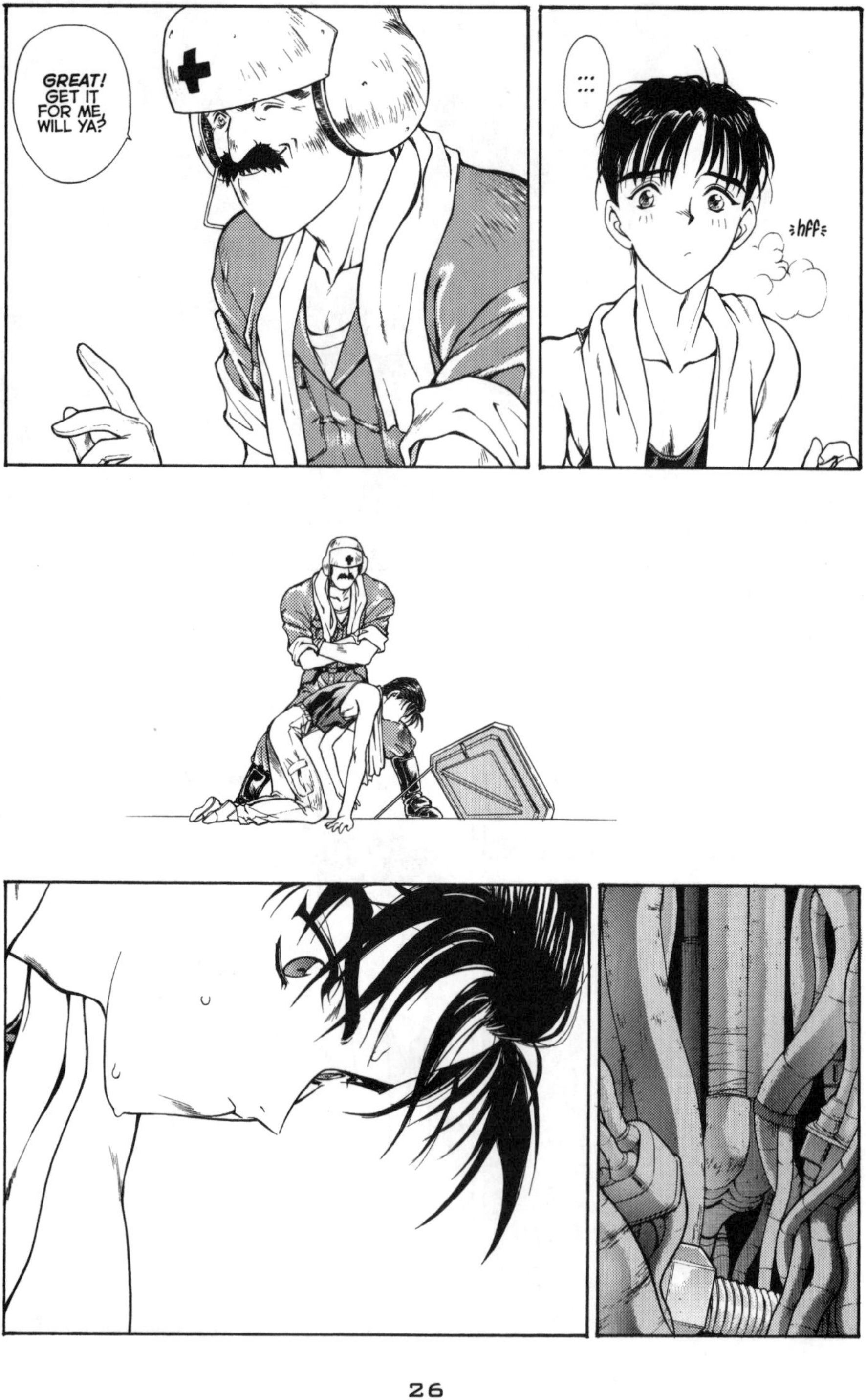
GREAT! GET IT FOR ME, WILL YA?
......
hff

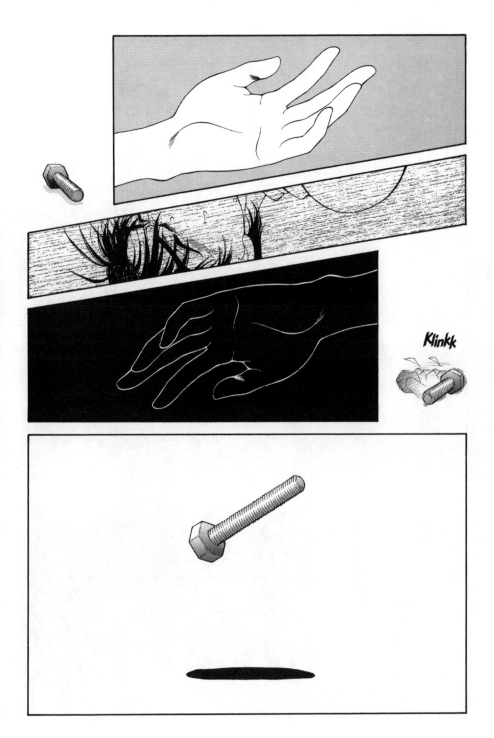

Klinkk

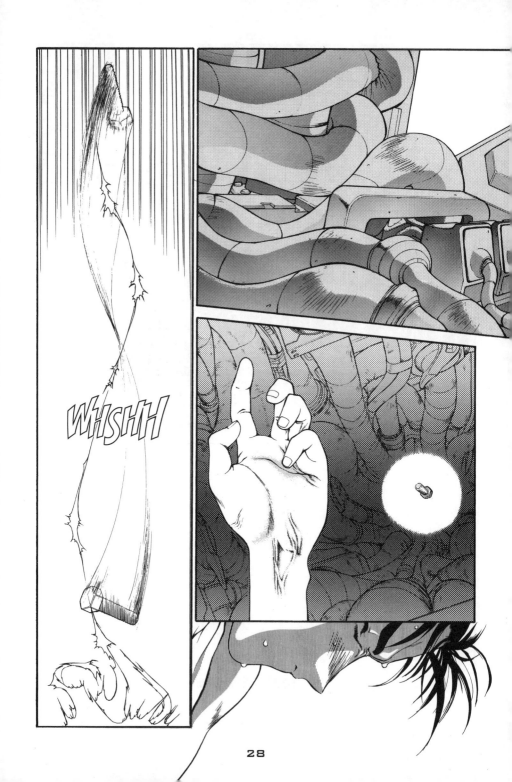

WHSHH

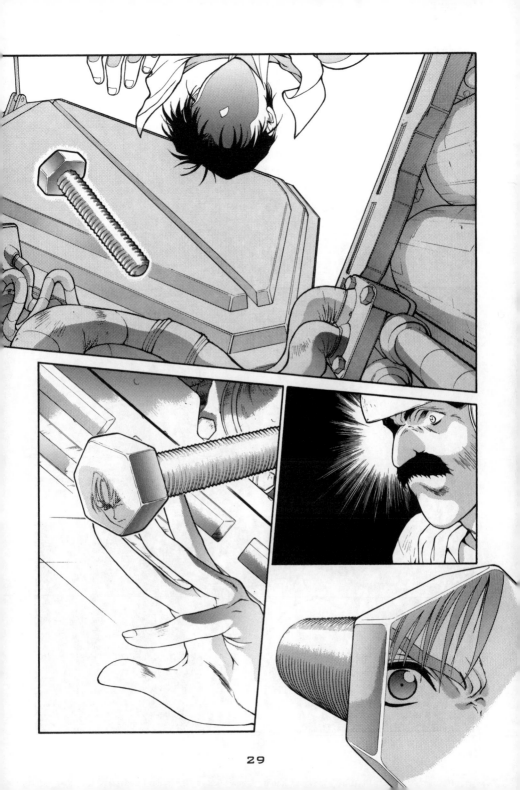

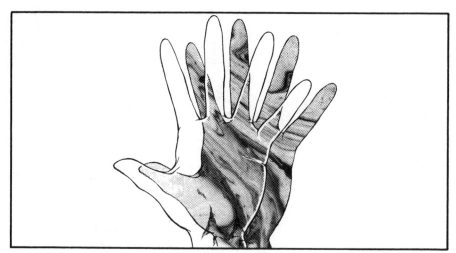

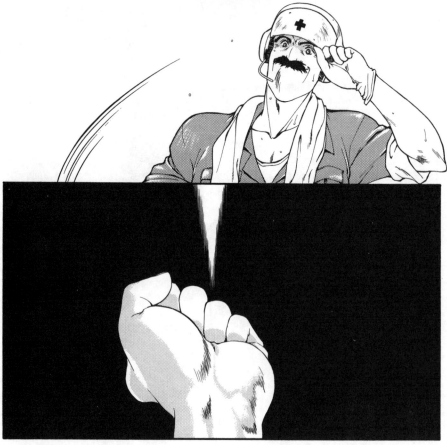

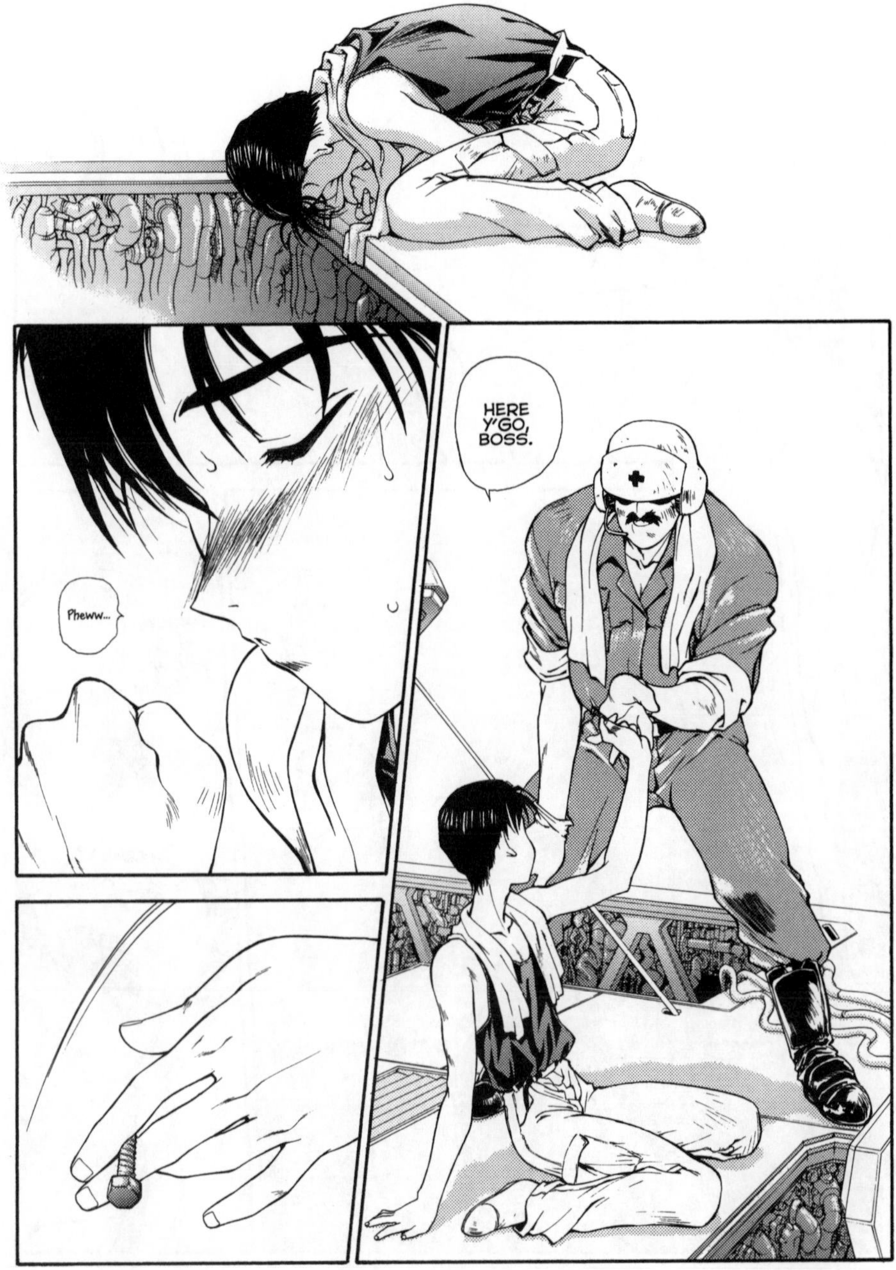
Pheww...
HERE Y'GO, BOSS.

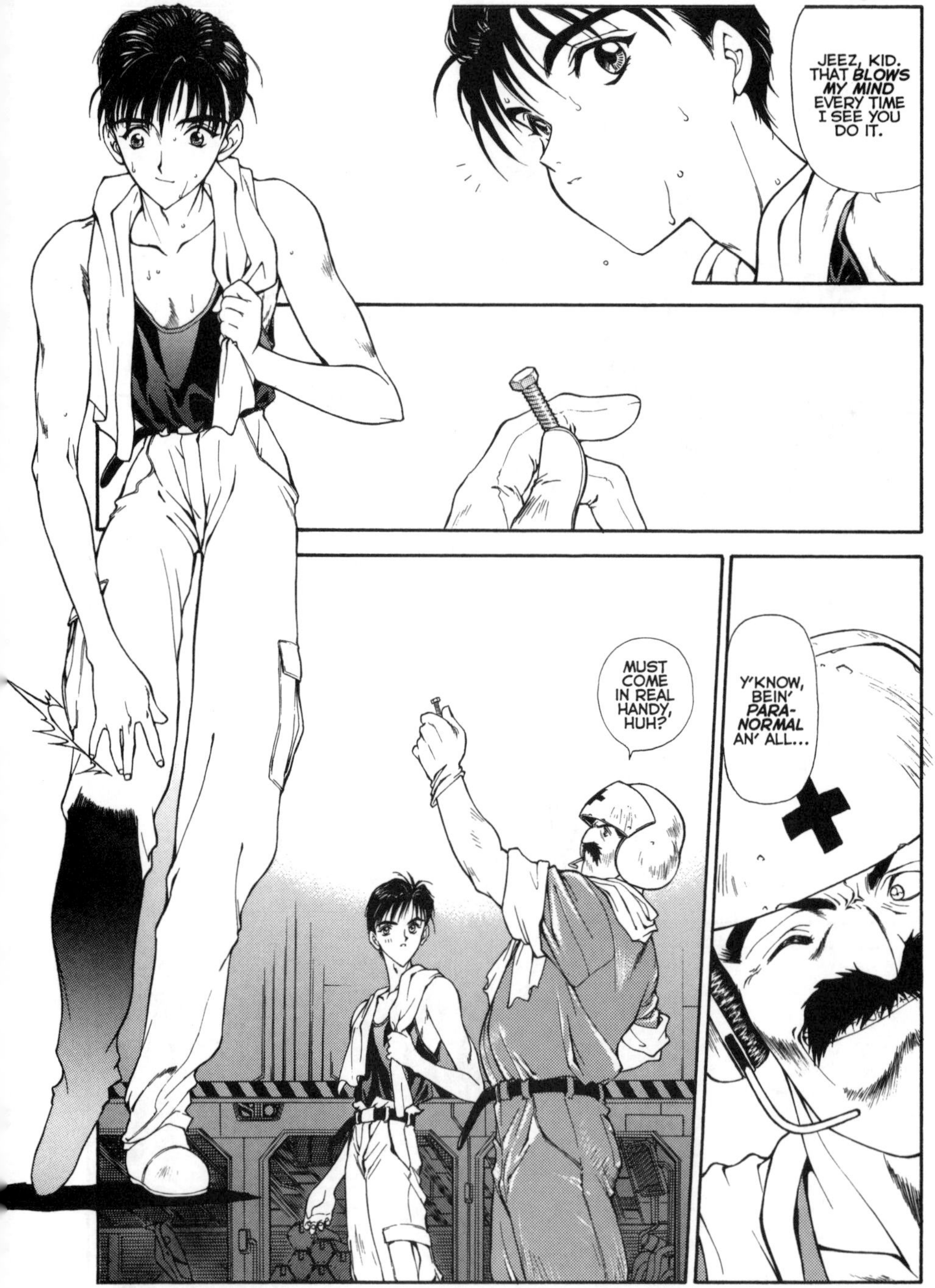
JEEZ, KID. THAT BLOWS MY MIND EVERY TIME I SEE YOU DO IT.
MUST COME IN REAL HANDY, HUH?
Y'KNOW, BEIN' PARA-NORMAL AN' ALL...

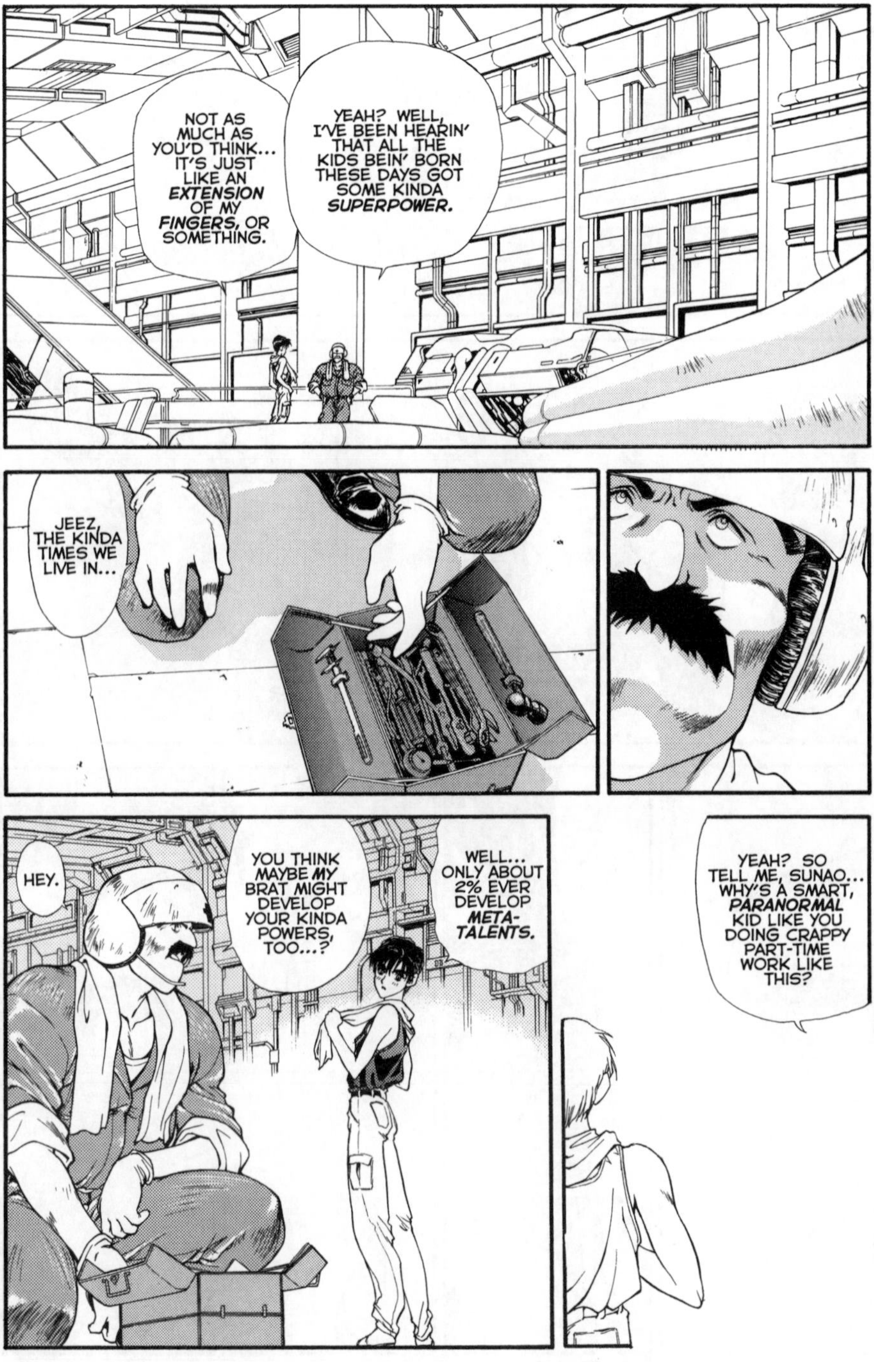
NOT AS MUCH AS YOU'D THINK... IT'S JUST LIKE AN EXTENSION OF MY FINGERS, OR SOMETHING.
YEAH? WELL, I'VE BEEN HEARIN' THAT ALL THE KIDS BEIN' BORN THESE DAYS GOT SOME KINDA SUPERPOWER.
JEEZ, THE KINDA TIMES WE LIVE IN...
HEY.
YOU THINK MAYBE MY BRAT MIGHT DEVELOP YOUR KINDA POWERS, TOO...?
WELL... ONLY ABOUT 2% EVER DEVELOP META-TALENTS.
YEAH? SO TELL ME, SUNAO... WHY'S A SMART, PARANORMAL KID LIKE YOU DOING CRAPPY PART-TIME WORK LIKE THIS?

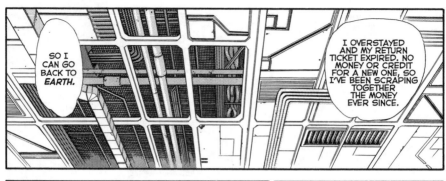

SO I CAN GO BACK TO *EARTH.*

I OVERSTAYED AND MY RETURN TICKET EXPIRED. NO MONEY OR CREDIT FOR A NEW ONE, SO I'VE BEEN SCRAPING TOGETHER THE MONEY EVER SINCE.

HUH. YOU'RE A WEIRD ONE, KID. WHY WOULD YOU WANNA GO BACK DOWN TO THAT *HELLHOLE,* ANYWAY?

THEN AGAIN, WHY DID YOU COME HERE IN THE *FIRST* PLACE?

I... I HAD TO VISIT THE GRAVE OF A CHILD-HOOD FRIEND.

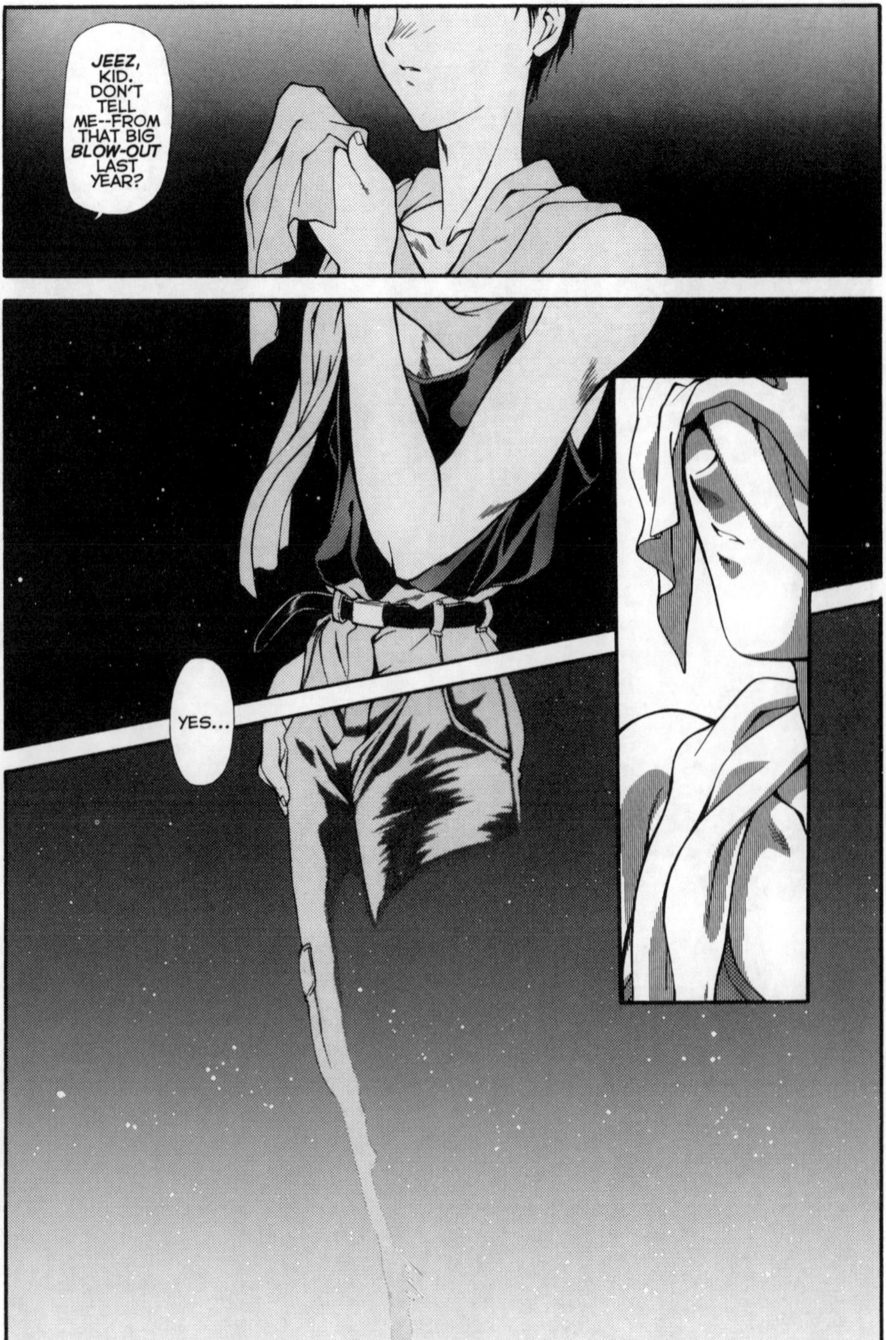
JEEZ, KID. DON'T TELL ME--FROM THAT BIG BLOW-OUT LAST YEAR?
YES...

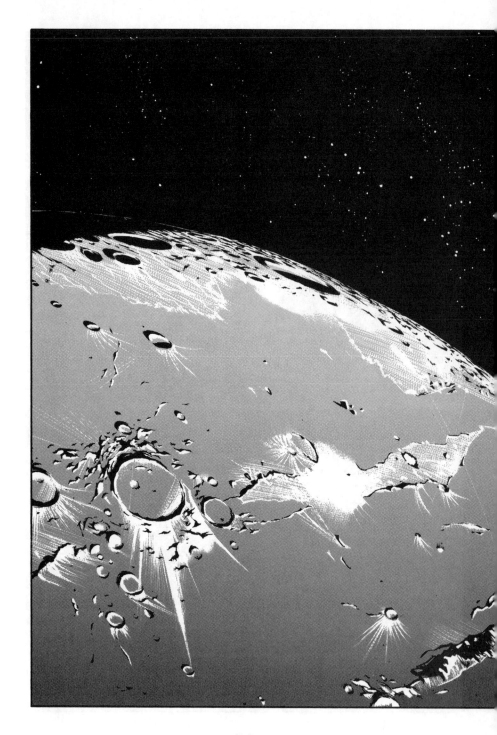

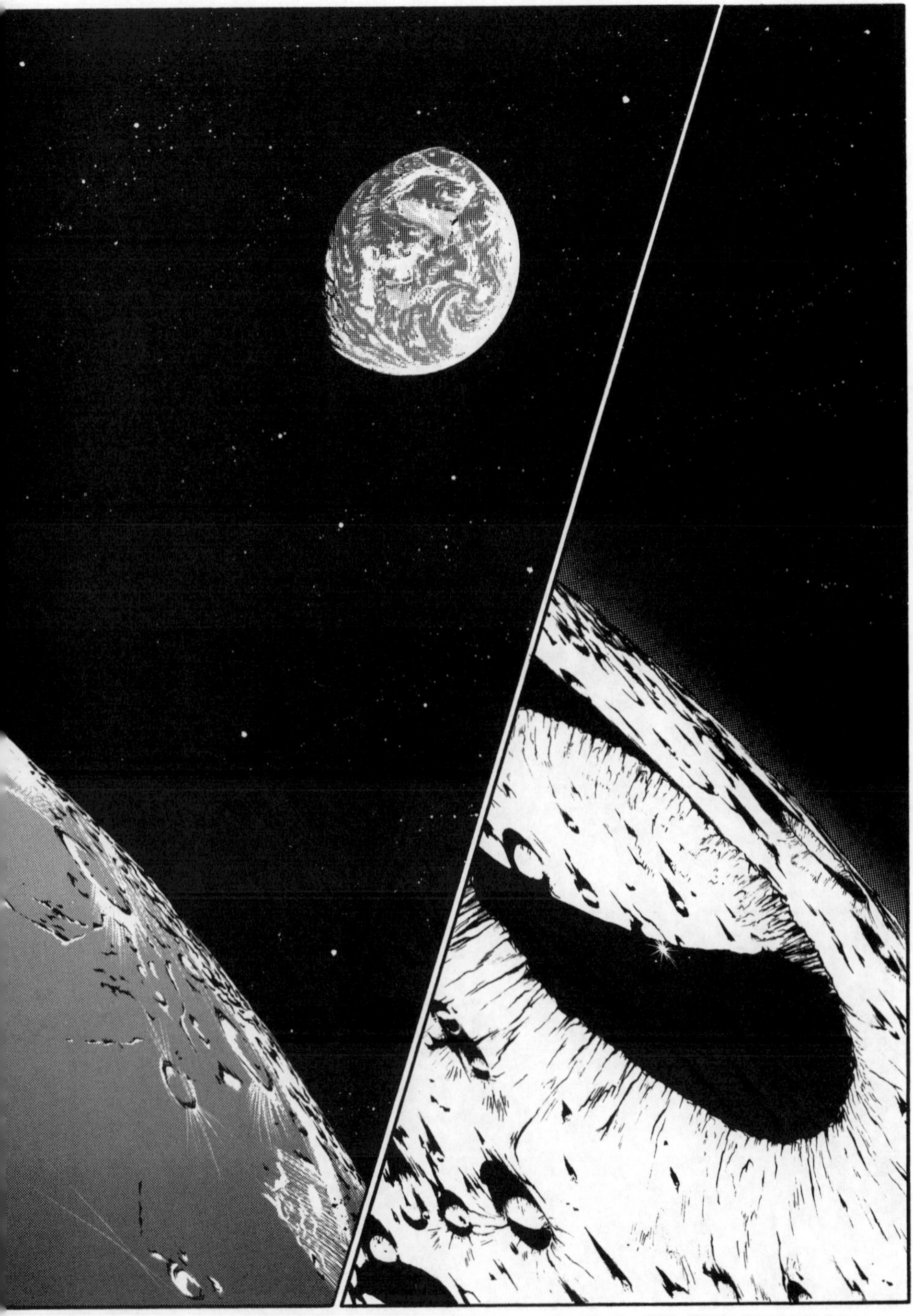

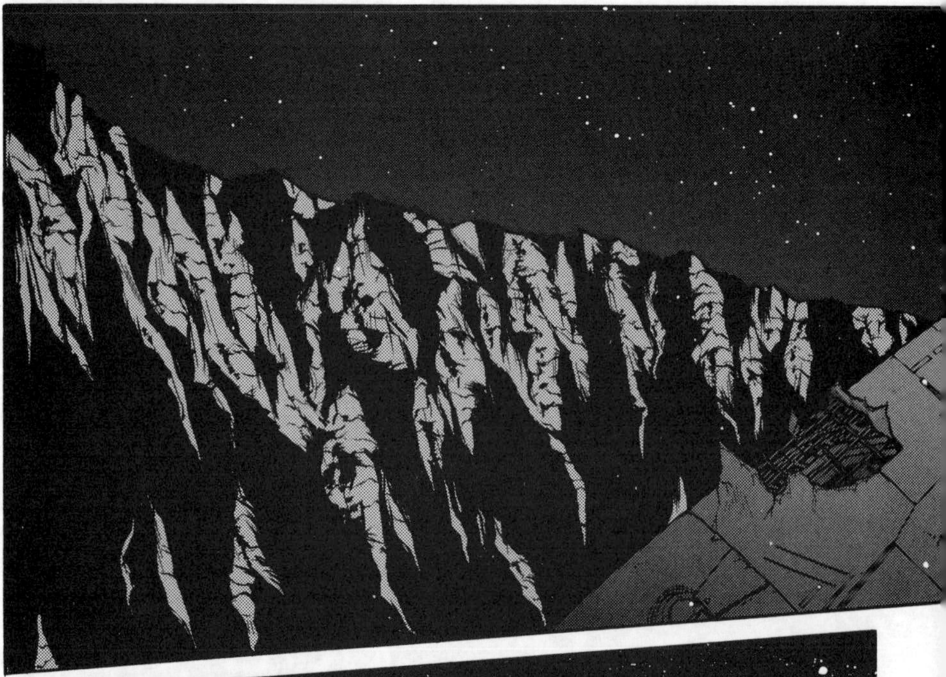

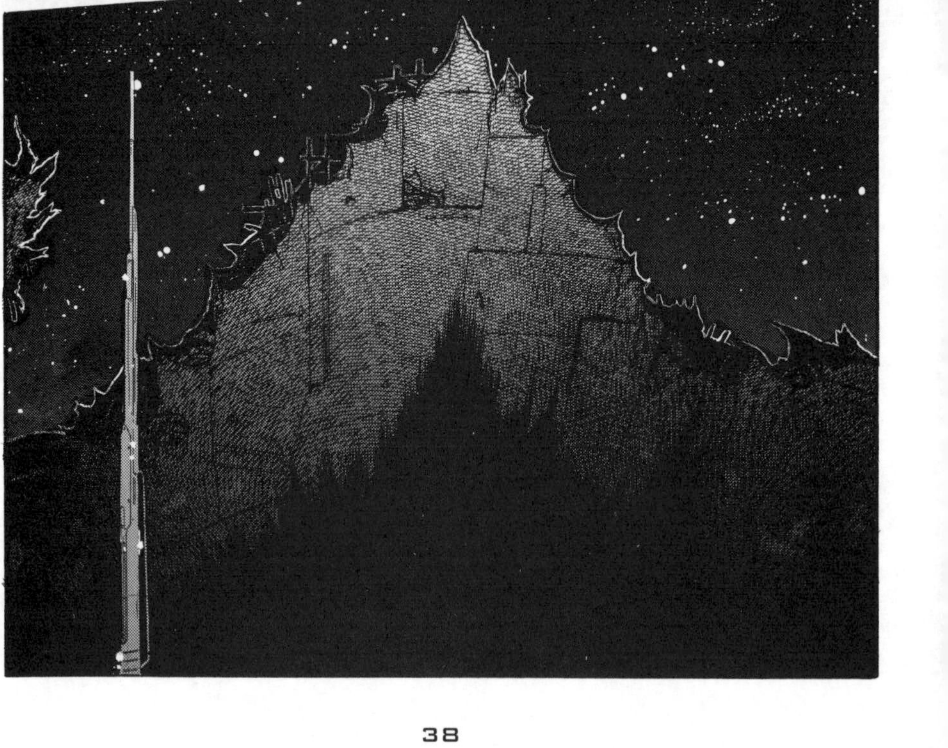

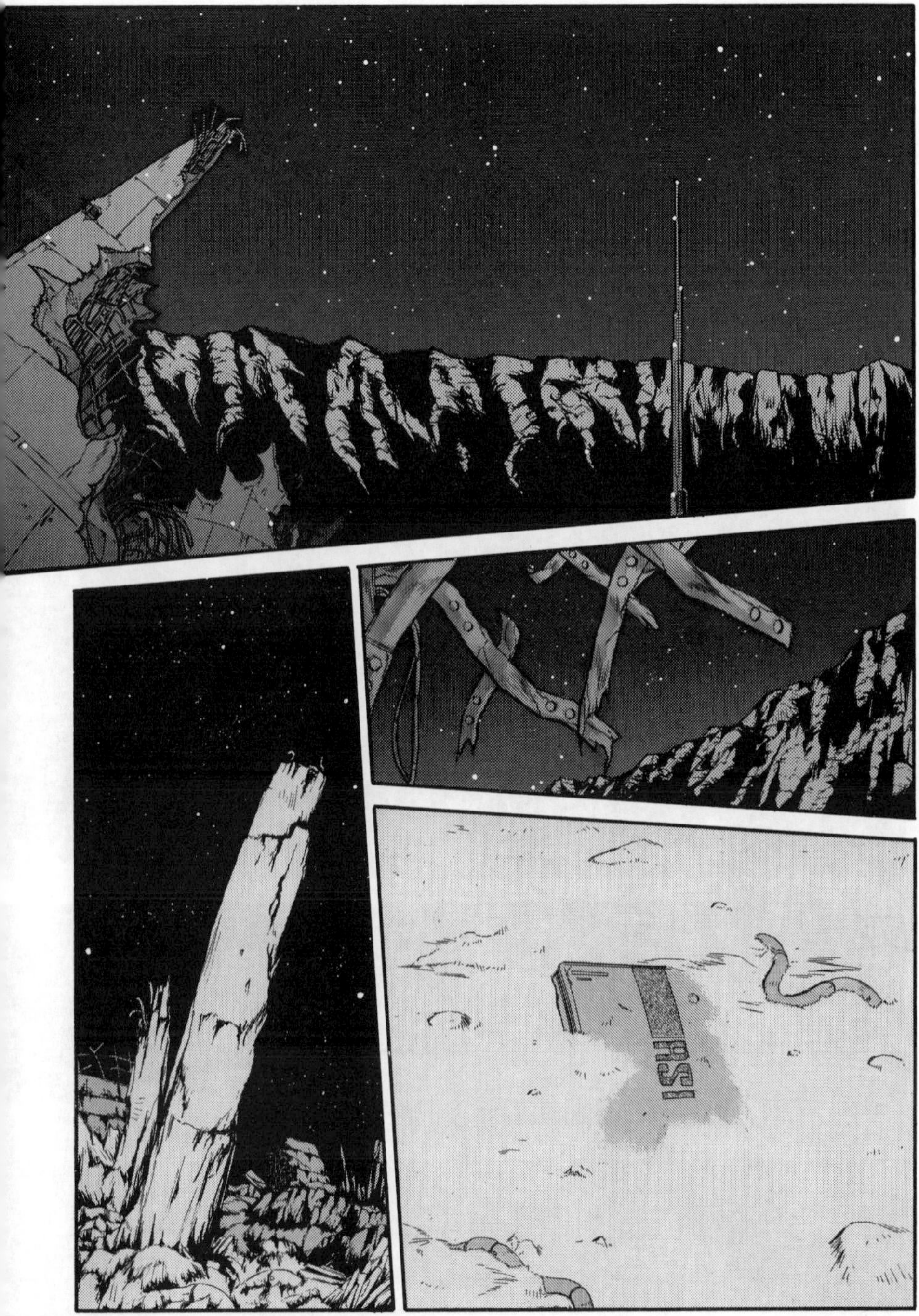

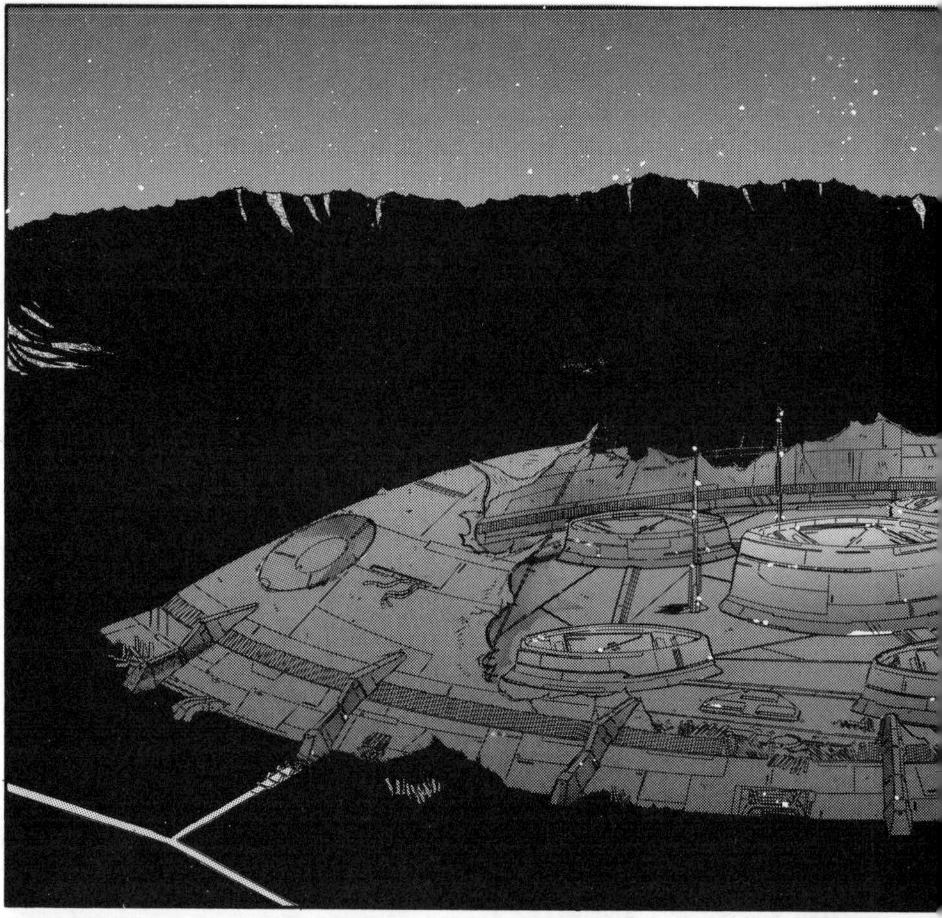

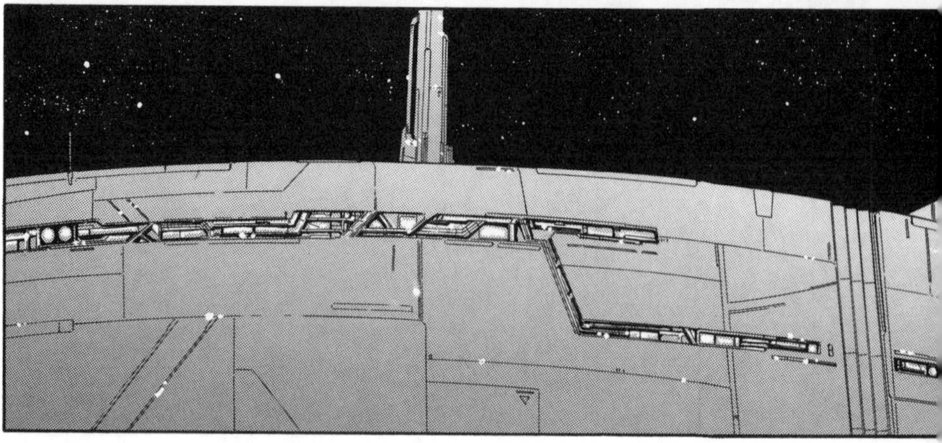

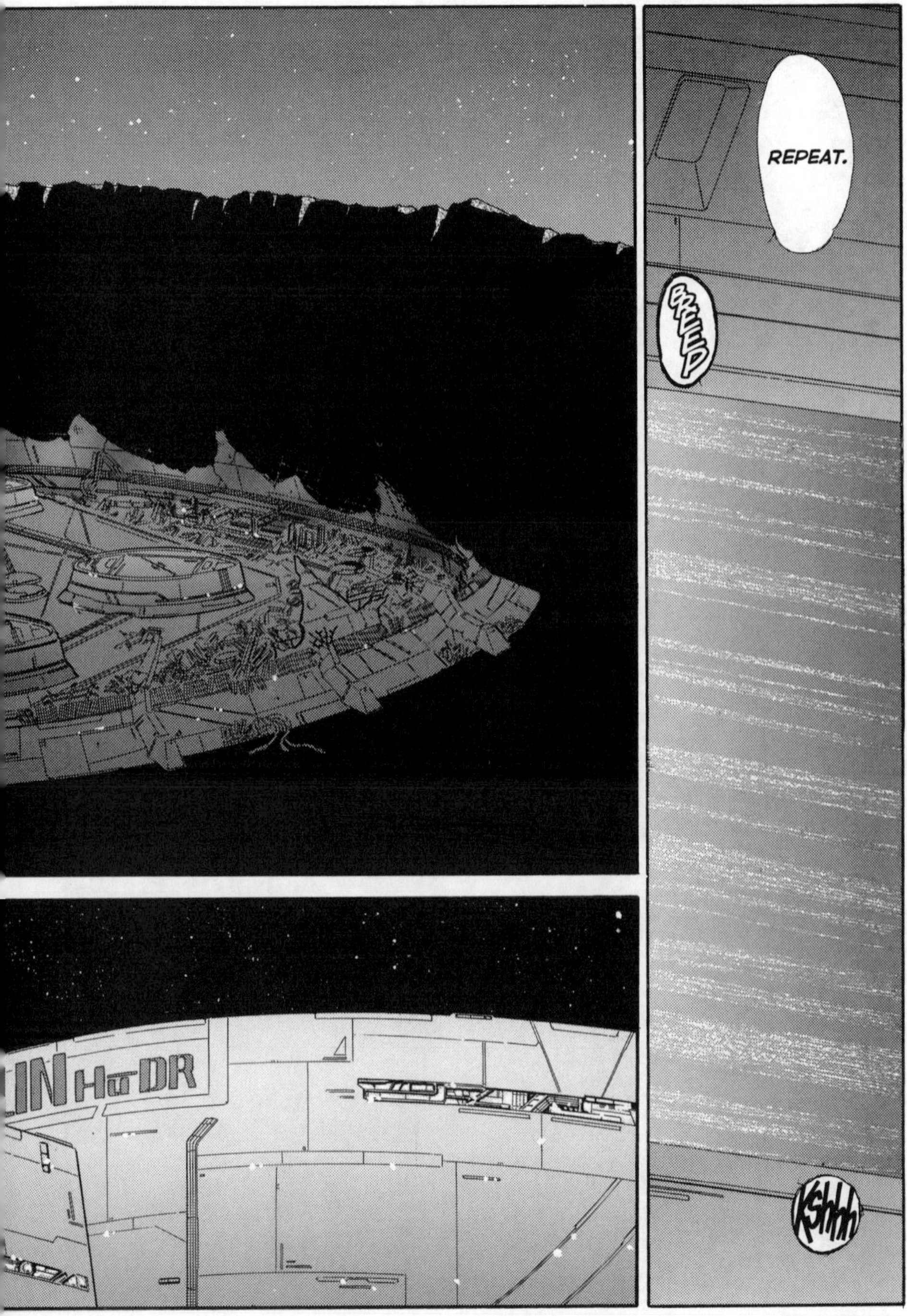
REPEAT.
BREEP
Kshhh

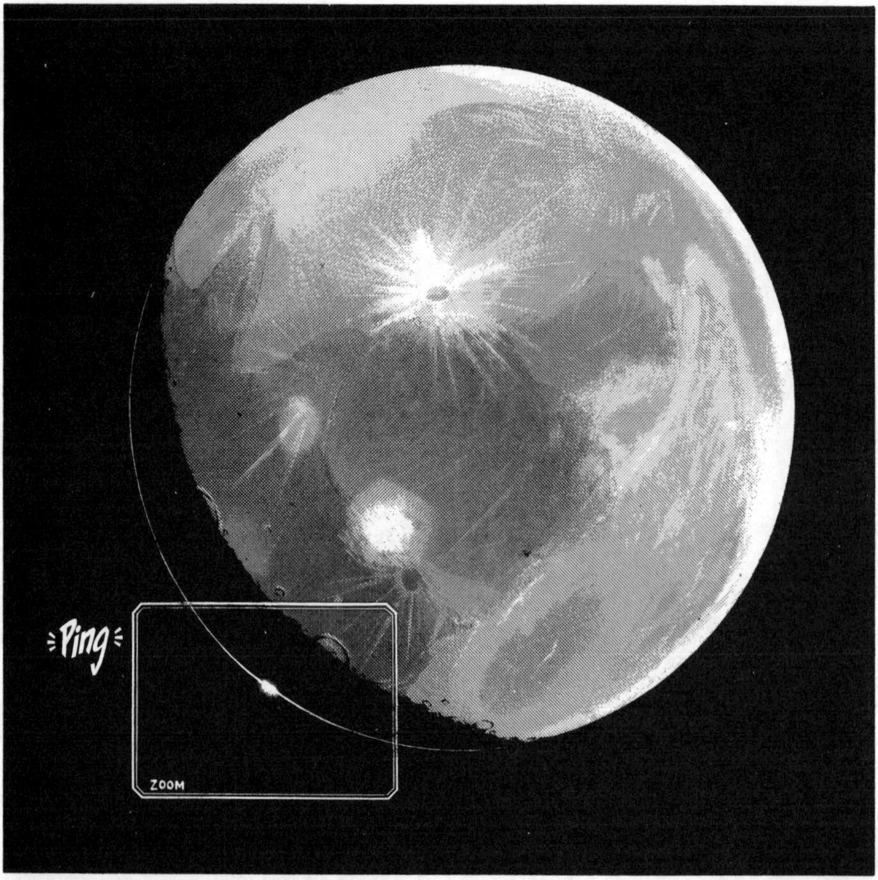
Ping
ZOOM

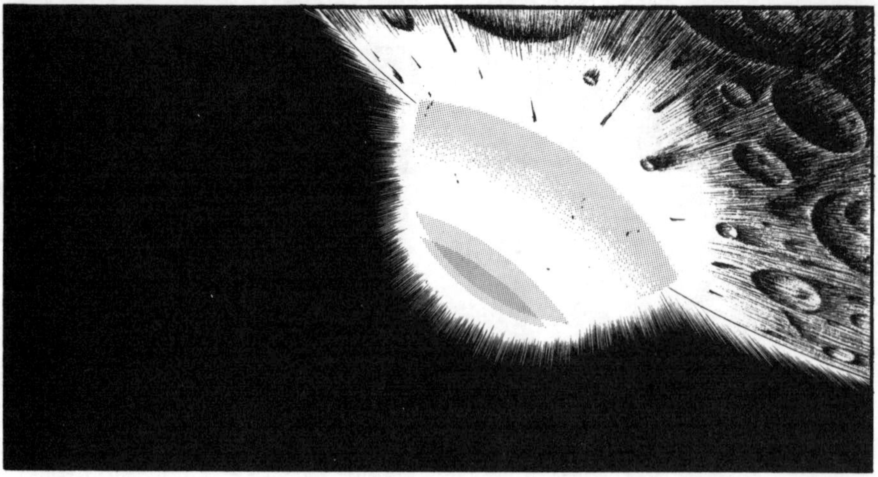

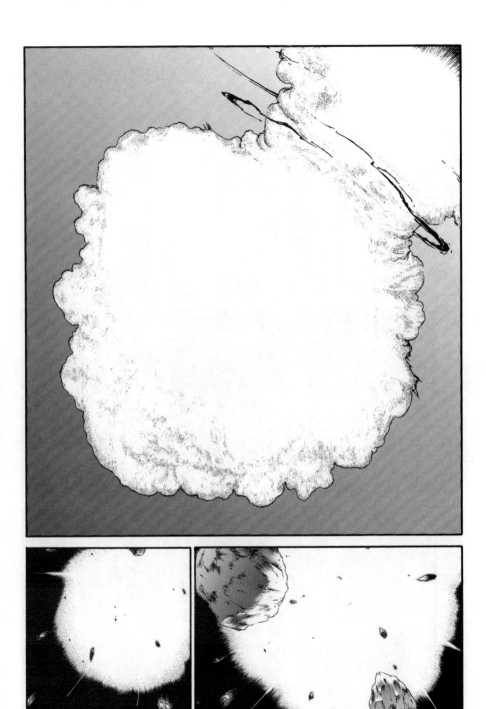

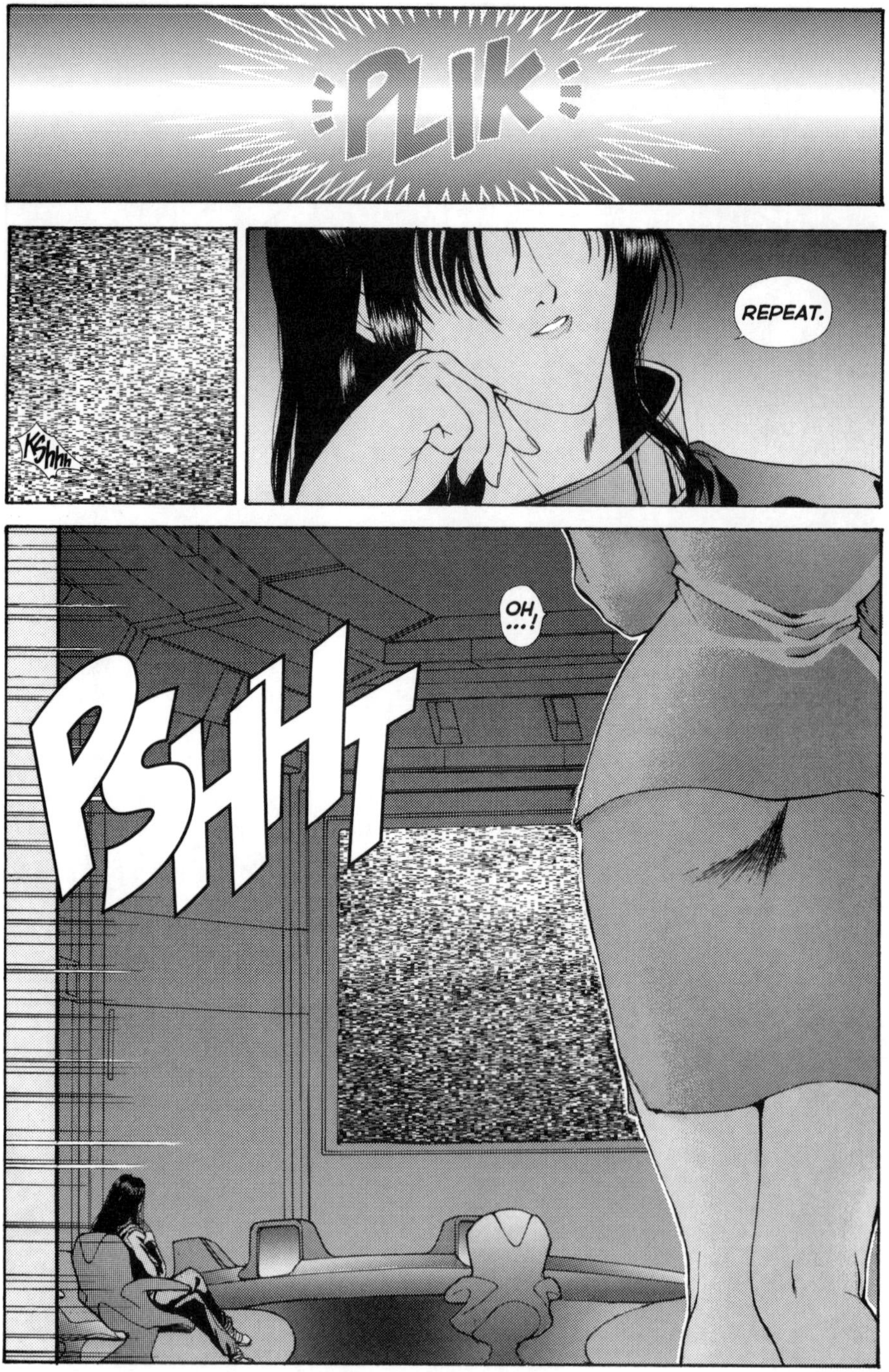
PLIK
KSHHH
REPEAT.
PSHHT
OH ...!

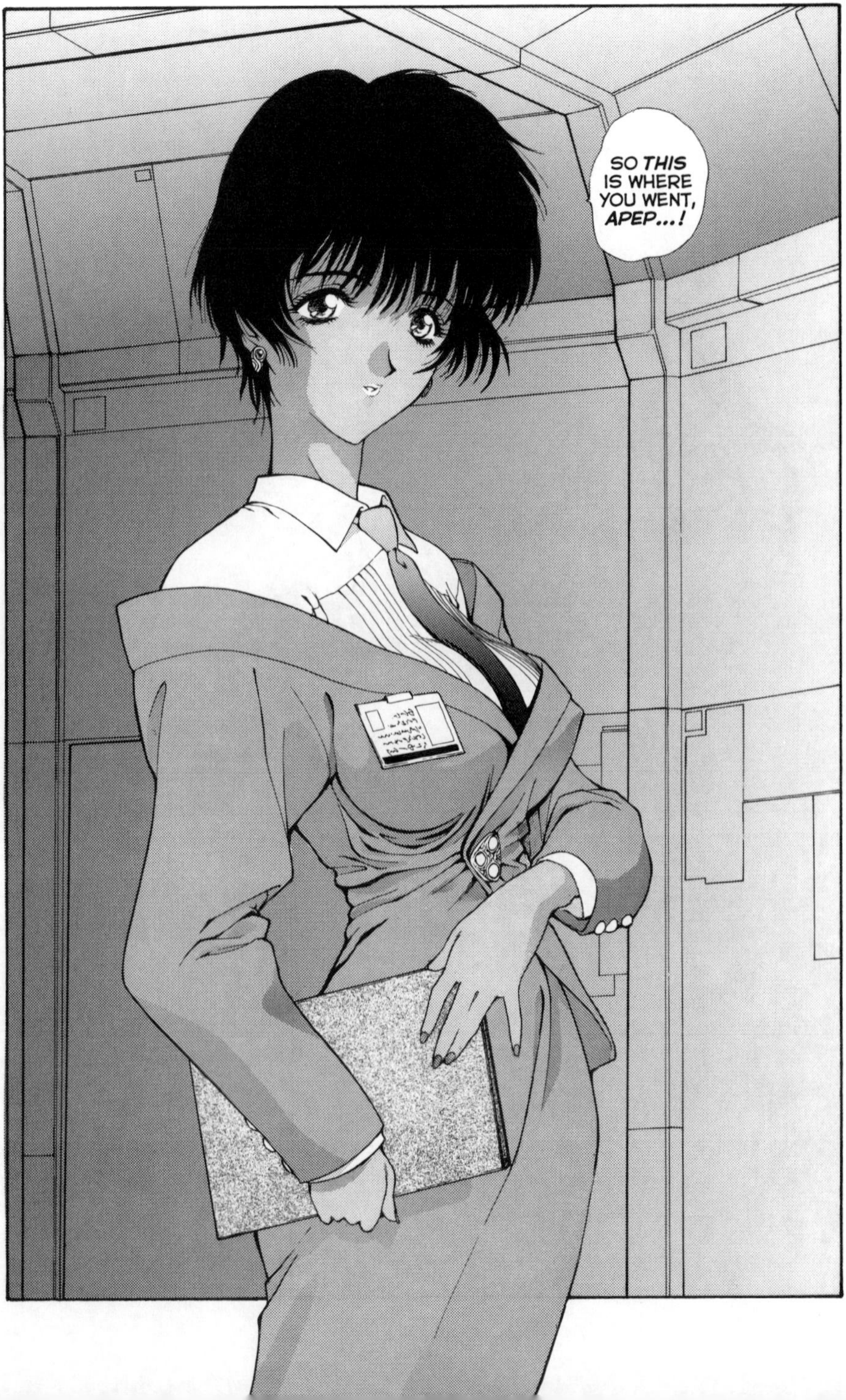
SO THIS IS WHERE YOU WENT, APEP...!

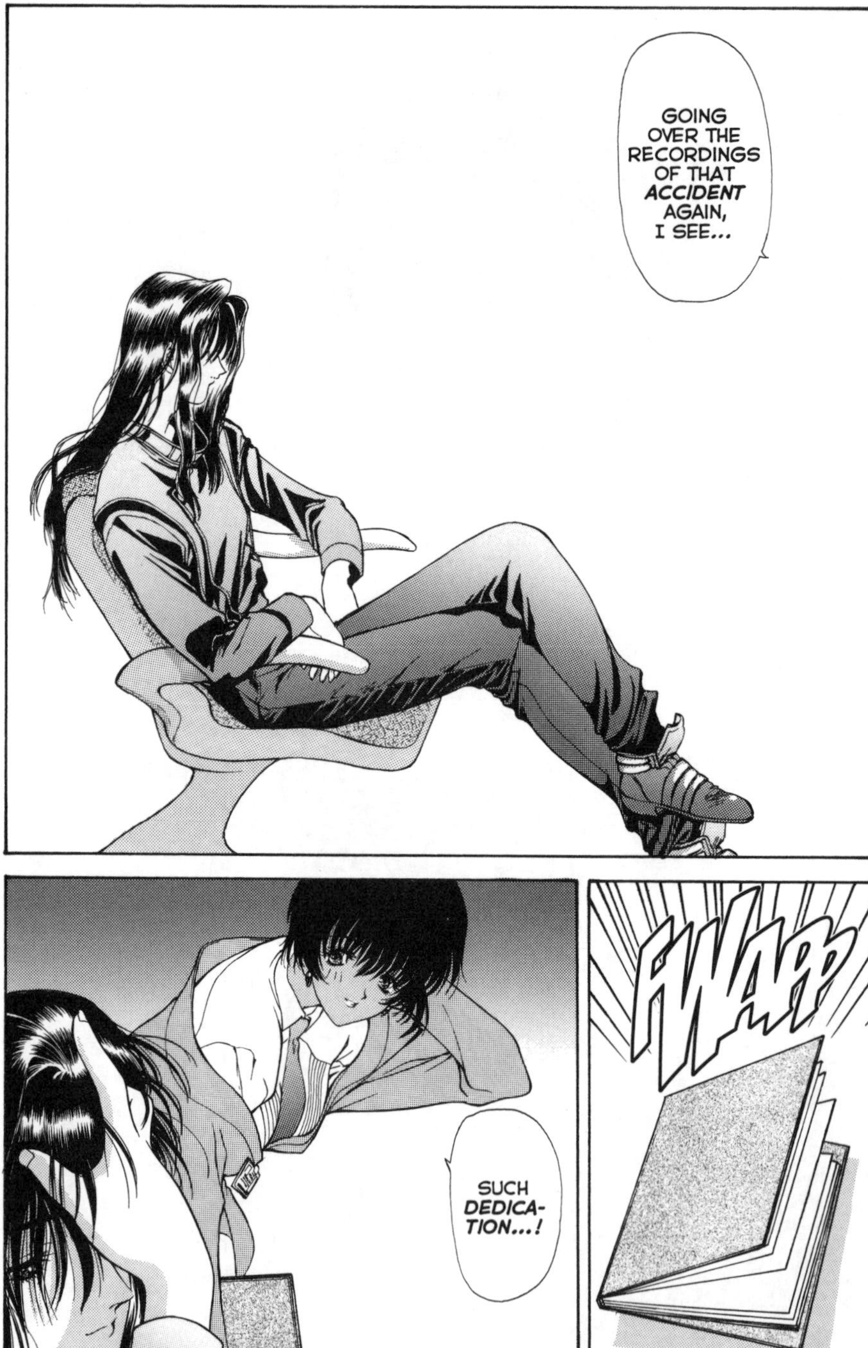
GOING OVER THE RECORDINGS OF THAT ACCIDENT AGAIN, I SEE...
SUCH DEDICA- TION...!
FWAPP

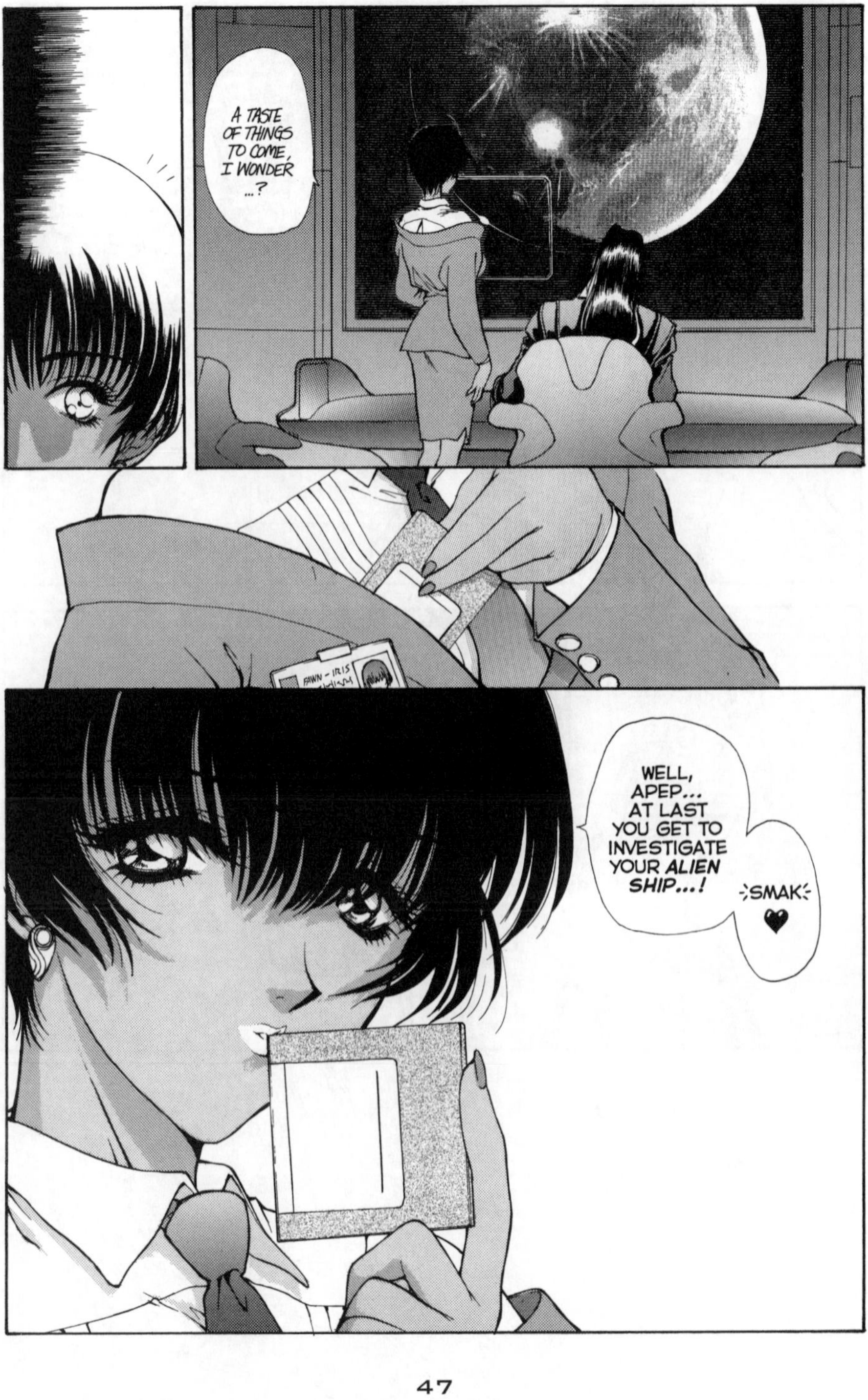
A TASTE OF THINGS TO COME, I WONDER ...?
FAWN - IRIS
WELL, APEP... AT LAST YOU GET TO INVESTIGATE YOUR *ALIEN* SHIP...!
SMAK

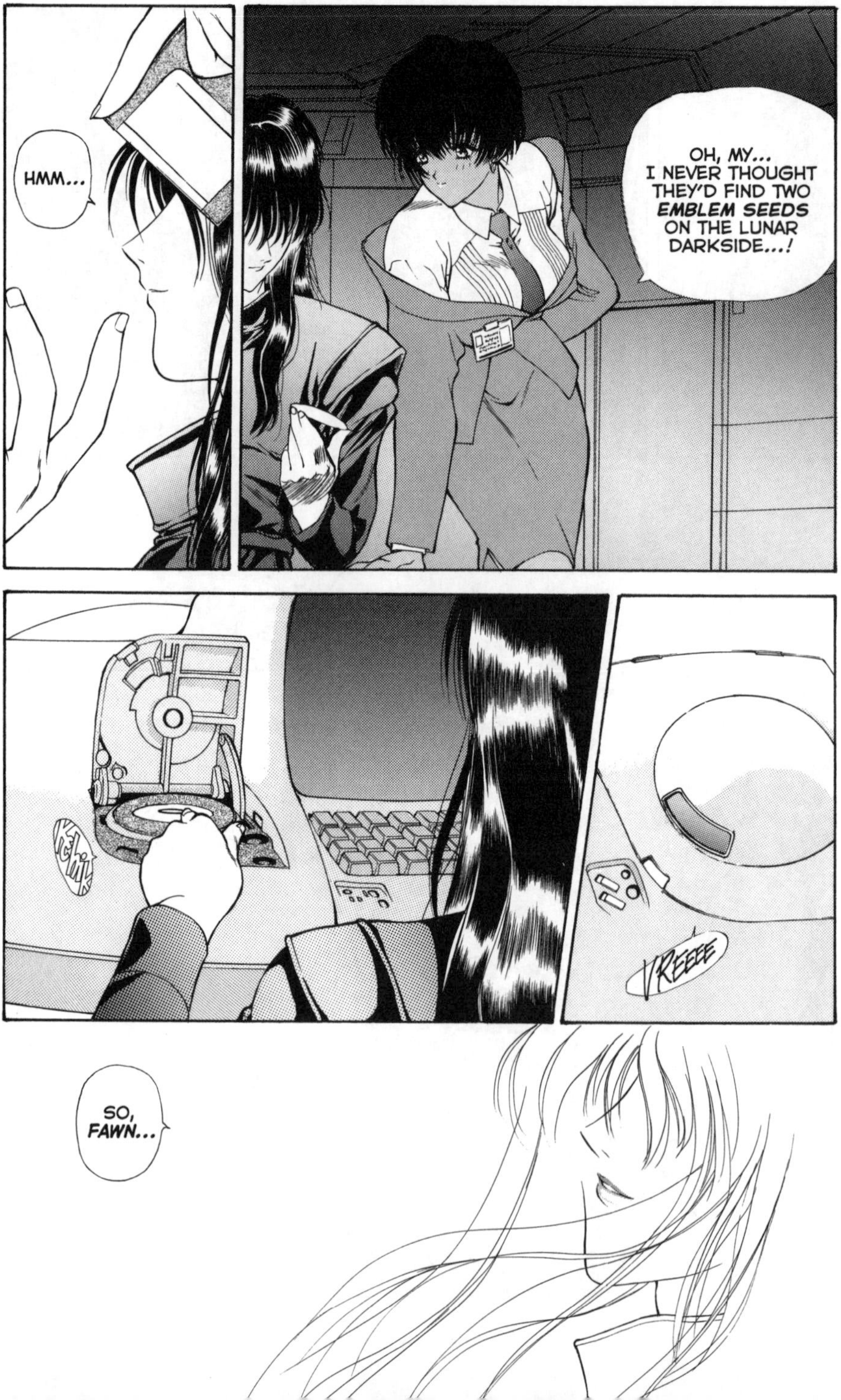
HMM...
OH, MY... I NEVER THOUGHT THEY'D FIND TWO ***EMBLEM SEEDS*** ON THE LUNAR DARKSIDE...!
KCHIK
VREEEE
SO, FAWN...

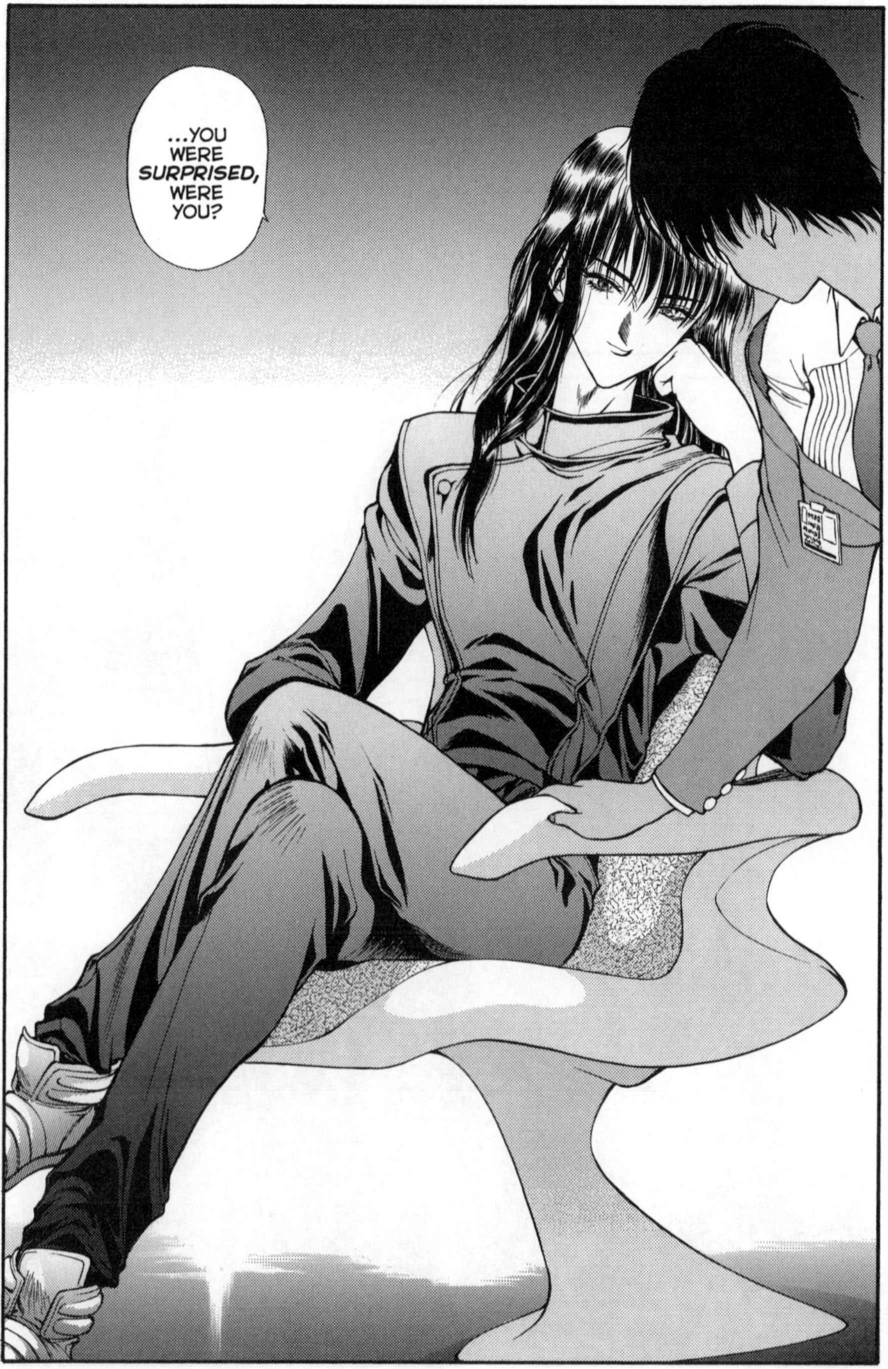
...YOU WERE SURPRISED, WERE YOU?

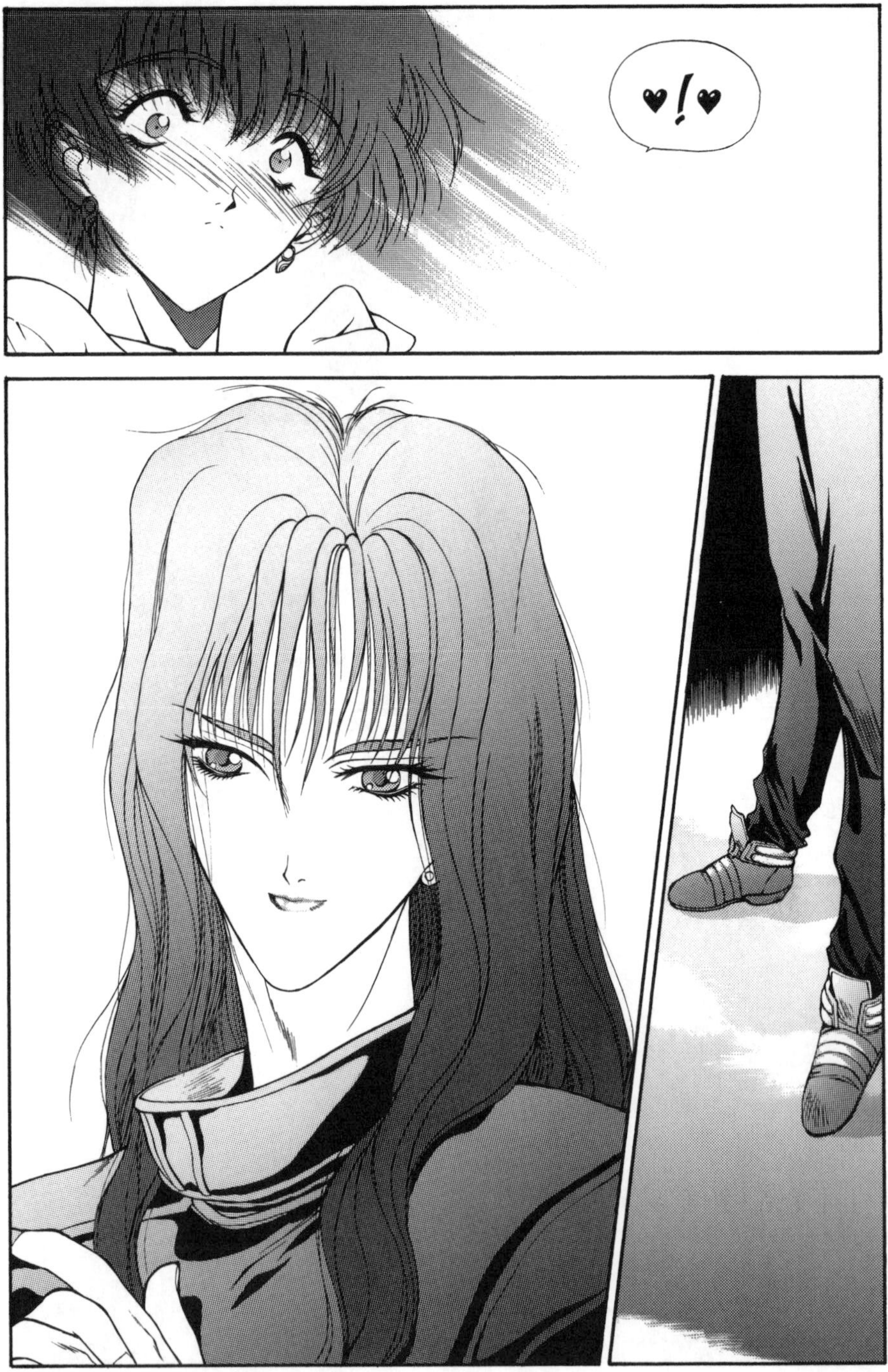
♥!♥

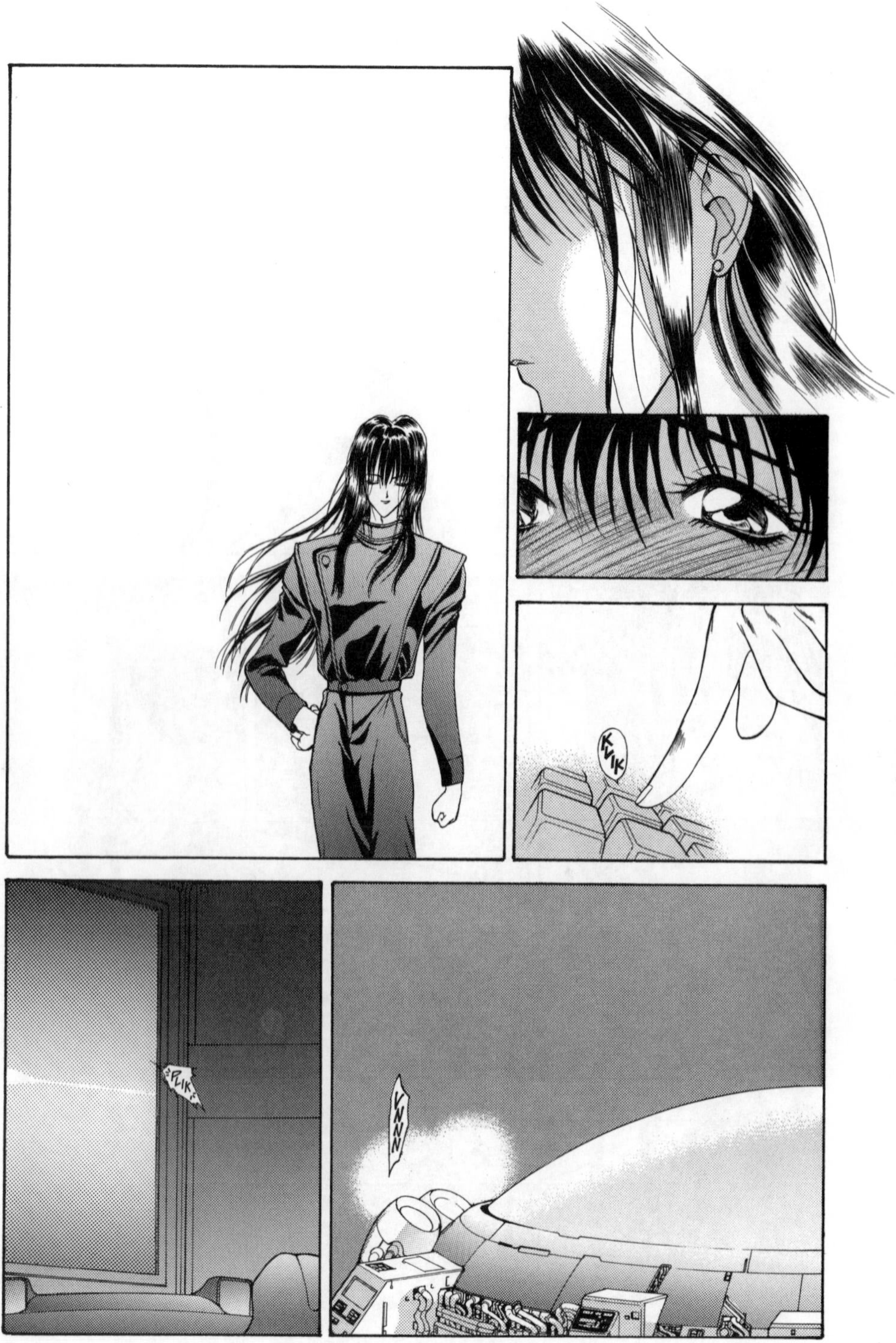
KVIK
PLIK
VNNN

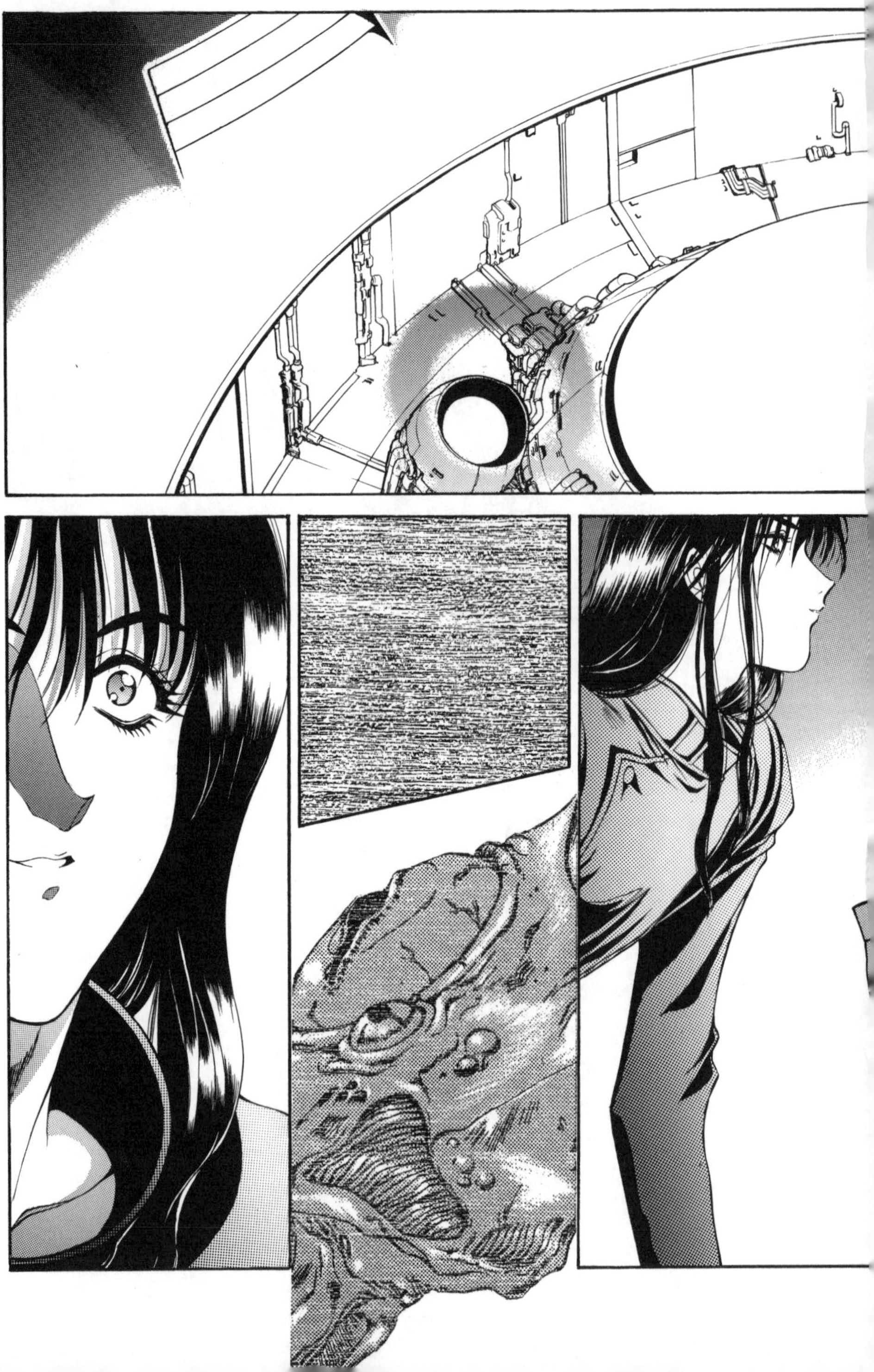

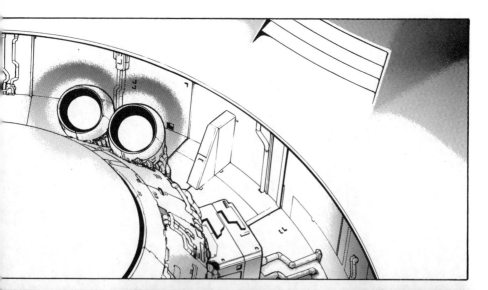

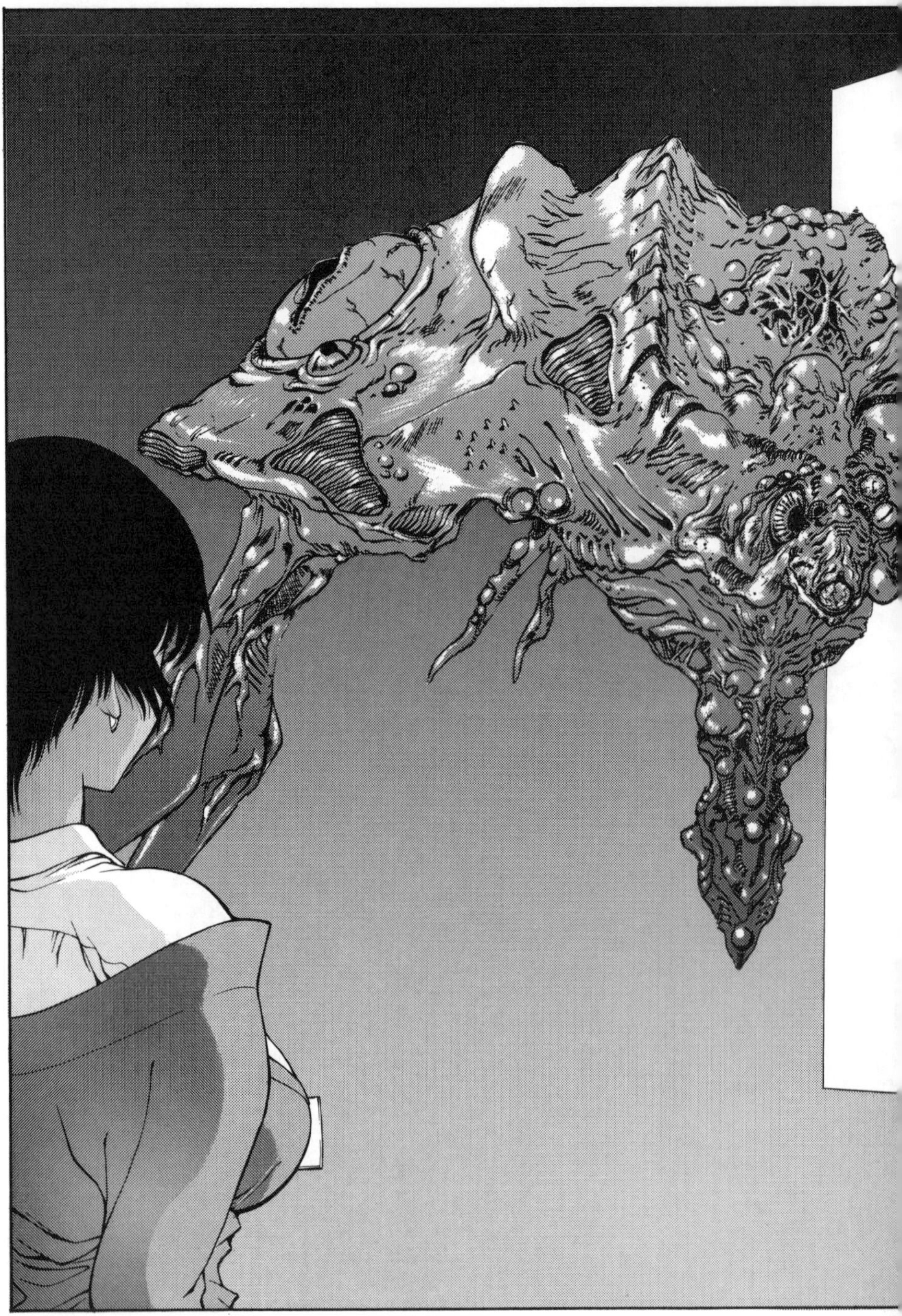

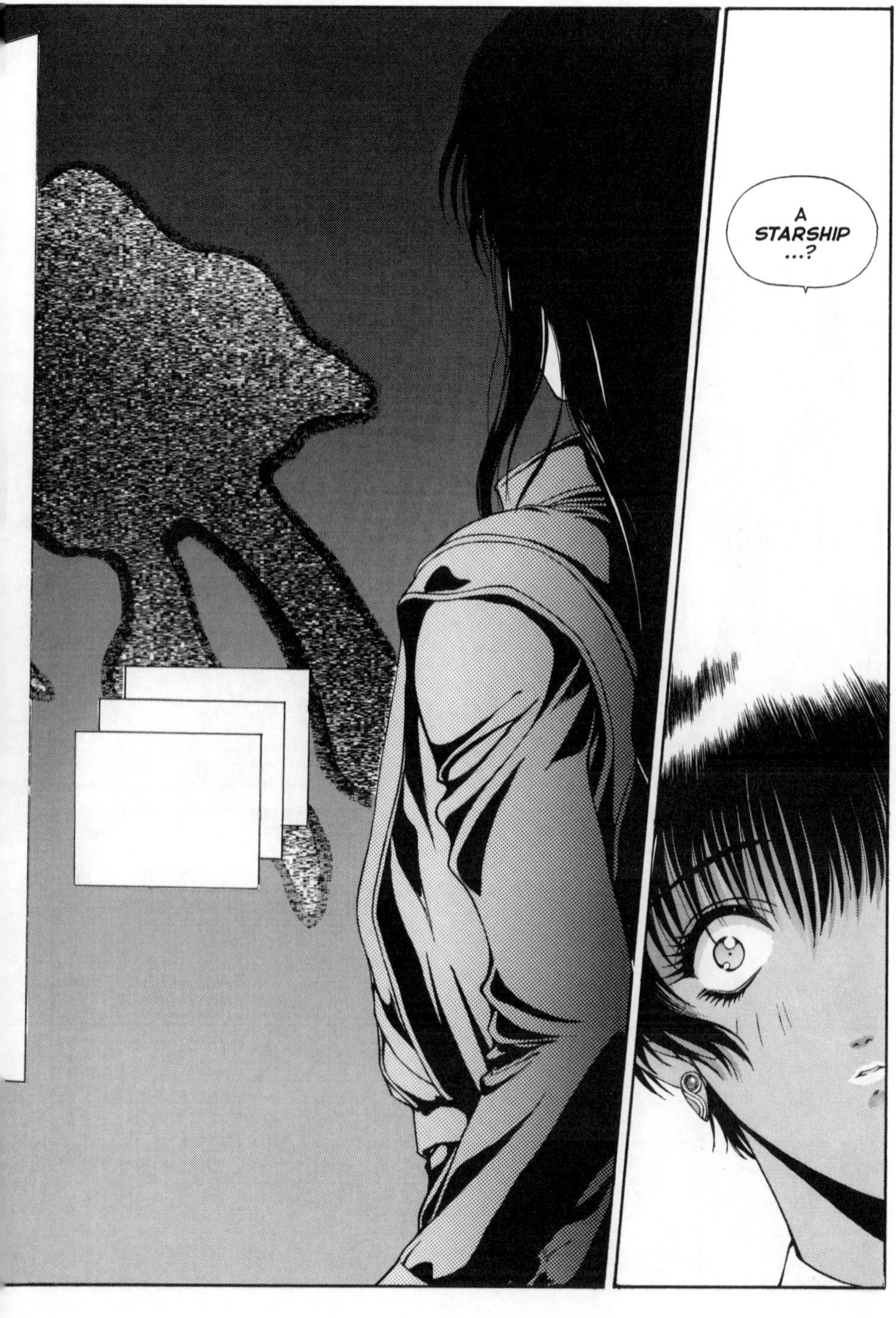
A STARSHIP ...?

APEP... IS THAT THING *REALLY* A SPACECRAFT OF SOME SORT?

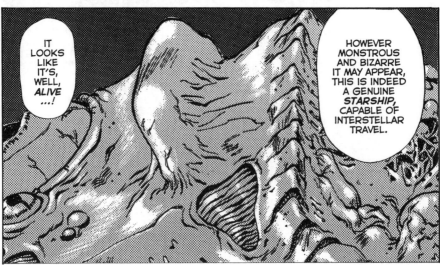

IT LOOKS LIKE IT'S, WELL, *ALIVE* ...!

HOWEVER MONSTROUS AND BIZARRE IT MAY APPEAR, THIS IS INDEED A GENUINE *STARSHIP,* CAPABLE OF INTERSTELLAR TRAVEL.

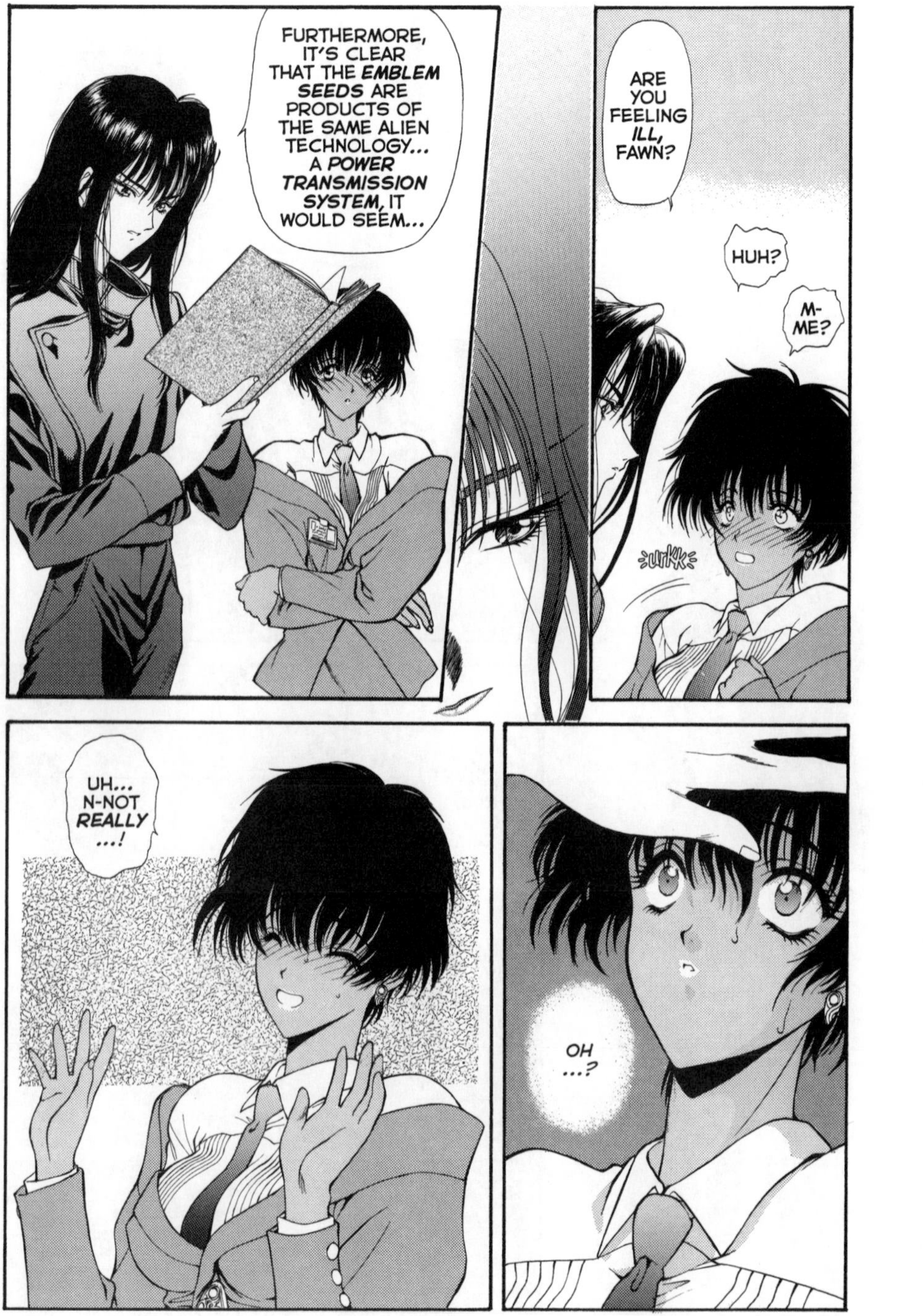
FURTHERMORE, IT'S CLEAR THAT THE **EMBLEM SEEDS** ARE PRODUCTS OF THE SAME ALIEN TECHNOLOGY... A **POWER TRANSMISSION SYSTEM,** IT WOULD SEEM...
ARE YOU FEELING **ILL,** FAWN?
HUH?
M-ME?
URKK
UH... N-NOT **REALLY** ...!
OH ...?

OHHH... ♥

HMM... YOU DON'T SEEM TO BE RUNNING A *FEVER.*

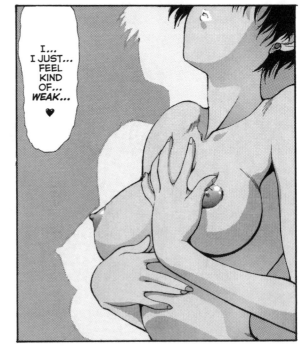

I... I JUST... FEEL KIND OF... *WEAK...* ♥

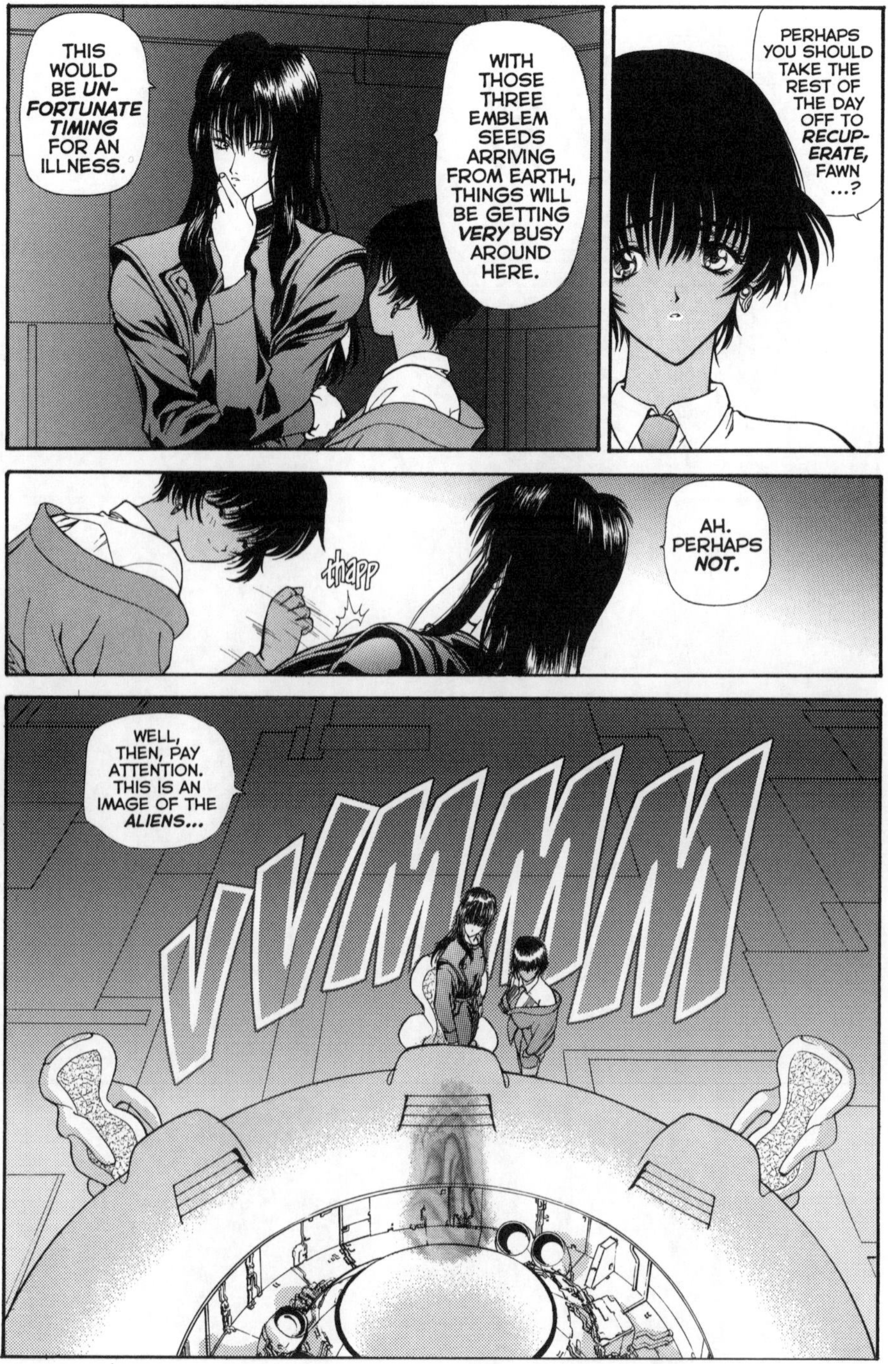
THIS WOULD BE UN-FORTUNATE TIMING FOR AN ILLNESS.
WITH THOSE THREE EMBLEM SEEDS ARRIVING FROM EARTH, THINGS WILL BE GETTING VERY BUSY AROUND HERE.
PERHAPS YOU SHOULD TAKE THE REST OF THE DAY OFF TO RECUP-ERATE, FAWN ...?
thapp
AH. PERHAPS NOT.
WELL, THEN, PAY ATTENTION. THIS IS AN IMAGE OF THE ALIENS...
VVMMMM

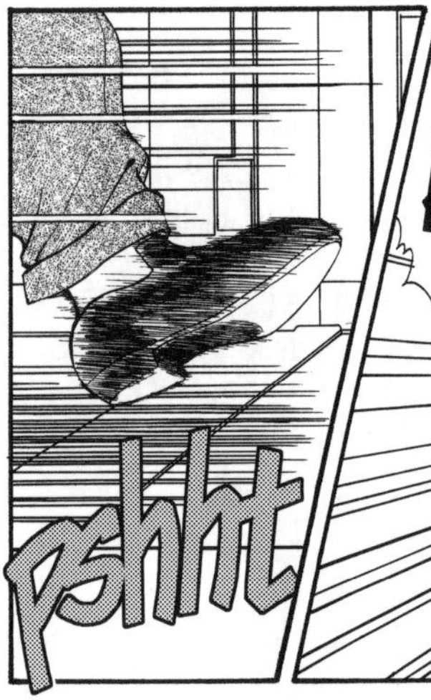
pshht

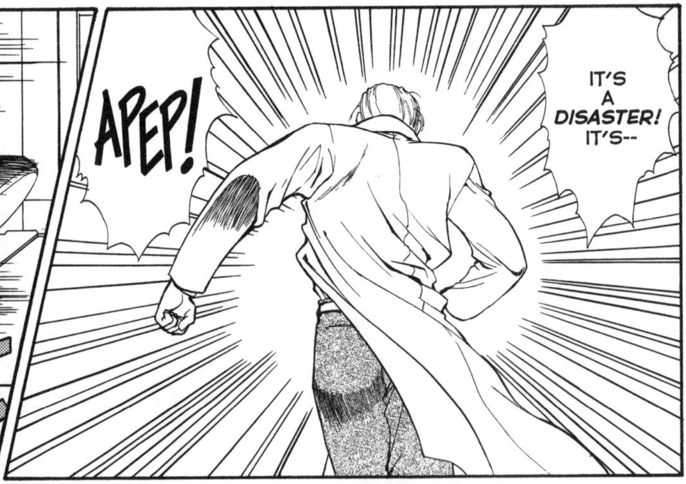
APEP!
IT'S A DISASTER! IT'S--

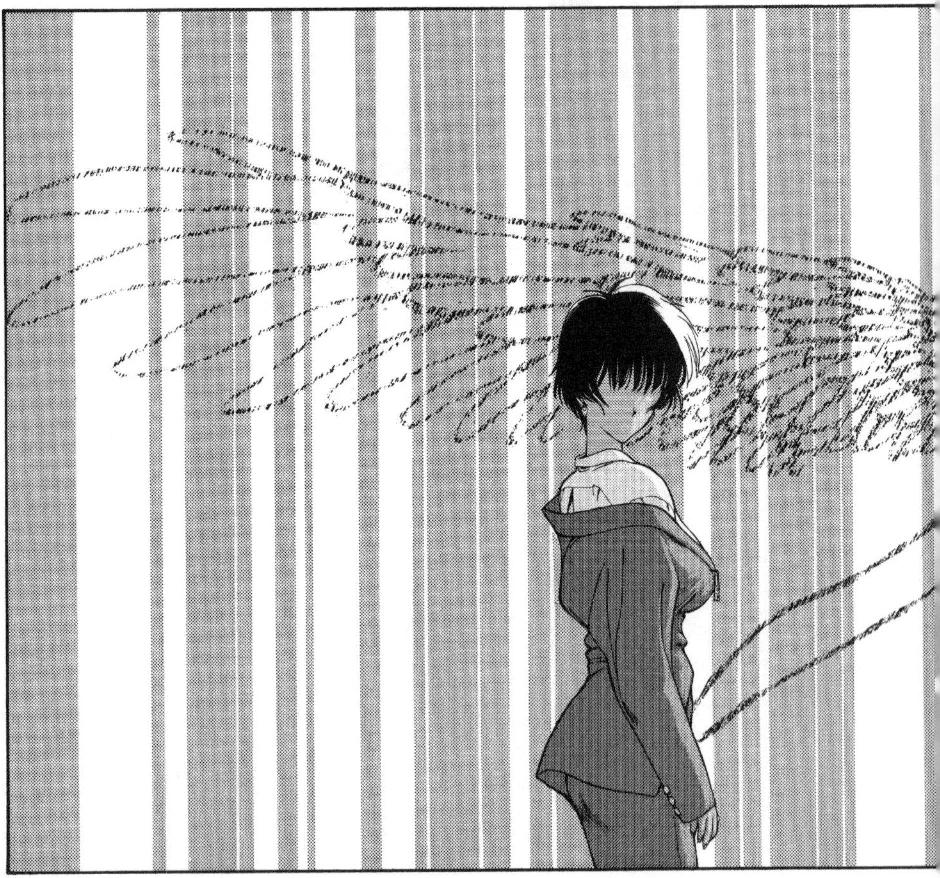

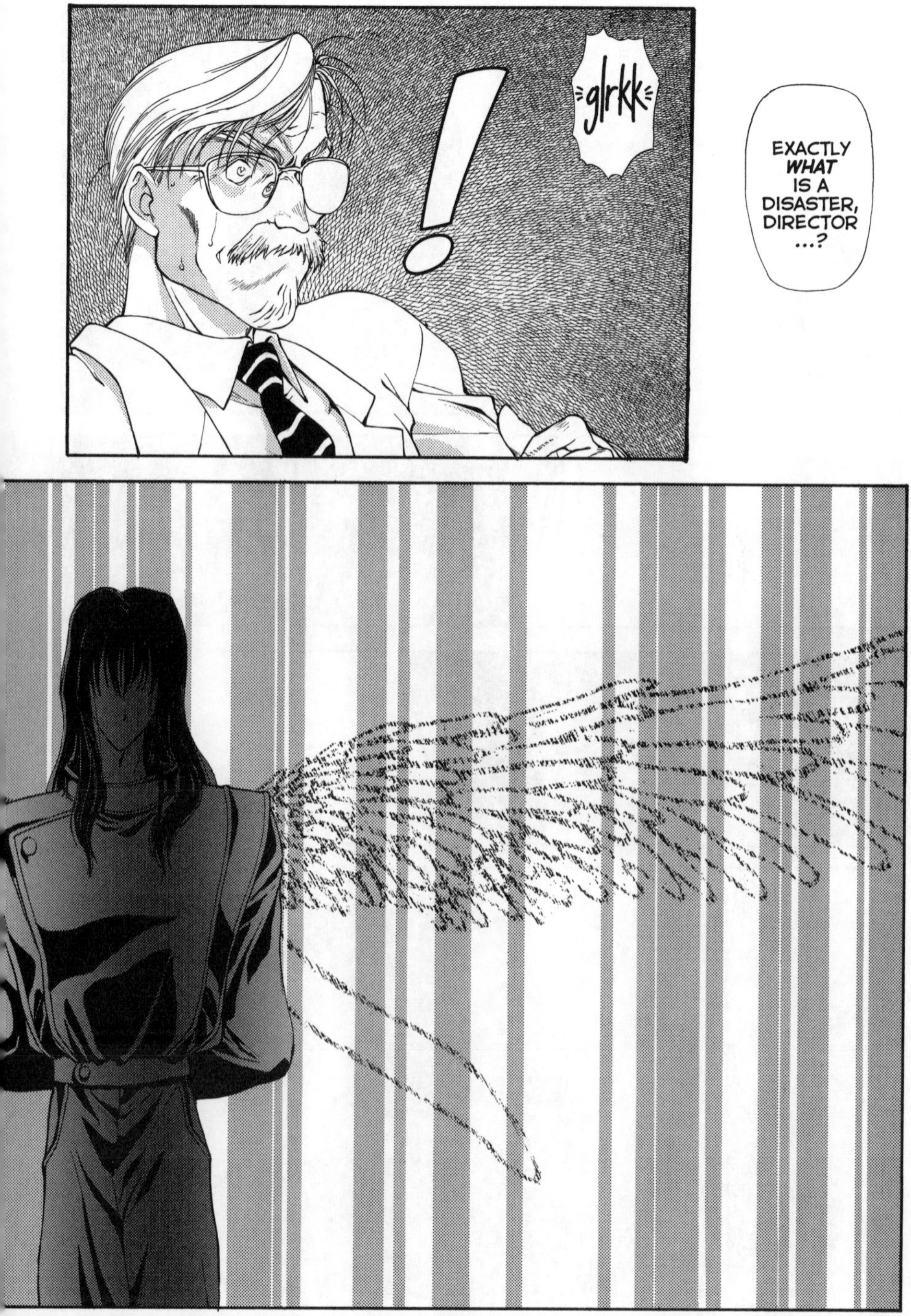
glrkk
EXACTLY WHAT IS A DISASTER, DIRECTOR ...?

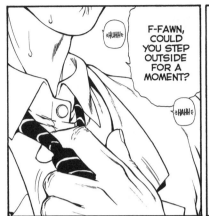

=HUHH=

F-FAWN, COULD YOU STEP OUTSIDE FOR A MOMENT?

=HAHH=

TAP

TAP
TAP

GET SOME REST, FAWN.

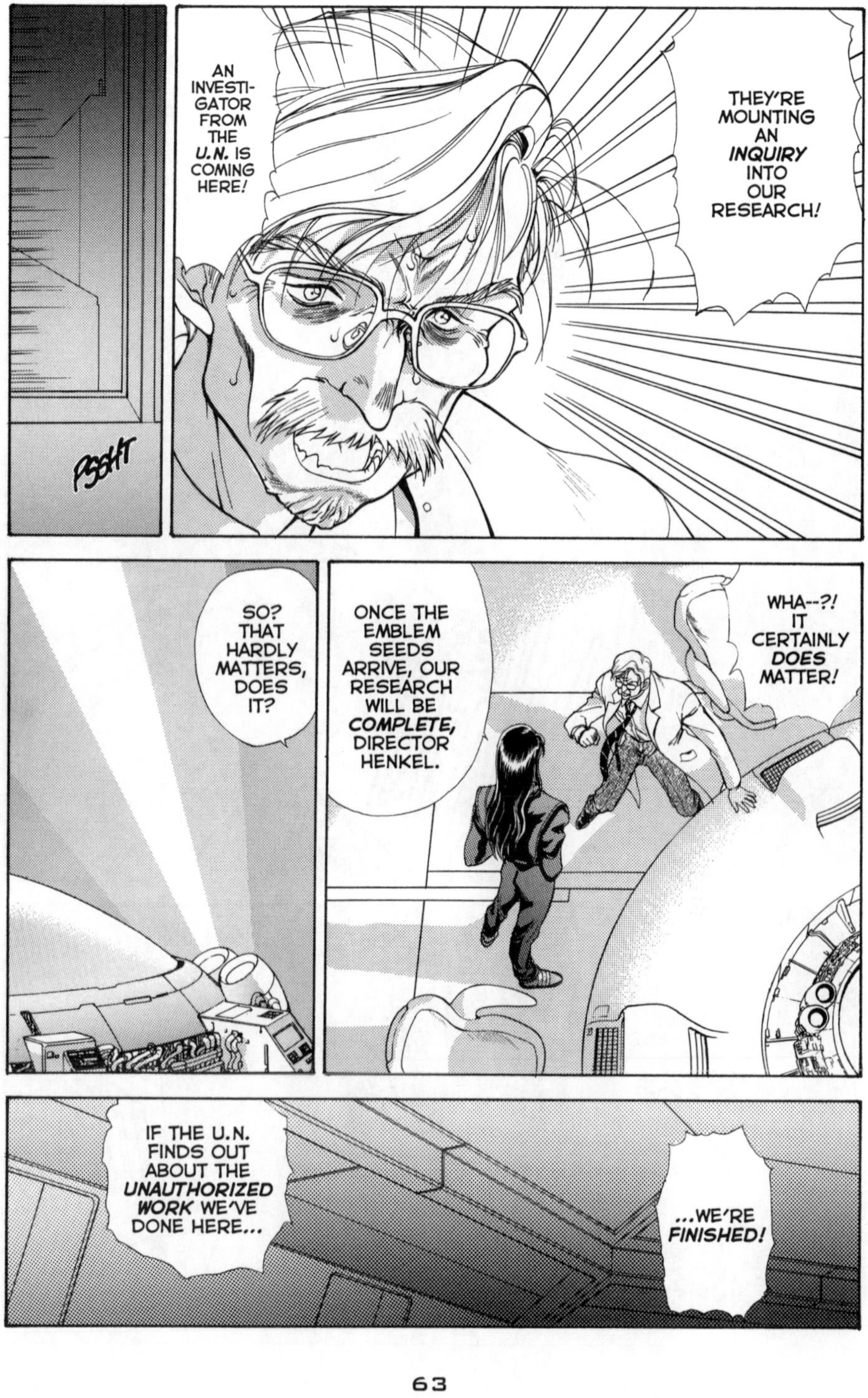
PSSHT
AN INVESTIGATOR FROM THE *U.N.* IS COMING HERE!
THEY'RE MOUNTING AN ***INQUIRY*** INTO OUR RESEARCH!
SO? THAT HARDLY MATTERS, DOES IT?
ONCE THE EMBLEM SEEDS ARRIVE, OUR RESEARCH WILL BE ***COMPLETE,*** DIRECTOR HENKEL.
WHA--?! IT CERTAINLY ***DOES*** MATTER!
IF THE U.N. FINDS OUT ABOUT THE ***UNAUTHORIZED WORK*** WE'VE DONE HERE...
...WE'RE ***FINISHED!***

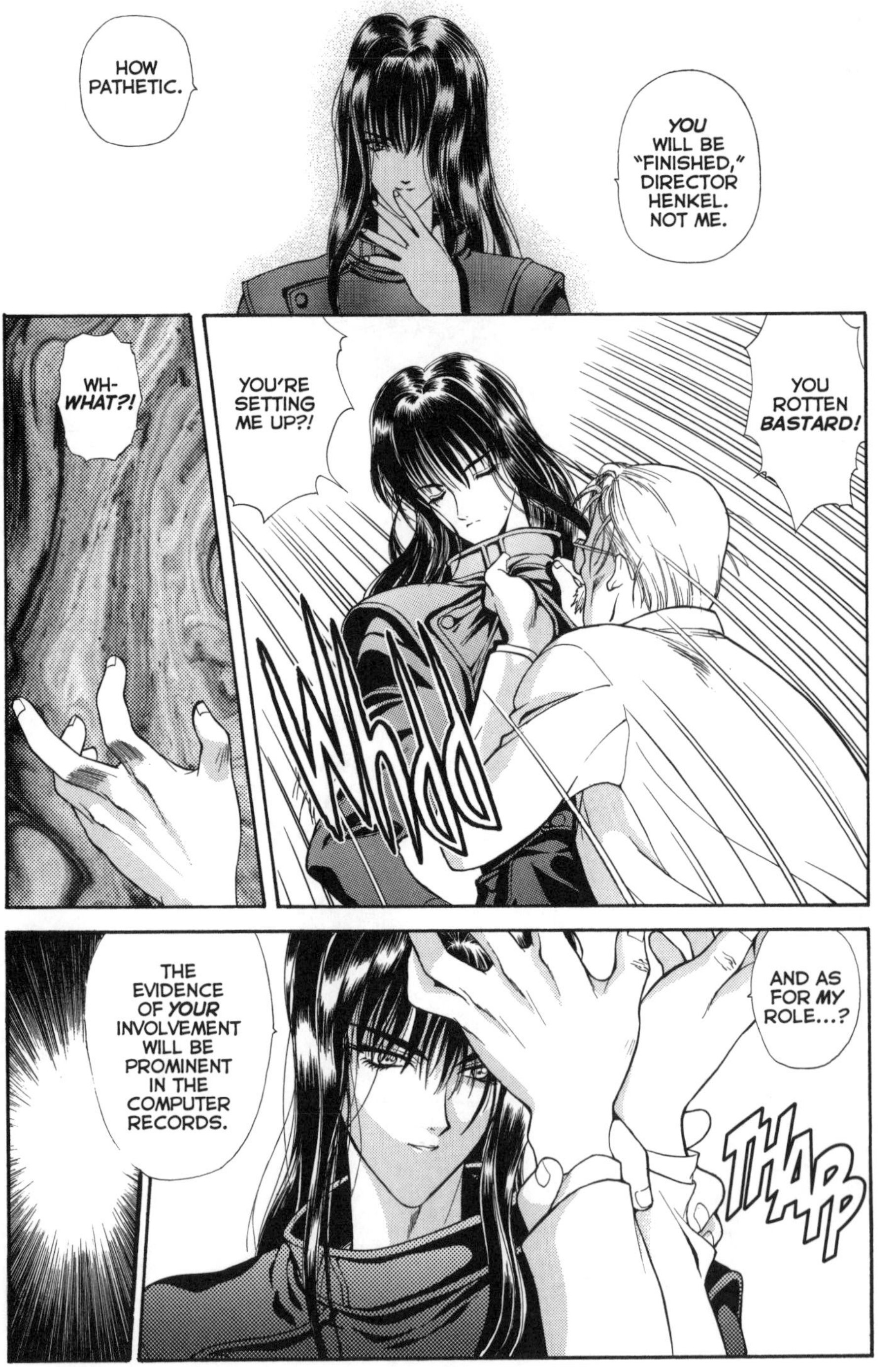
HOW PATHETIC.
YOU WILL BE "FINISHED," DIRECTOR HENKEL. NOT ME.
WH- *WHAT?!*
YOU'RE SETTING ME UP?!
YOU ROTTEN *BASTARD!*
WHUD
THE EVIDENCE OF *YOUR* INVOLVEMENT WILL BE PROMINENT IN THE COMPUTER RECORDS.
AND AS FOR *MY* ROLE...?
THAP

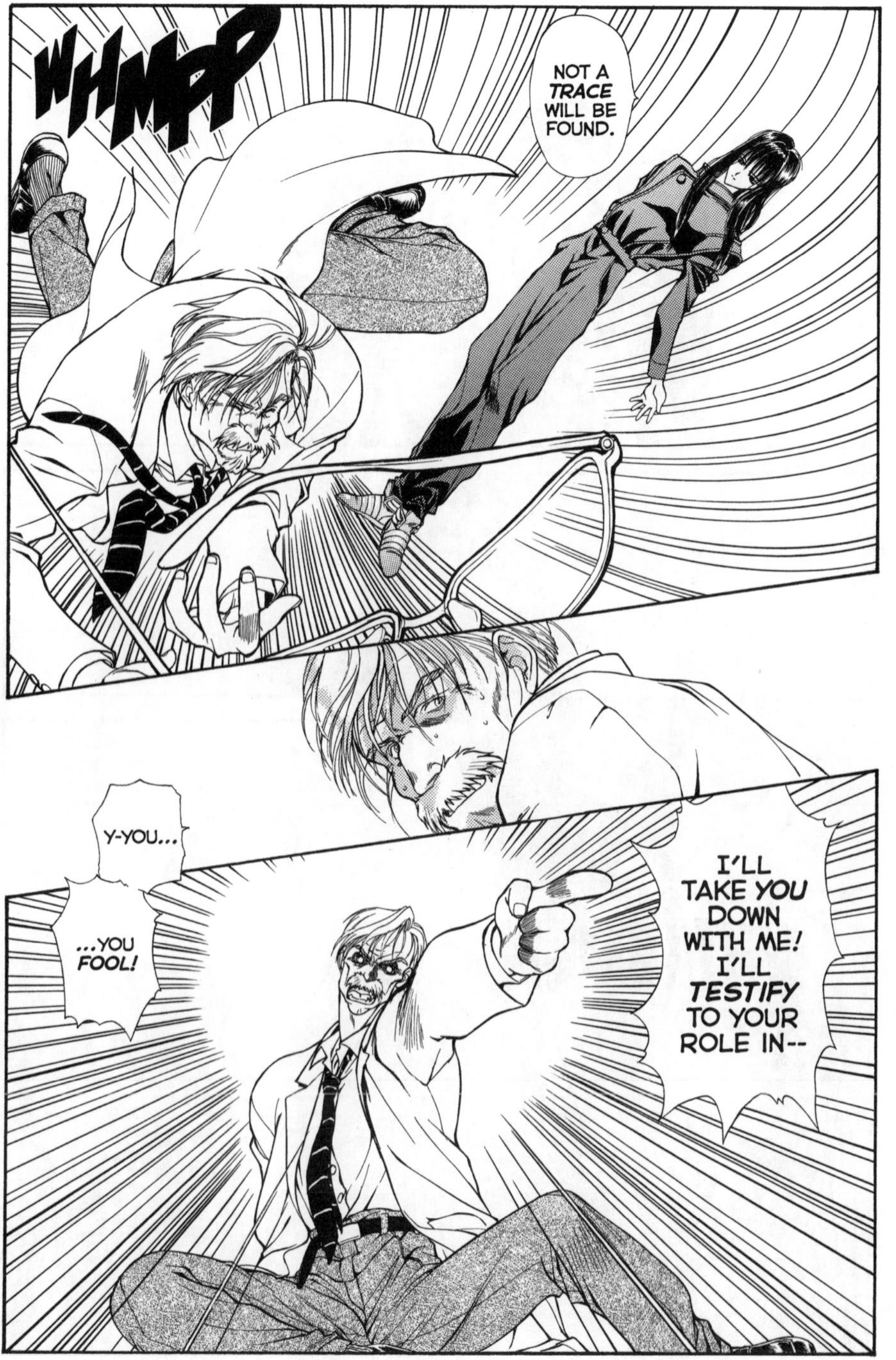
WHMPP
NOT A *TRACE* WILL BE FOUND.
Y-YOU...
...YOU *FOOL!*
I'LL TAKE *YOU* DOWN WITH ME! I'LL *TESTIFY* TO YOUR ROLE IN--

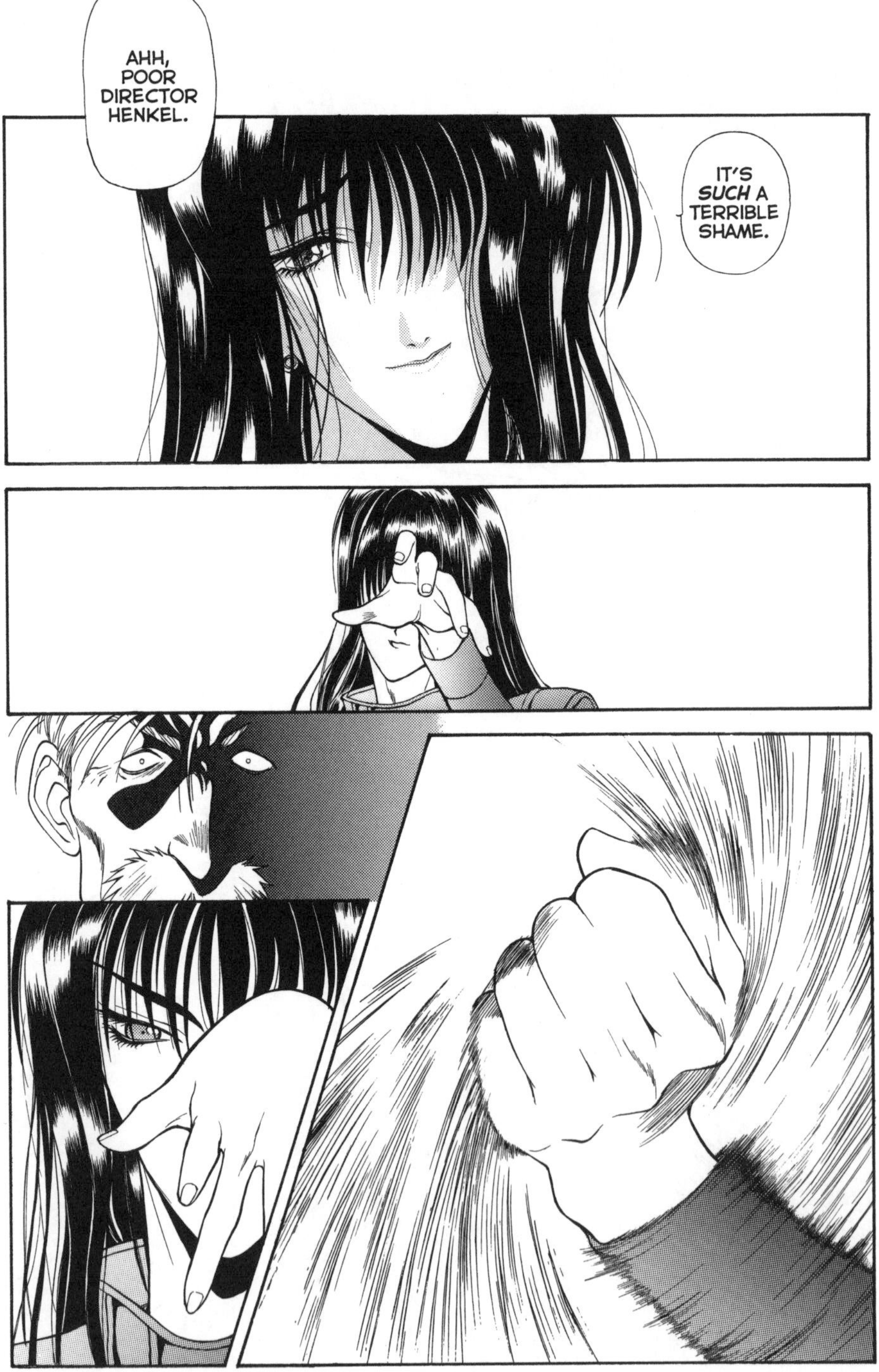
AHH, POOR DIRECTOR HENKEL.
IT'S SUCH A TERRIBLE SHAME.

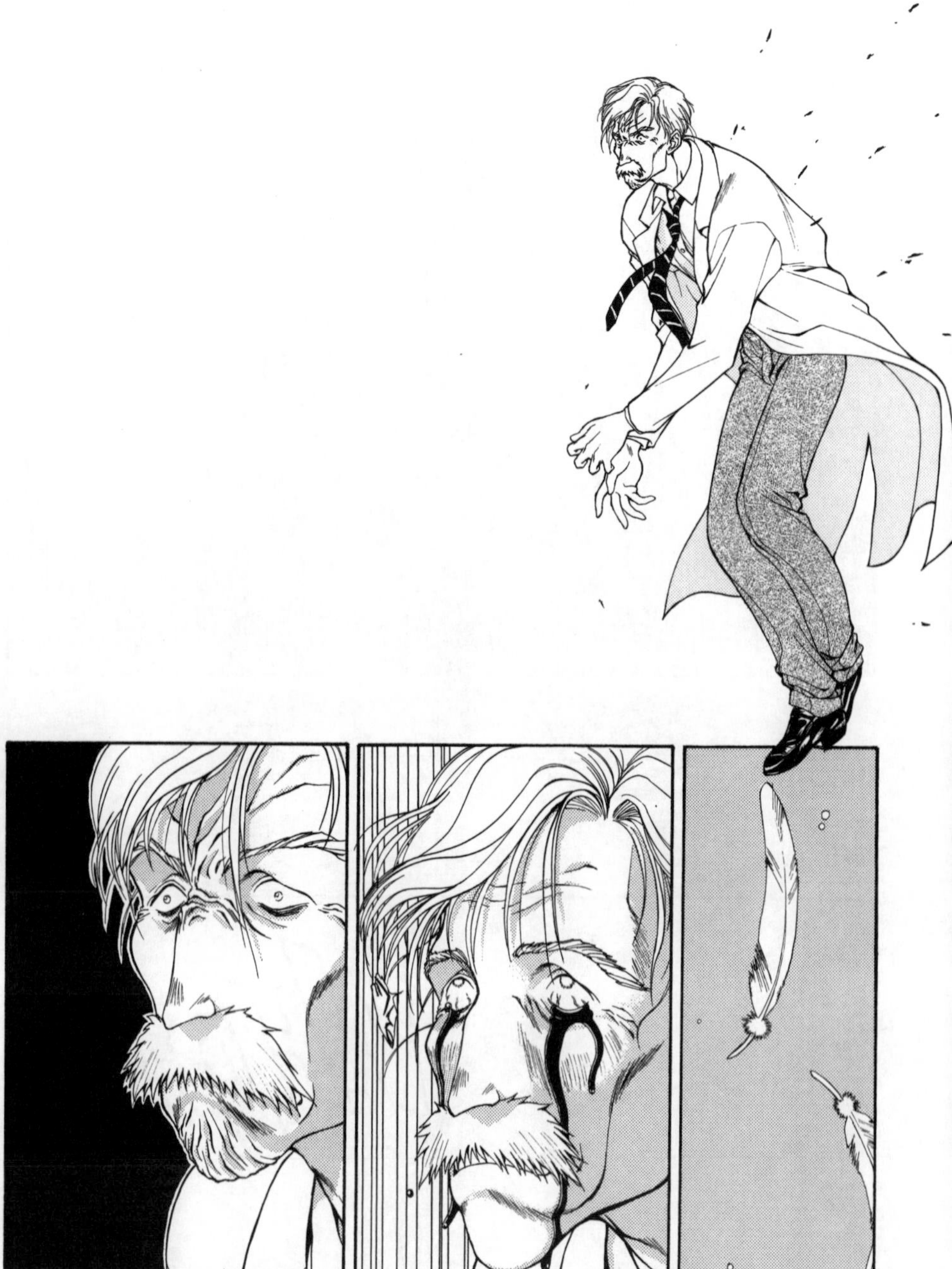

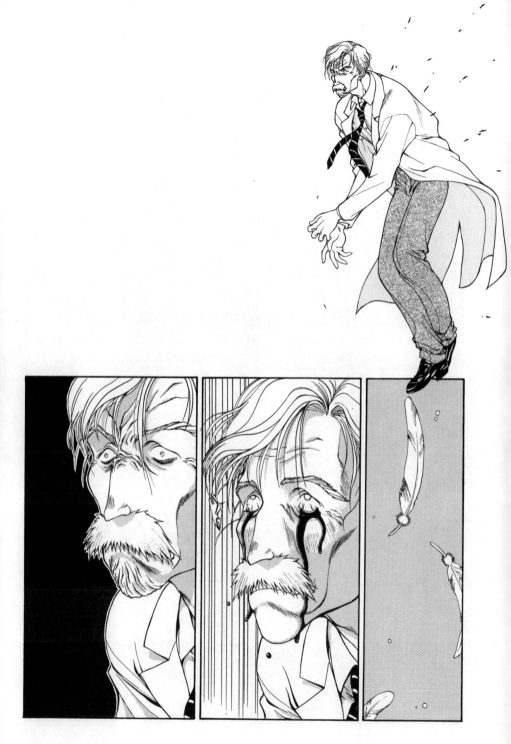

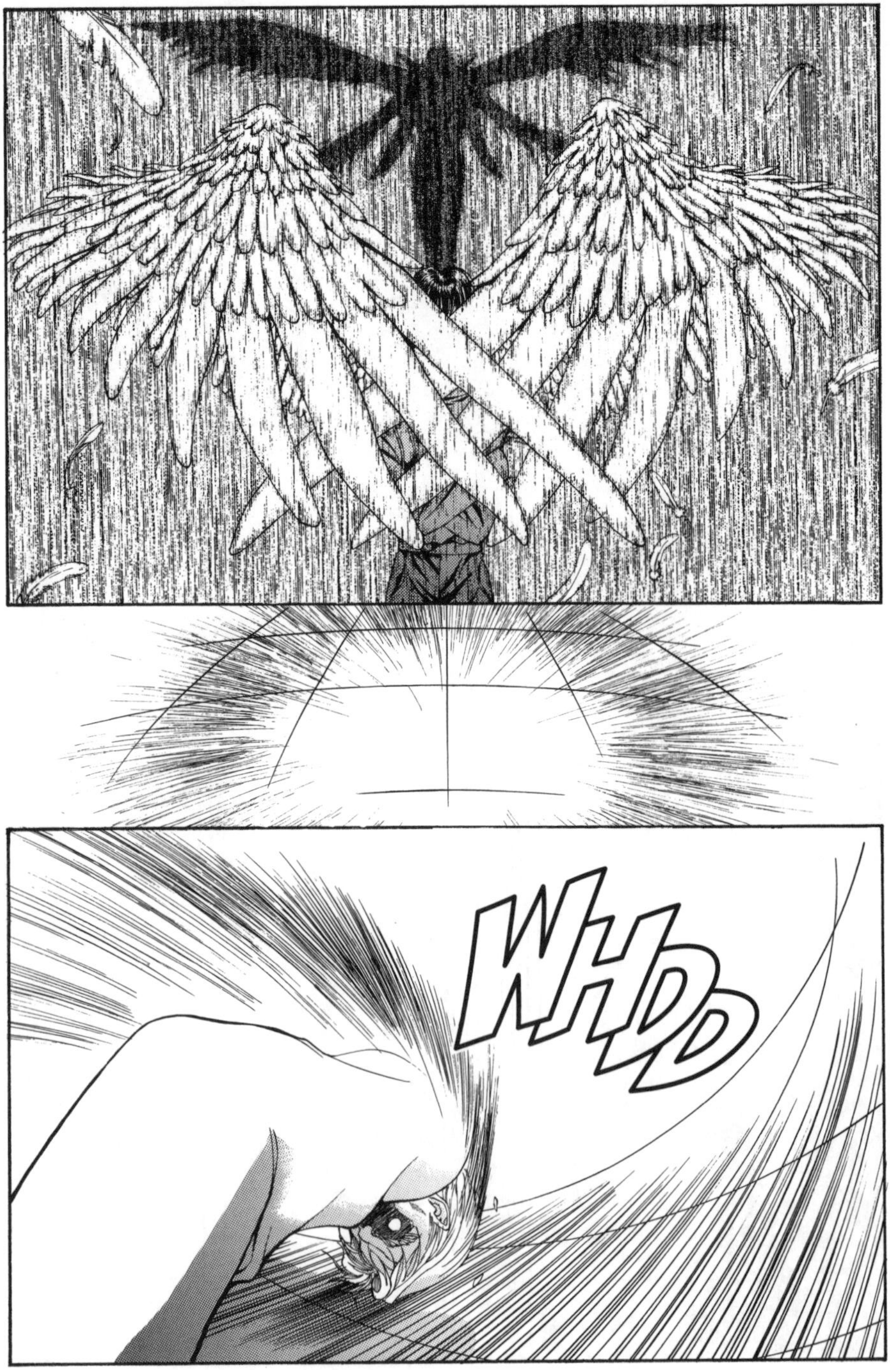
WHDD

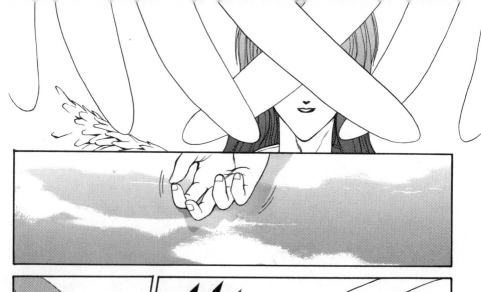

FHHH

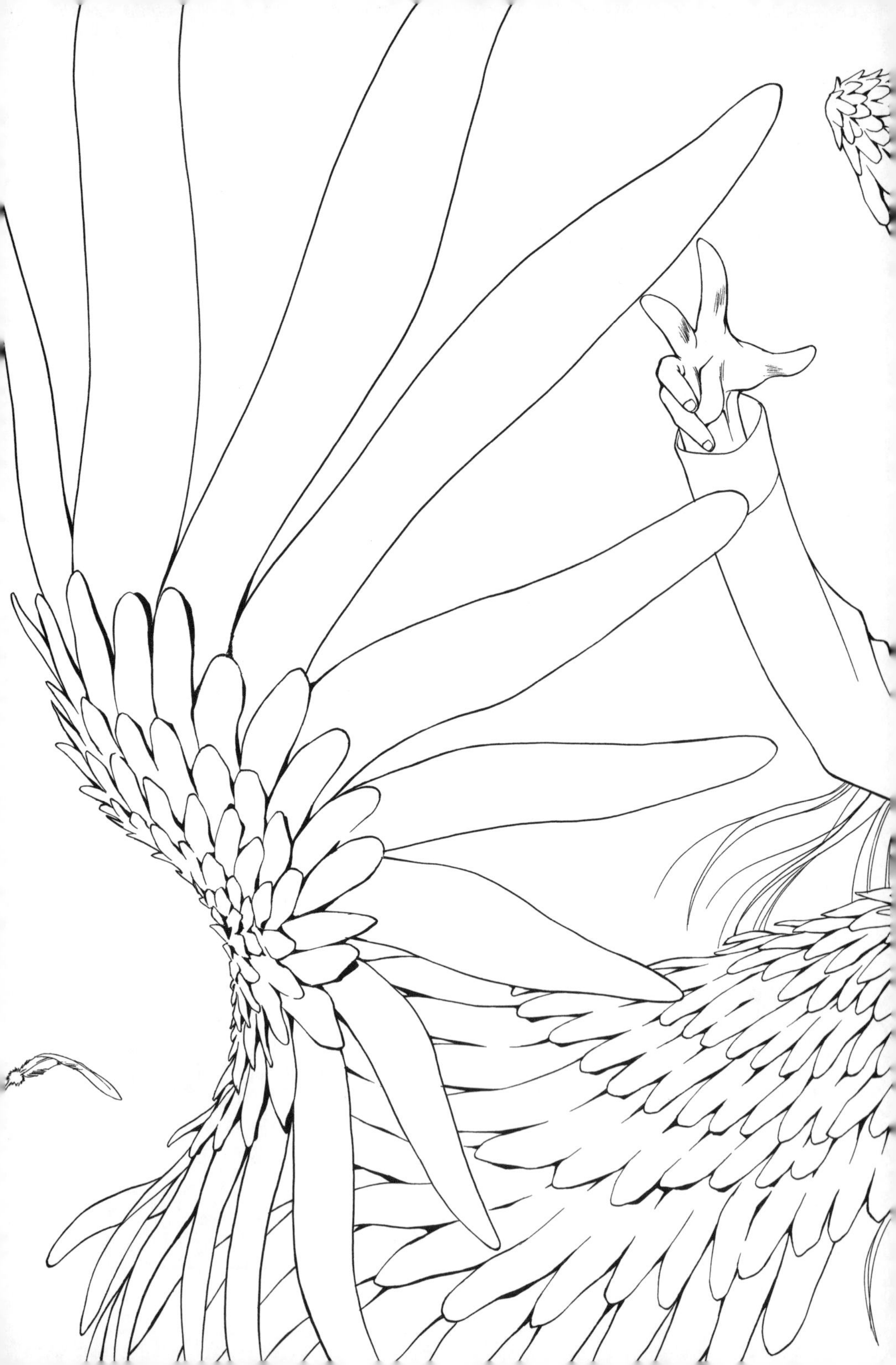

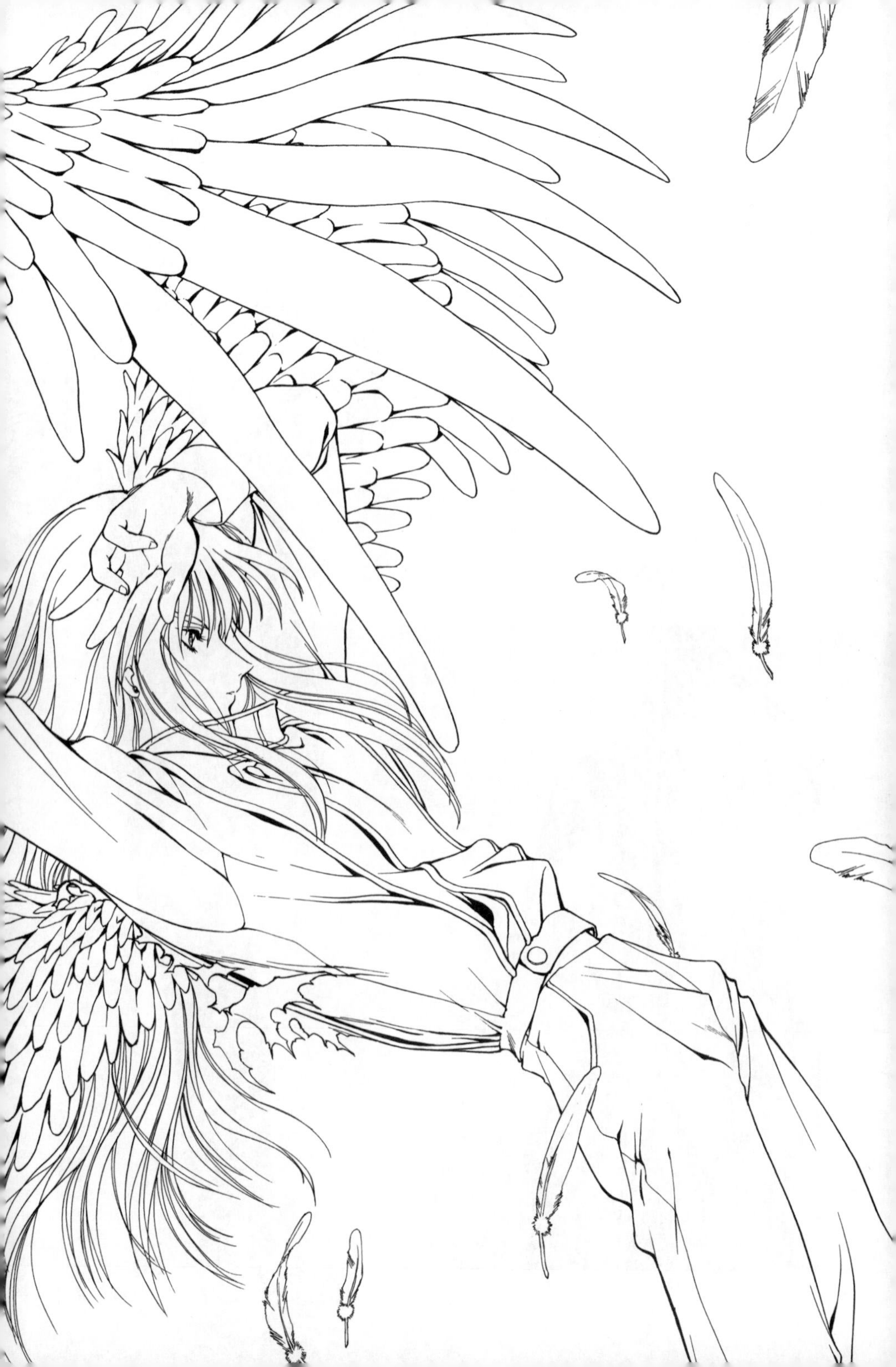

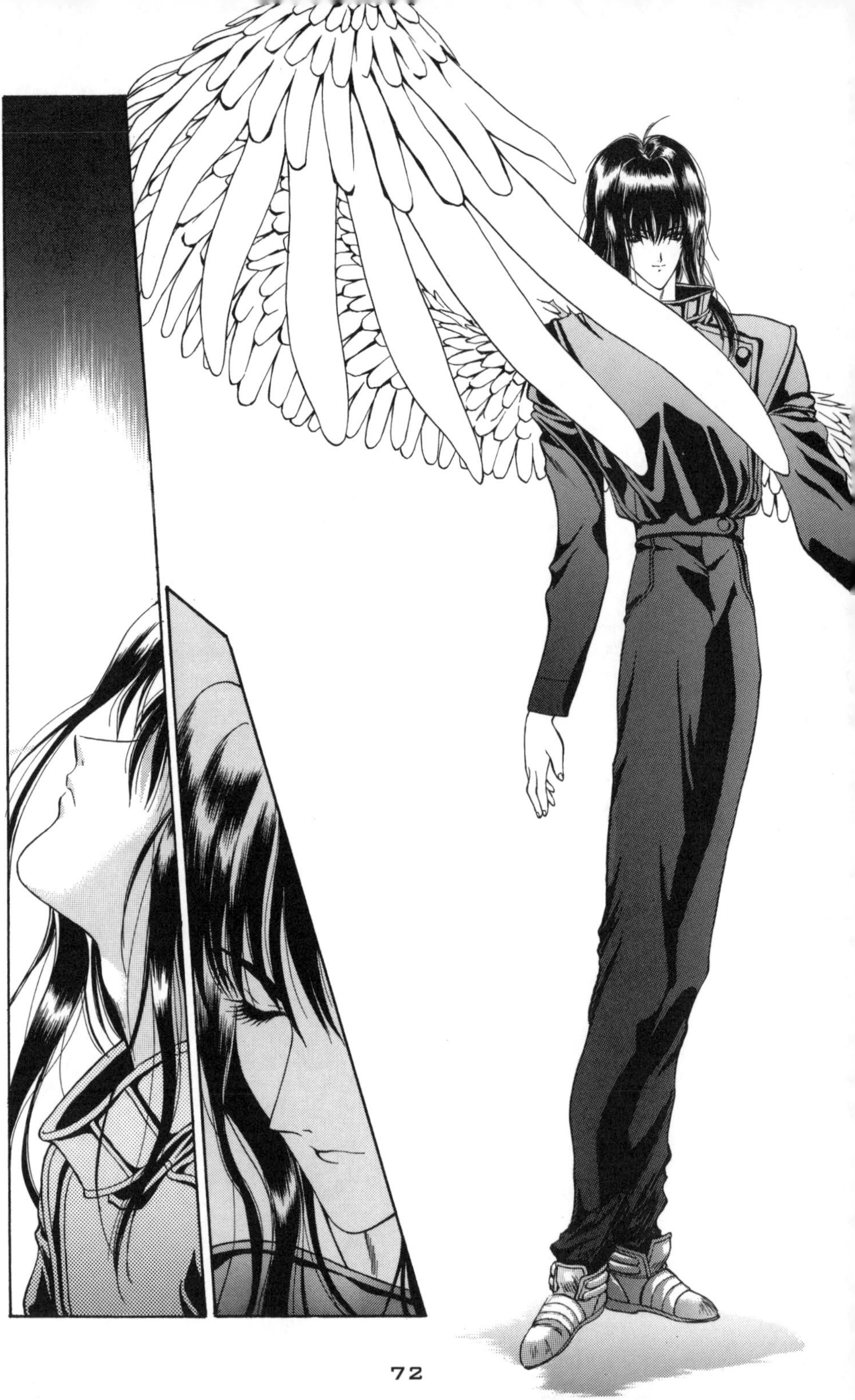

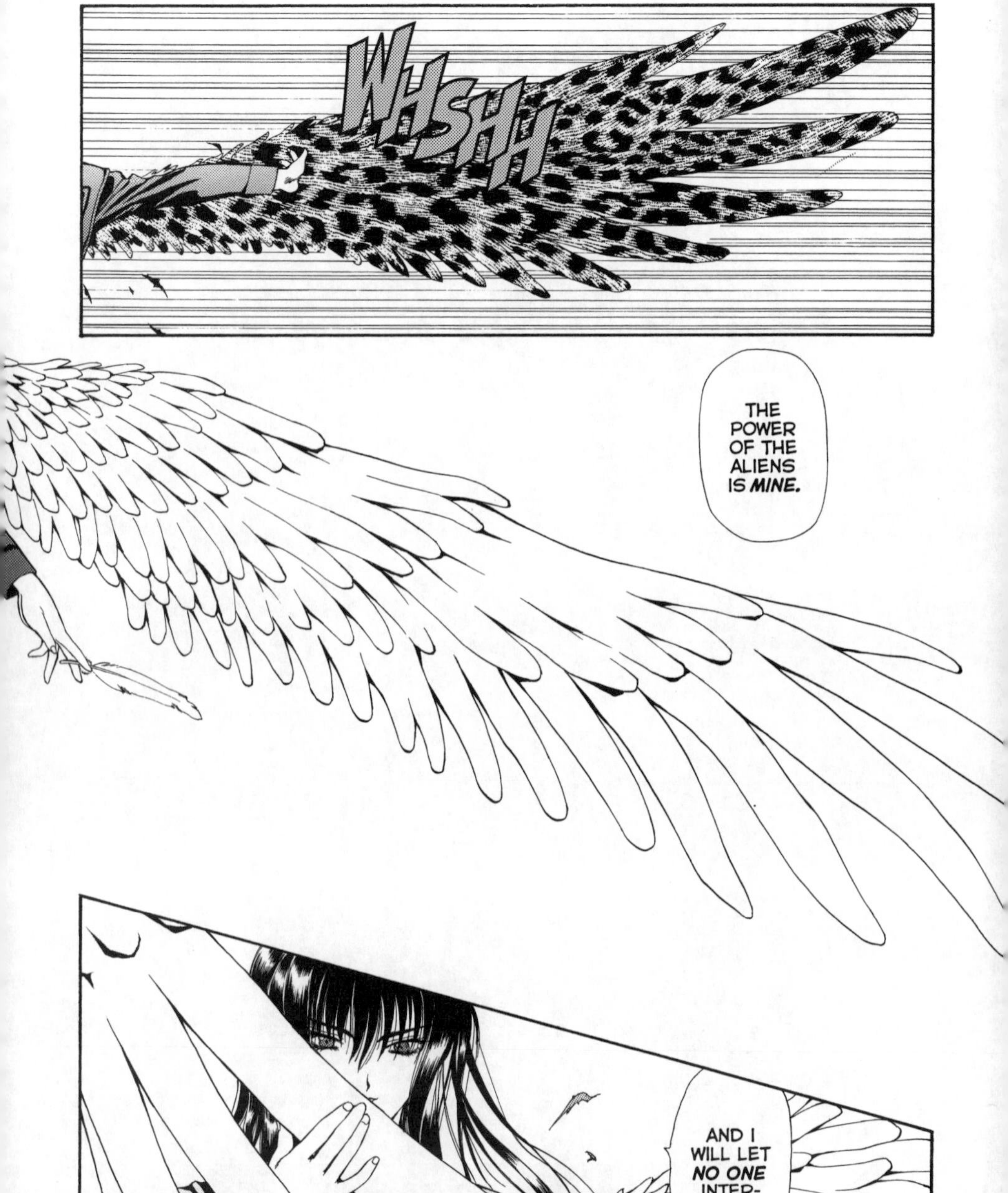
WHSHH
THE POWER OF THE ALIENS IS *MINE.*
AND I WILL LET *NO ONE* INTER-FERE...

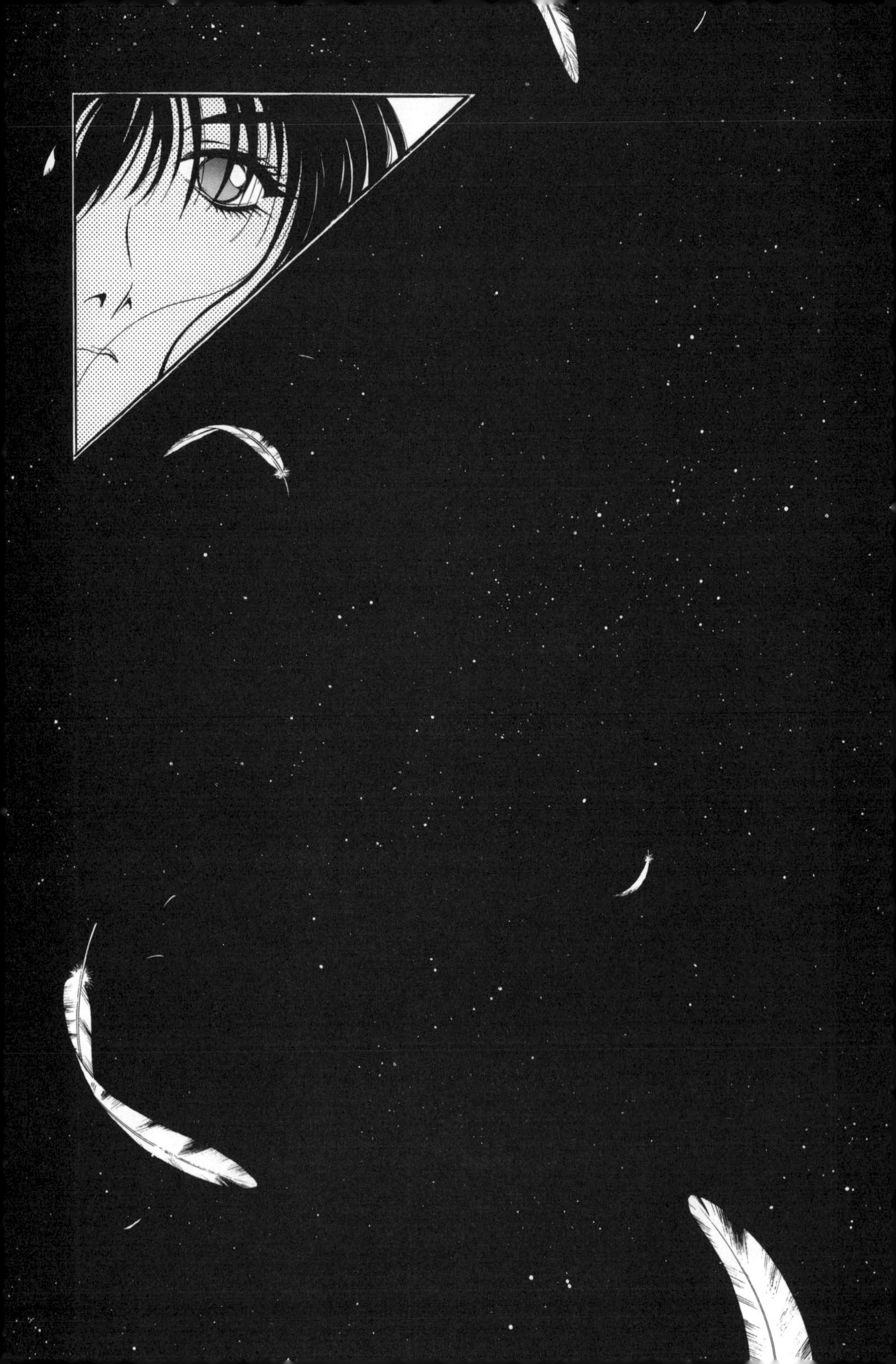

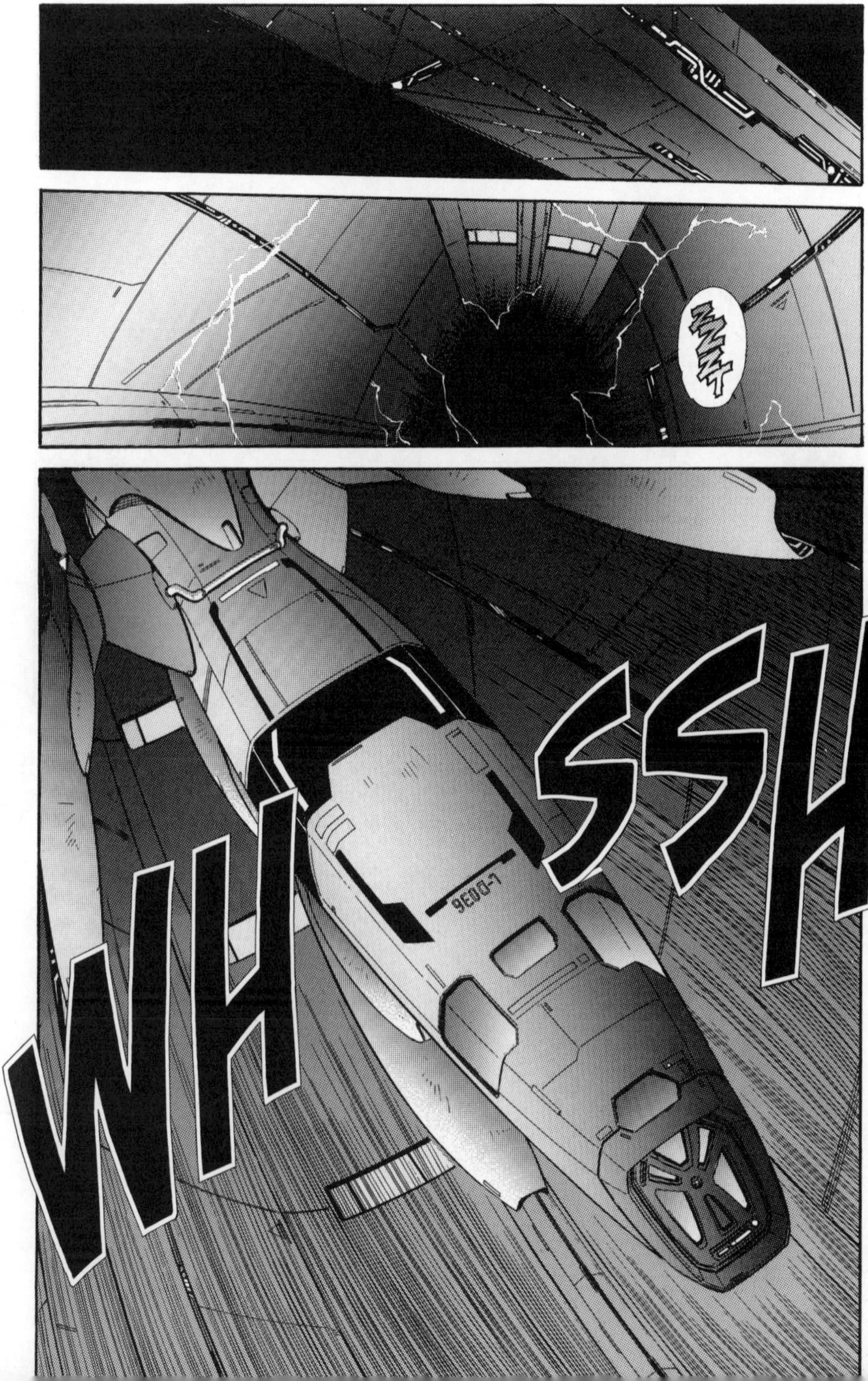
NNNT
WHSSH
L-D036

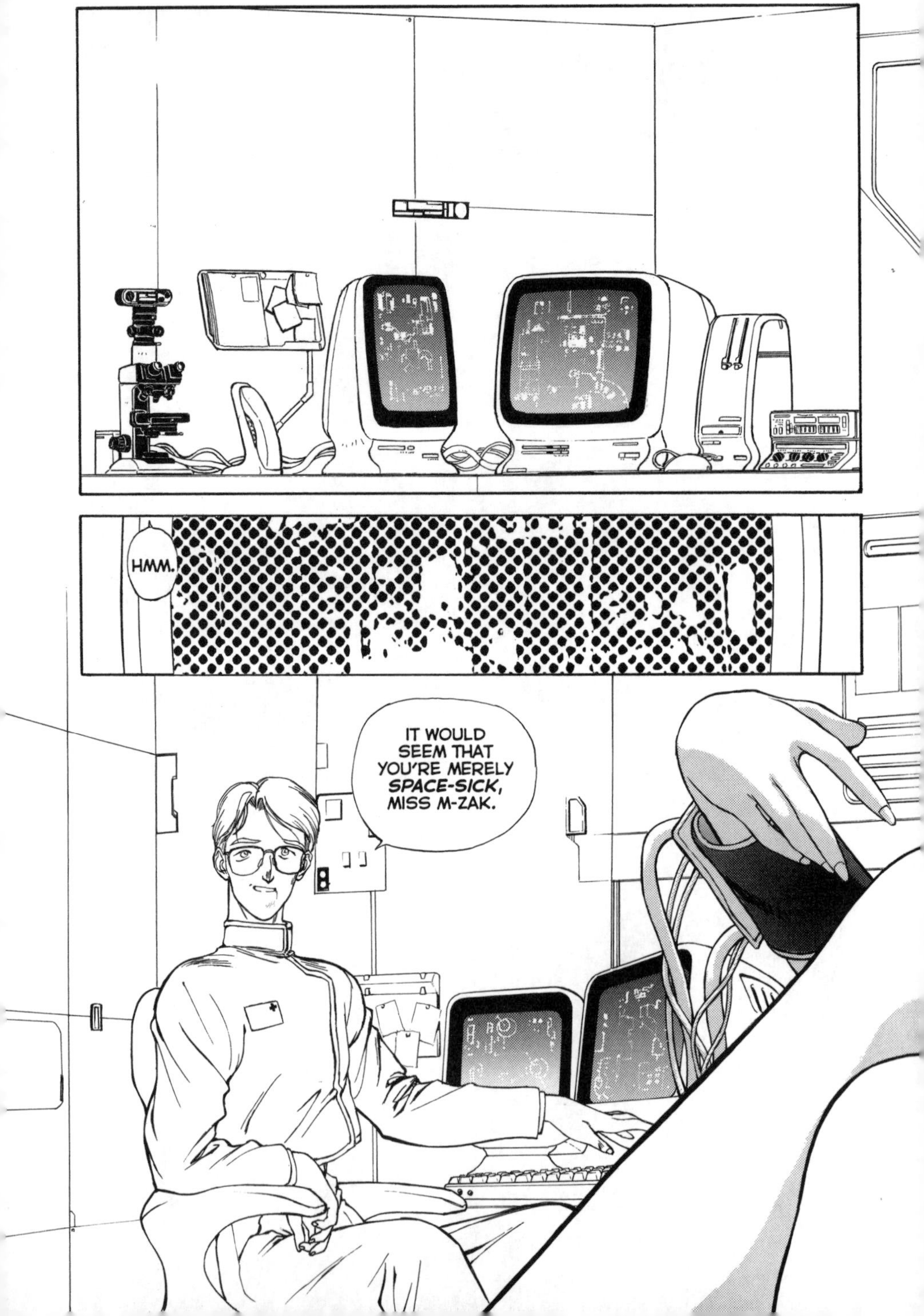
HMM.
IT WOULD SEEM THAT YOU'RE MERELY *SPACE-SICK*, MISS M-ZAK.

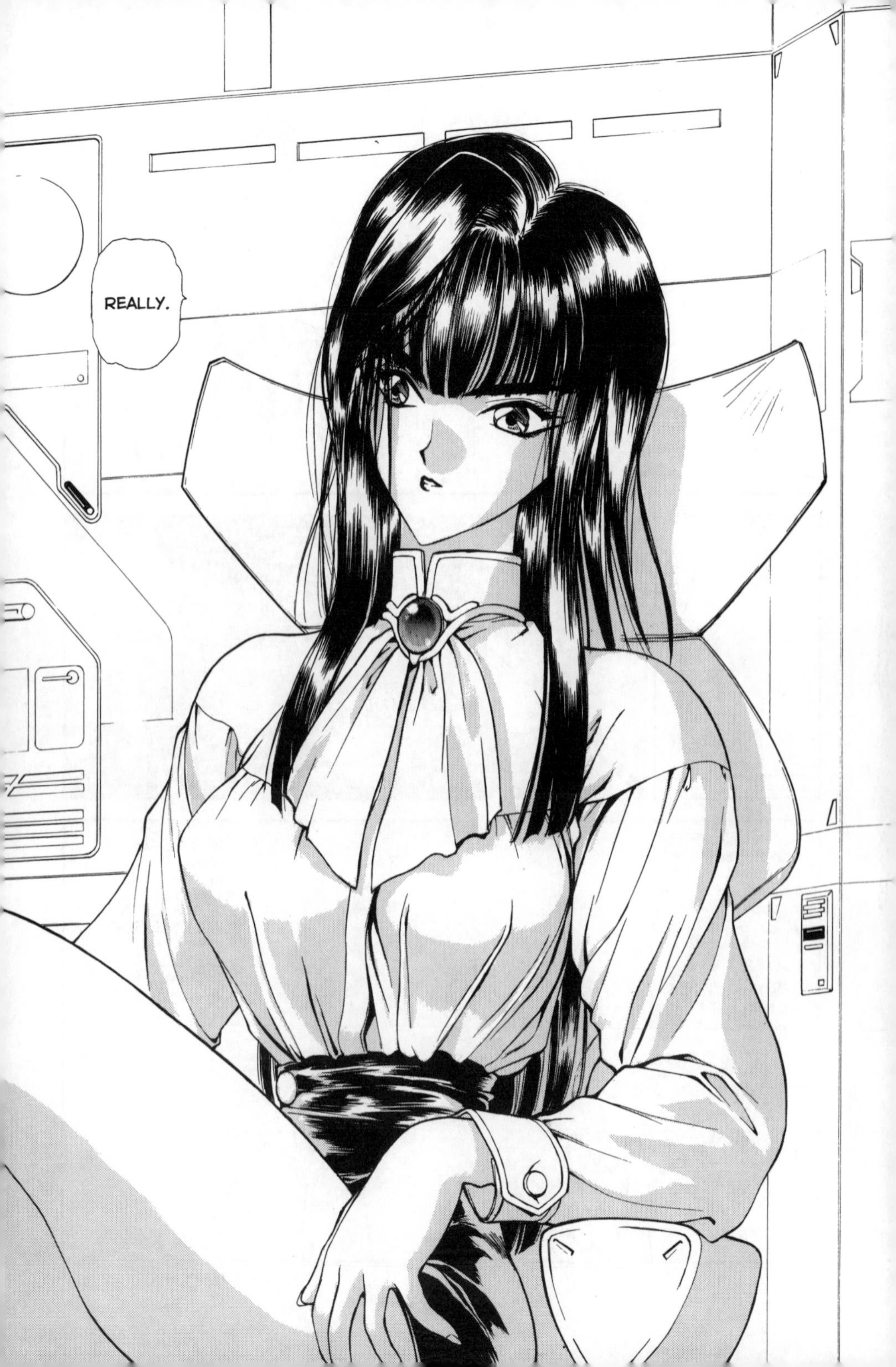
REALLY.

STILL...WHO WOULD'VE THOUGHT THAT A *UNITED NATIONS SPECIAL INVESTIGATOR* WOULD GET SPACE-SICK...?

SHRIP

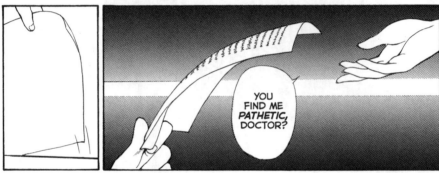

YOU FIND ME *PATHETIC*, DOCTOR?

NOT AT *ALL*, MISS M-ZAK. PERHAPS THAT *AUGMENTED BODY* OF YOURS IS SIMPLY *REJECTING* THE STANDARD ANTI-NAUSEA INJECTION.

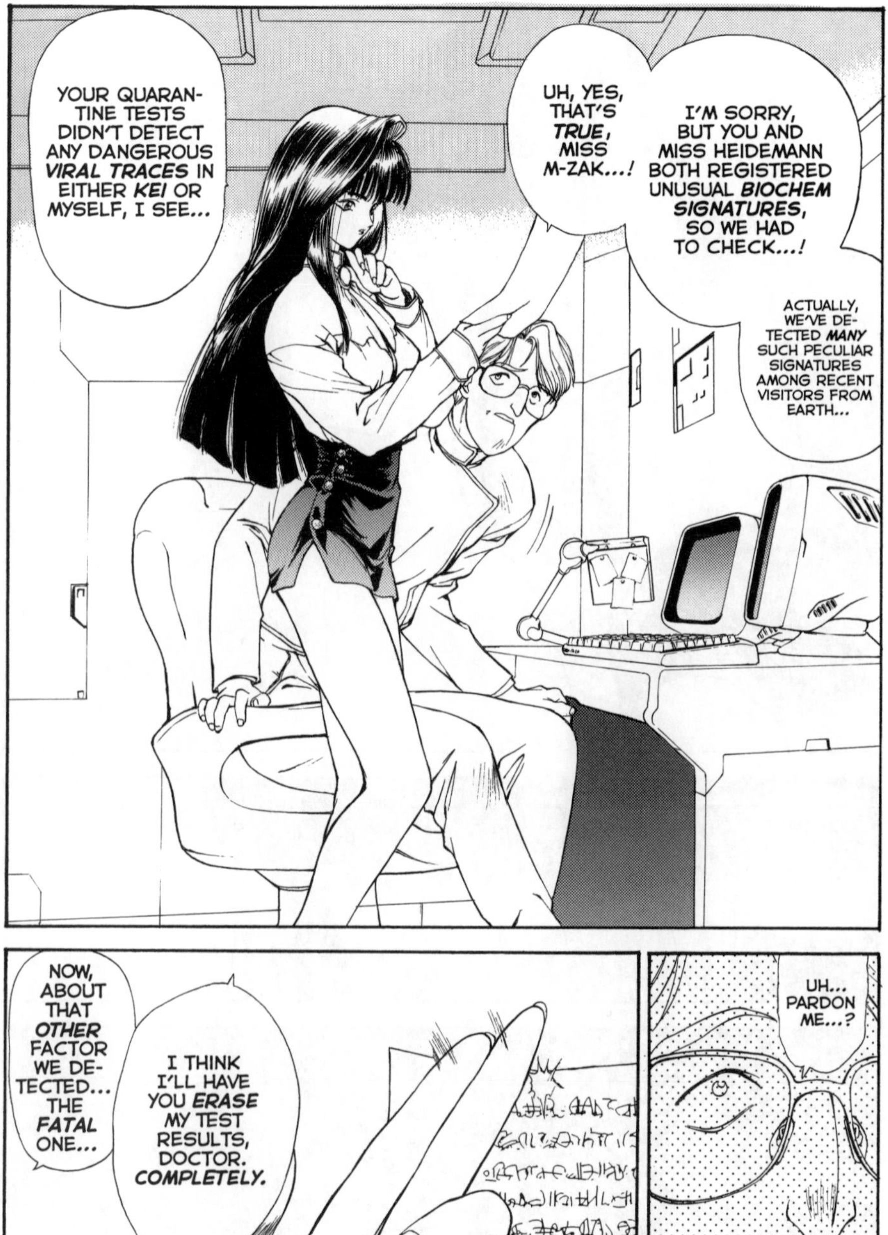
YOUR QUARANTINE TESTS DIDN'T DETECT ANY DANGEROUS *VIRAL TRACES* IN EITHER *KEI* OR MYSELF, I SEE...
UH, YES, THAT'S *TRUE*, MISS M-ZAK...!
I'M SORRY, BUT YOU AND MISS HEIDEMANN BOTH REGISTERED UNUSUAL *BIOCHEM SIGNATURES*, SO WE HAD TO CHECK...!
ACTUALLY, WE'VE DETECTED *MANY* SUCH PECULIAR SIGNATURES AMONG RECENT VISITORS FROM EARTH...
NOW, ABOUT THAT *OTHER* FACTOR WE DETECTED... THE *FATAL* ONE...
I THINK I'LL HAVE YOU *ERASE* MY TEST RESULTS, DOCTOR. *COMPLETELY.*
UH... PARDON ME...?

WE WOULDN'T WANT SOMEONE *ANALYZING* SUCH *INTRIGUING* DATA LATER, NOW, WOULD WE?

NOT THAT *YOU* WOULD CONSIDER SUCH A THING...

...WOULD YOU.

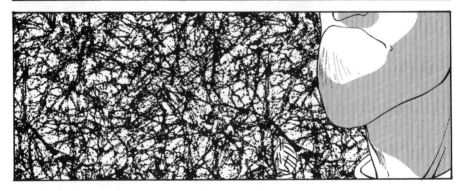

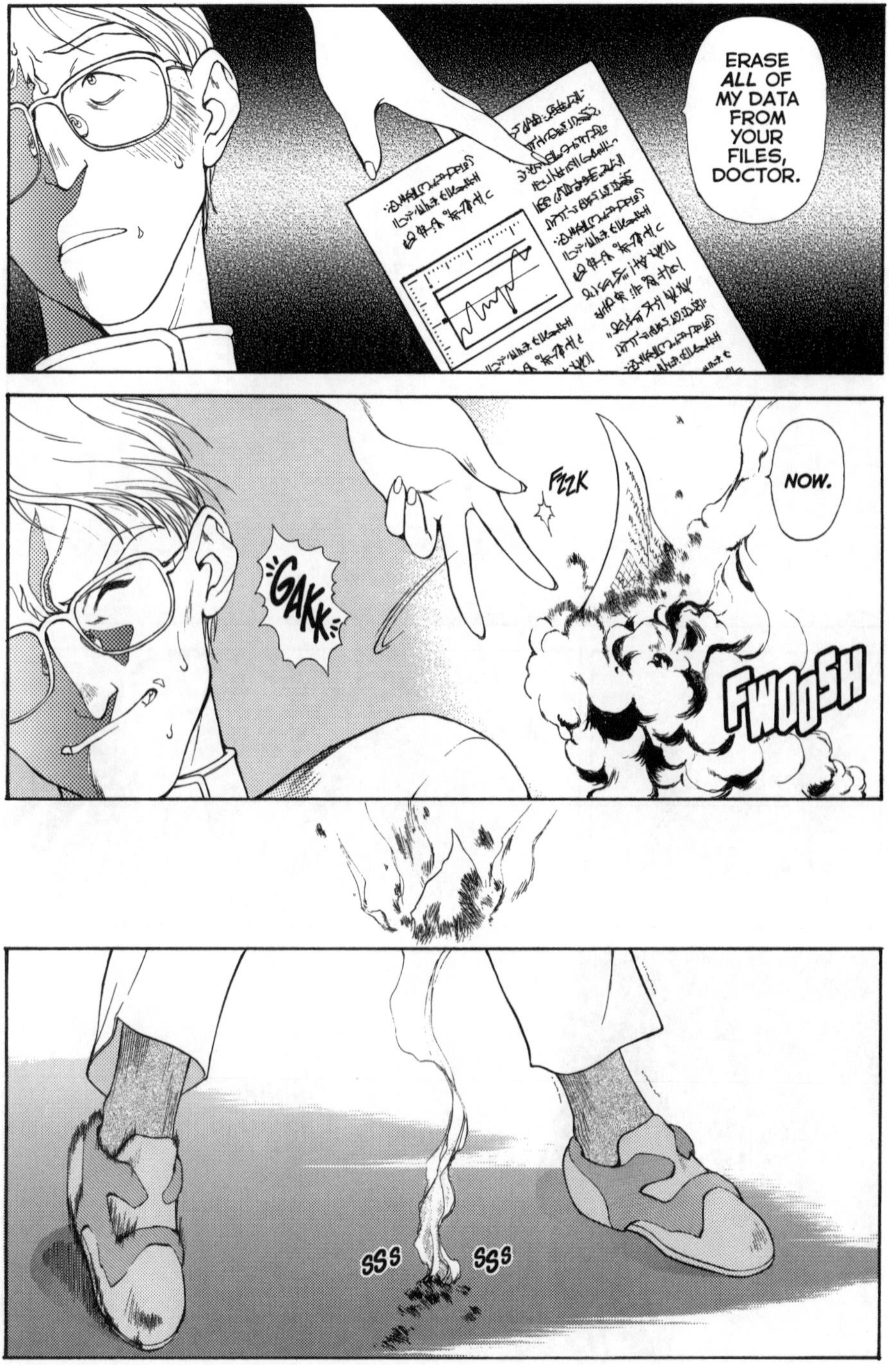
ERASE ALL OF MY DATA FROM YOUR FILES, DOCTOR.
FZZK
NOW.
GAKK
FWOOSH
SSS
SSS

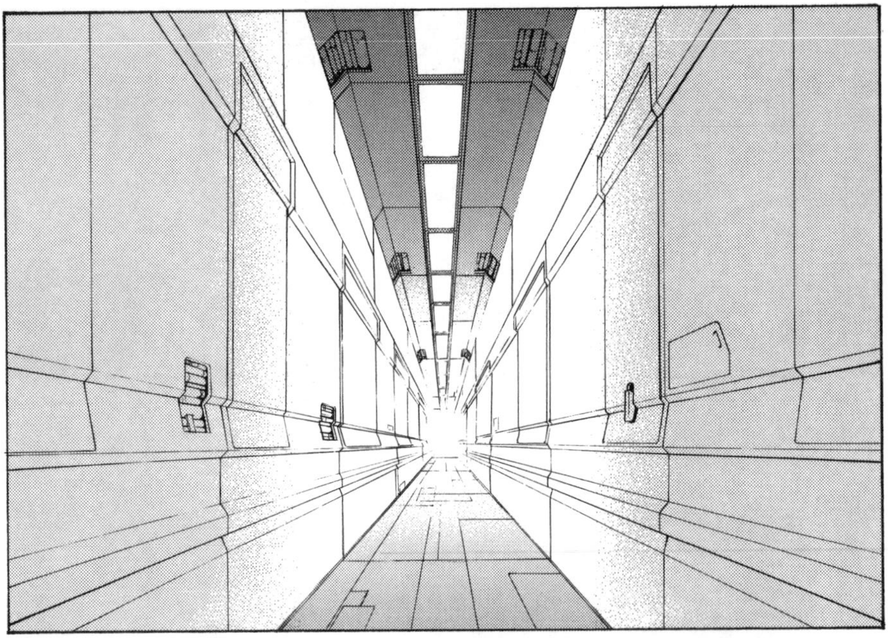
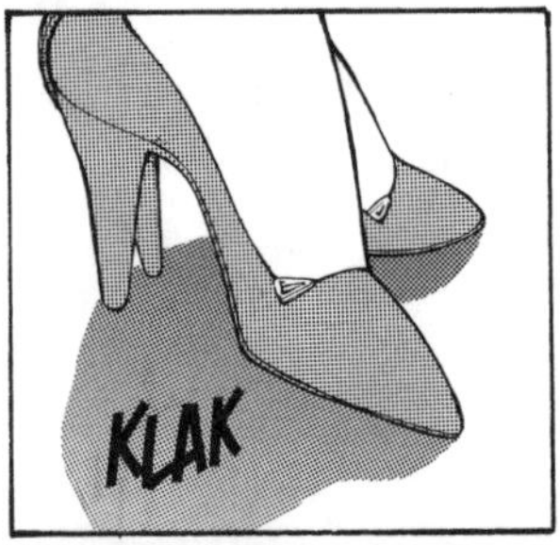
KLAK
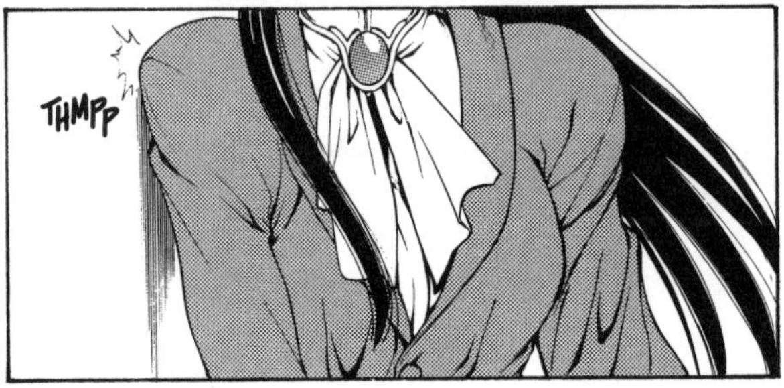
THMPP
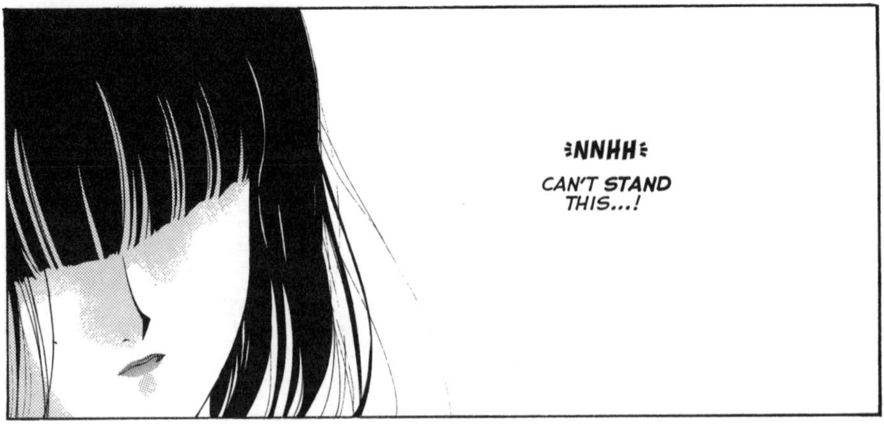
NNHH
CAN'T STAND THIS...!

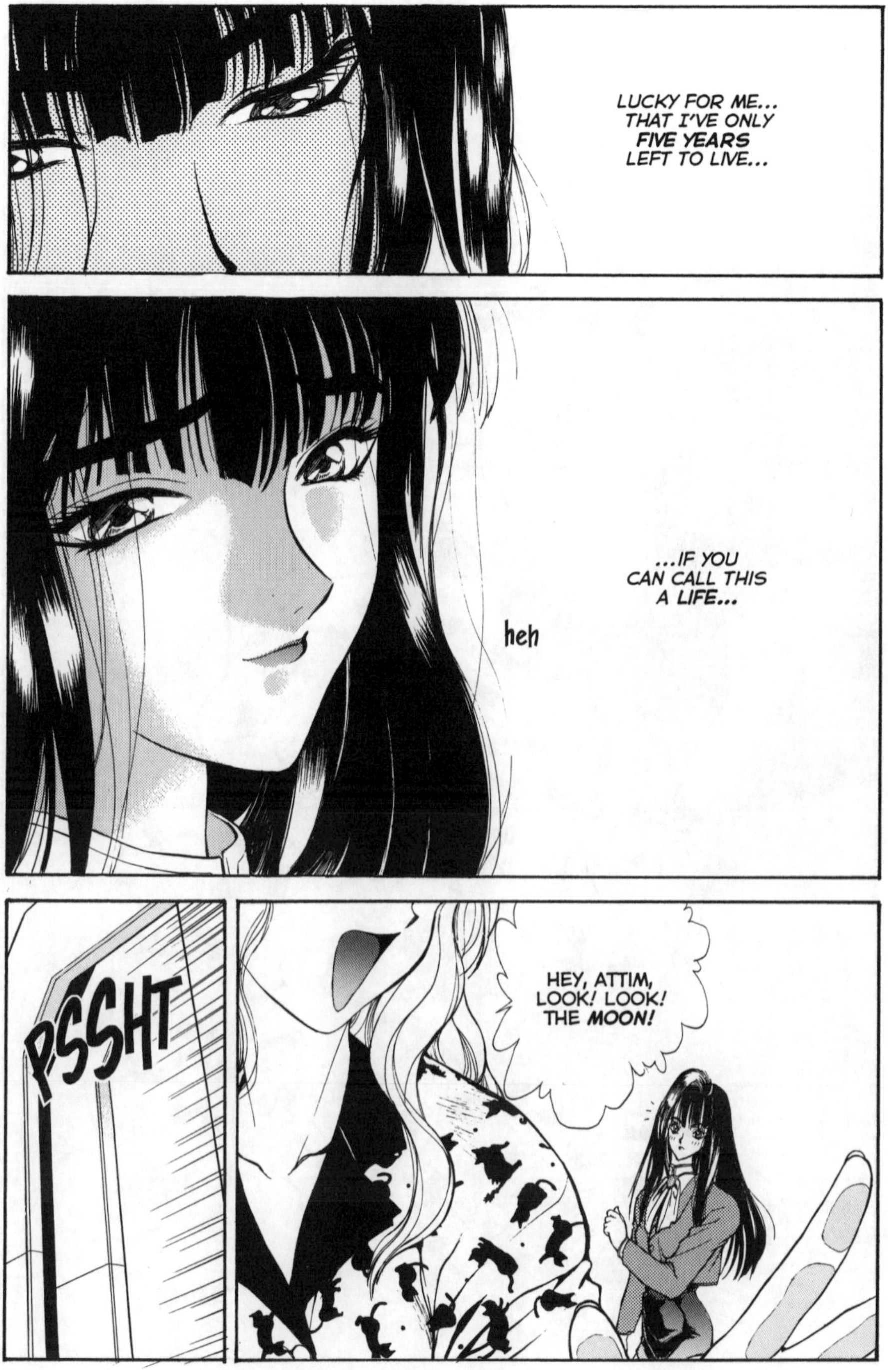
LUCKY FOR ME... THAT I'VE ONLY FIVE YEARS LEFT TO LIVE...
heh
...IF YOU CAN CALL THIS A LIFE...
PSSHT
HEY, ATTIM, LOOK! LOOK! THE MOON!

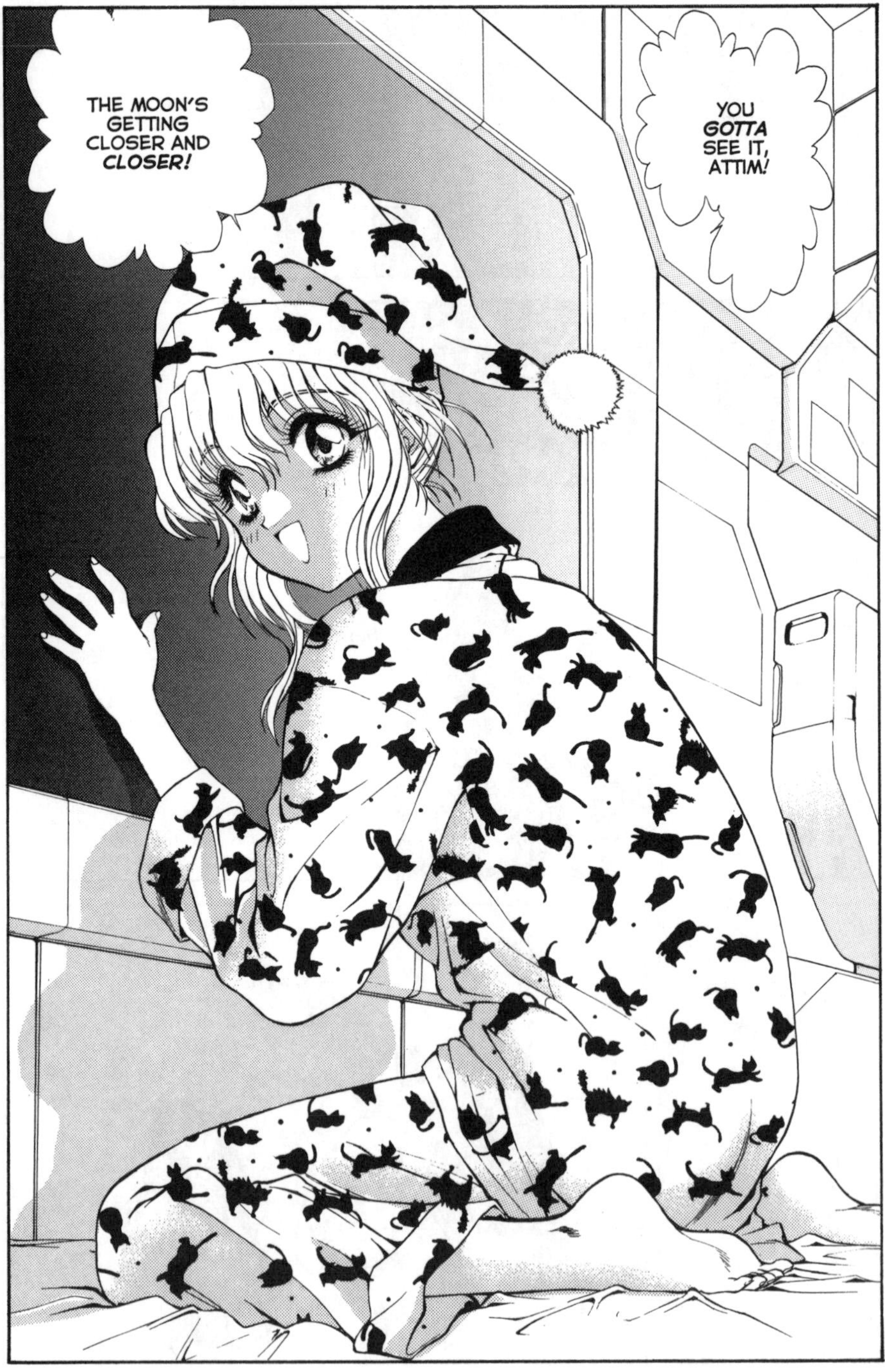
THE MOON'S GETTING CLOSER AND *CLOSER!*
YOU *GOTTA* SEE IT, ATTIM!

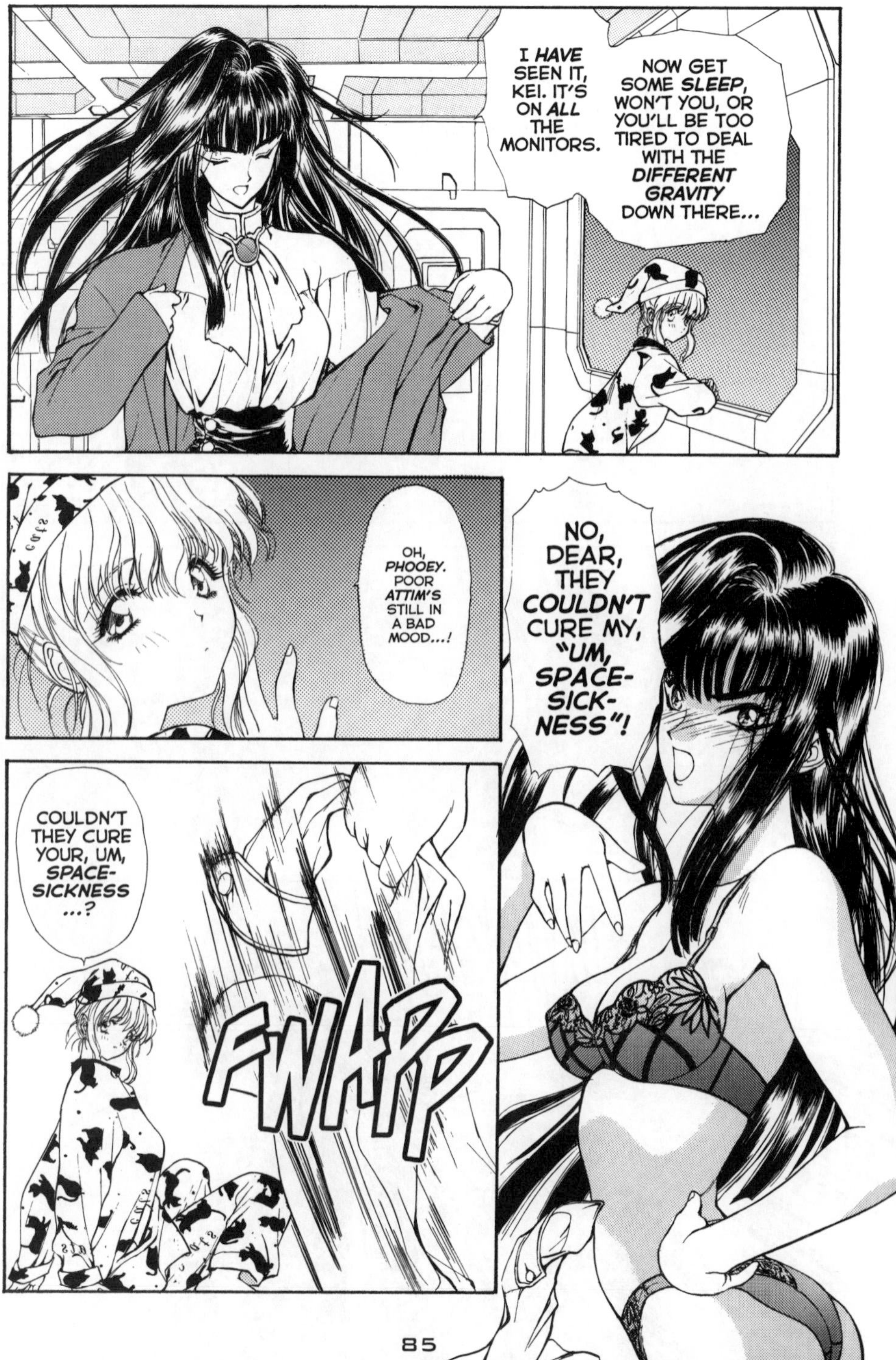
I HAVE SEEN IT, KEI. IT'S ON ALL THE MONITORS.
NOW GET SOME SLEEP, WON'T YOU, OR YOU'LL BE TOO TIRED TO DEAL WITH THE DIFFERENT GRAVITY DOWN THERE...
OH, PHOOEY. POOR ATTIM'S STILL IN A BAD MOOD...!
NO, DEAR, THEY COULDN'T CURE MY, "UM, SPACE-SICKNESS"!
COULDN'T THEY CURE YOUR, UM, SPACE-SICKNESS ...?
FWAPP

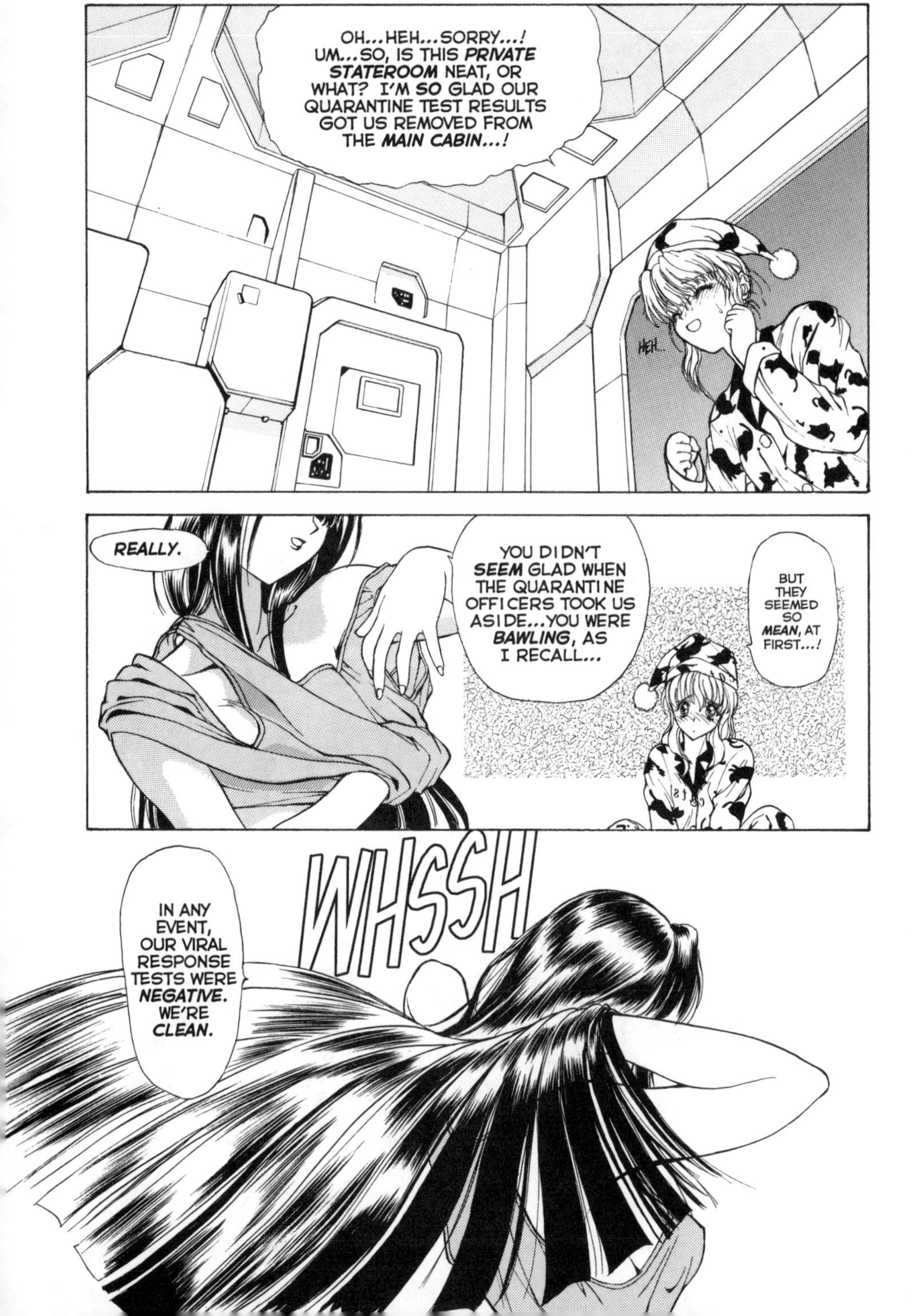
OH...HEH...SORRY...! UM...SO, IS THIS PRIVATE STATEROOM NEAT, OR WHAT? I'M SO GLAD OUR QUARANTINE TEST RESULTS GOT US REMOVED FROM THE MAIN CABIN...!
HEH...
REALLY.
YOU DIDN'T SEEM GLAD WHEN THE QUARANTINE OFFICERS TOOK US ASIDE...YOU WERE BAWLING, AS I RECALL...
BUT THEY SEEMED SO MEAN, AT FIRST...!
WHSSH
IN ANY EVENT, OUR VIRAL RESPONSE TESTS WERE NEGATIVE. WE'RE CLEAN.

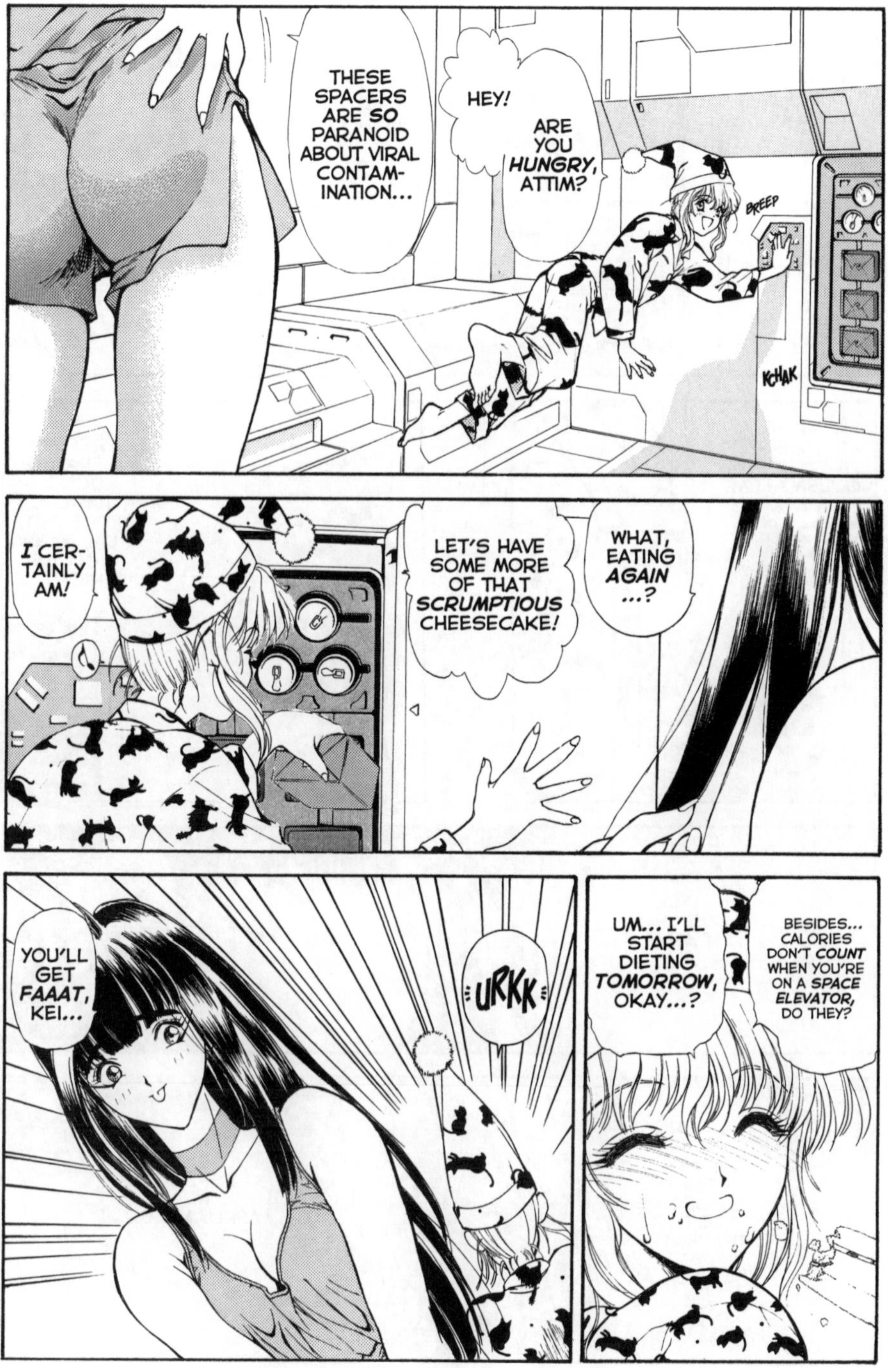
THESE SPACERS ARE SO PARANOID ABOUT VIRAL CONTAMINATION...
HEY!
ARE YOU HUNGRY, ATTIM?
BREEP
KCHAK
I CERTAINLY AM!
LET'S HAVE SOME MORE OF THAT SCRUMPTIOUS CHEESECAKE!
WHAT, EATING AGAIN ...?
YOU'LL GET FAAAT, KEI...
URKK
UM... I'LL START DIETING TOMORROW, OKAY...?
BESIDES... CALORIES DON'T COUNT WHEN YOU'RE ON A SPACE ELEVATOR, DO THEY?

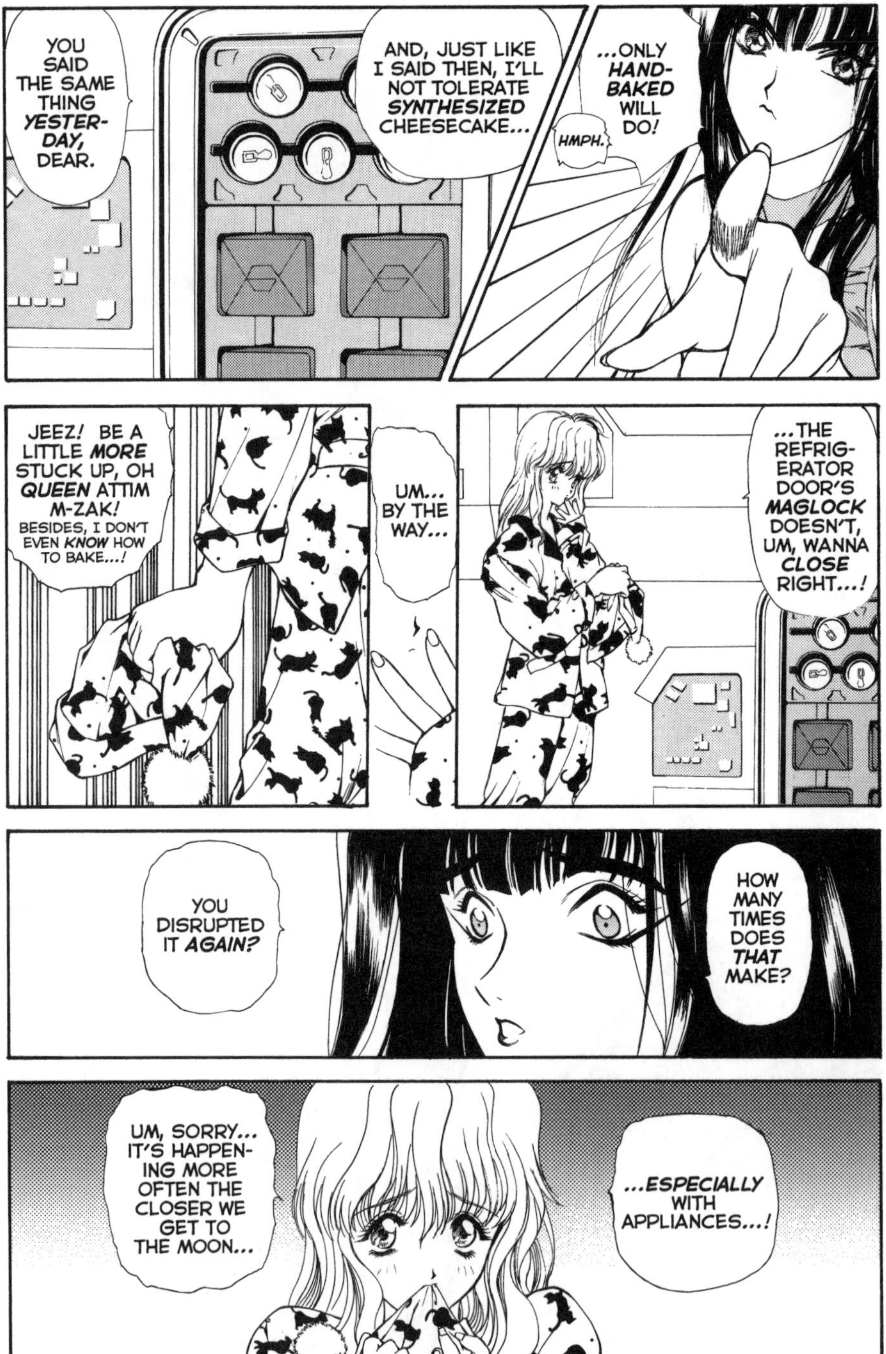
YOU SAID THE SAME THING YESTER-DAY, DEAR.
AND, JUST LIKE I SAID THEN, I'LL NOT TOLERATE SYNTHESIZED CHEESECAKE...
HMPH.
...ONLY HAND-BAKED WILL DO!
JEEZ! BE A LITTLE MORE STUCK UP, OH QUEEN ATTIM M-ZAK! BESIDES, I DON'T EVEN KNOW HOW TO BAKE...!
UM... BY THE WAY...
...THE REFRIG-ERATOR DOOR'S MAGLOCK DOESN'T, UM, WANNA CLOSE RIGHT...!
YOU DISRUPTED IT AGAIN?
HOW MANY TIMES DOES THAT MAKE?
UM, SORRY... IT'S HAPPEN-ING MORE OFTEN THE CLOSER WE GET TO THE MOON...
...ESPECIALLY WITH APPLIANCES...!

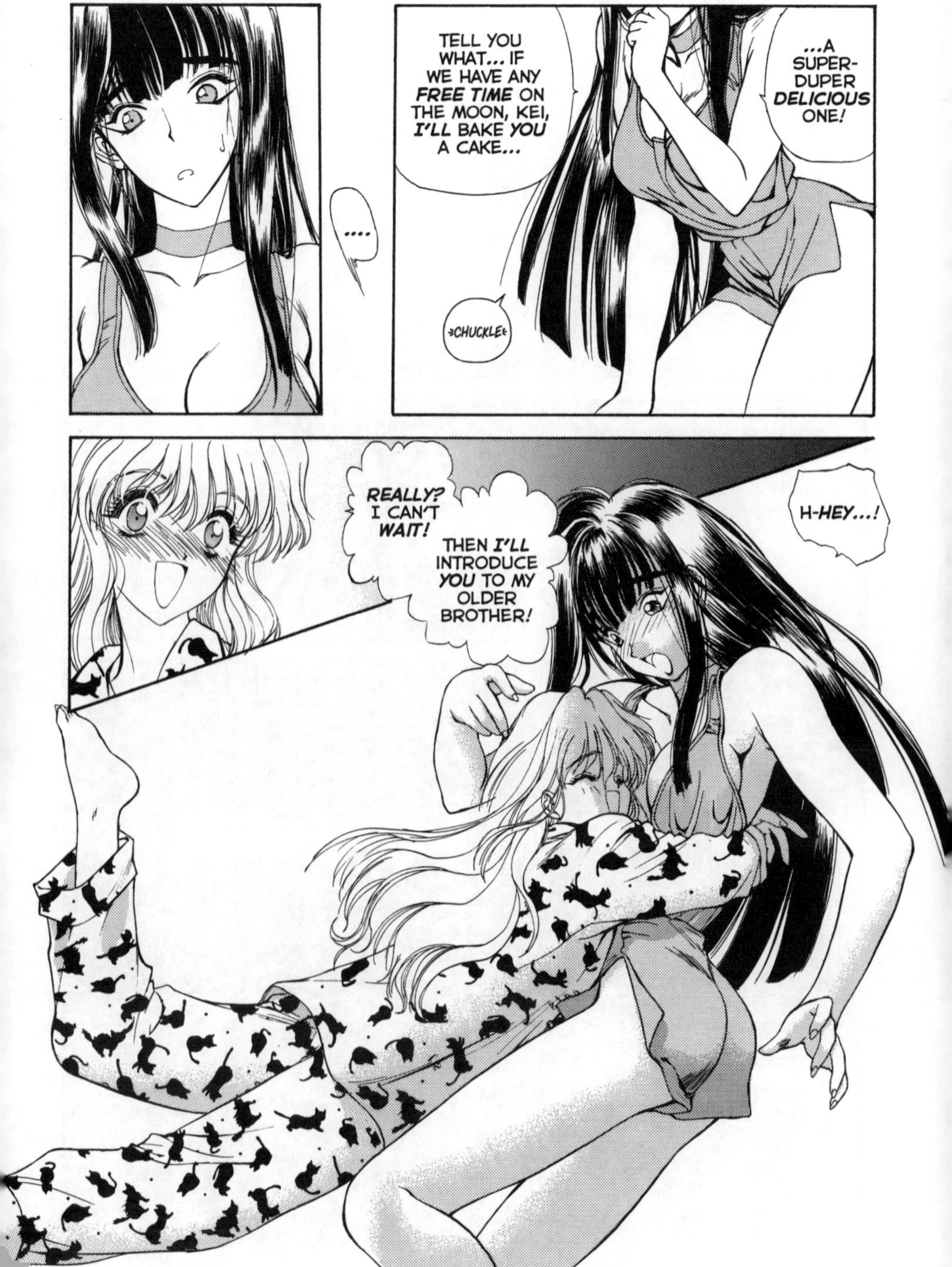
....
TELL YOU WHAT... IF WE HAVE ANY FREE TIME ON THE MOON, KEI, I'LL BAKE YOU A CAKE...
...A SUPER-DUPER DELICIOUS ONE!
CHUCKLE
REALLY? I CAN'T WAIT!
THEN I'LL INTRODUCE YOU TO MY OLDER BROTHER!
H-HEY...!

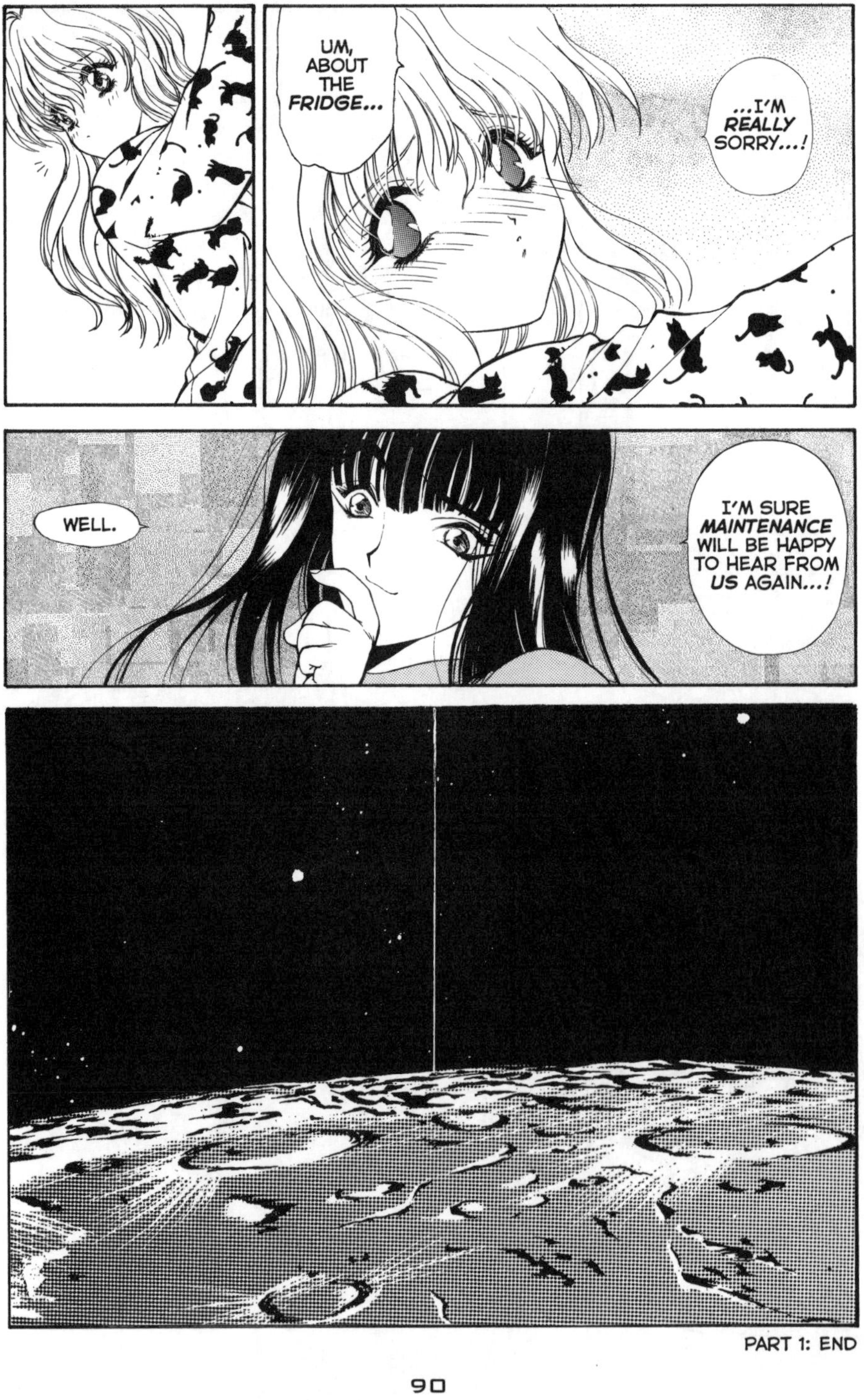
UM, ABOUT THE FRIDGE...
...I'M REALLY SORRY...!
WELL.
I'M SURE MAINTENANCE WILL BE HAPPY TO HEAR FROM US AGAIN...!

PART 1: END

ACT 2

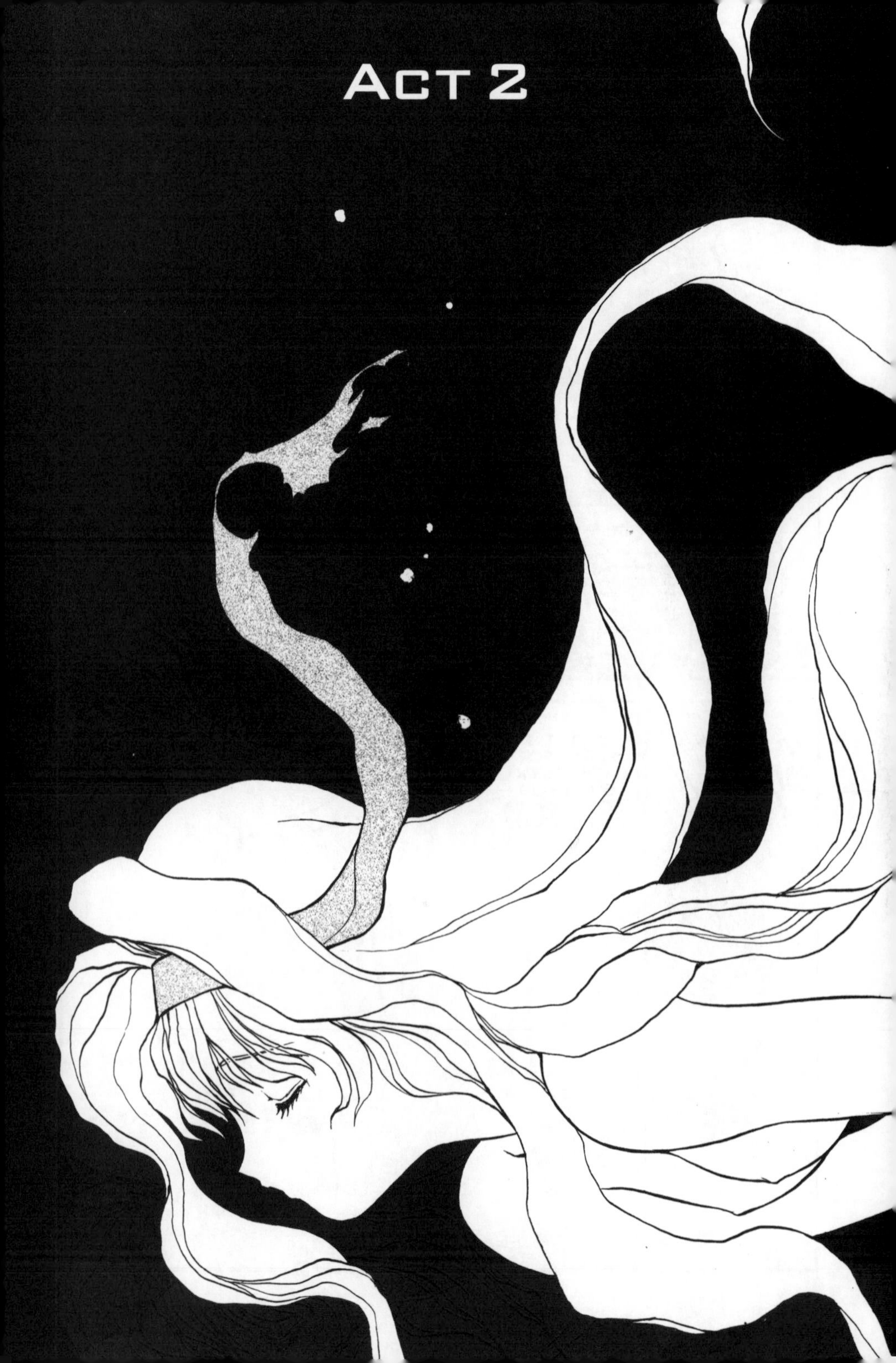

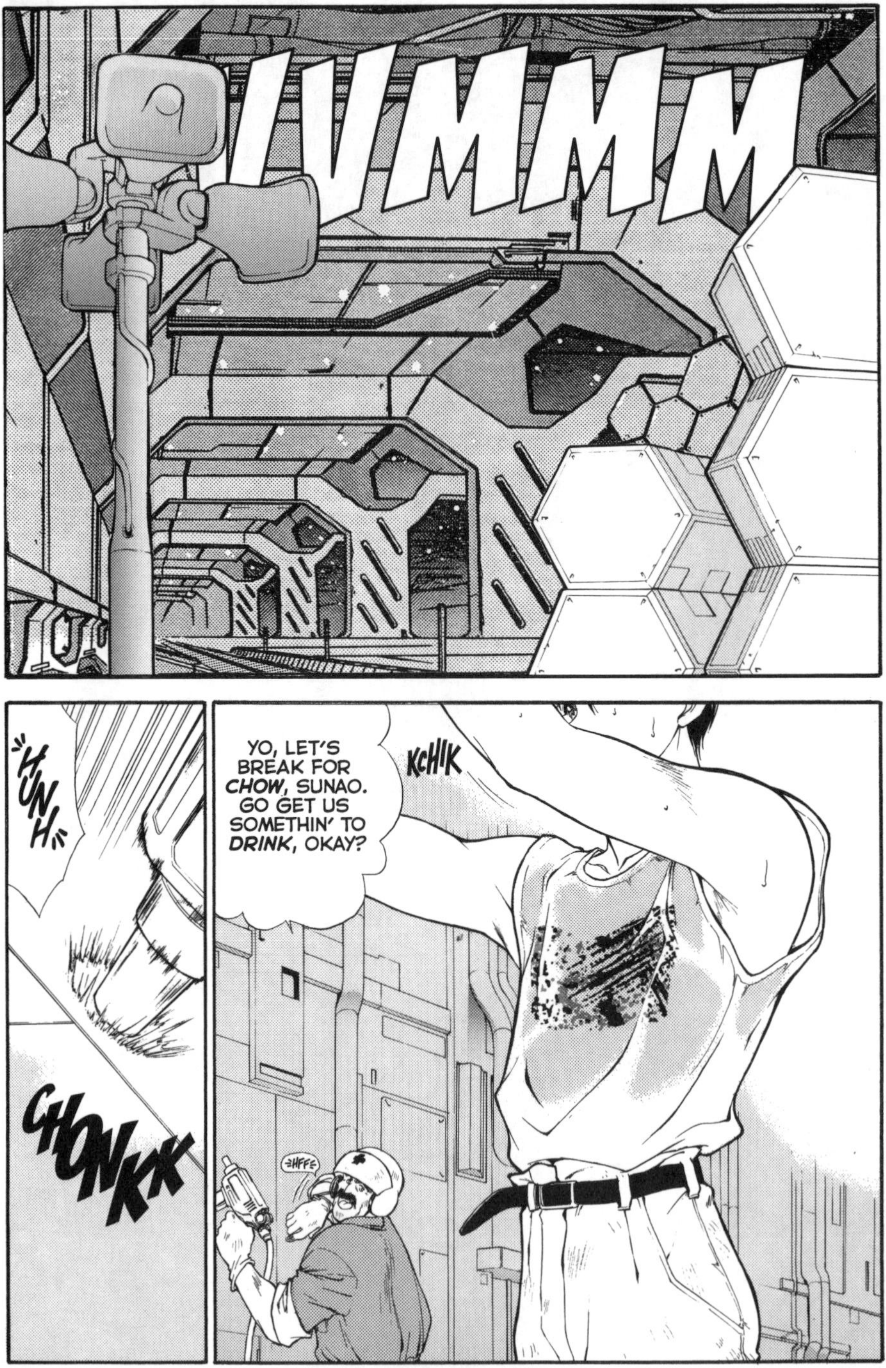
VMMMM
HUNH
CHONKK
YO, LET'S BREAK FOR *CHOW*, SUNAO. GO GET US SOMETHIN' TO *DRINK*, OKAY?
KCHIK
HFF

UH, *SURE,* BOSS... BUT...

KCHIK KCHIK

...ACTUALLY, I'VE GOT SOME *TOUR GUIDE* WORK THIS AFTERNOON...!

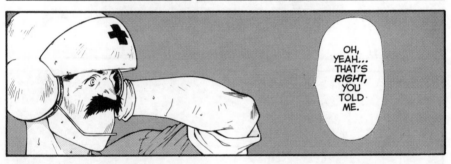

OH, YEAH... THAT'S *RIGHT,* YOU TOLD ME.

WELL, DAMN. GOT TOO MANY *LUNCH BOXES,* THEN.

AW, WHAT THE HELL... TAKE IT AND HAVE AN OFFWORK *FEAST,* KID!

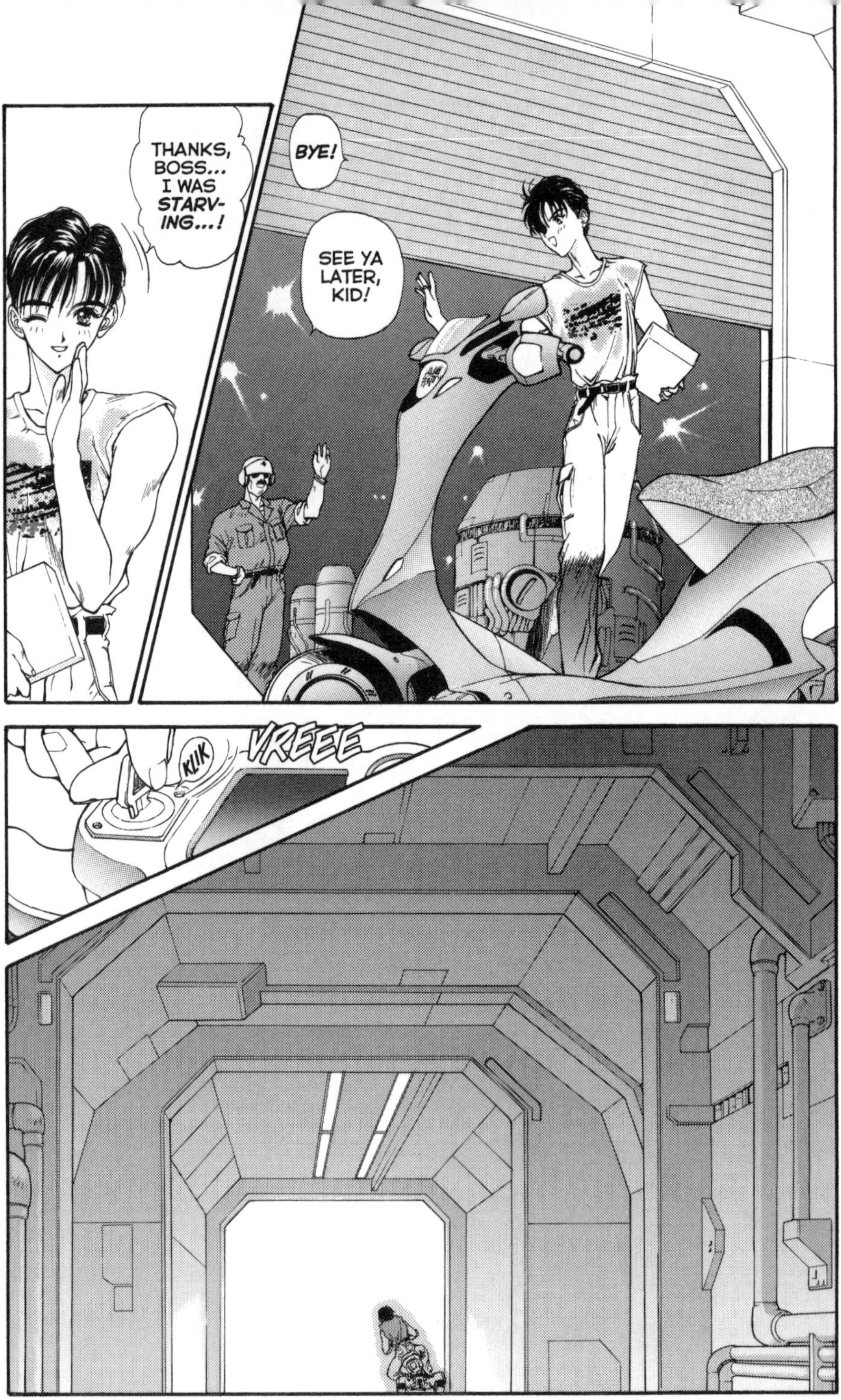
THANKS, BOSS... I WAS STARV-ING...!
BYE!
SEE YA LATER, KID!
KLIK
VREEE

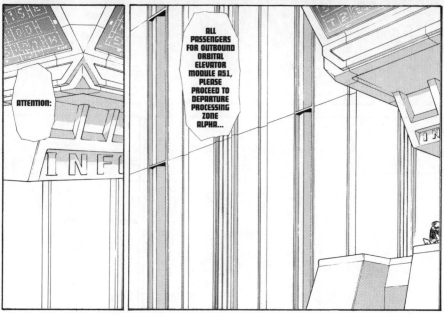

ATTENTION:

ALL PASSENGERS FOR OUTBOUND ORBITAL ELEVATOR MODULE A51, PLEASE PROCEED TO DEPARTURE PROCESSING ZONE ALPHA...

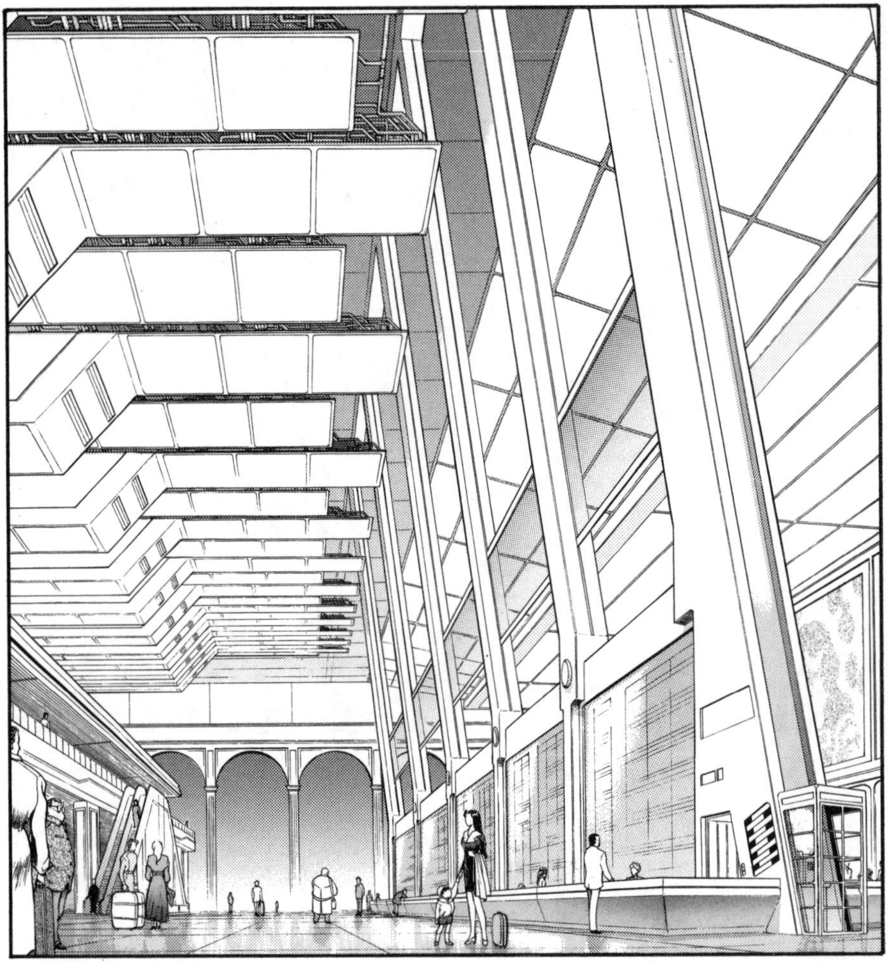

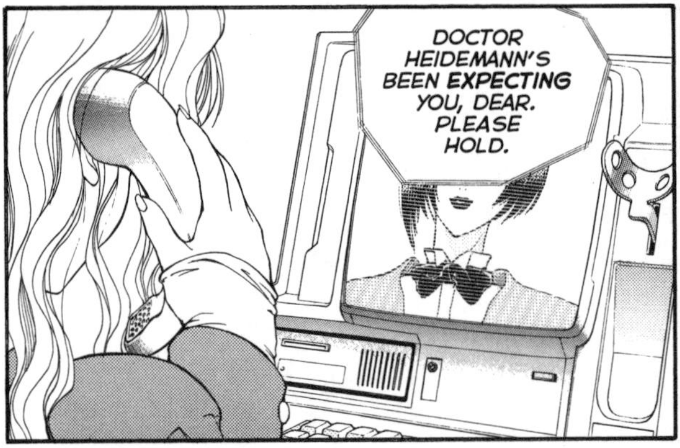
DOCTOR HEIDEMANN'S BEEN **EXPECTING** YOU, DEAR. PLEASE HOLD.

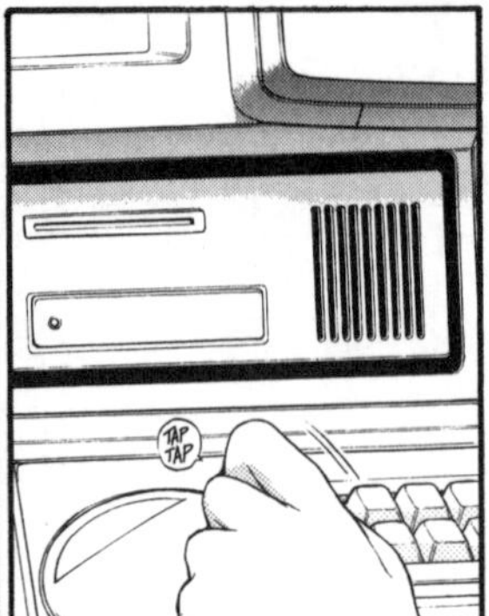
TAP TAP

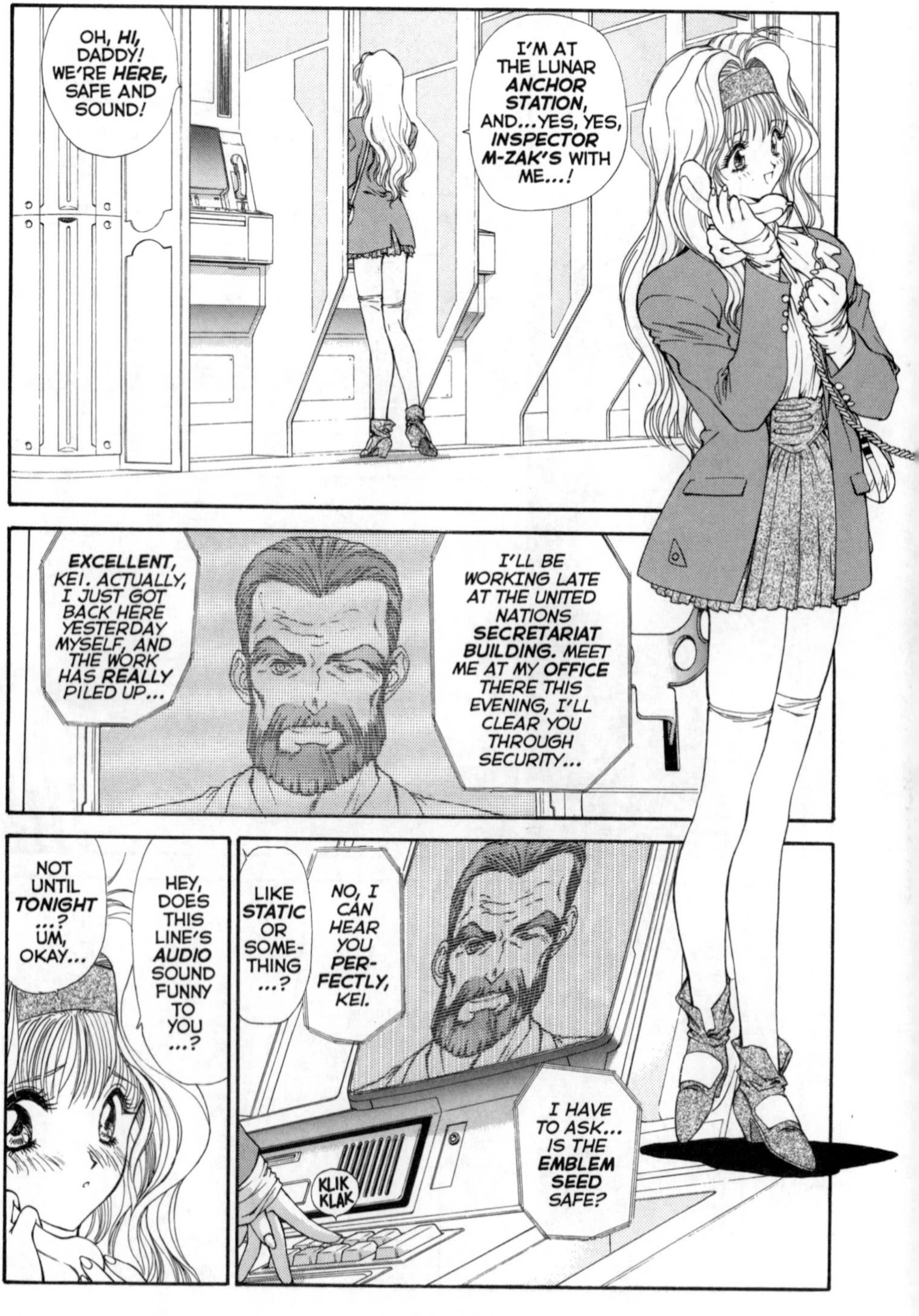
OH, HI, DADDY! WE'RE HERE, SAFE AND SOUND!
I'M AT THE LUNAR ANCHOR STATION, AND...YES, YES, INSPECTOR M-ZAK'S WITH ME...!
EXCELLENT, KEI. ACTUALLY, I JUST GOT BACK HERE YESTERDAY MYSELF, AND THE WORK HAS REALLY PILED UP...
I'LL BE WORKING LATE AT THE UNITED NATIONS SECRETARIAT BUILDING. MEET ME AT MY OFFICE THERE THIS EVENING, I'LL CLEAR YOU THROUGH SECURITY...
NOT UNTIL TONIGHT ...? UM, OKAY...
HEY, DOES THIS LINE'S AUDIO SOUND FUNNY TO YOU ...?
LIKE STATIC OR SOME-THING ...?
NO, I CAN HEAR YOU PER-FECTLY, KEI.
KLIK KLAK
I HAVE TO ASK... IS THE EMBLEM SEED SAFE?

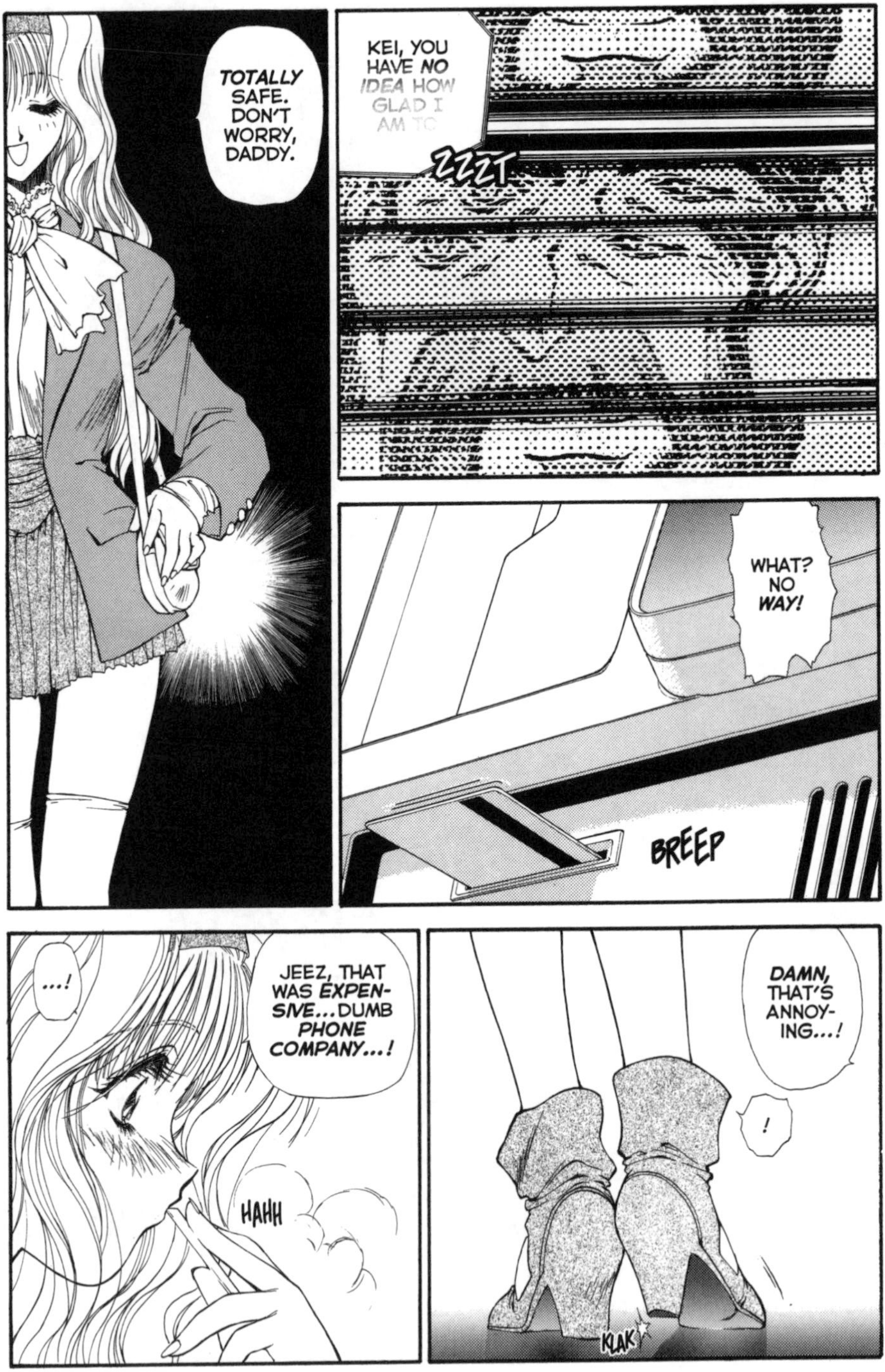
TOTALLY SAFE. DON'T WORRY, DADDY.
KEI, YOU HAVE NO IDEA HOW GLAD I AM TO
ZZZT
WHAT? NO WAY!
BREEP
...!
JEEZ, THAT WAS EXPENSIVE...DUMB PHONE COMPANY...!
HAHH
DAMN, THAT'S ANNOYING...!
!
KLAK

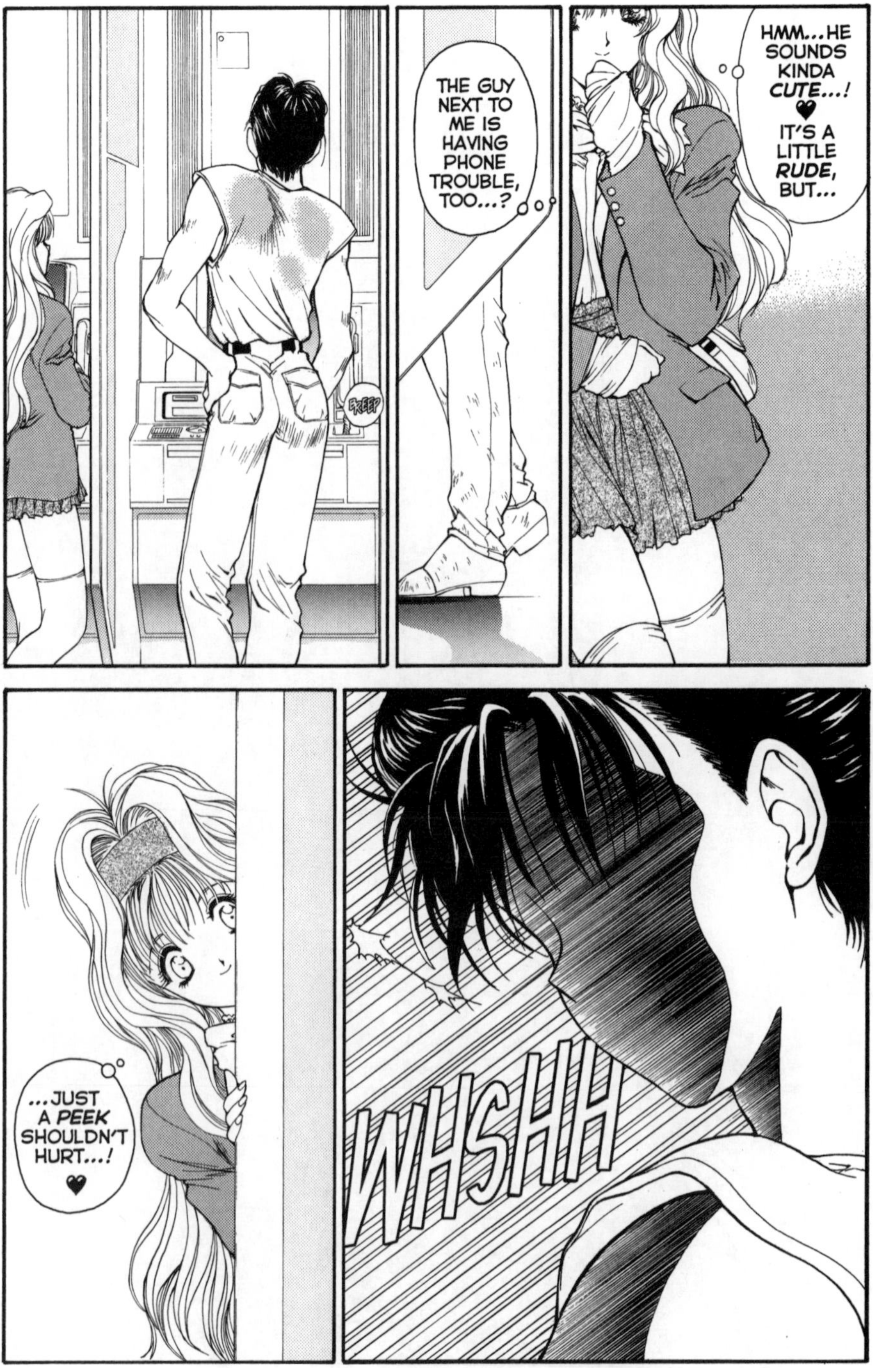
BREEP
THE GUY NEXT TO ME IS HAVING PHONE TROUBLE, TOO...?
HMM...HE SOUNDS KINDA *CUTE*...! ♥ IT'S A LITTLE *RUDE*, BUT...
...JUST A *PEEK* SHOULDN'T HURT...! ♥
WHSHH

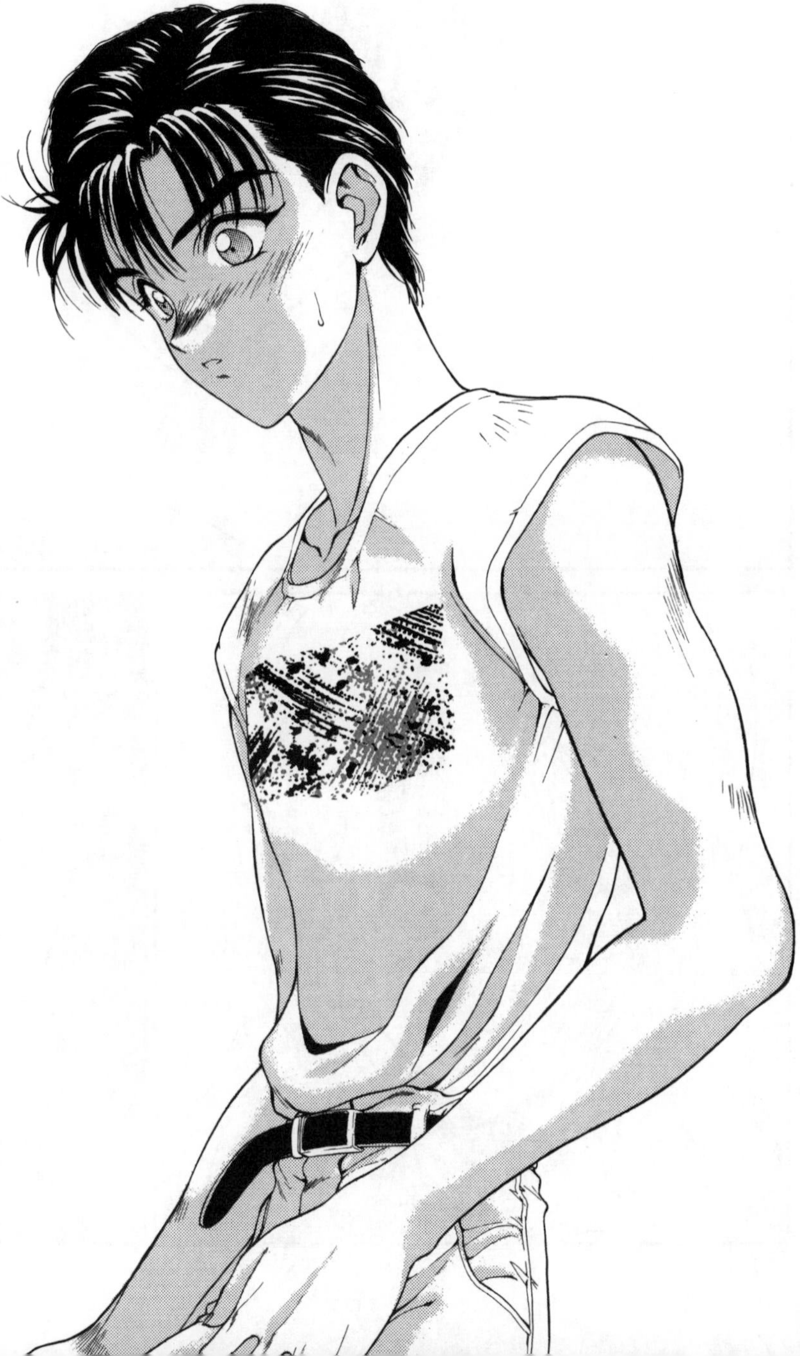

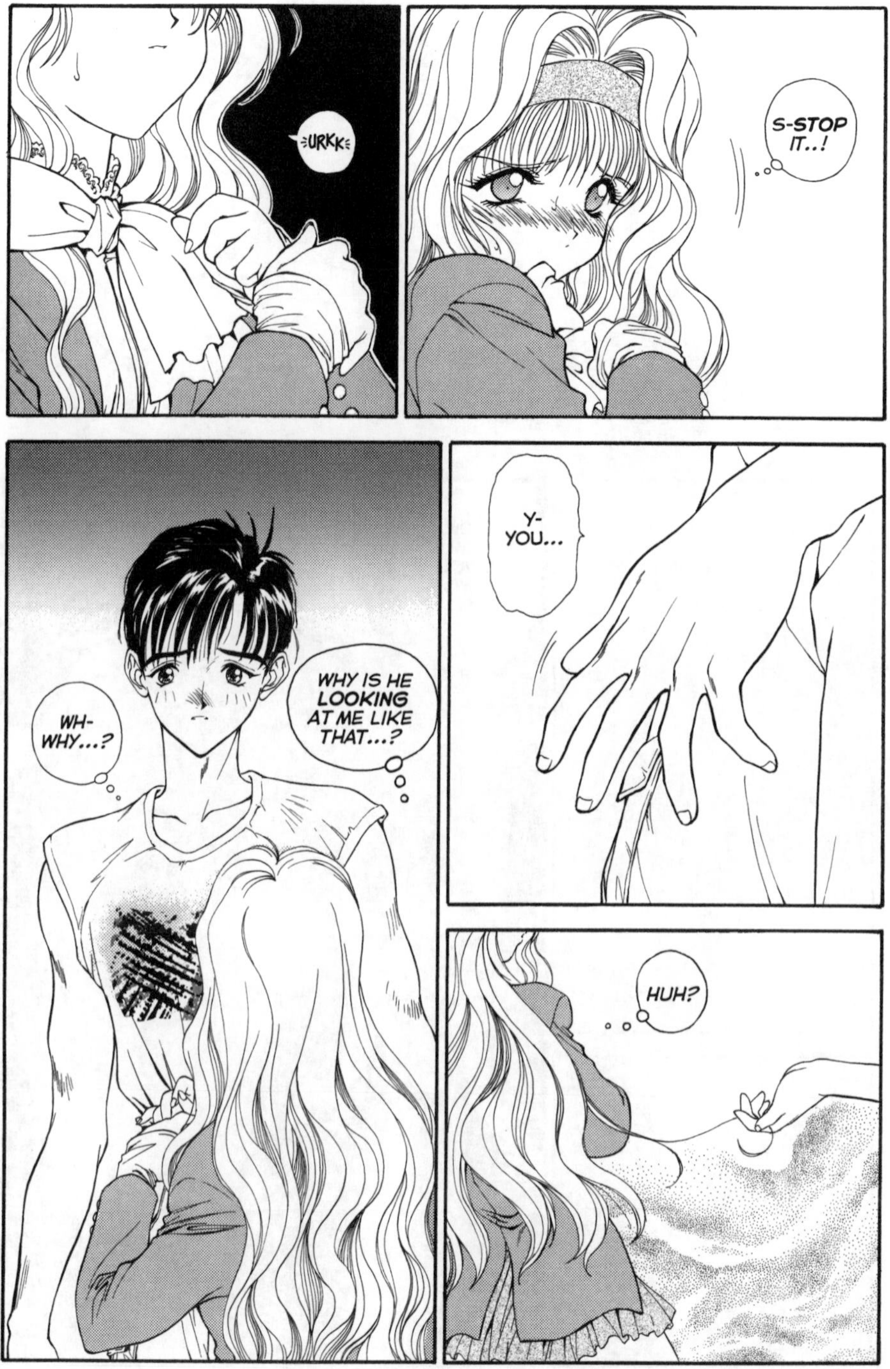
URKK
S-STOP IT..!
WH-WHY...?
WHY IS HE LOOKING AT ME LIKE THAT...?
Y-YOU...
HUH?

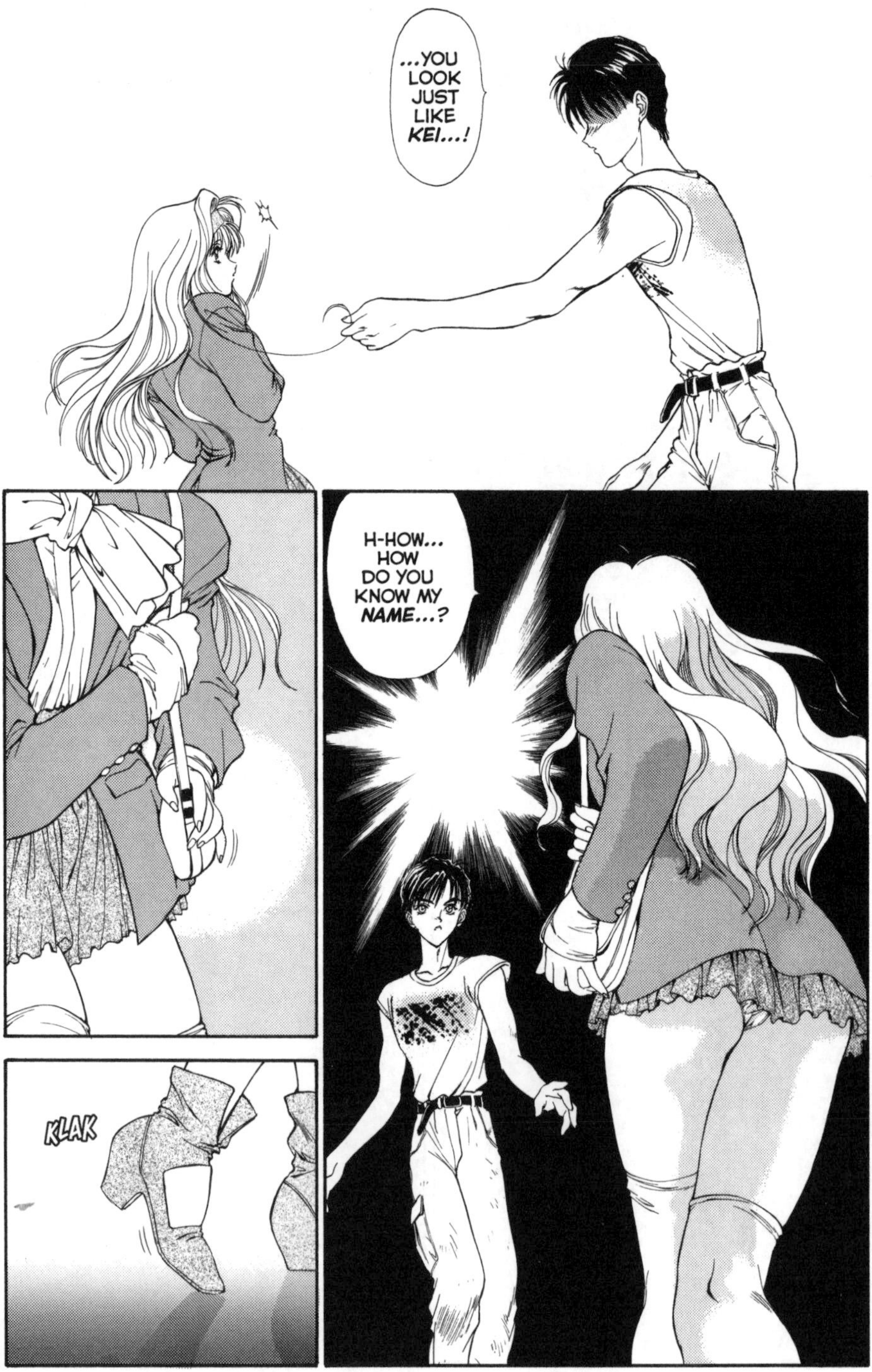
...YOU LOOK JUST LIKE *KEI*...!
KLAK
H-HOW... HOW DO YOU KNOW MY *NAME*...?

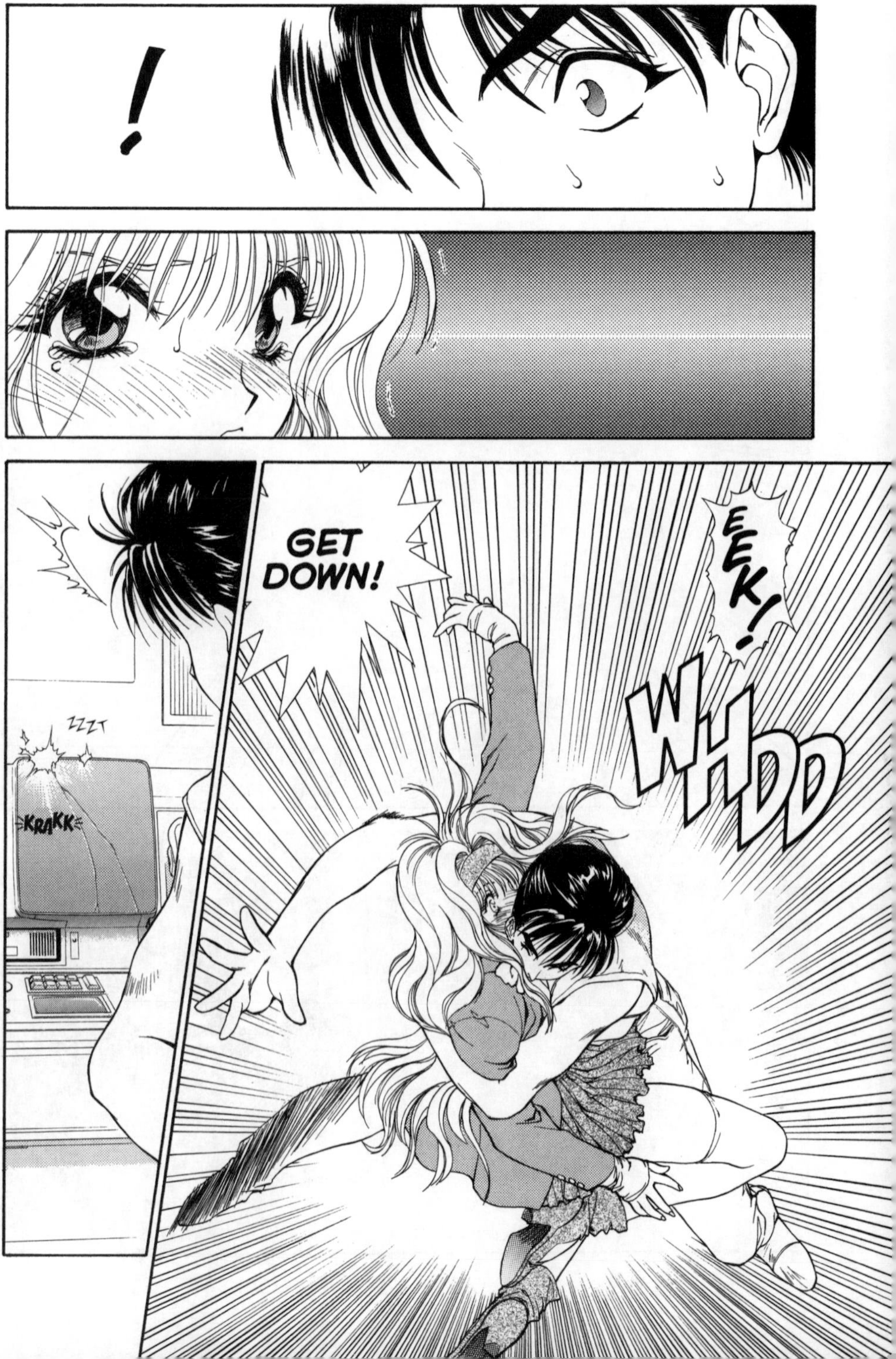
!
GET DOWN!
EEK!!
ZZZT
KRAKK
WHDD

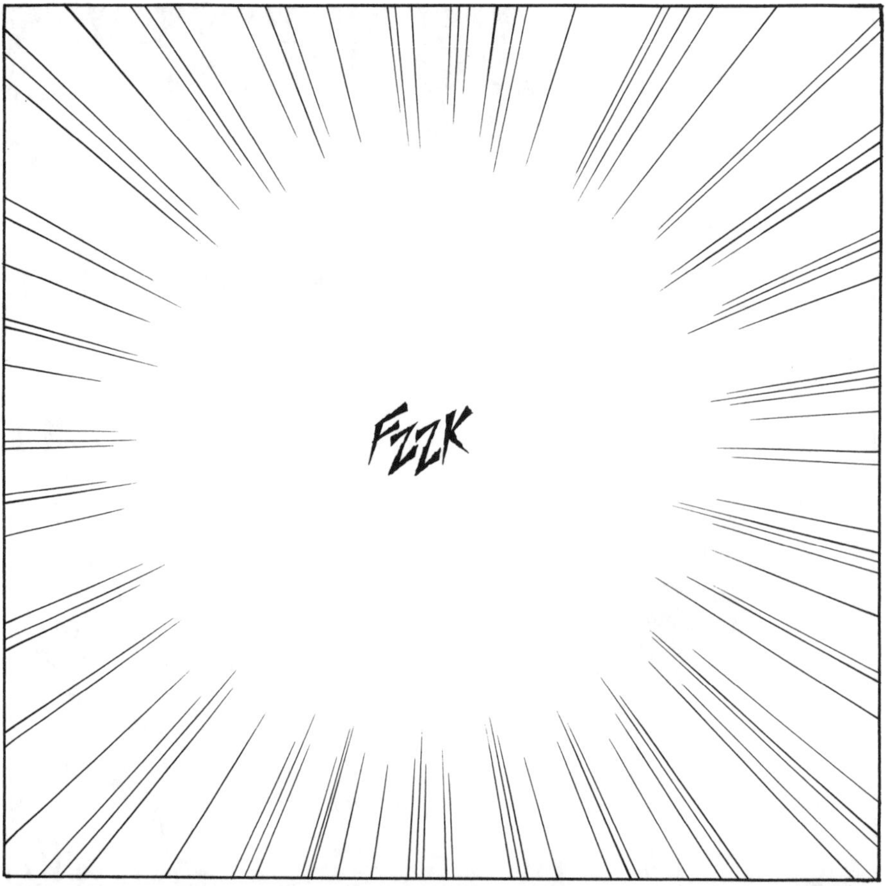
FZZK

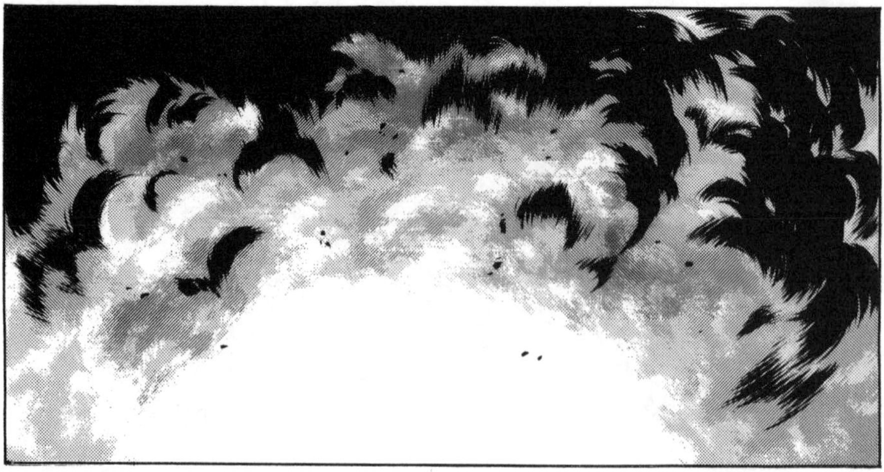

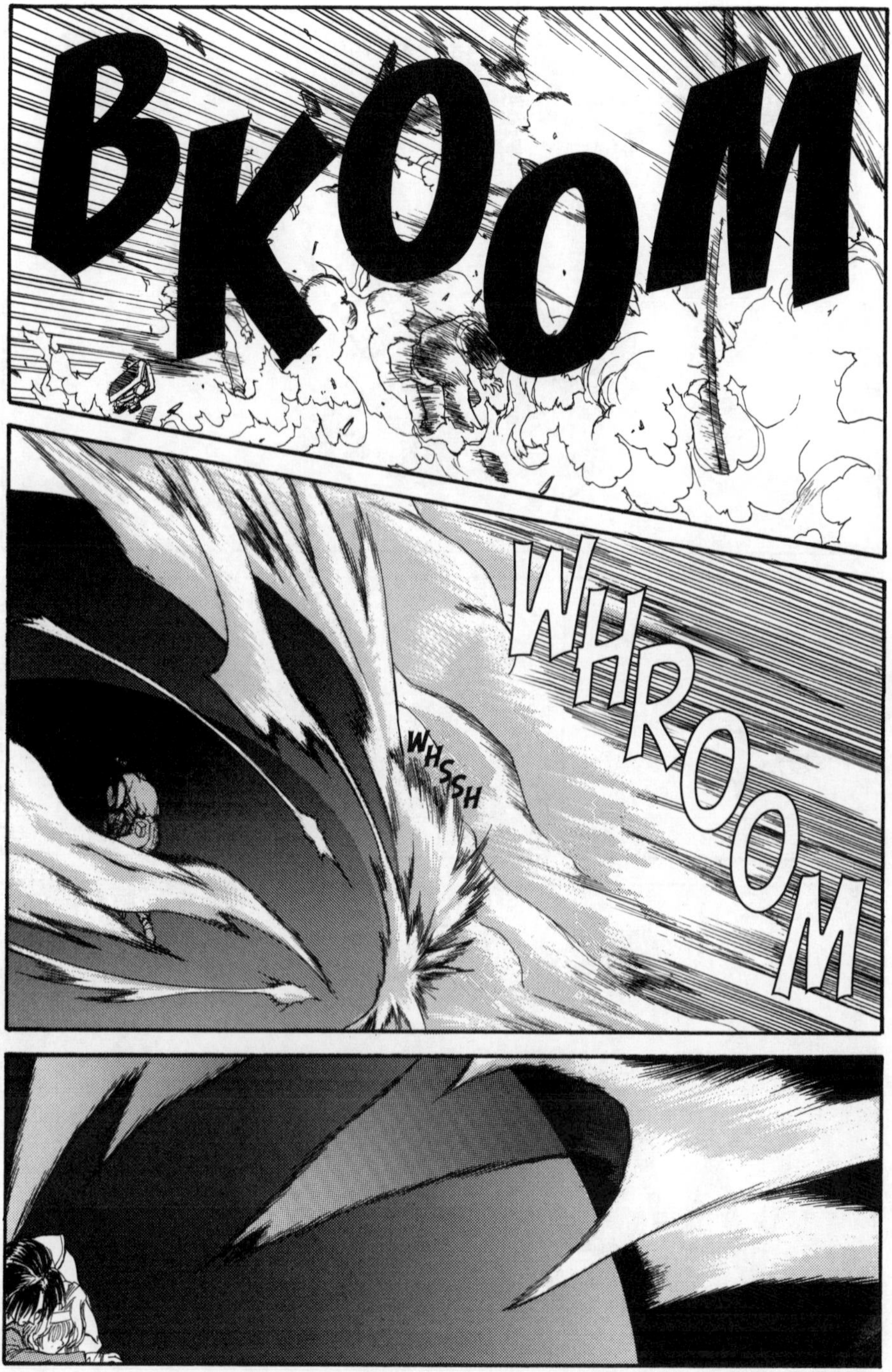
BKOOM
WHROOM
WHSSSH

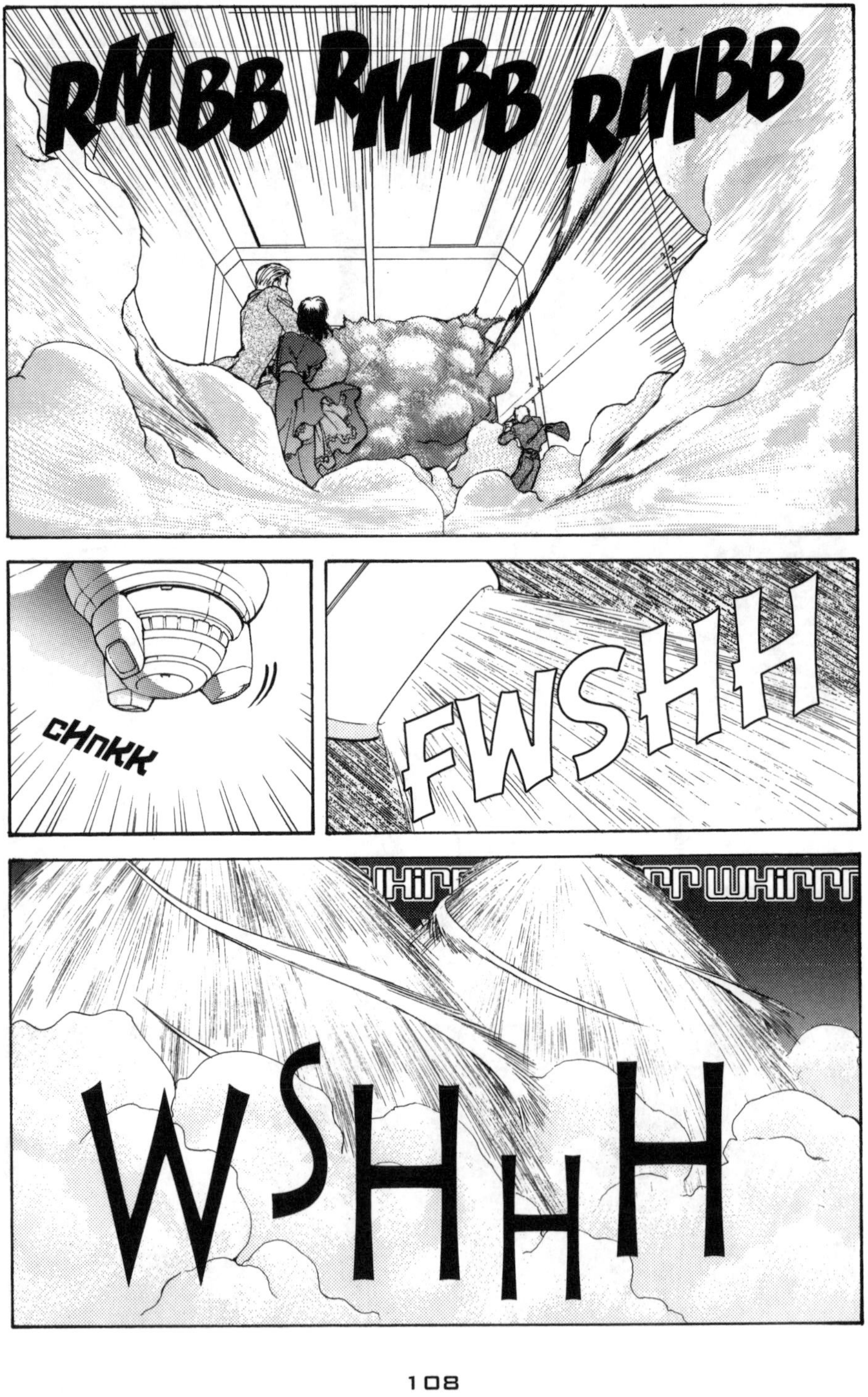
RMBB RMBB RMBB
CHNKK
FWSHH
WHIRRR
WSHHH

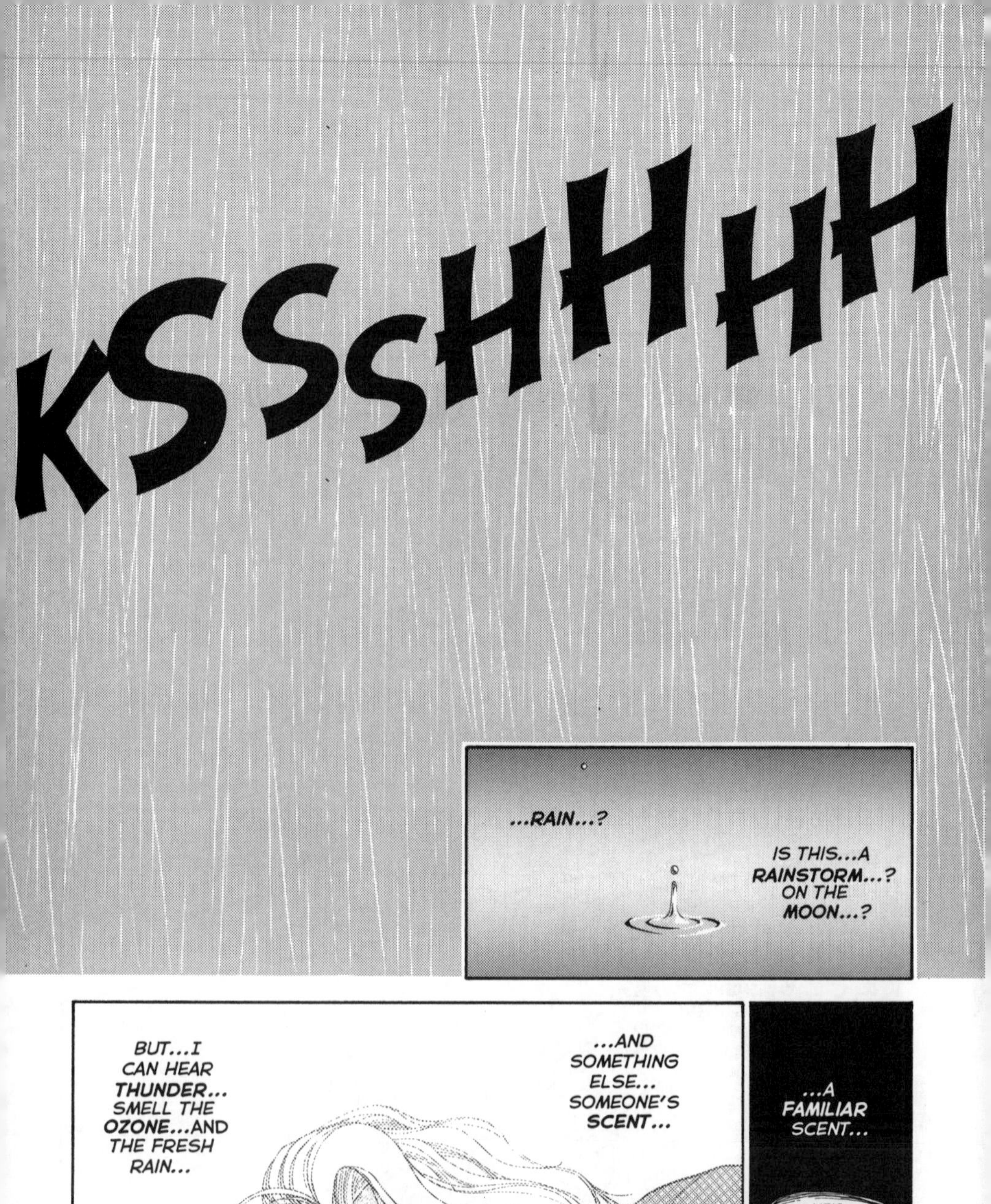
KSSHHHH
...RAIN...?
IS THIS...A RAINSTORM...? ON THE MOON...?
BUT...I CAN HEAR THUNDER... SMELL THE OZONE...AND THE FRESH RAIN...
...AND SOMETHING ELSE... SOMEONE'S SCENT...
...A FAMILIAR SCENT...
KEI?

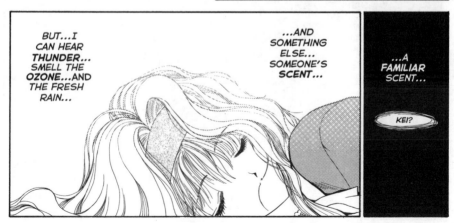

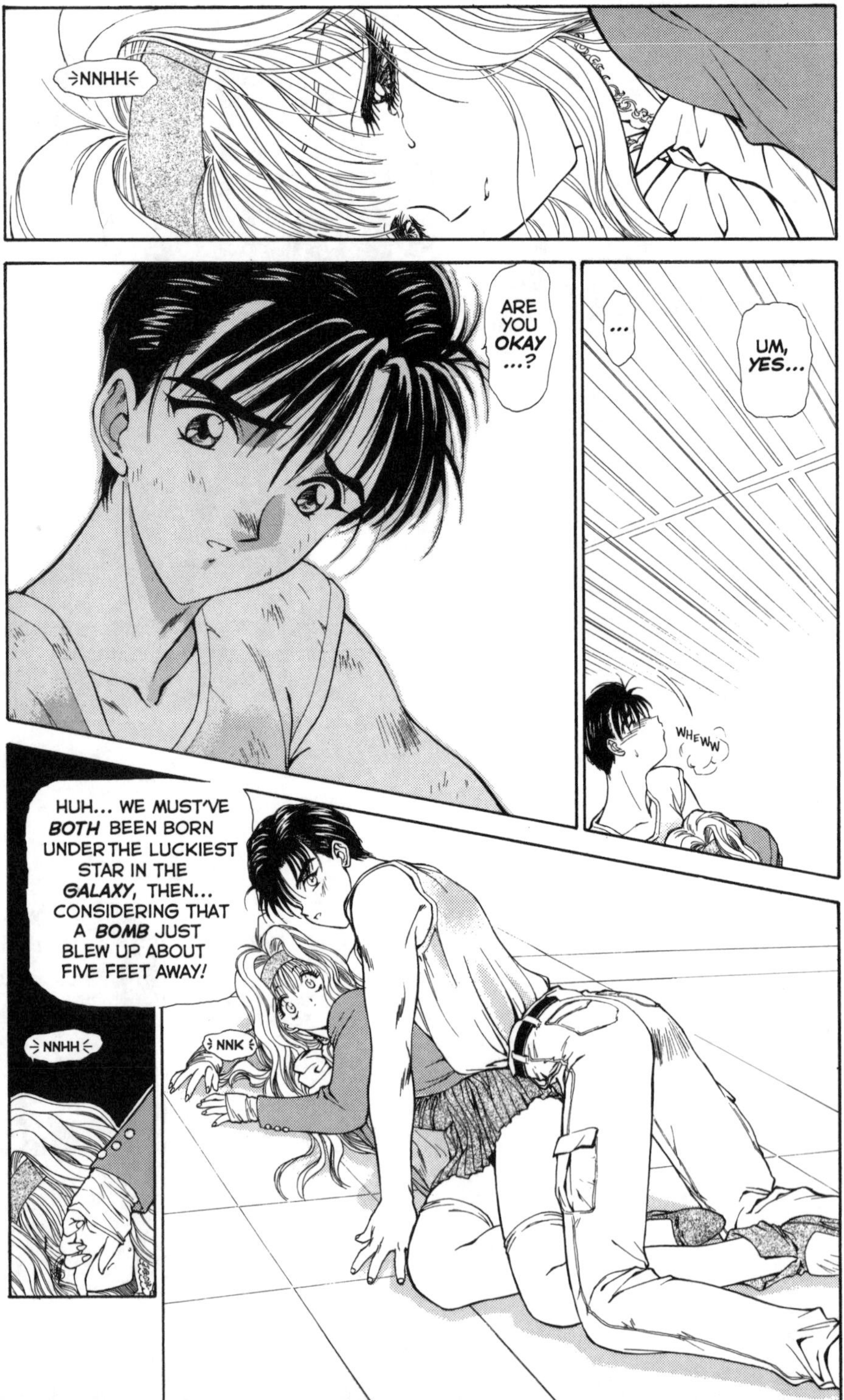
NNHH
ARE YOU OKAY ...?
...
UM, YES...
WHEWW
HUH... WE MUST'VE BOTH BEEN BORN UNDER THE LUCKIEST STAR IN THE GALAXY, THEN... CONSIDERING THAT A BOMB JUST BLEW UP ABOUT FIVE FEET AWAY!
NNHH
NNK

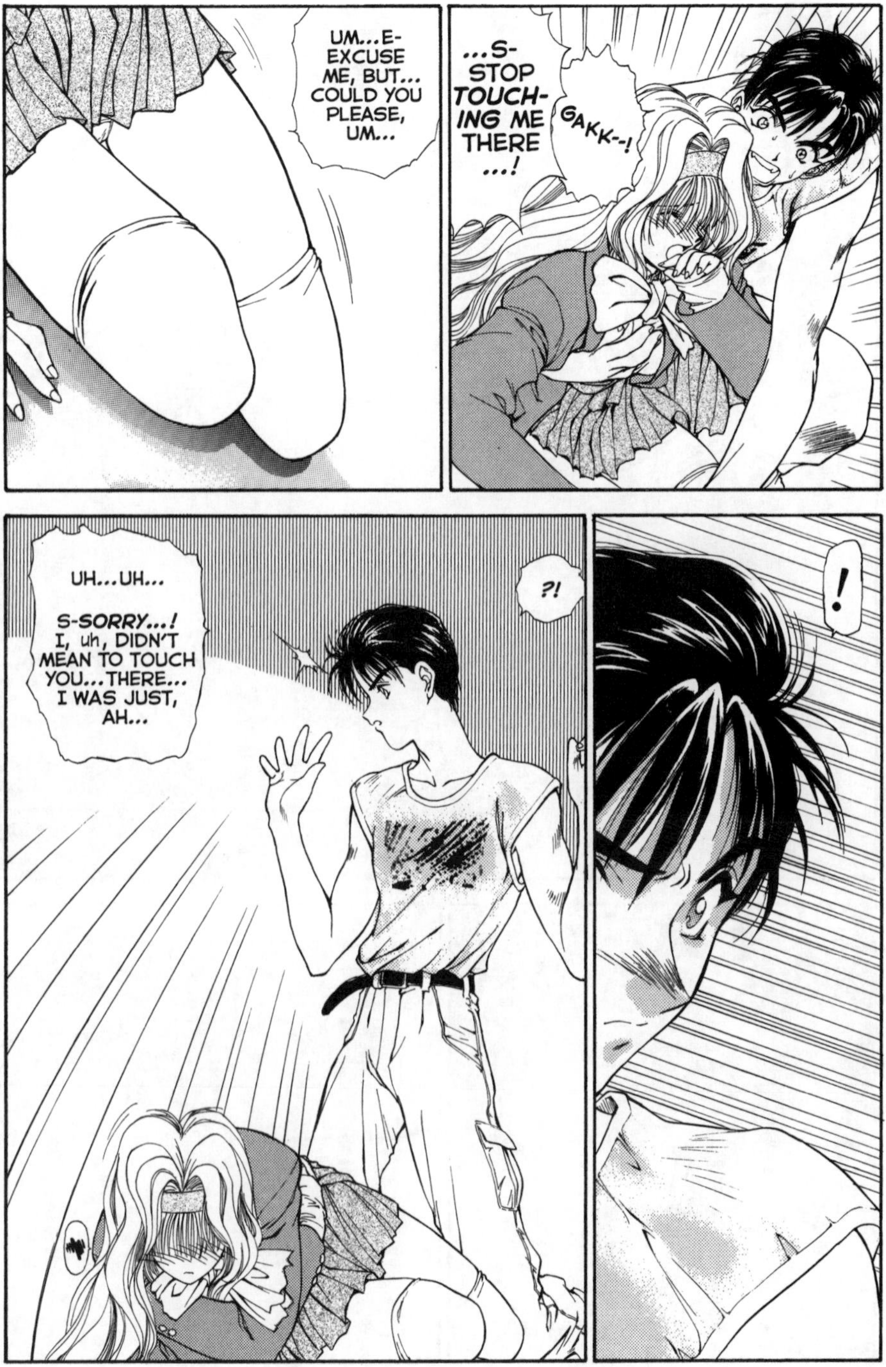
UM...E-EXCUSE ME, BUT... COULD YOU PLEASE, UM...
...S-STOP TOUCHING ME THERE ...!
GAKK--!
UH...UH...
S-SORRY...! I, uh, DIDN'T MEAN TO TOUCH YOU...THERE... I WAS JUST, AH...
?!
!

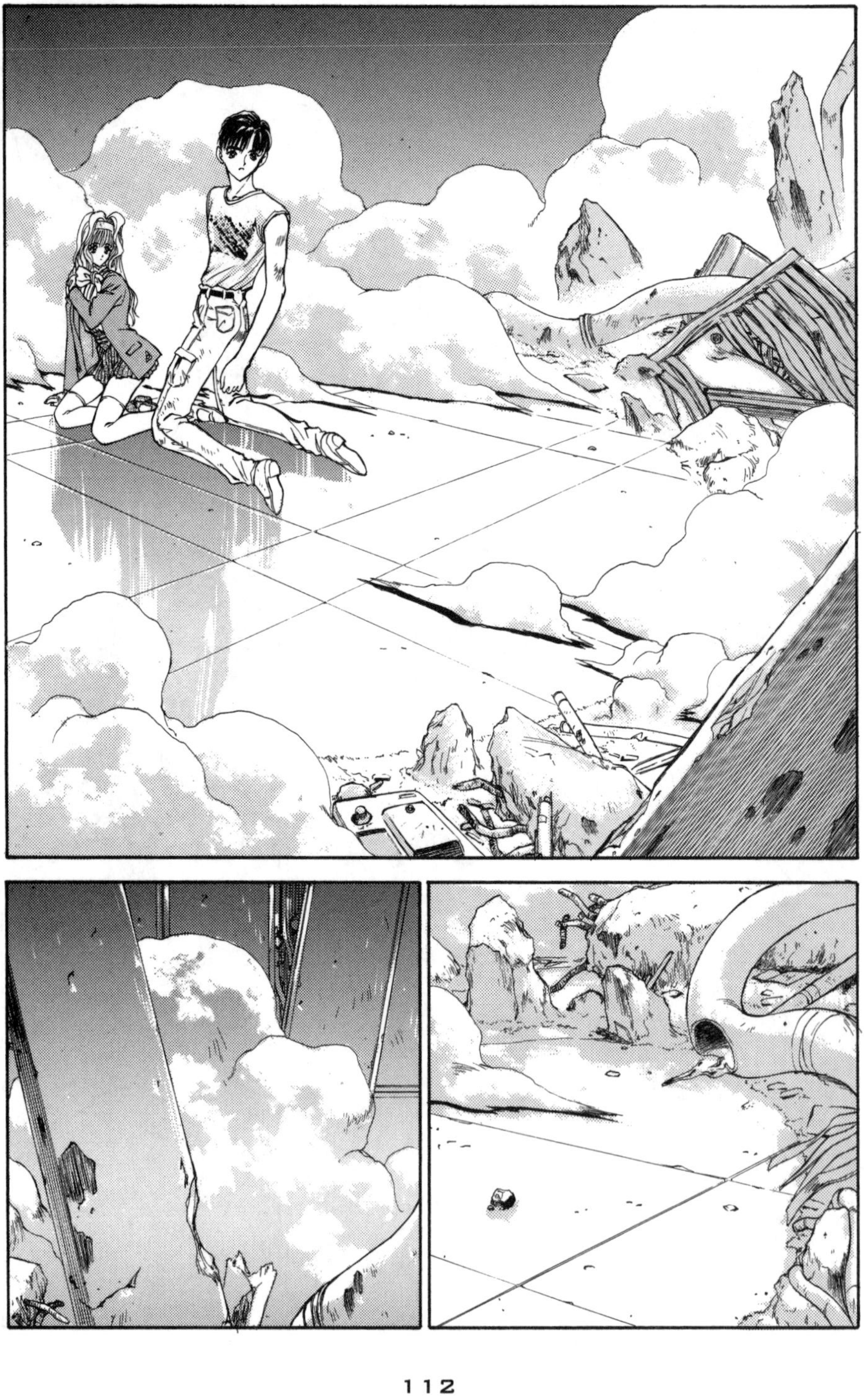

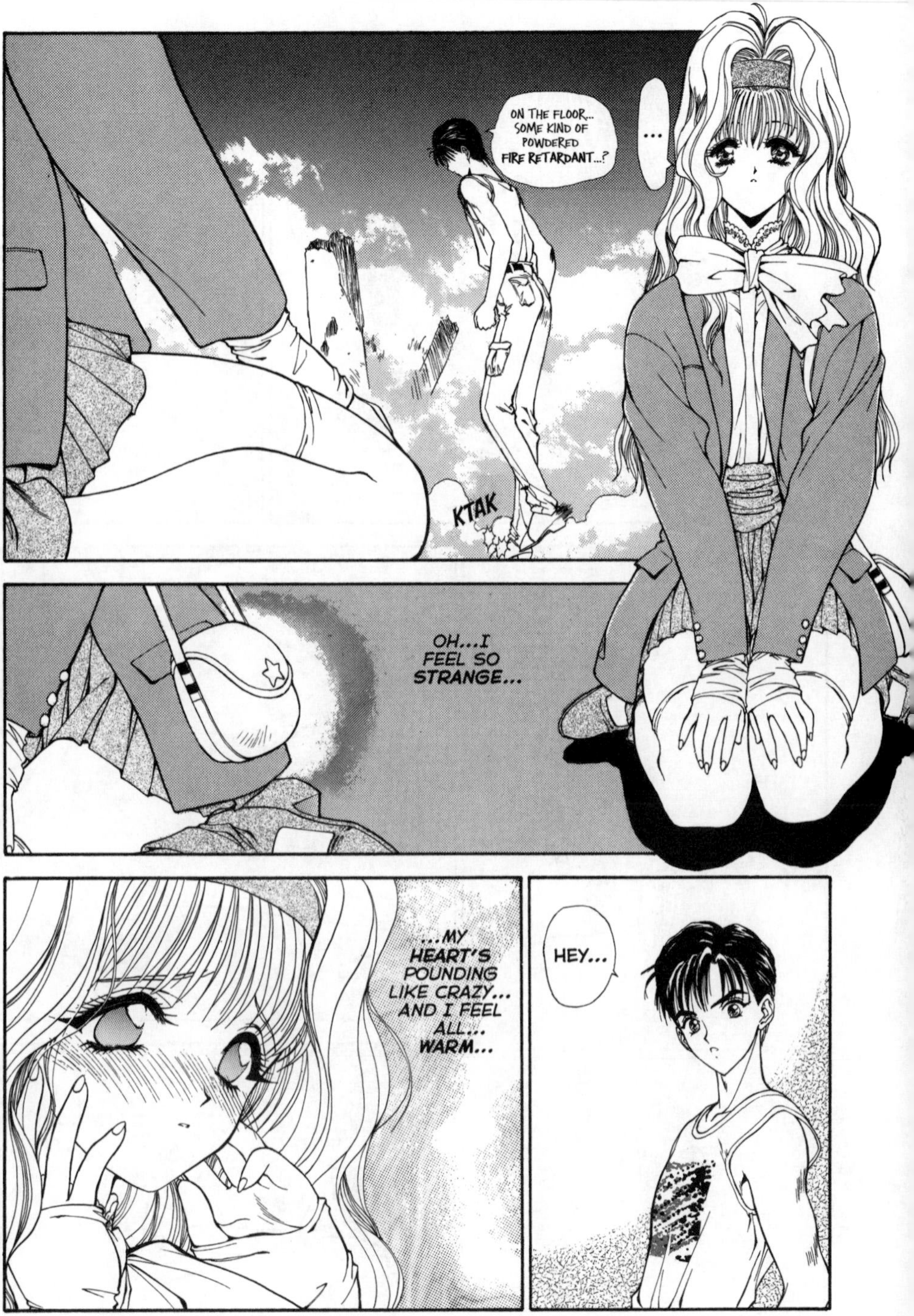
...
ON THE FLOOR... SOME KIND OF POWDERED FIRE RETARDANT...?
KTAK
OH...I FEEL SO STRANGE...
...MY HEART'S POUNDING LIKE CRAZY... AND I FEEL ALL... WARM...
HEY...

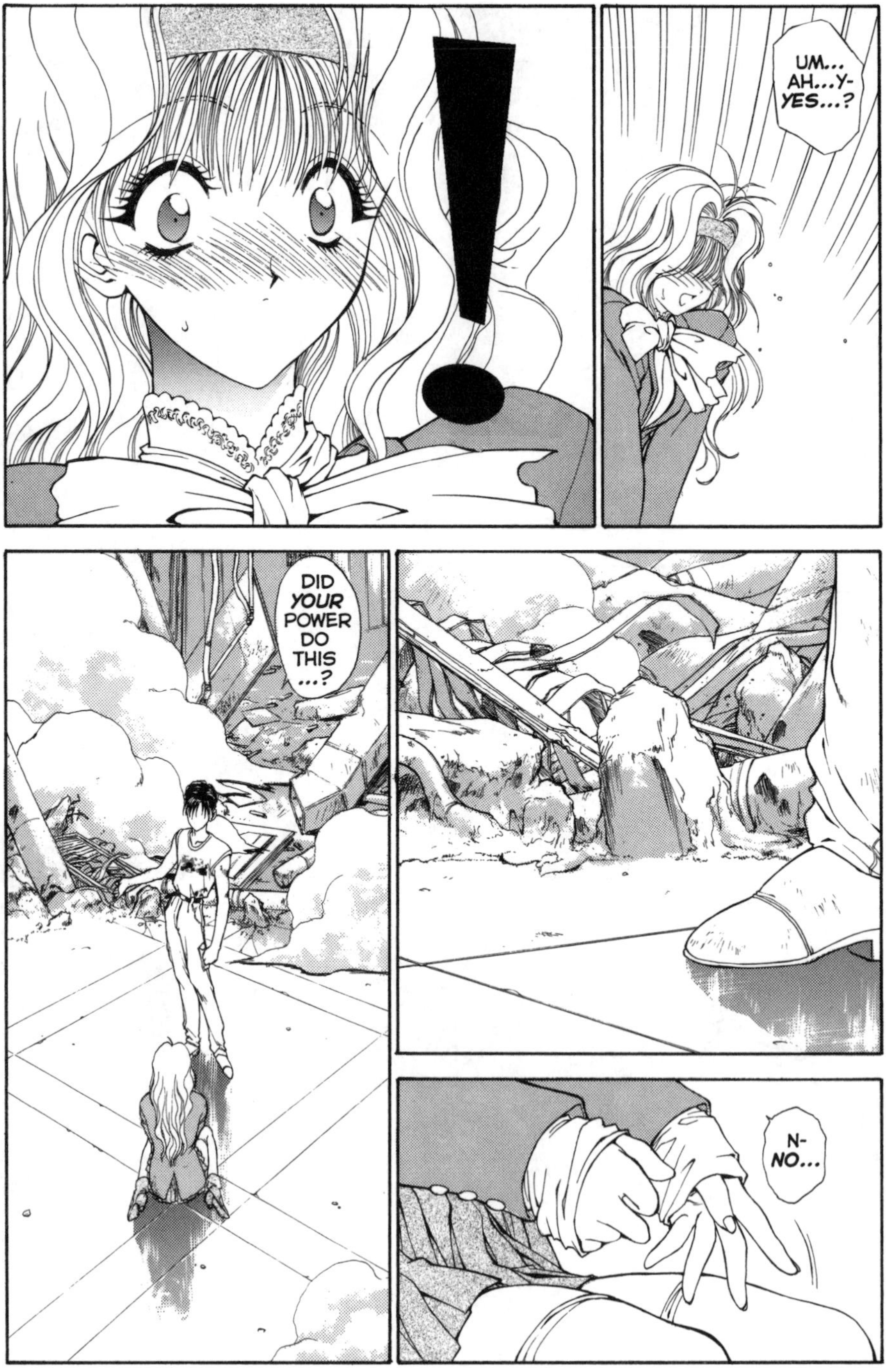
UM... AH...Y-YES...?
DID YOUR POWER DO THIS ...?
N-NO...

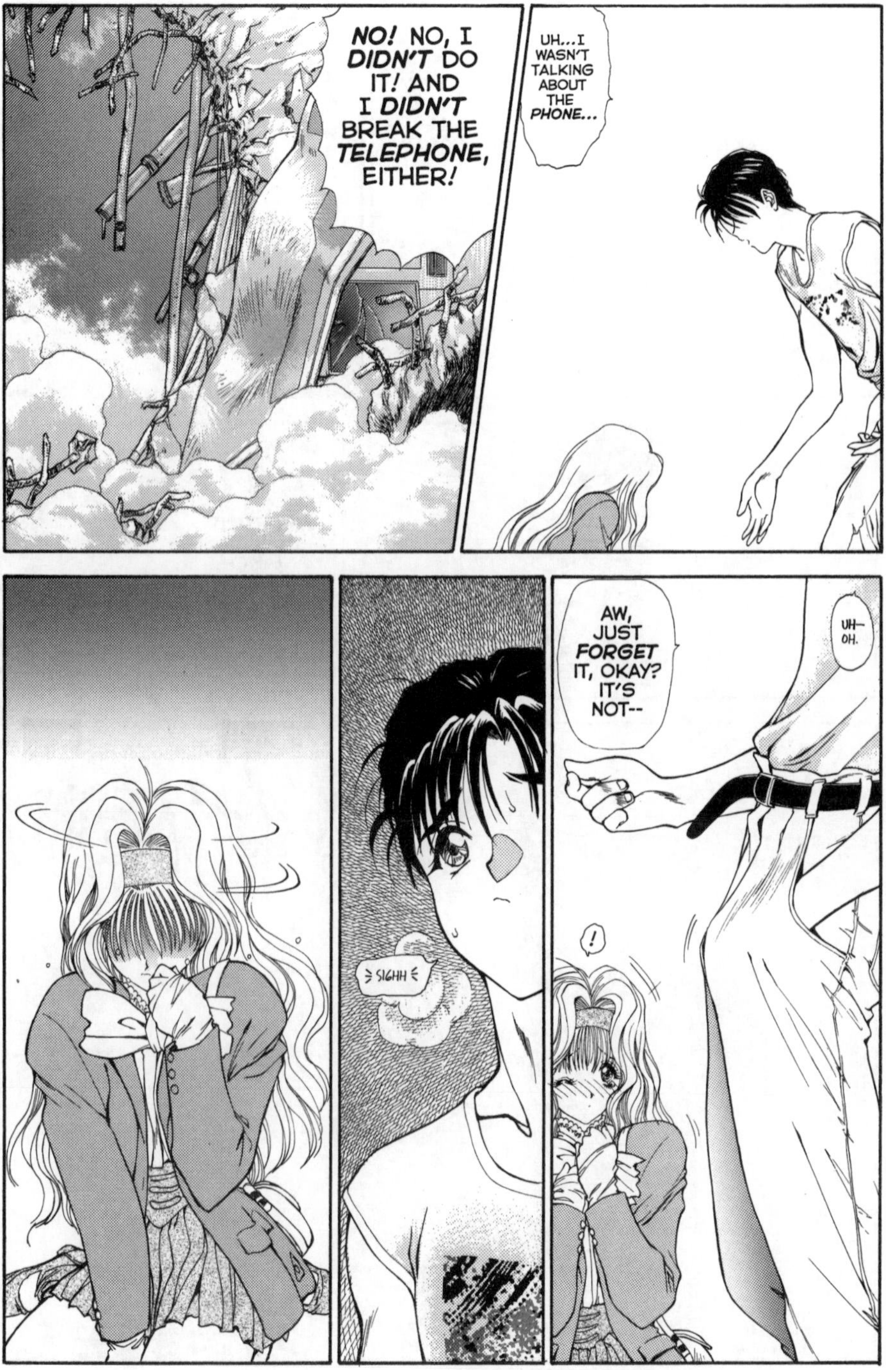
NO! NO, I DIDN'T DO IT! AND I DIDN'T BREAK THE TELEPHONE, EITHER!
UH...I WASN'T TALKING ABOUT THE PHONE...
SIGHH
AW, JUST FORGET IT, OKAY? IT'S NOT--
UH-OH.
!

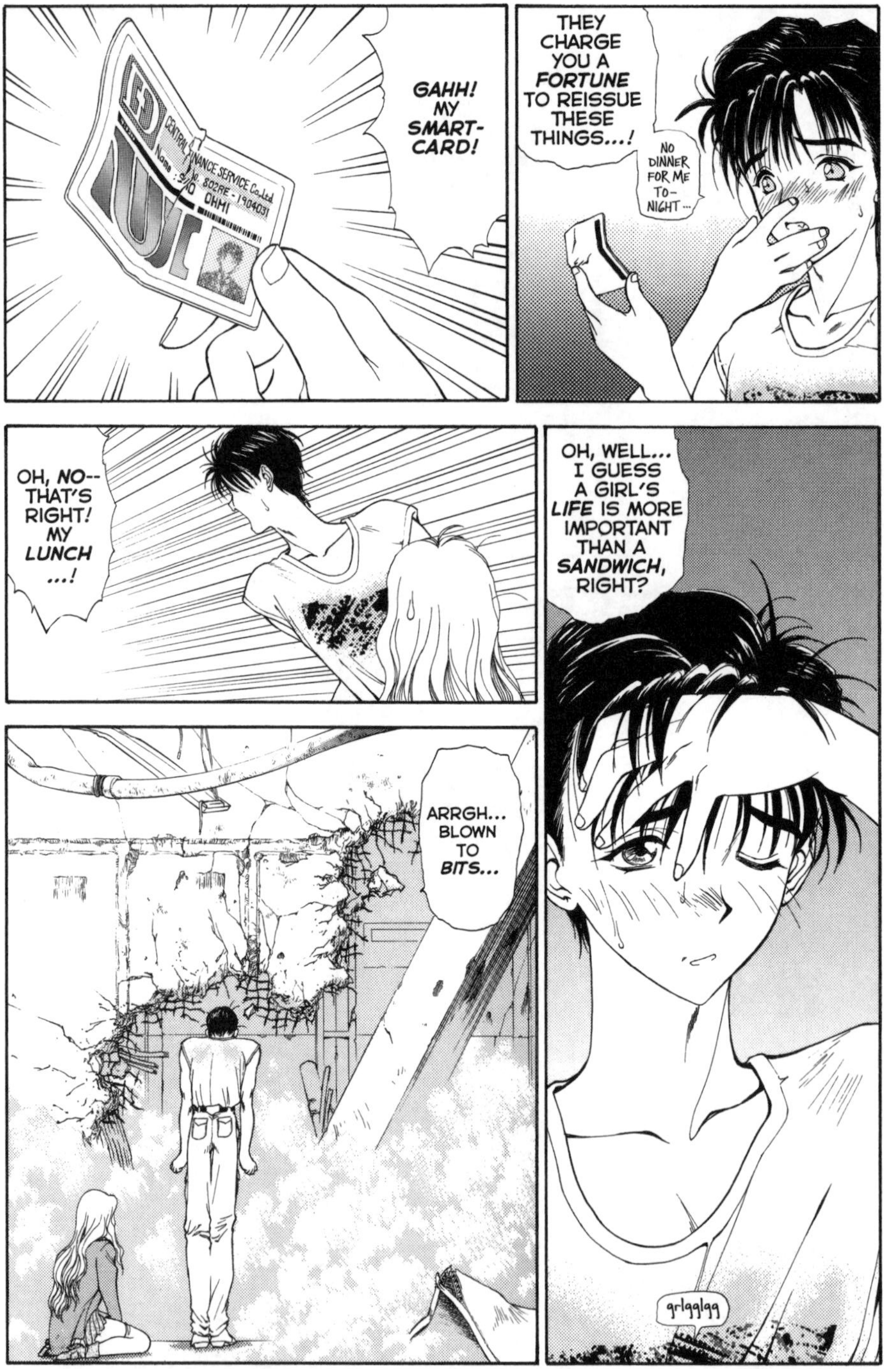
GAHH! MY SMART-CARD!
THEY CHARGE YOU A *FORTUNE* TO REISSUE THESE THINGS...!
NO DINNER FOR ME TO-NIGHT...
OH, *NO*-- THAT'S RIGHT! MY *LUNCH*...!
ARRGH... BLOWN TO *BITS*...
OH, WELL... I GUESS A GIRL'S *LIFE* IS MORE IMPORTANT THAN A *SANDWICH*, RIGHT?
grlgglgg

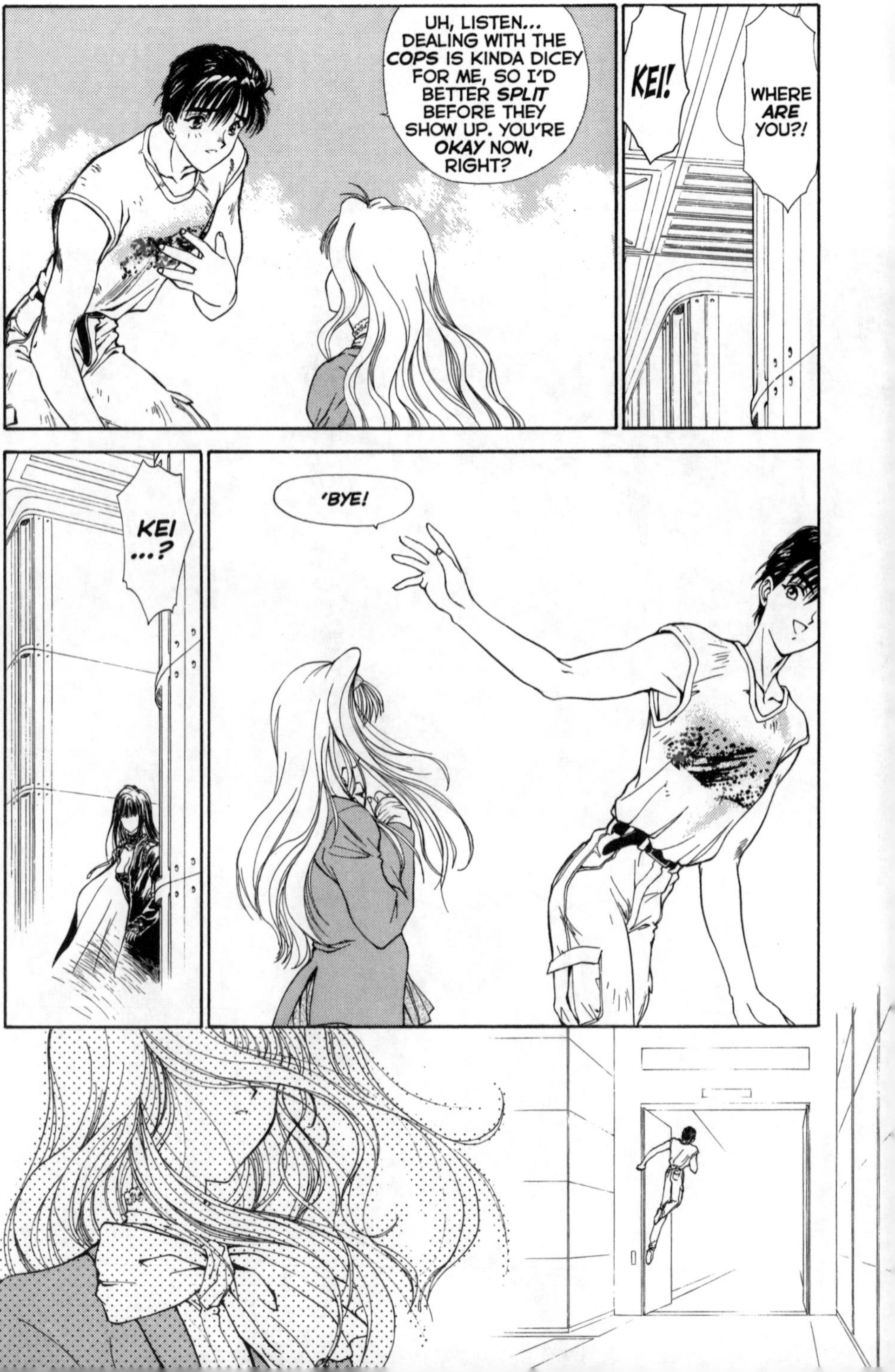
UH, LISTEN... DEALING WITH THE COPS IS KINDA DICEY FOR ME, SO I'D BETTER SPLIT BEFORE THEY SHOW UP. YOU'RE OKAY NOW, RIGHT?
KEI!
WHERE ARE YOU?!
KEI ...?
'BYE!

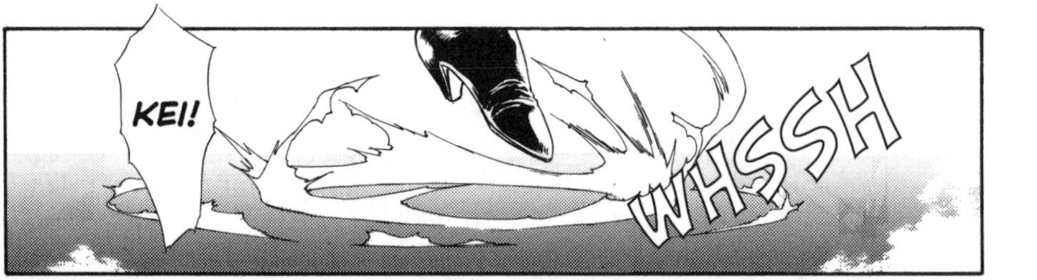
KEI!
WHSSH

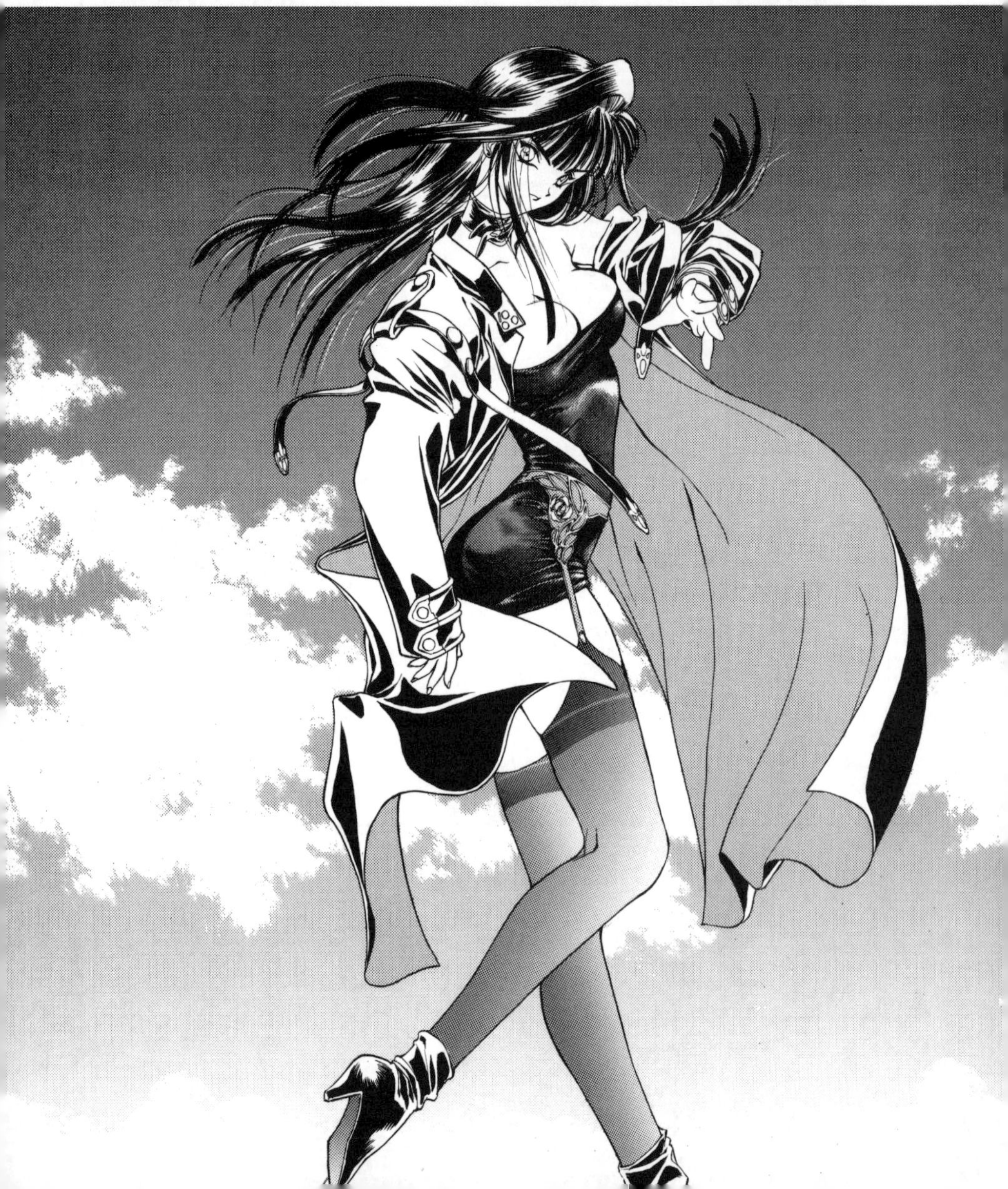

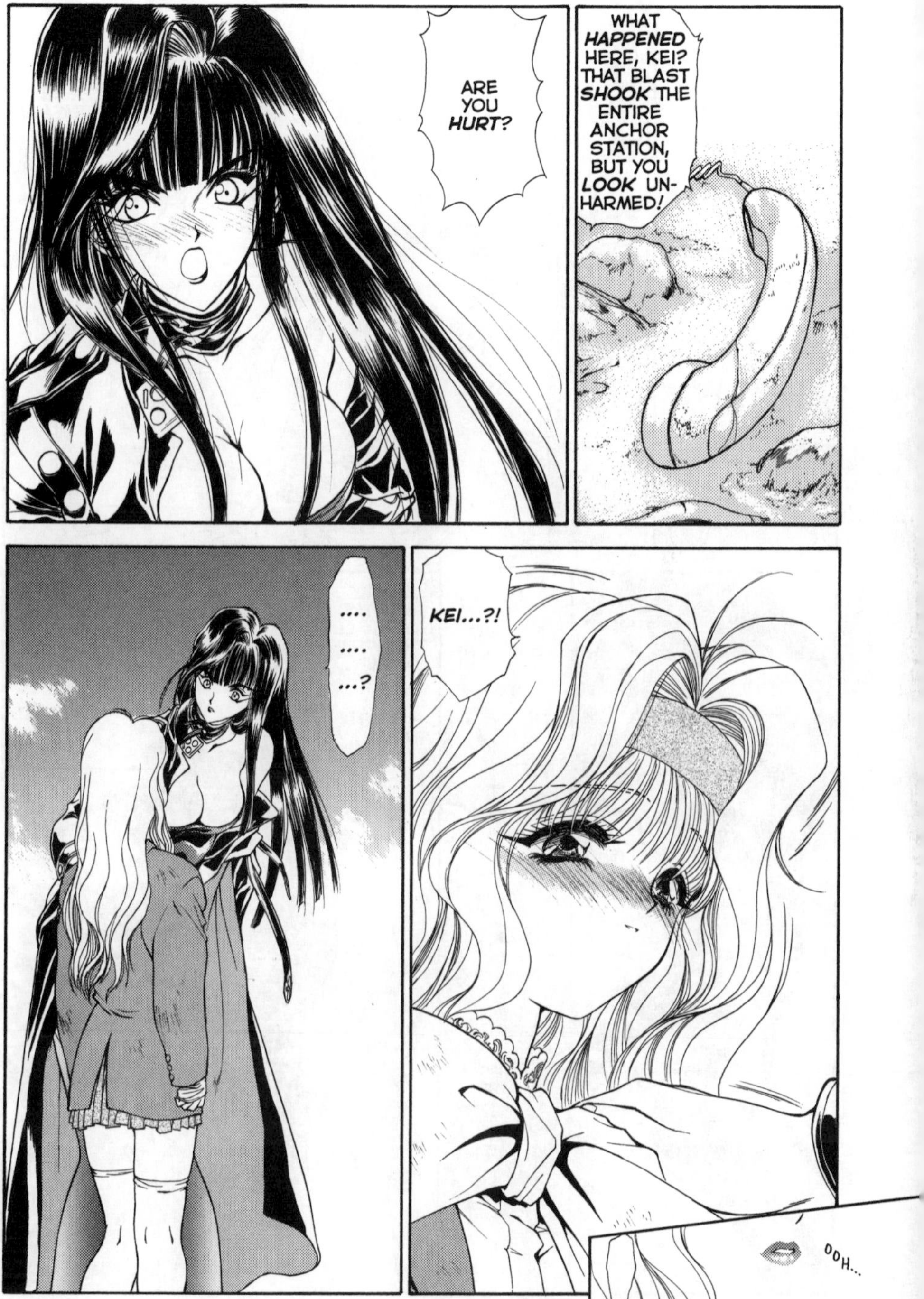

ARE YOU HURT?
WHAT HAPPENED HERE, KEI? THAT BLAST SHOOK THE ENTIRE ANCHOR STATION, BUT YOU LOOK UN-HARMED!
....?
KEI...?!
OOH...

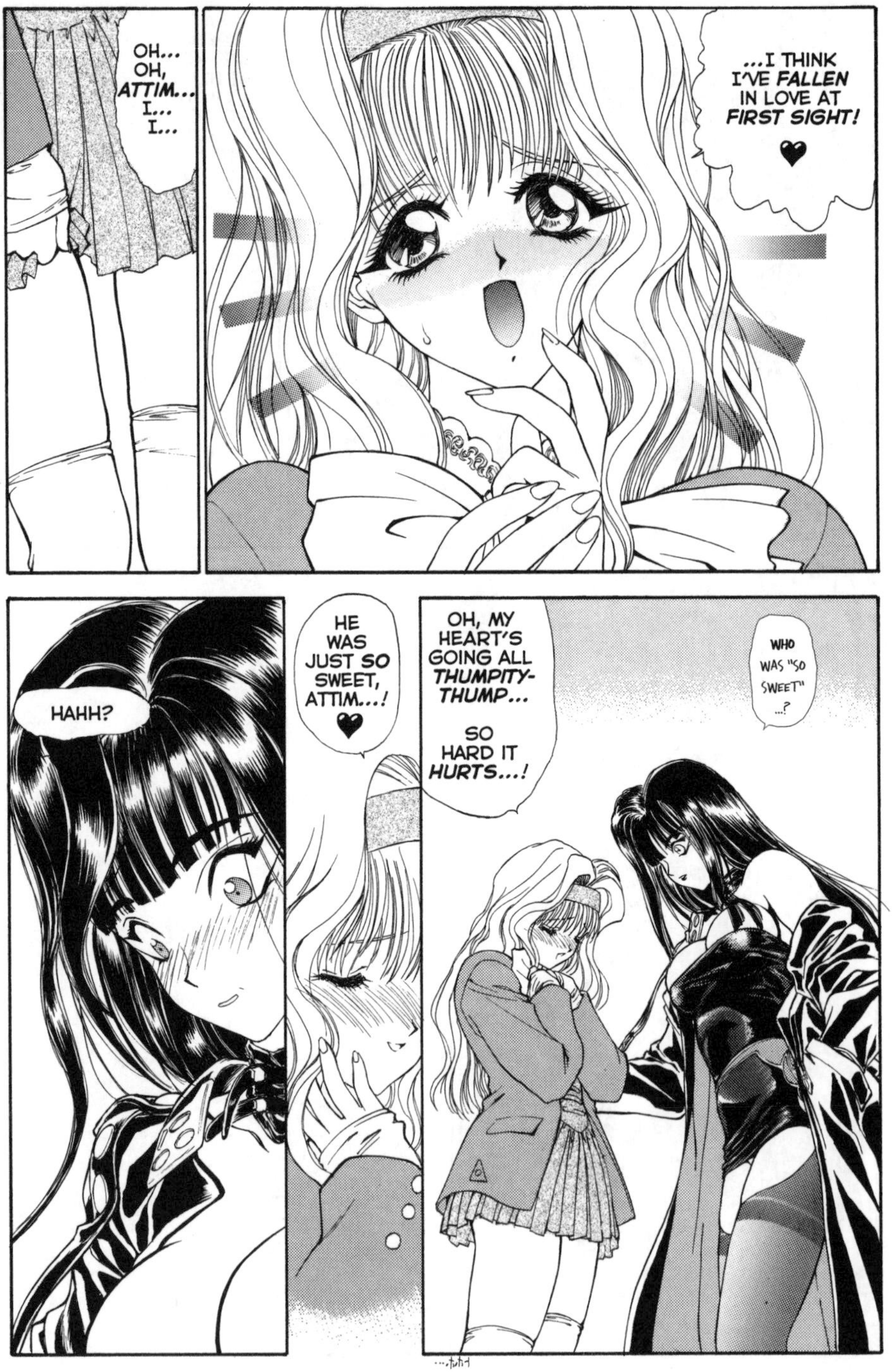
OH... OH, ATTIM... I... I...
...I THINK I'VE FALLEN IN LOVE AT FIRST SIGHT! ♥
HAHH?
HE WAS JUST SO SWEET, ATTIM...! ♥
OH, MY HEART'S GOING ALL THUMPITY-THUMP...
SO HARD IT HURTS...!
WHO WAS "SO SWEET" ...?

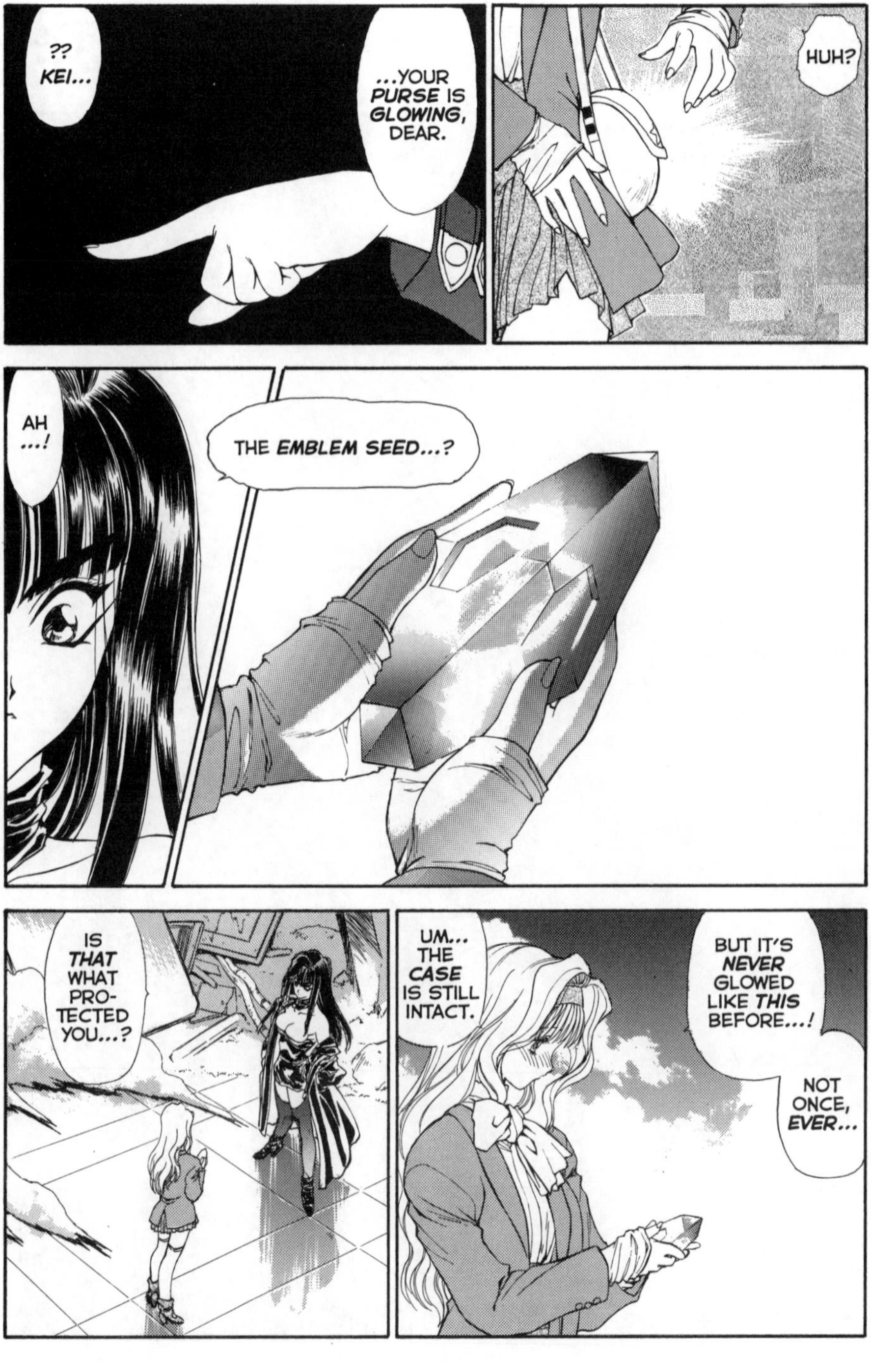

?? KEI...
...YOUR PURSE IS GLOWING, DEAR.
HUH?
AH ...!
THE EMBLEM SEED...?
IS THAT WHAT PRO-TECTED YOU...?
UM... THE CASE IS STILL INTACT.
BUT IT'S NEVER GLOWED LIKE THIS BEFORE...!
NOT ONCE, EVER...

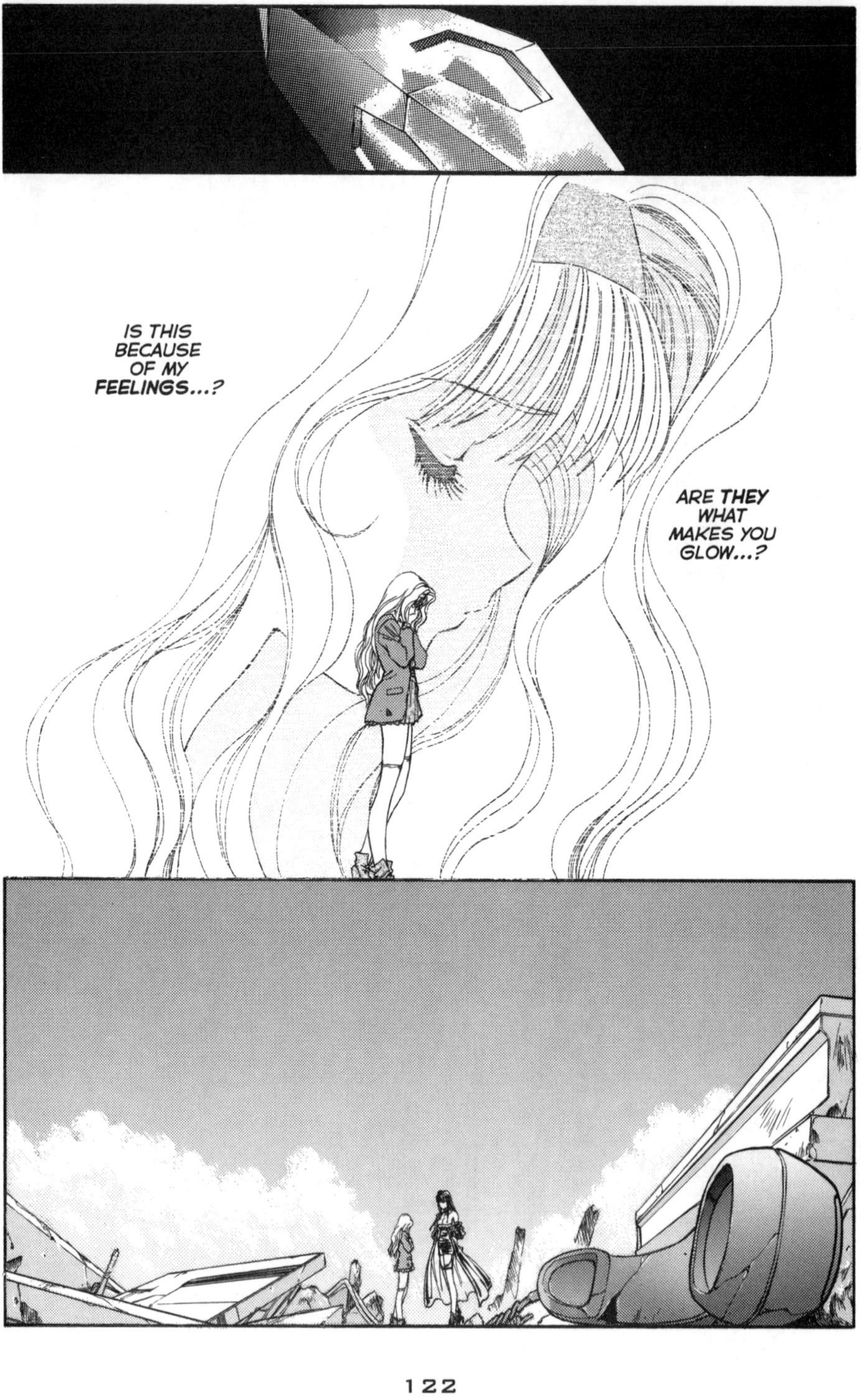
IS THIS BECAUSE OF MY FEELINGS...?
ARE THEY WHAT MAKES YOU GLOW...?

ACT 3

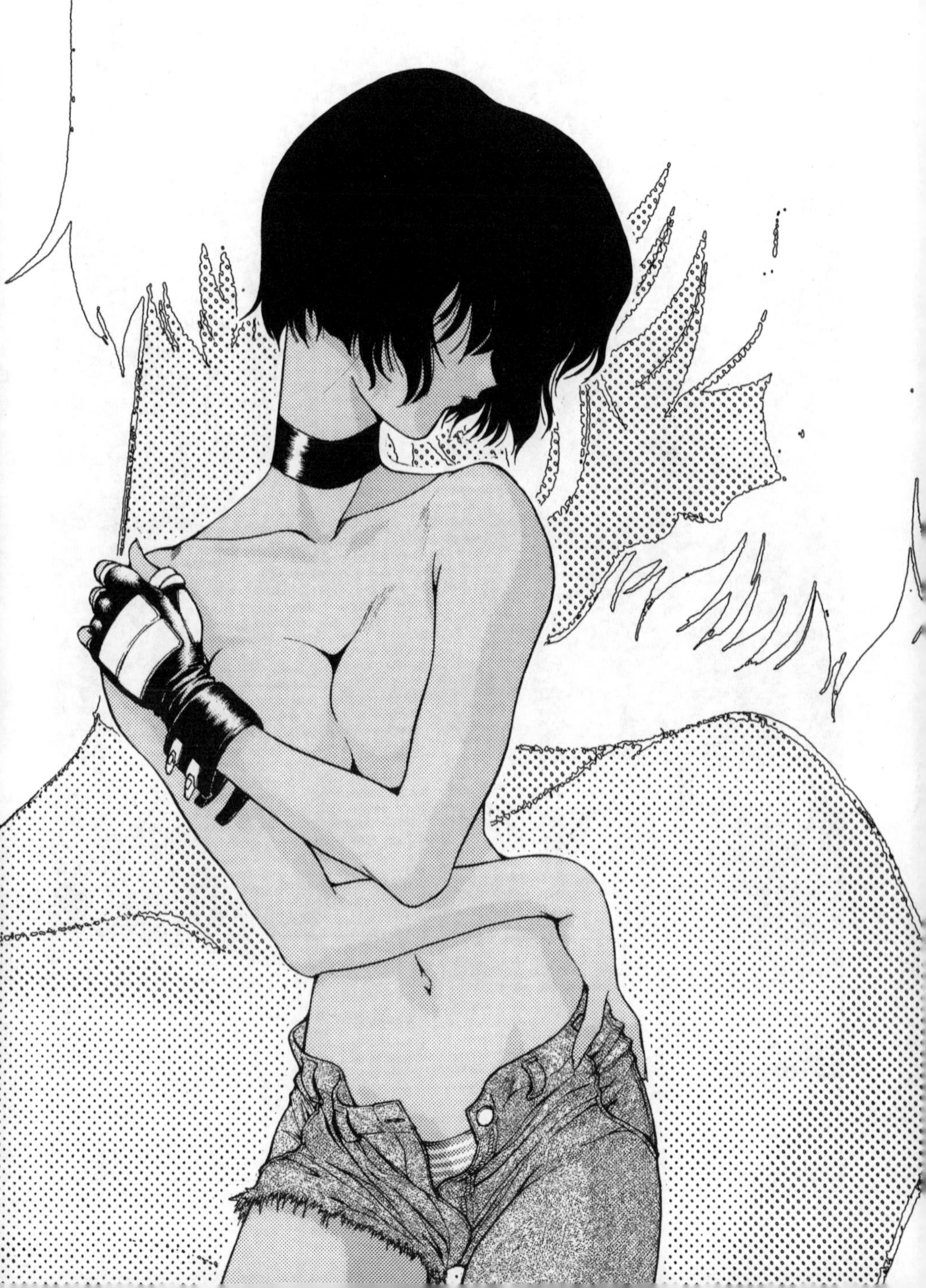

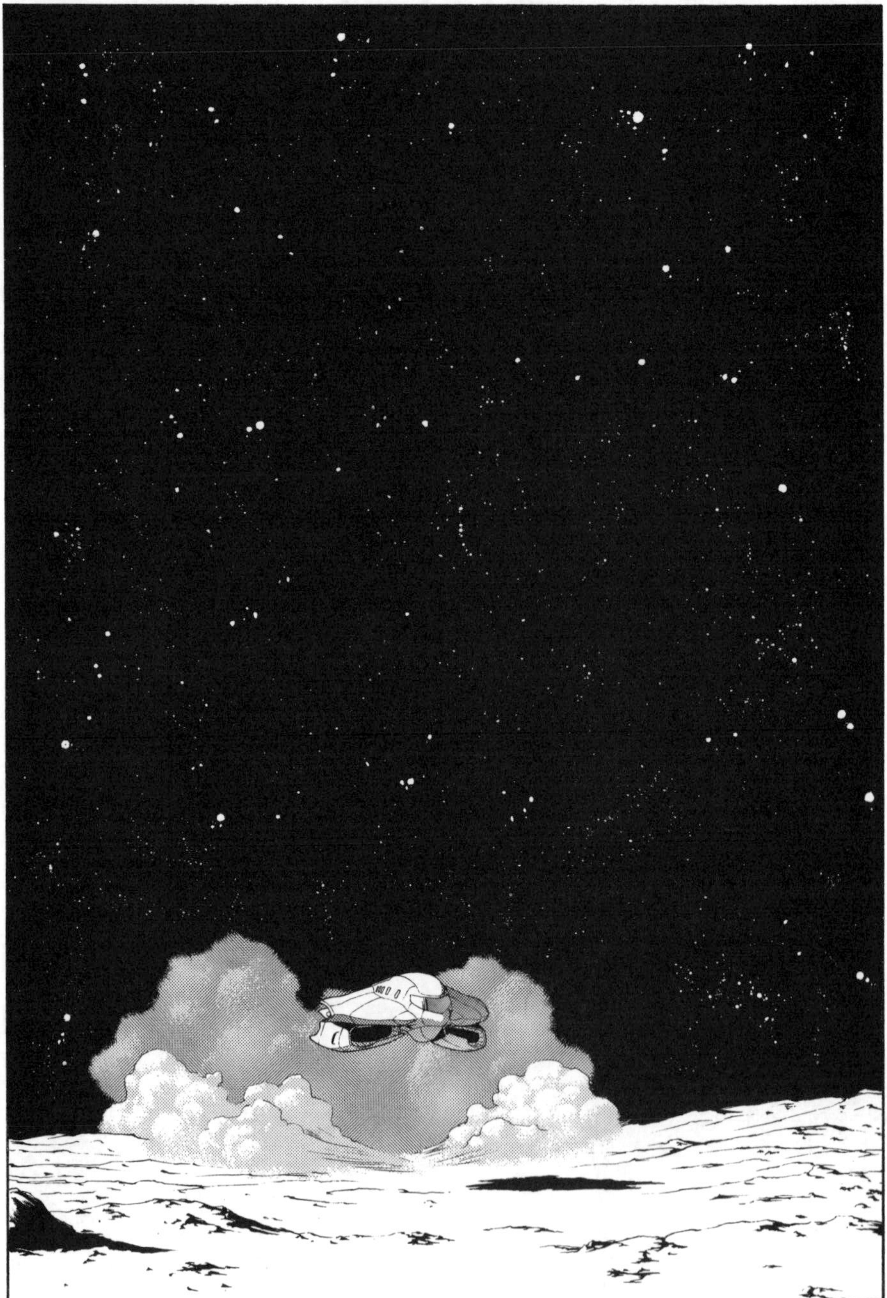

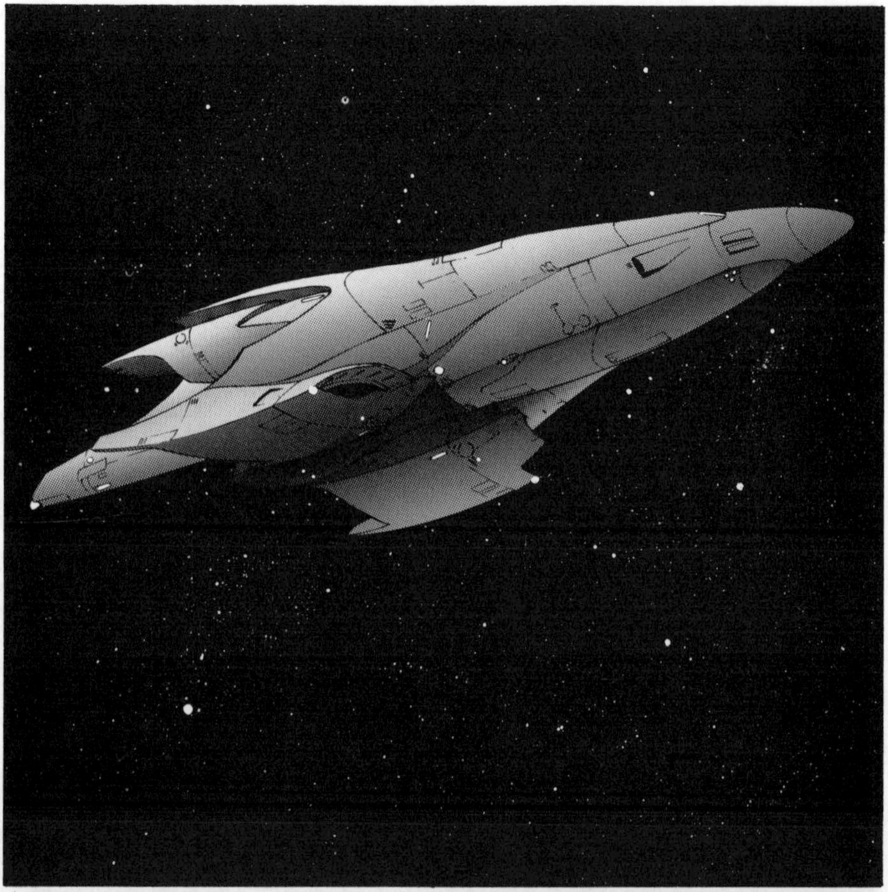

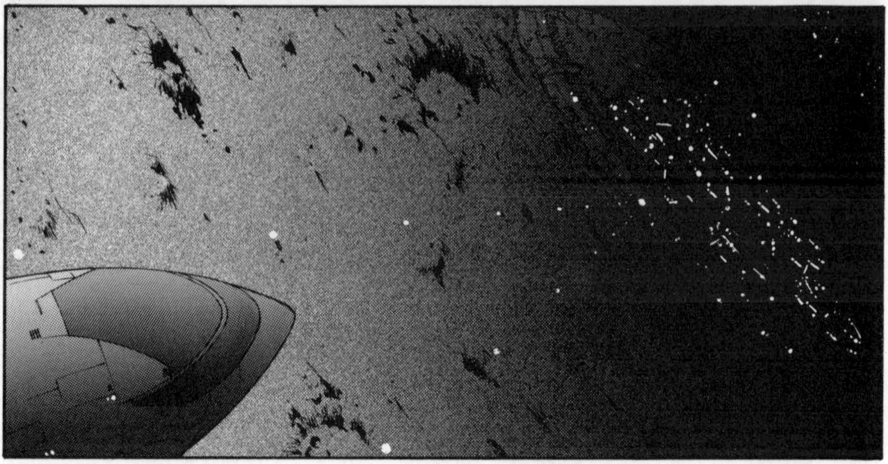

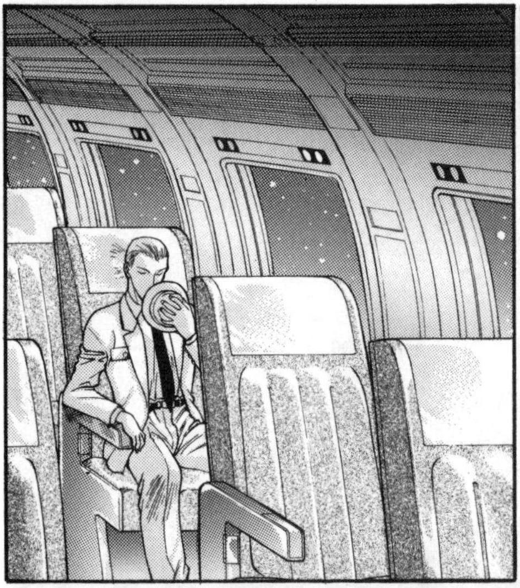

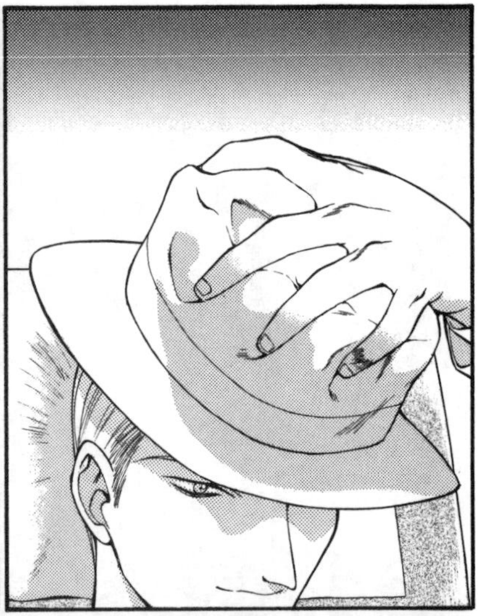

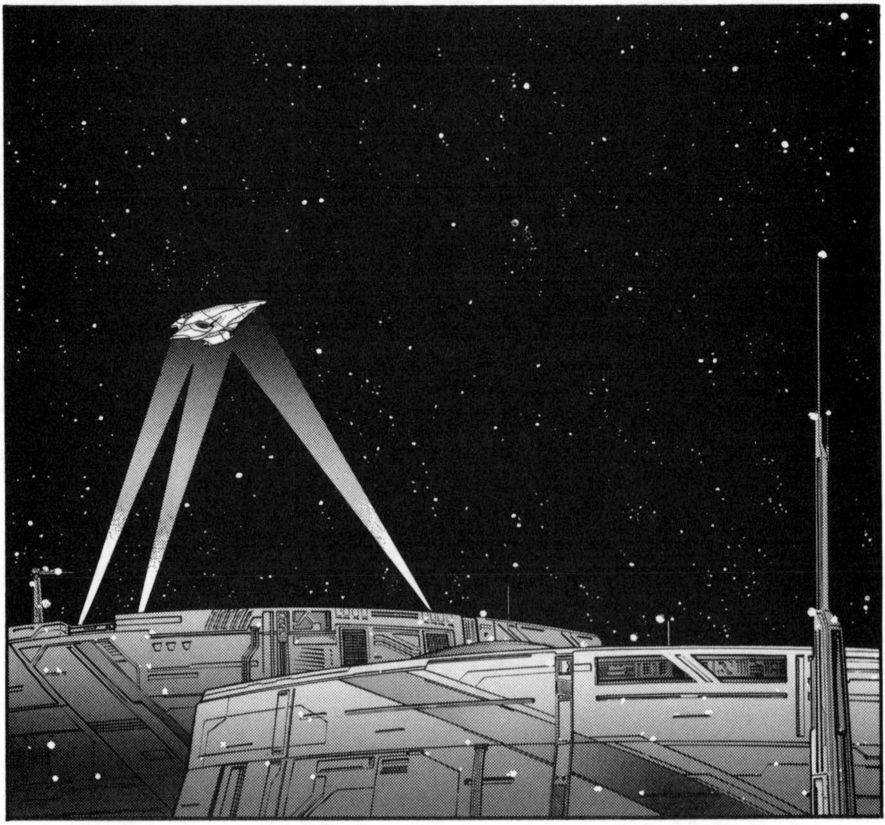

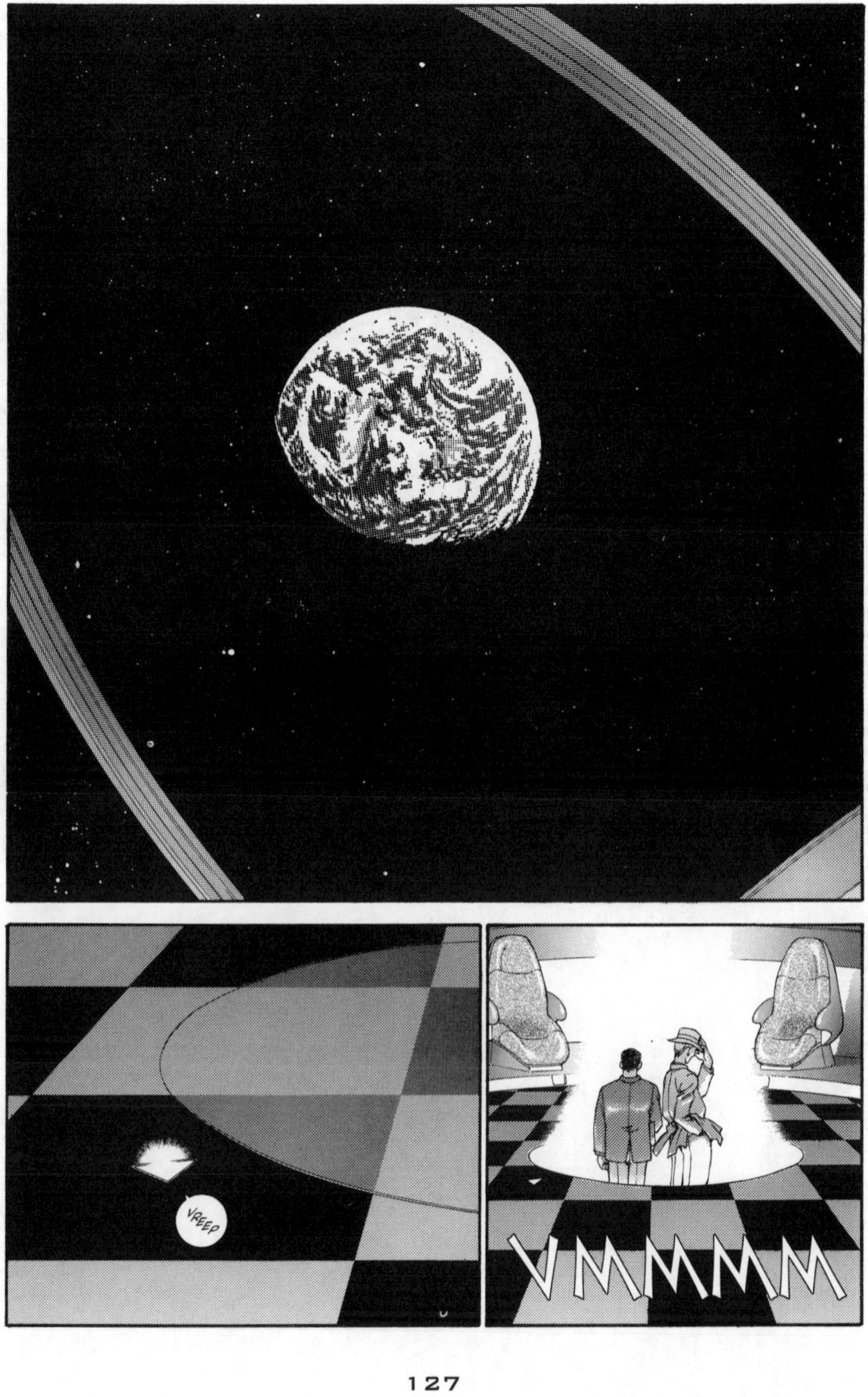
VREEP
VMMMMM

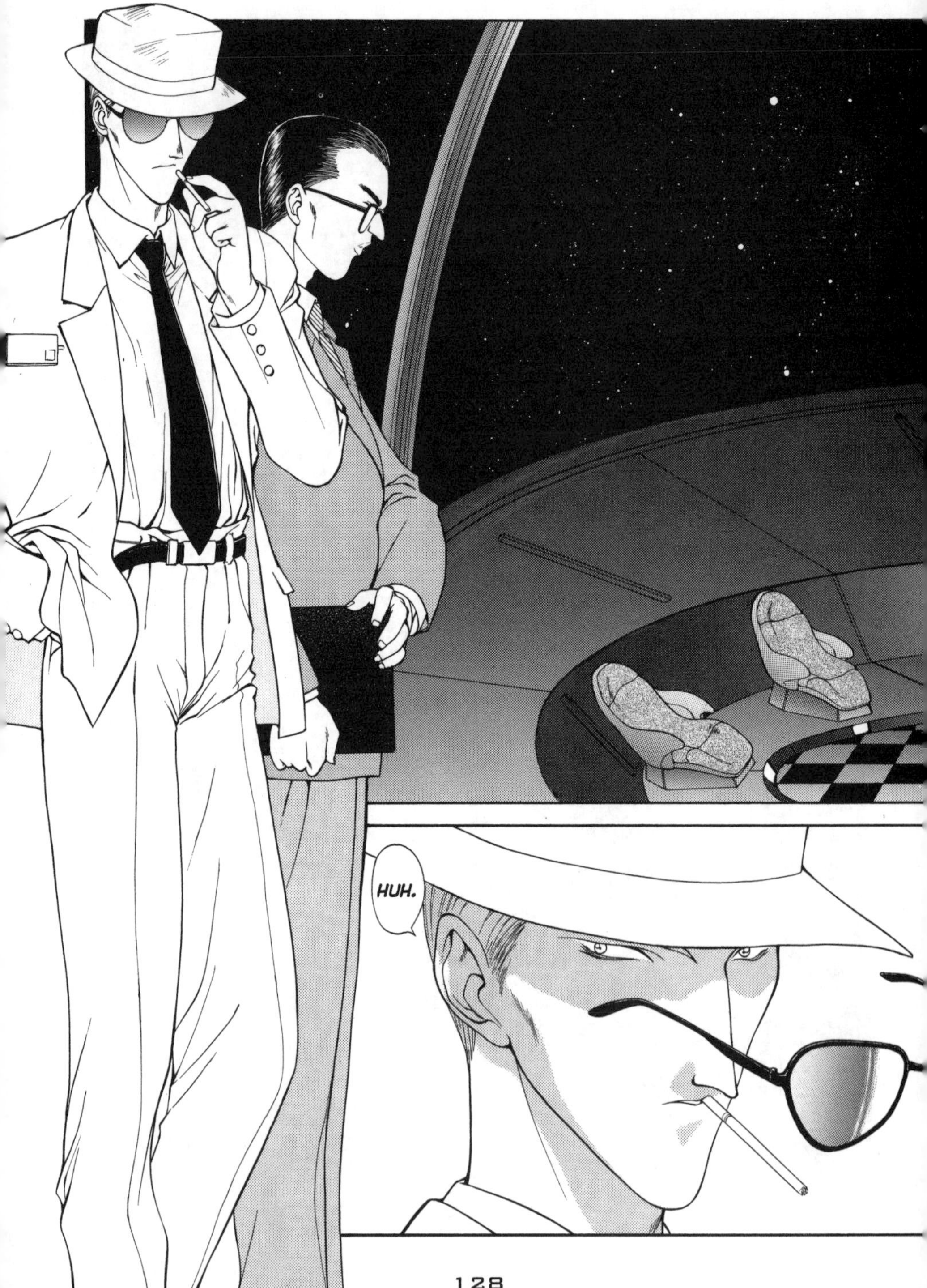
HUH.

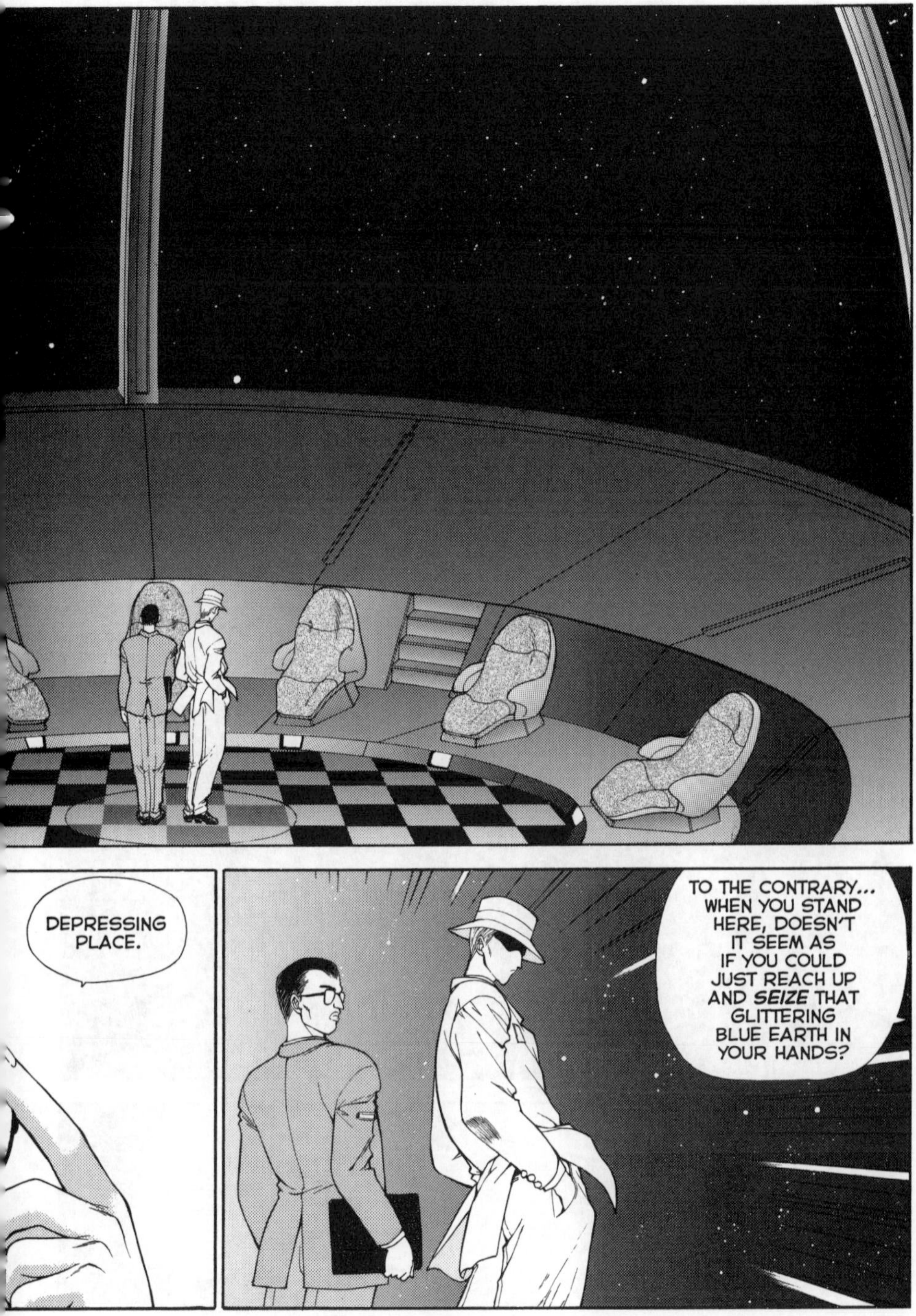
DEPRESSING PLACE.
TO THE CONTRARY... WHEN YOU STAND HERE, DOESN'T IT SEEM AS IF YOU COULD JUST REACH UP AND *SEIZE* THAT GLITTERING BLUE EARTH IN YOUR HANDS?

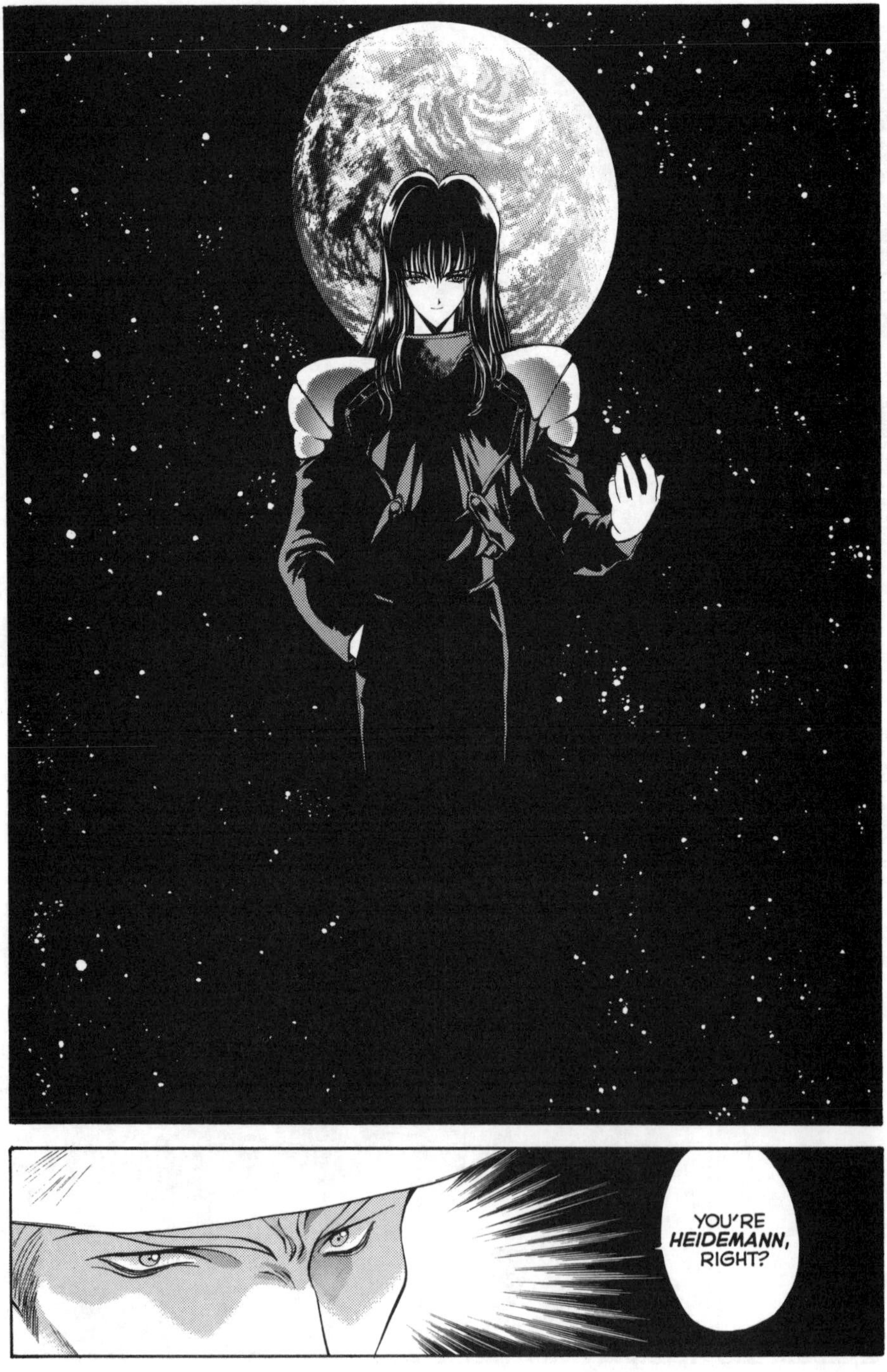
YOU'RE HEIDEMANN, RIGHT?

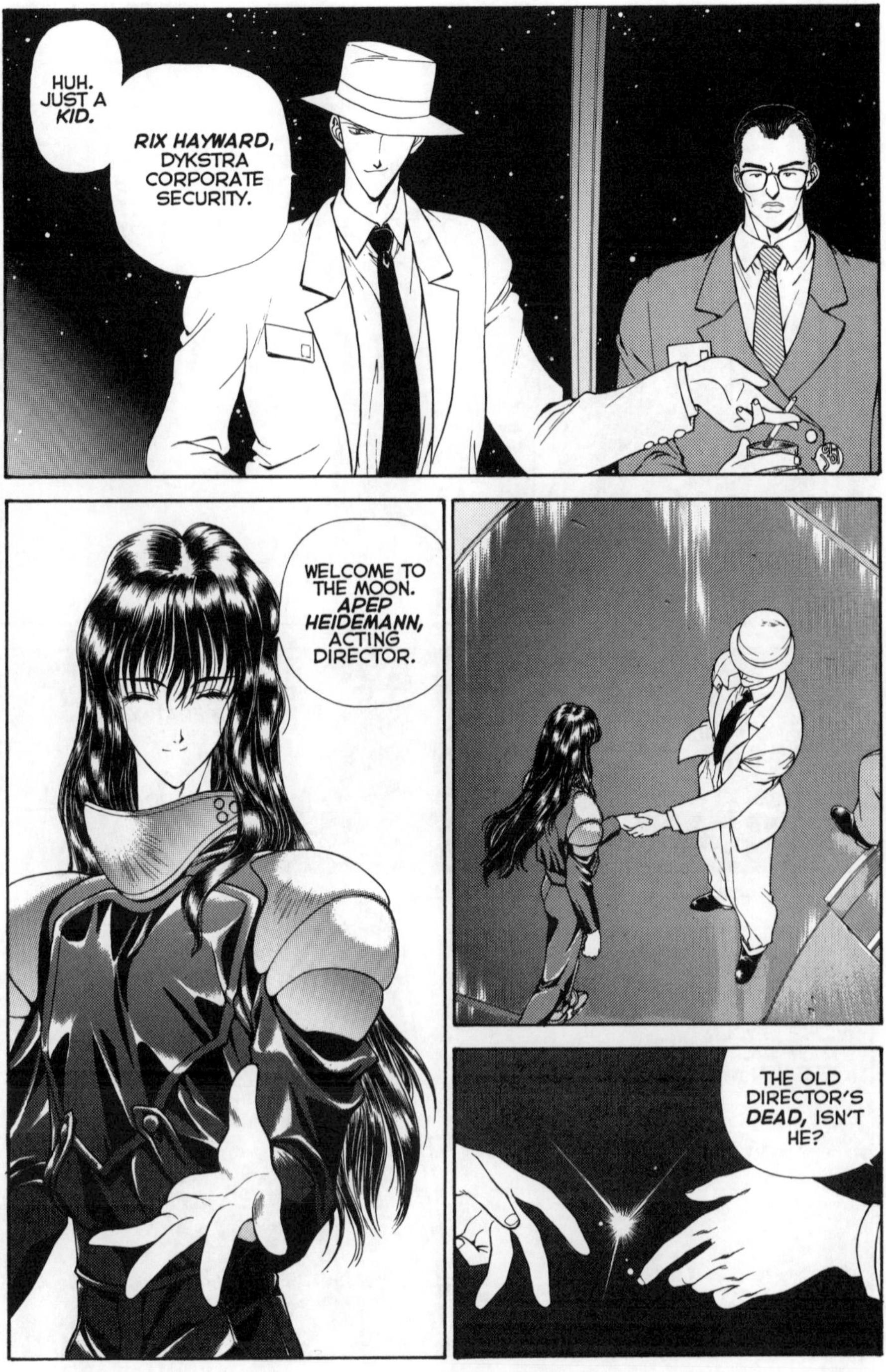
HUH. JUST A KID.
RIX HAYWARD, DYKSTRA CORPORATE SECURITY.
WELCOME TO THE MOON. APEP HEIDEMANN, ACTING DIRECTOR.
THE OLD DIRECTOR'S DEAD, ISN'T HE?

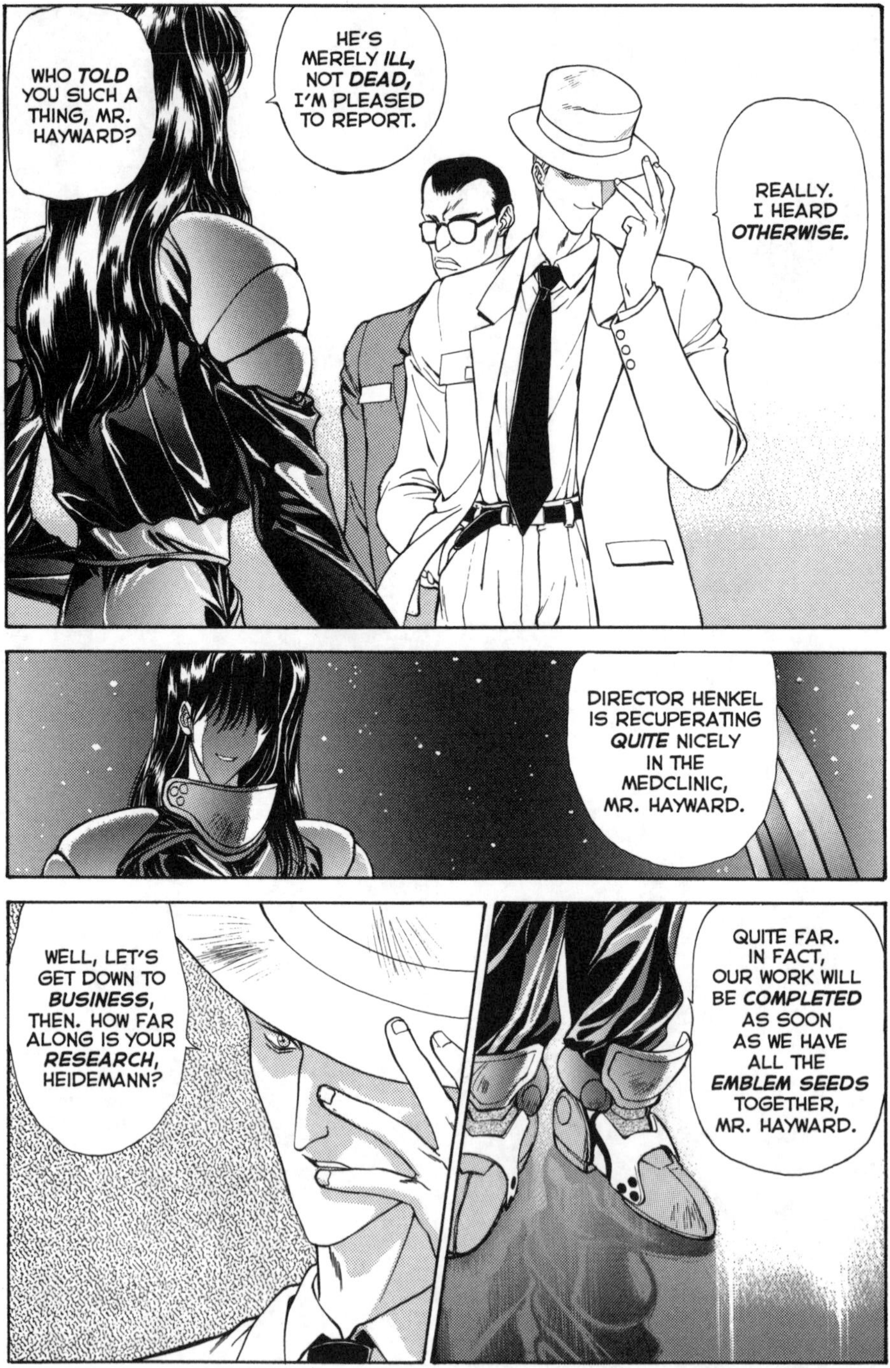
WHO *TOLD* YOU SUCH A THING, MR. HAYWARD?
HE'S MERELY *ILL,* NOT *DEAD,* I'M PLEASED TO REPORT.
REALLY. I HEARD *OTHERWISE.*
DIRECTOR HENKEL IS RECUPERATING *QUITE* NICELY IN THE MEDCLINIC, MR. HAYWARD.
WELL, LET'S GET DOWN TO *BUSINESS,* THEN. HOW FAR ALONG IS YOUR *RESEARCH,* HEIDEMANN?
QUITE FAR. IN FACT, OUR WORK WILL BE *COMPLETED* AS SOON AS WE HAVE ALL THE *EMBLEM SEEDS* TOGETHER, MR. HAYWARD.

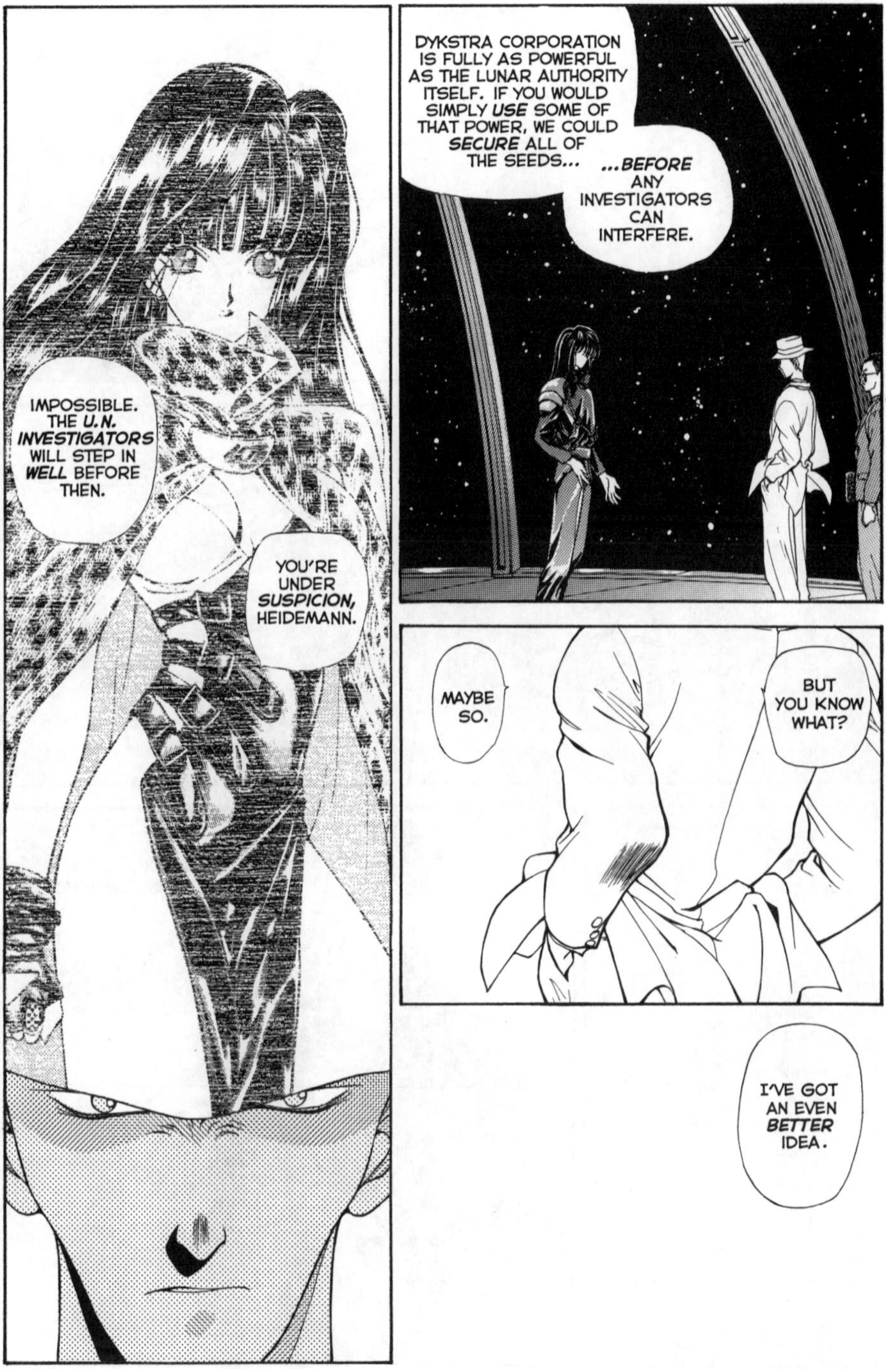
IMPOSSIBLE. THE U.N. INVESTIGATORS WILL STEP IN WELL BEFORE THEN.
YOU'RE UNDER SUSPICION, HEIDEMANN.
DYKSTRA CORPORATION IS FULLY AS POWERFUL AS THE LUNAR AUTHORITY ITSELF. IF YOU WOULD SIMPLY USE SOME OF THAT POWER, WE COULD SECURE ALL OF THE SEEDS...
...BEFORE ANY INVESTIGATORS CAN INTERFERE.
MAYBE SO.
BUT YOU KNOW WHAT?
I'VE GOT AN EVEN BETTER IDEA.

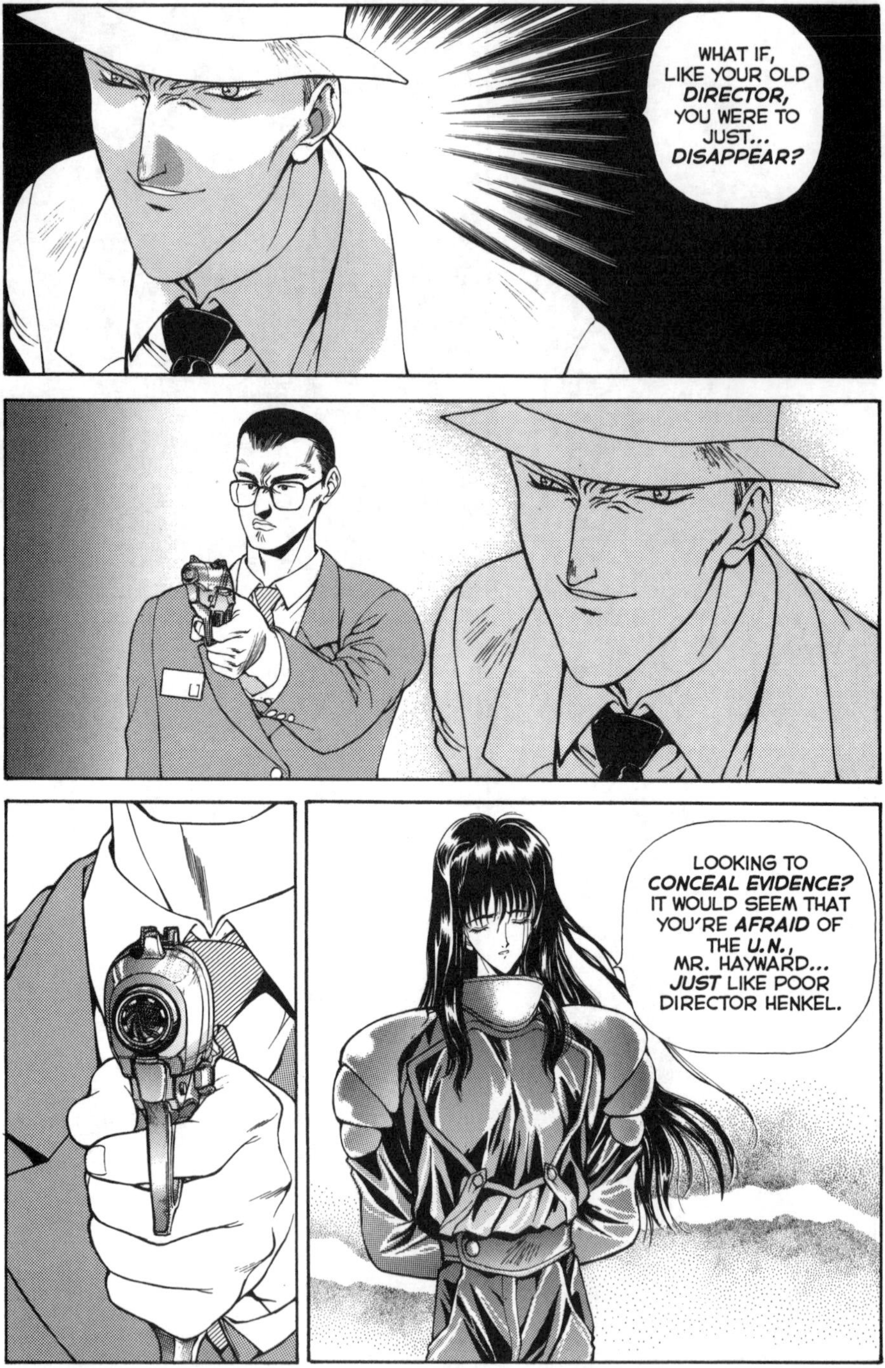
WHAT IF, LIKE YOUR OLD DIRECTOR, YOU WERE TO JUST... DISAPPEAR?
LOOKING TO CONCEAL EVIDENCE? IT WOULD SEEM THAT YOU'RE AFRAID OF THE U.N., MR. HAYWARD... JUST LIKE POOR DIRECTOR HENKEL.

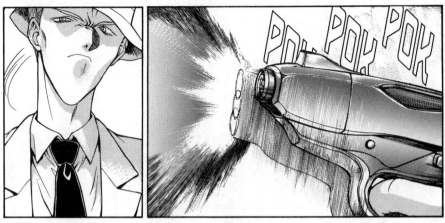

WH--

WHAT--?!

YOU SHOULD BE MORE *CAREFUL*, GENTLEMEN.

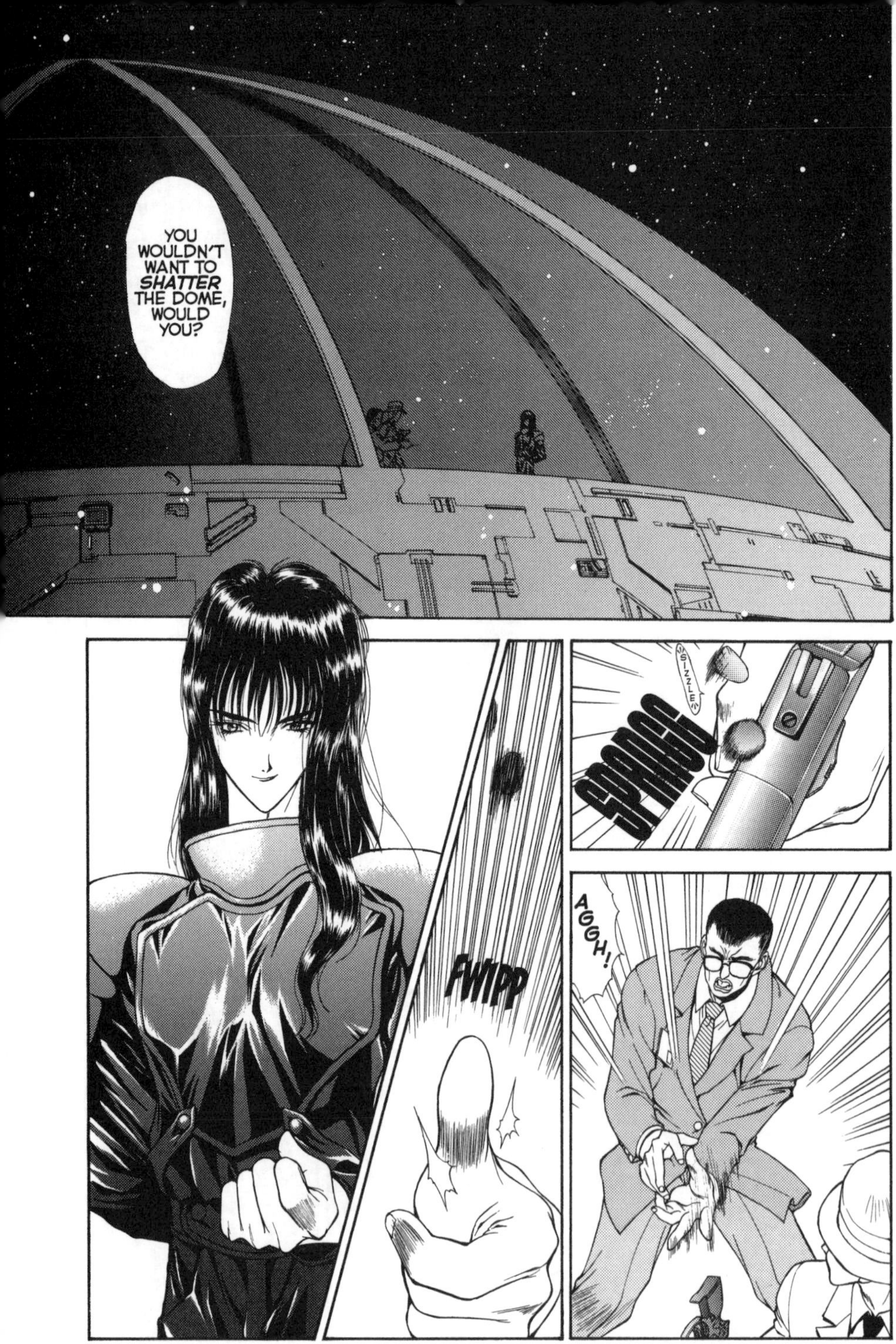
YOU WOULDN'T WANT TO *SHATTER* THE DOME, WOULD YOU?
FWIPP
SPROGG
SIZZLE
AGGH!

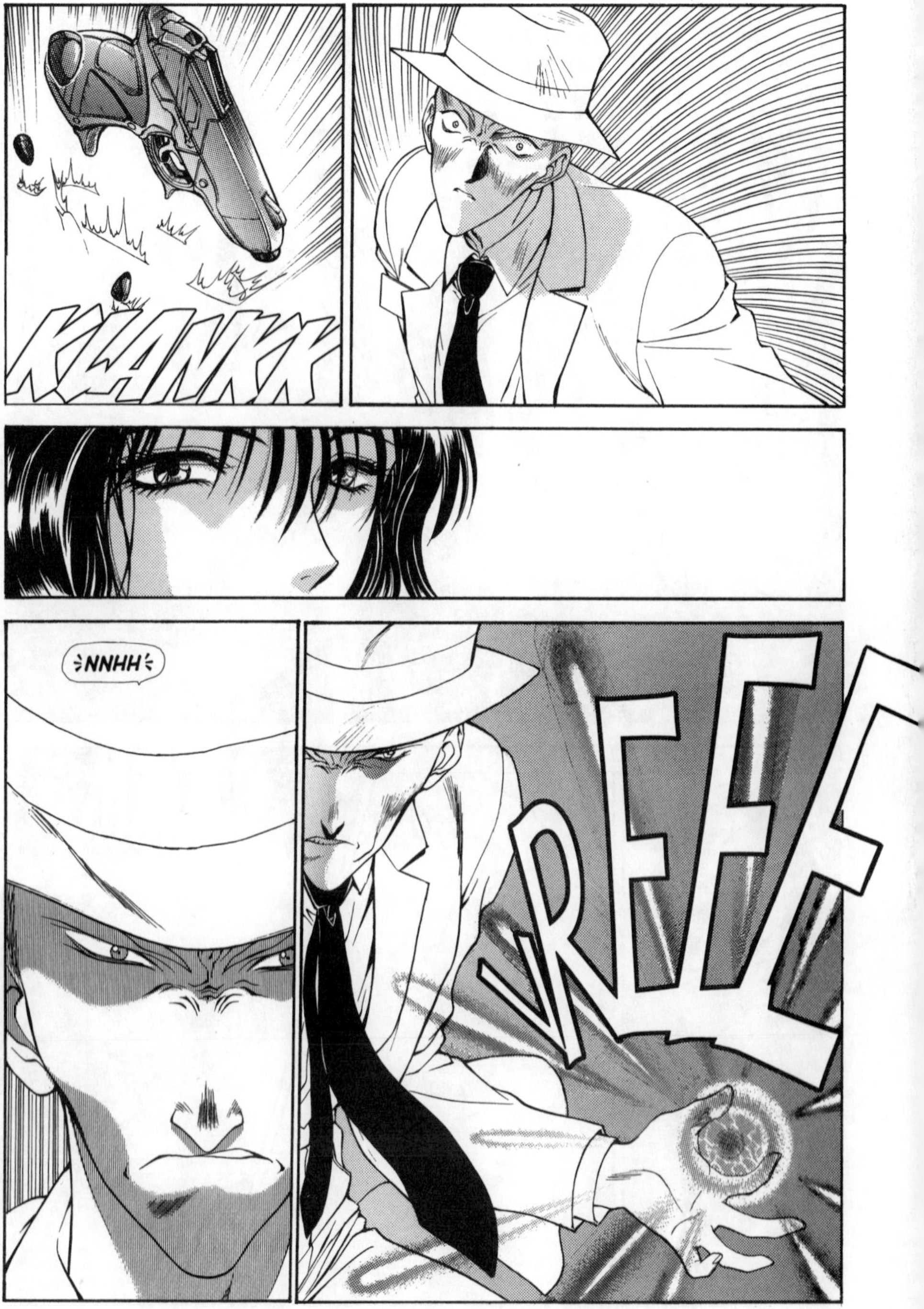
KLANKK
NNHH
VREEEE

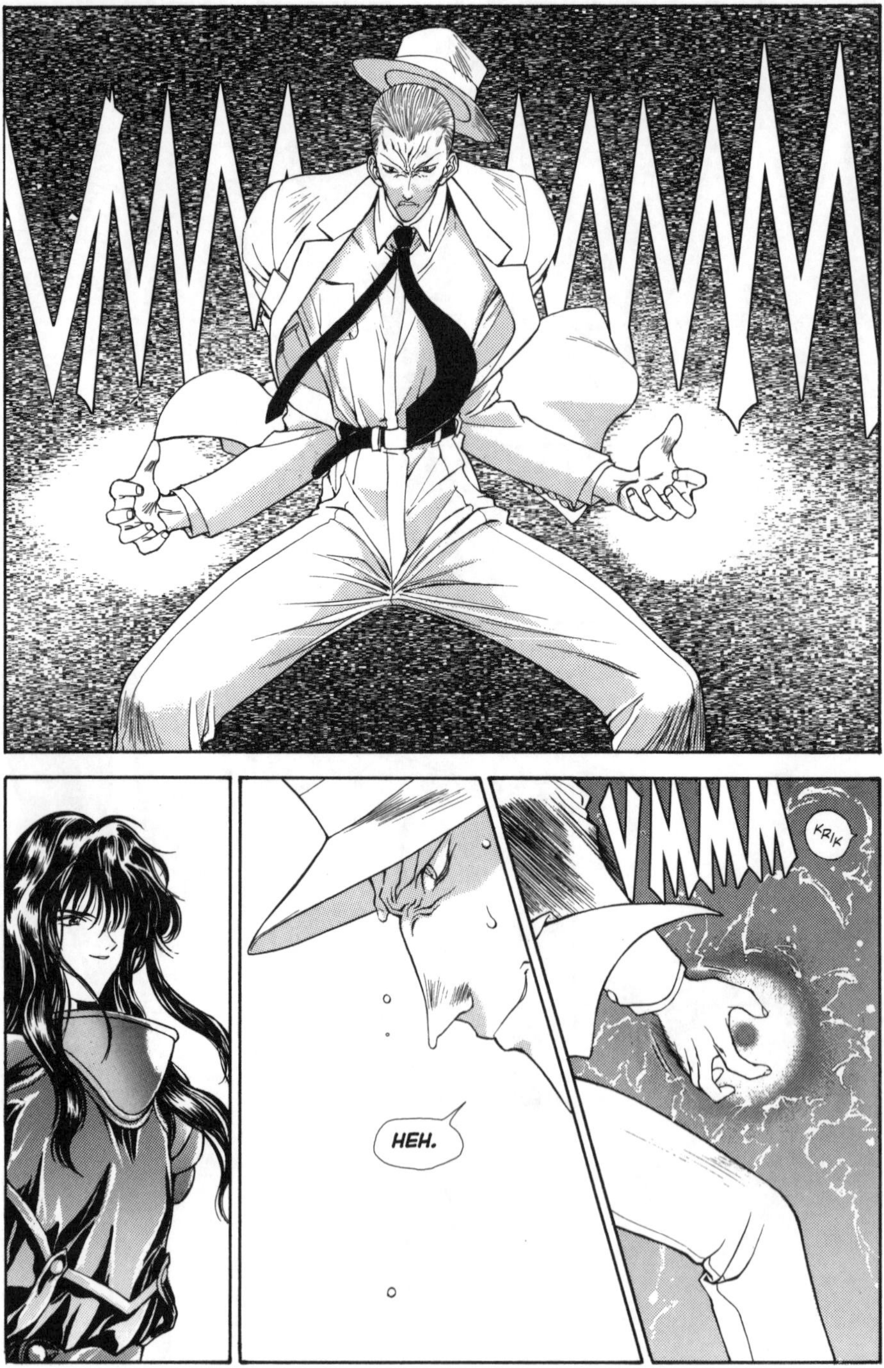
HEH.
VMMM
KRIK

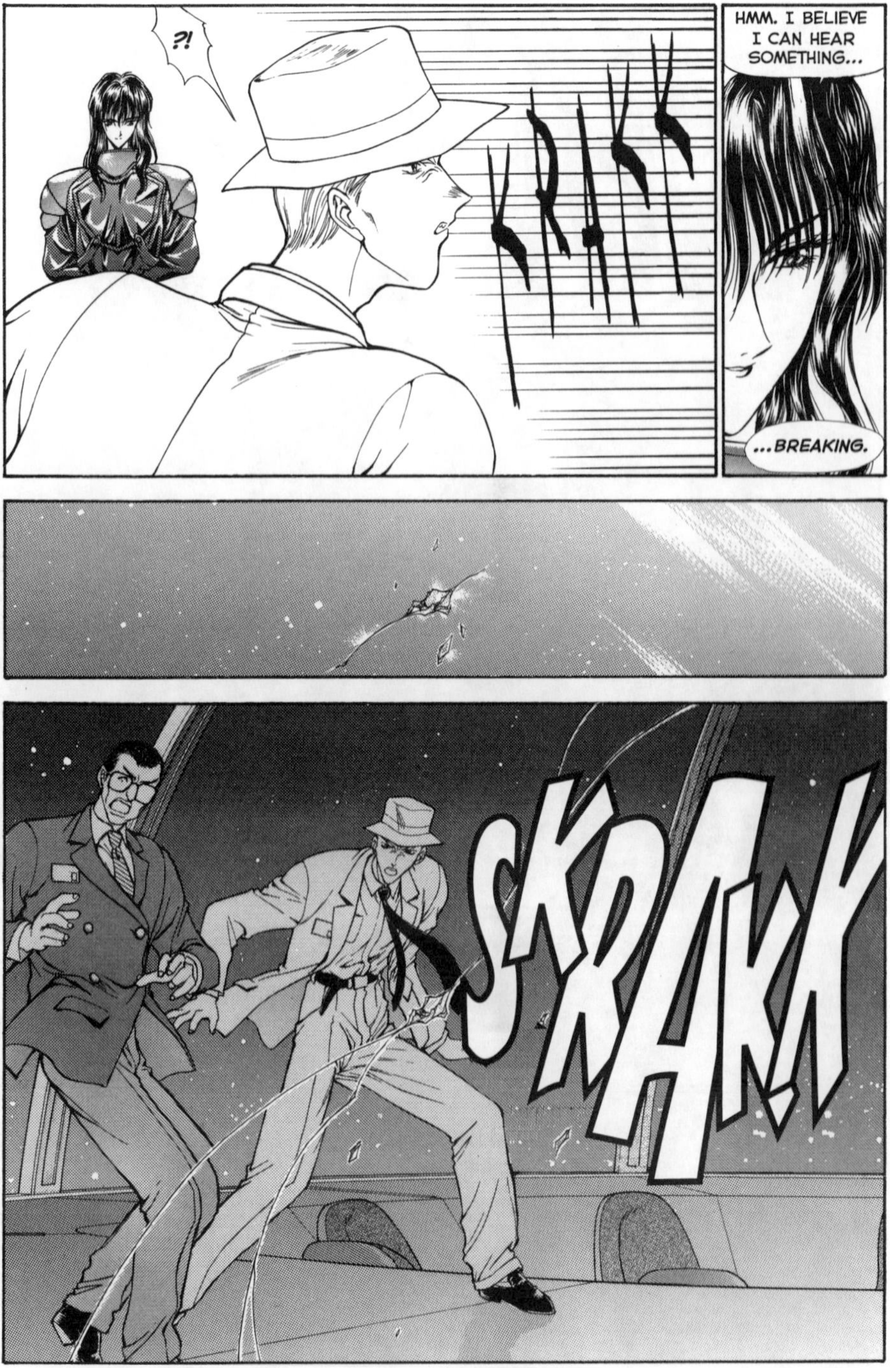
?!
KRAKK
HMM. I BELIEVE I CAN HEAR SOMETHING...
...BREAKING.
SKRAKK

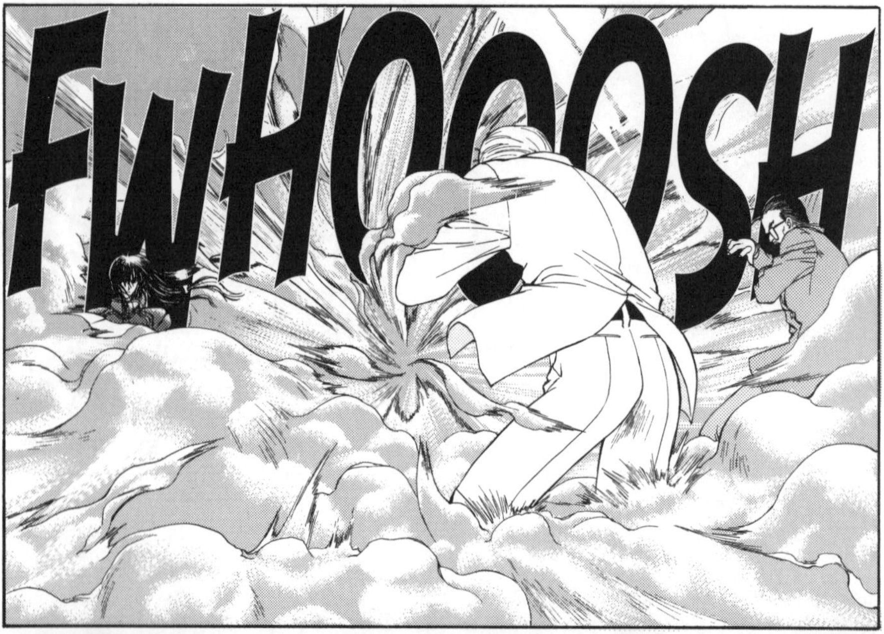
FWHOOOSH
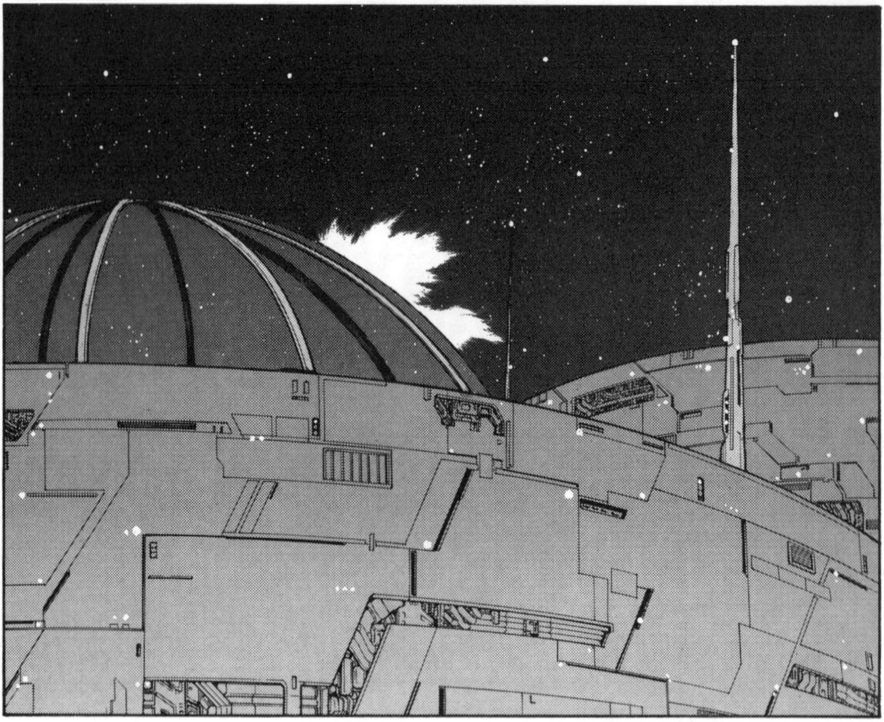

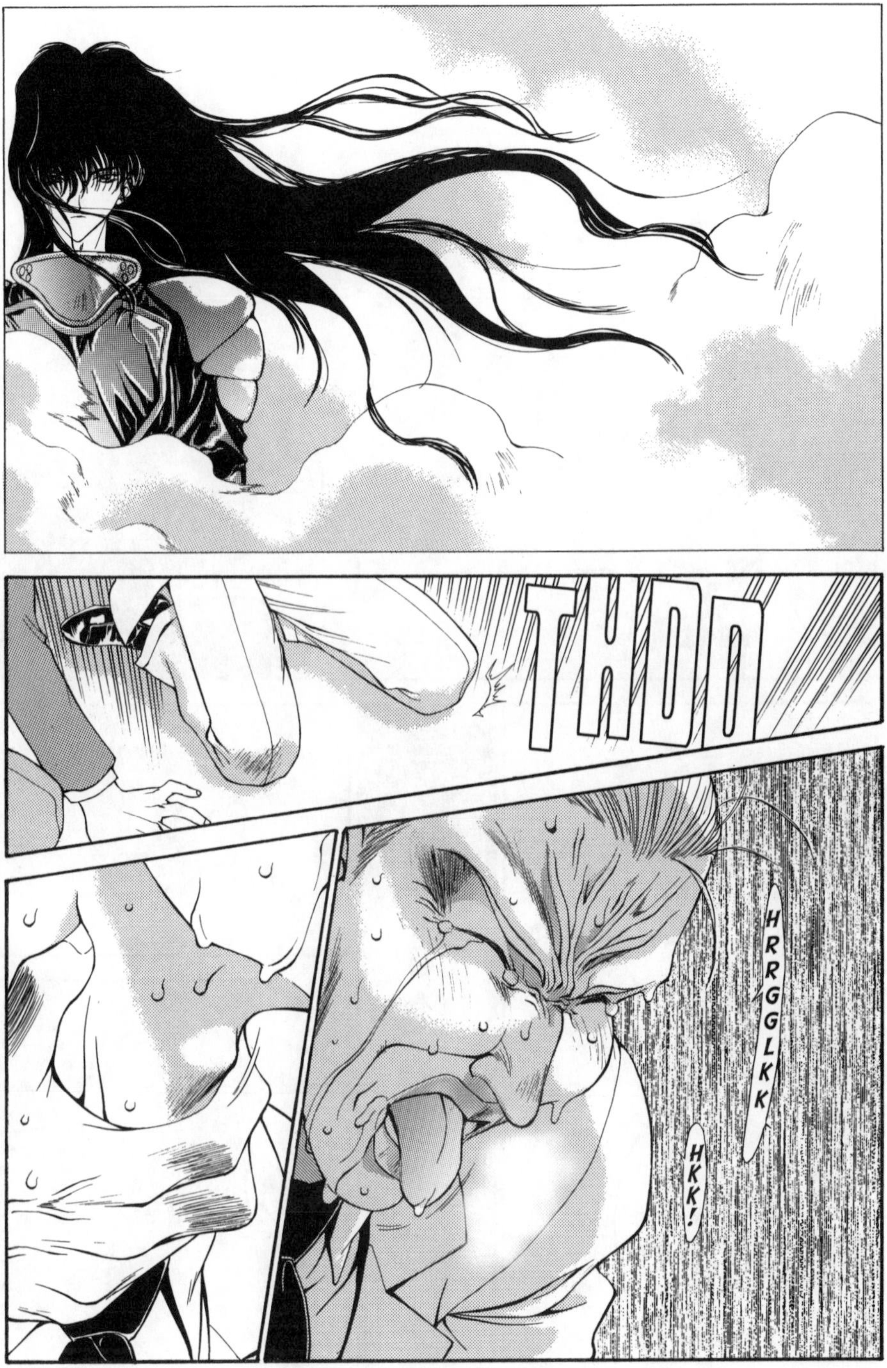
THDD
HRRGGLKK
HKK!

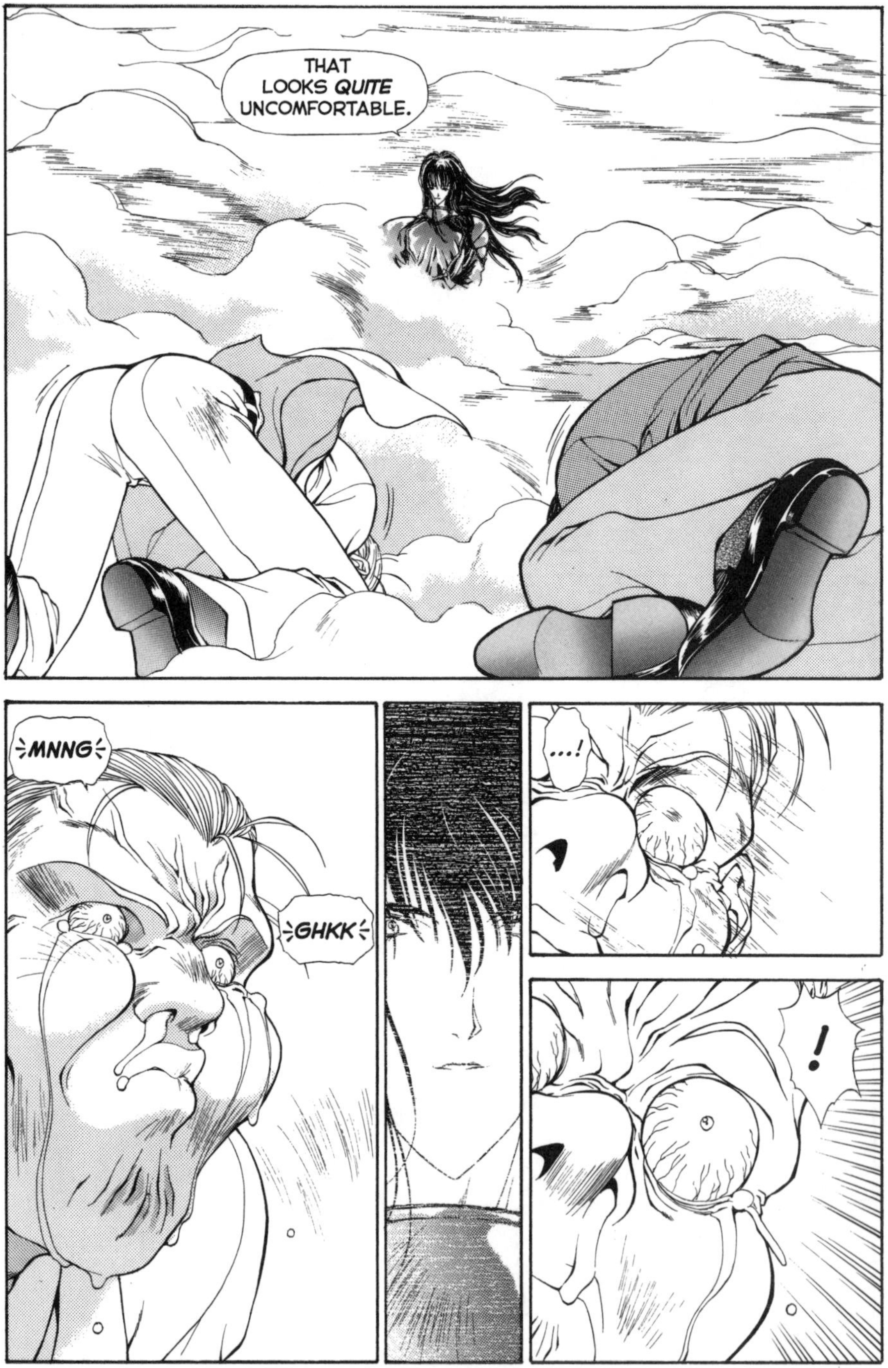
THAT LOOKS QUITE UNCOMFORTABLE.
MNNG
GHKK
...!
!

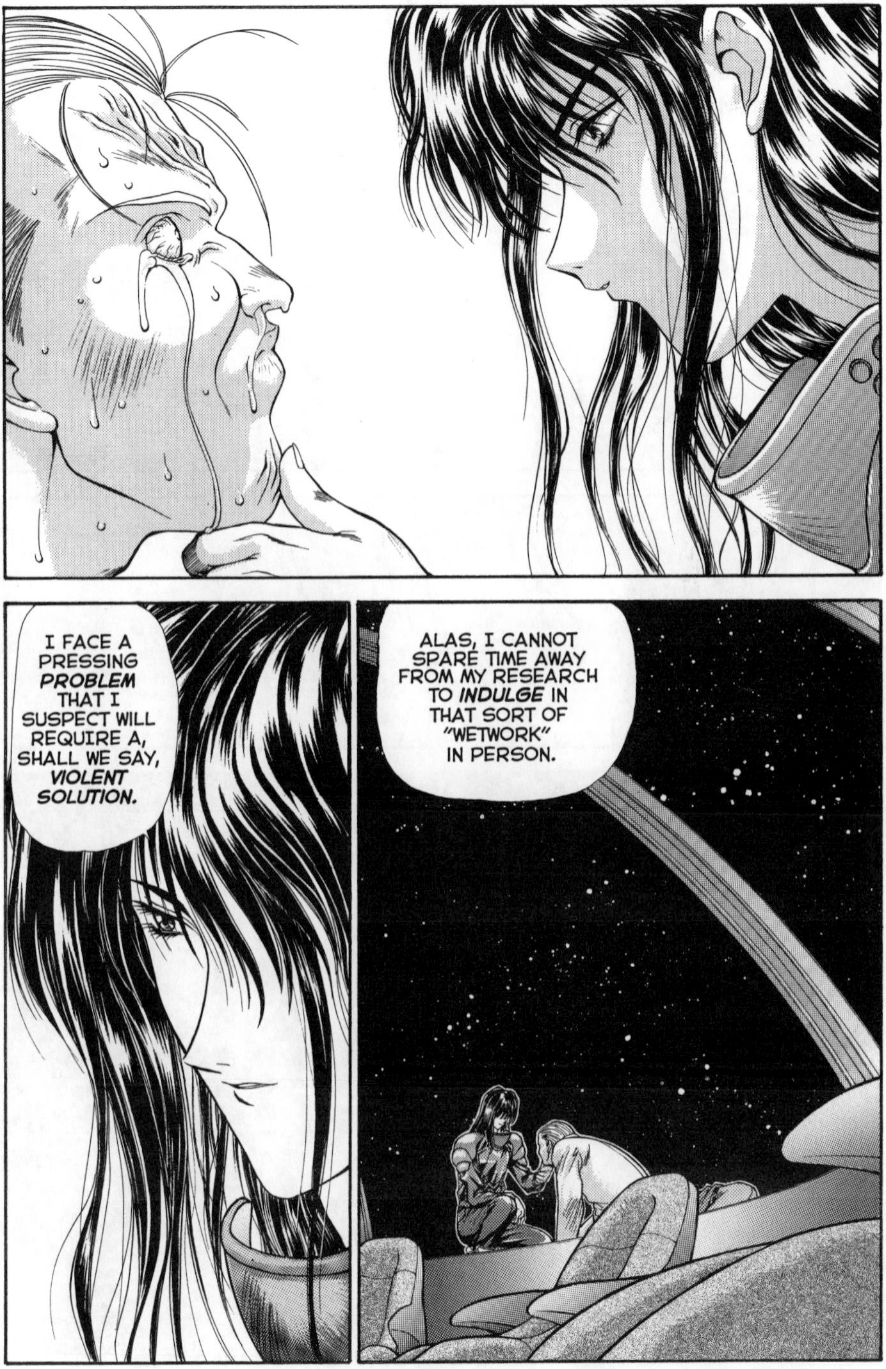
I FACE A PRESSING ***PROBLEM*** THAT I SUSPECT WILL REQUIRE A, SHALL WE SAY, ***VIOLENT SOLUTION.***
ALAS, I CANNOT SPARE TIME AWAY FROM MY RESEARCH TO ***INDULGE*** IN THAT SORT OF "WETWORK" IN PERSON.

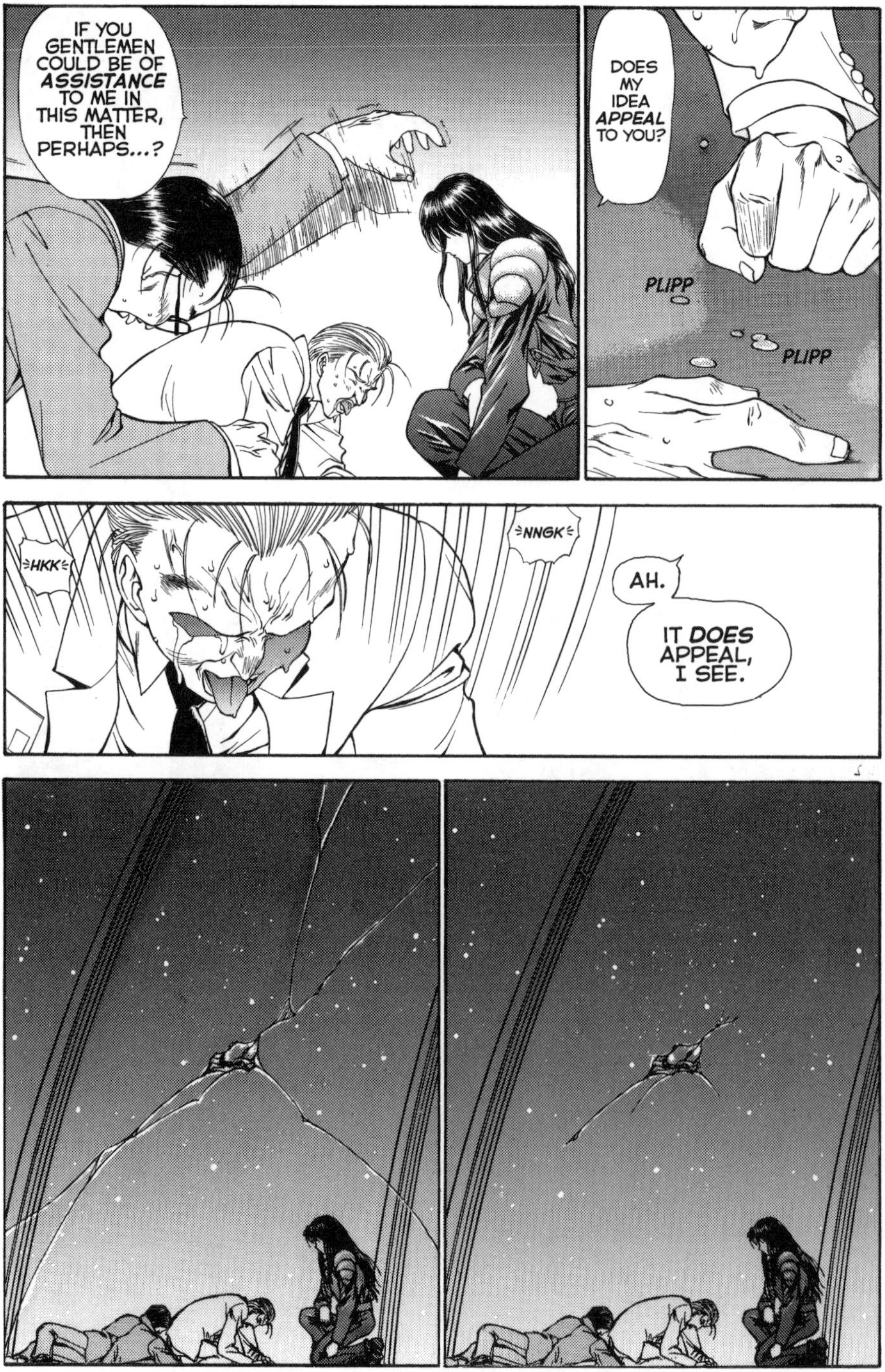
IF YOU GENTLEMEN COULD BE OF ***ASSISTANCE*** TO ME IN THIS MATTER, THEN PERHAPS...?
DOES MY IDEA ***APPEAL*** TO YOU?
PLIPP
PLIPP
HKK
NNGK
AH.
IT ***DOES*** APPEAL, I SEE.

HAAAHH!
WHDD
THE AIR PRESSURE... RESTORED... LIKE MAGIC...
KLAK
HAHH
HUHH

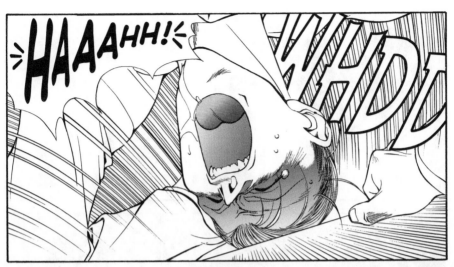

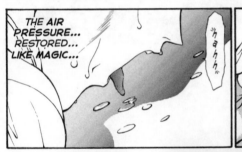

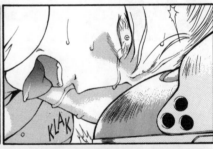

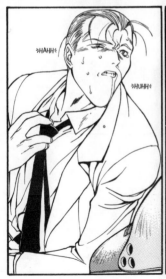

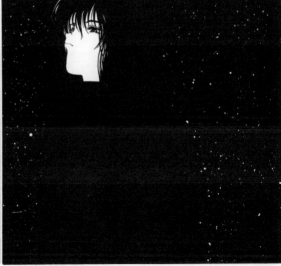

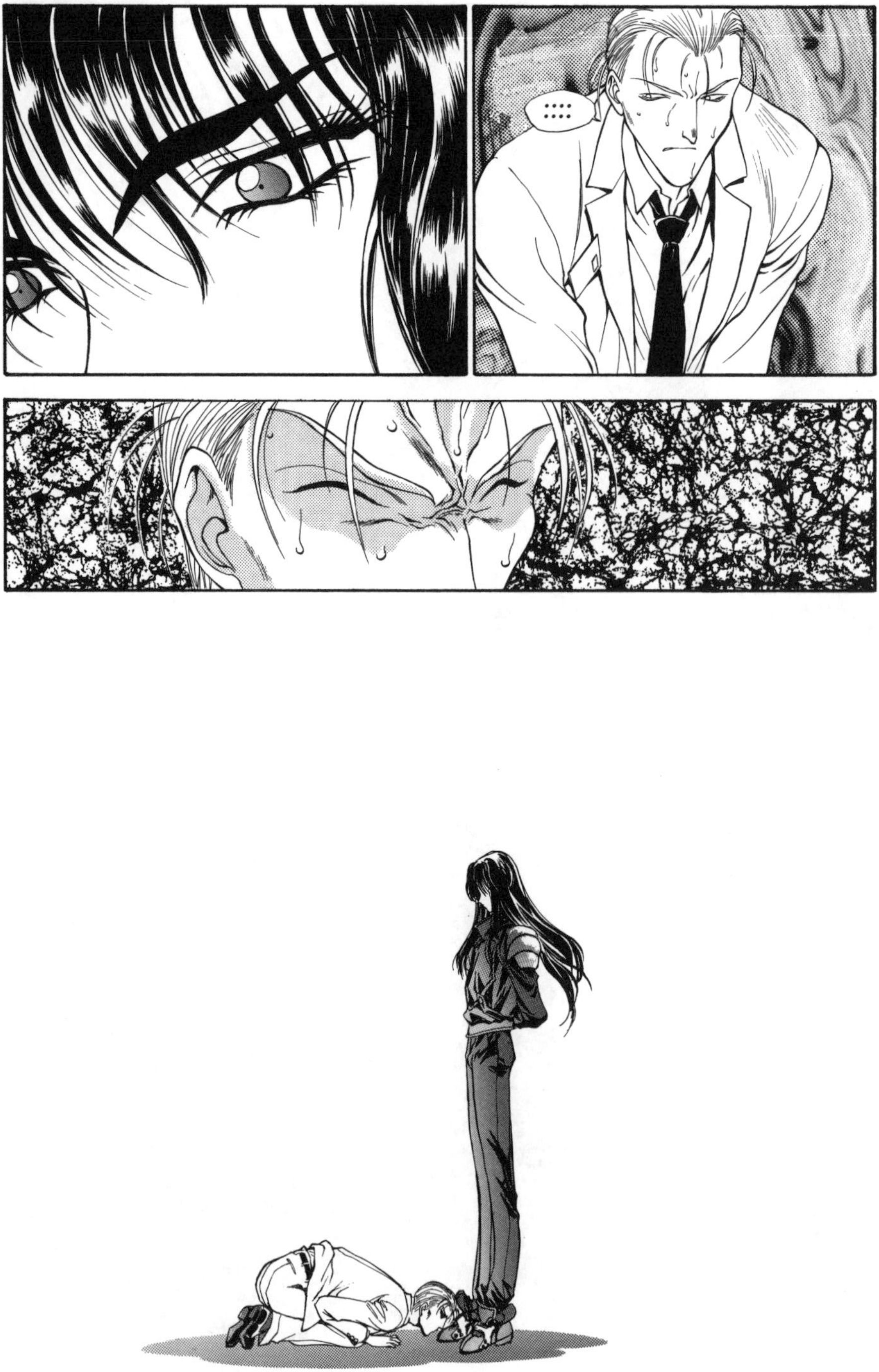
……

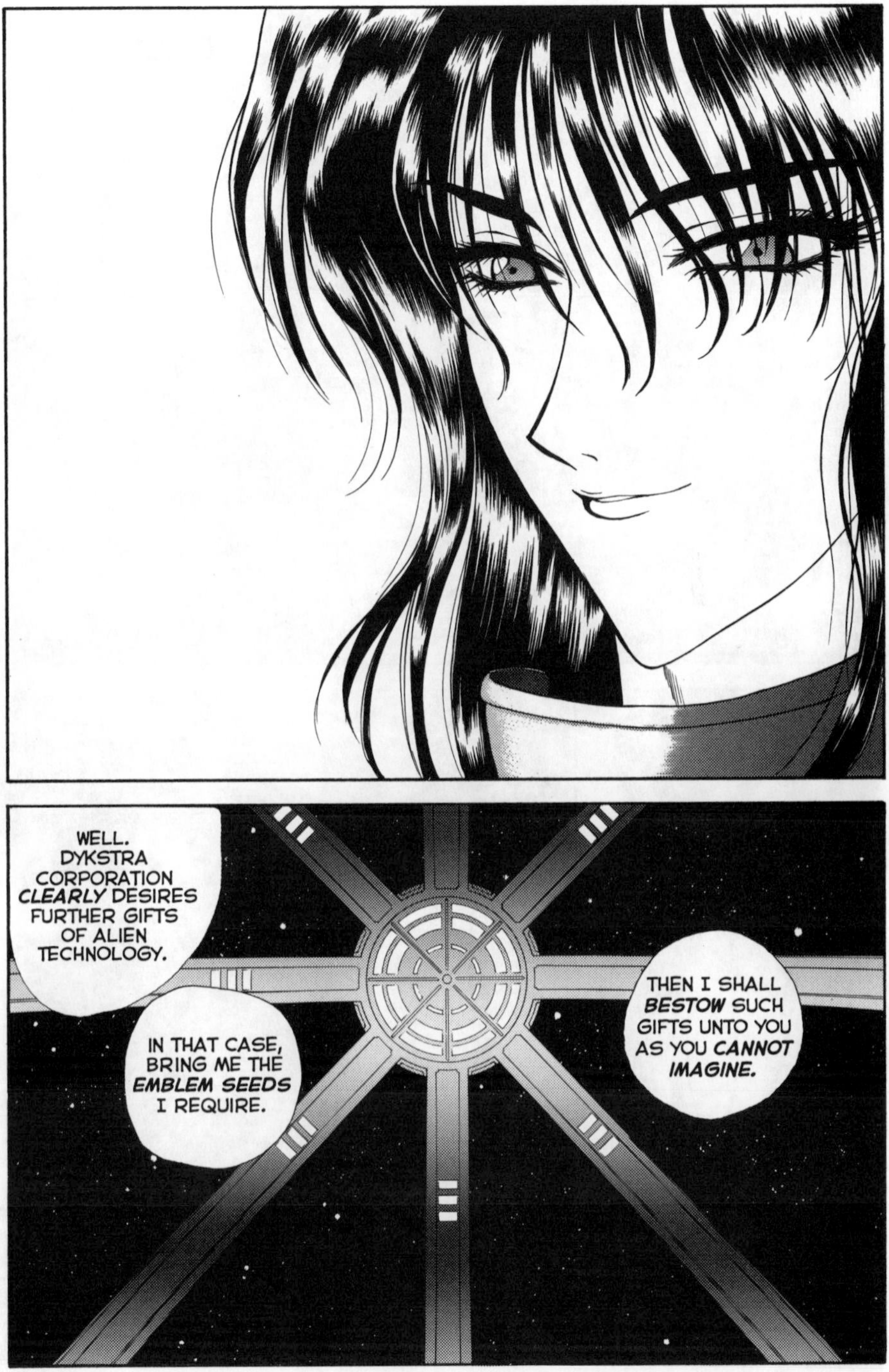
WELL. DYKSTRA CORPORATION *CLEARLY* DESIRES FURTHER GIFTS OF ALIEN TECHNOLOGY.
IN THAT CASE, BRING ME THE *EMBLEM SEEDS* I REQUIRE.
THEN I SHALL *BESTOW* SUCH GIFTS UNTO YOU AS YOU *CANNOT IMAGINE.*

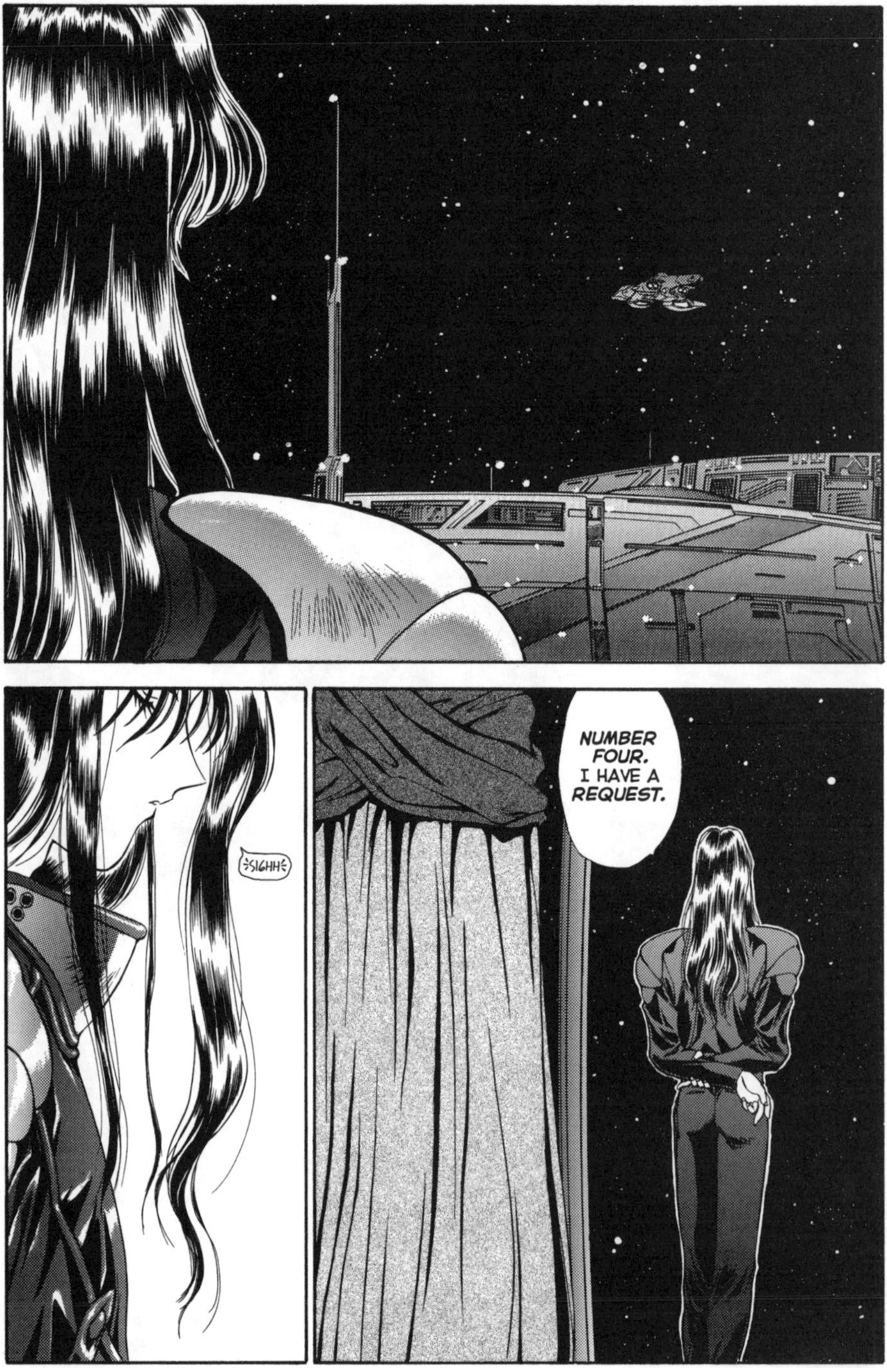

NUMBER FOUR. I HAVE A REQUEST.
SIGHH

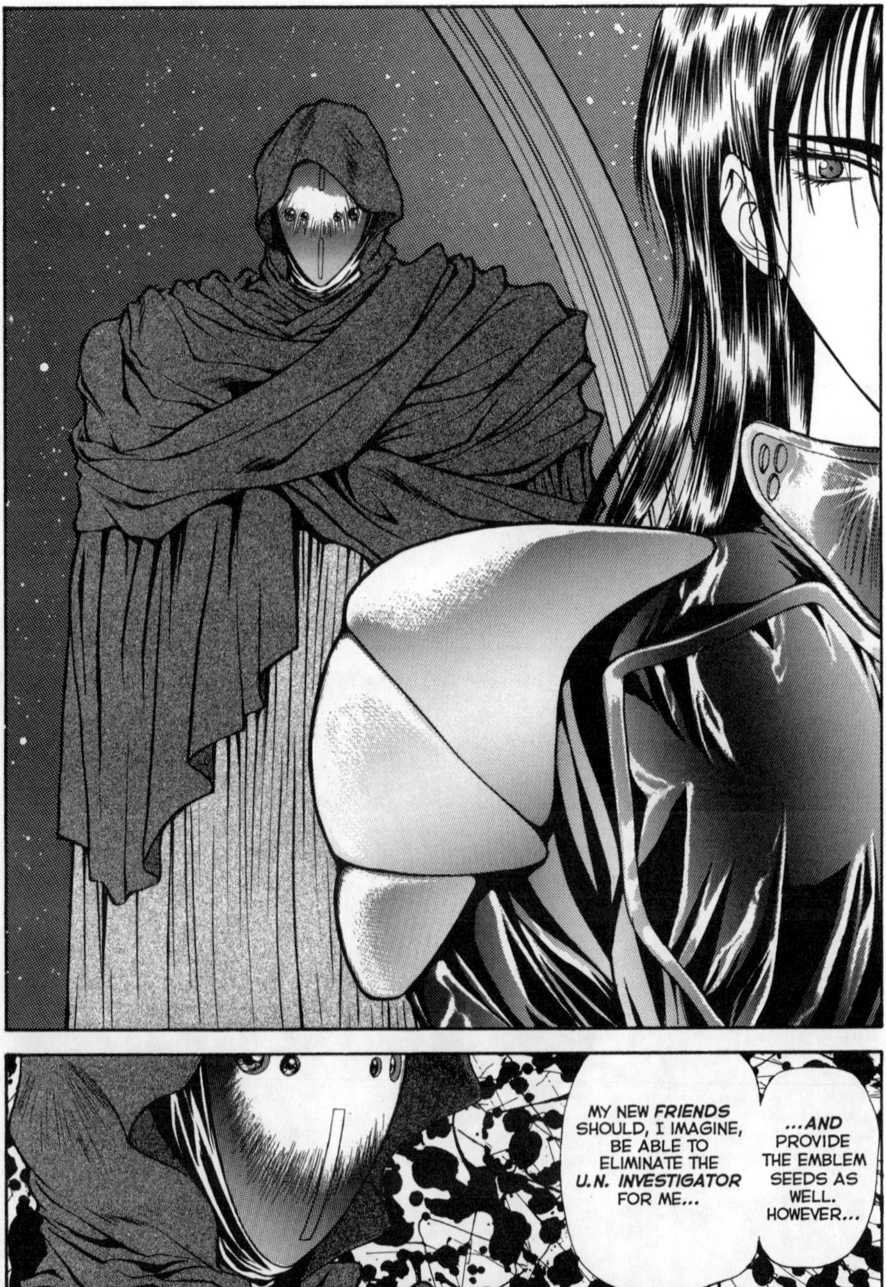
MY NEW *FRIENDS* SHOULD, I IMAGINE, BE ABLE TO ELIMINATE THE *U.N. INVESTIGATOR* FOR ME...
...AND PROVIDE THE EMBLEM SEEDS AS WELL. HOWEVER...

...THAT LEAVES ONE *OTHER* ISSUE UNRESOLVED.

AND THE RESOLUTION OF *THAT* MATTER...

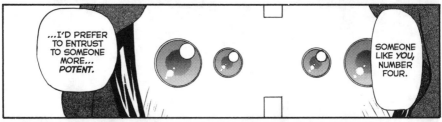

...I'D PREFER TO ENTRUST TO SOMEONE MORE... *POTENT.*

SOMEONE LIKE *YOU,* NUMBER FOUR.

ACT 4

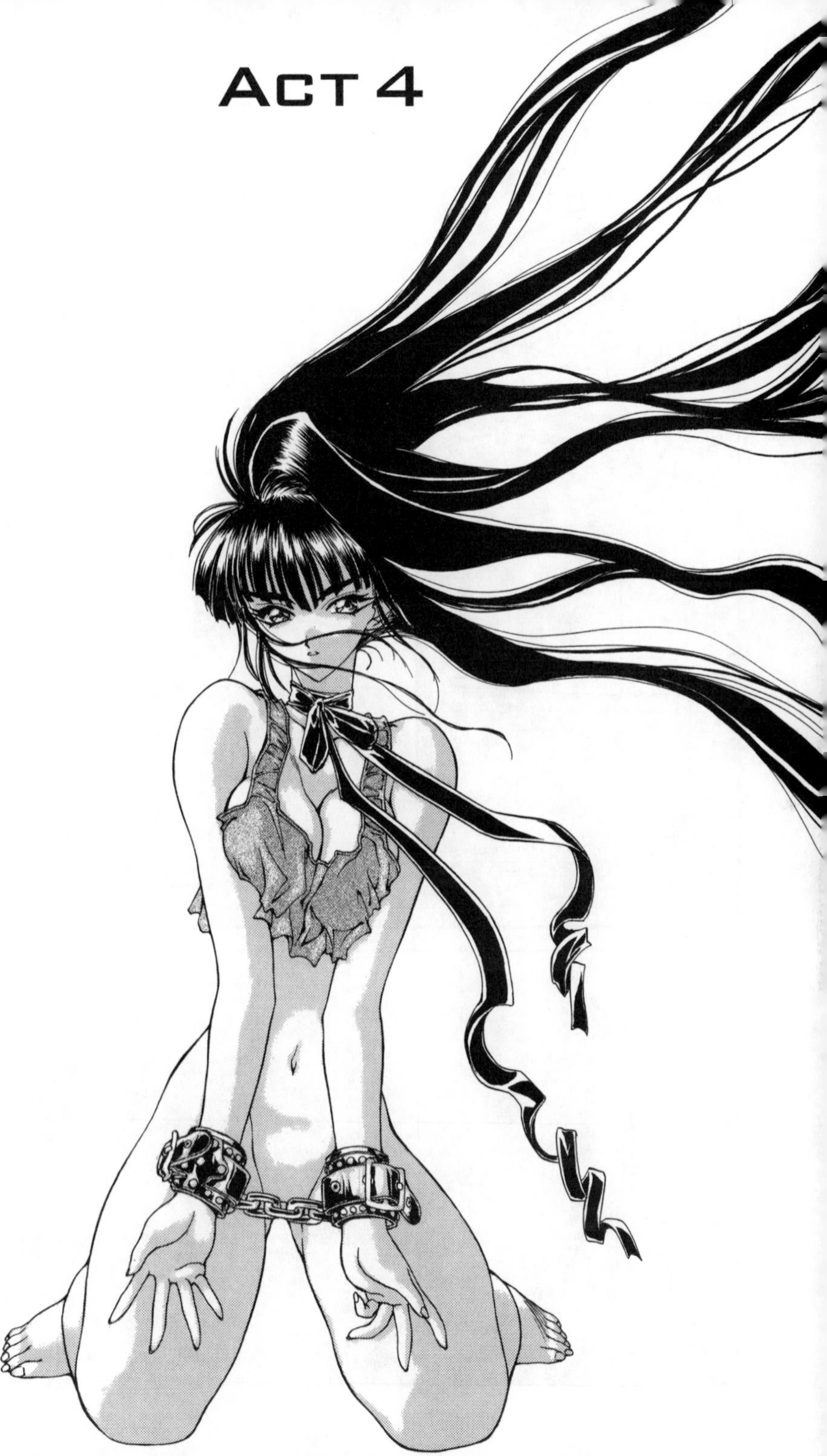

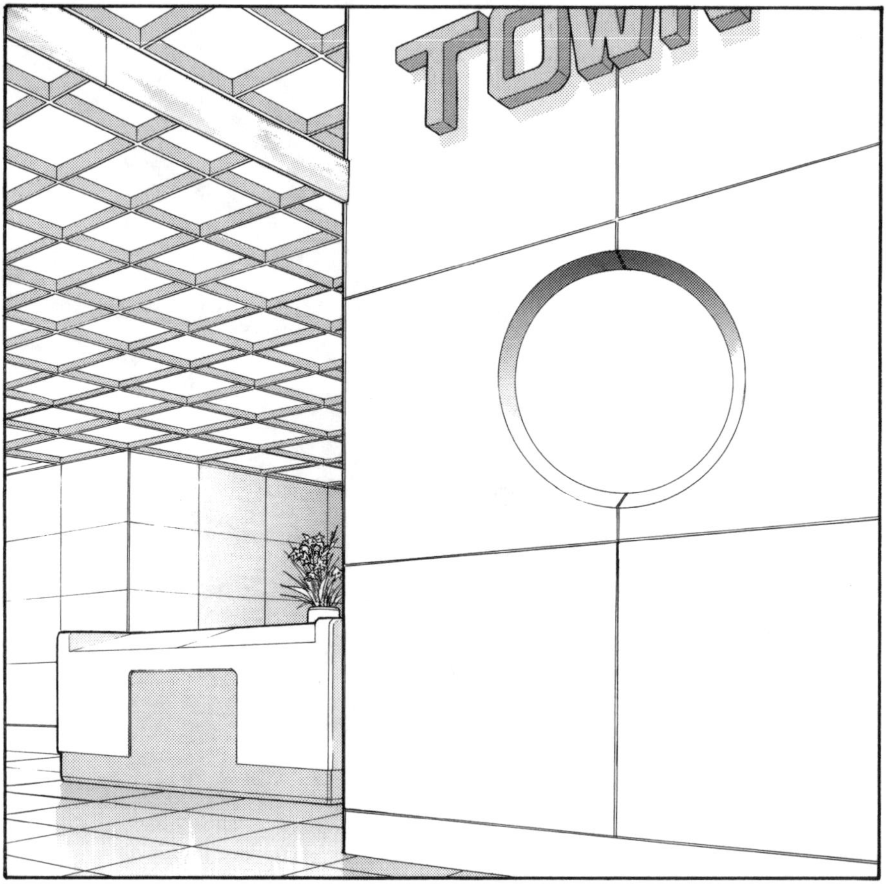
TOW

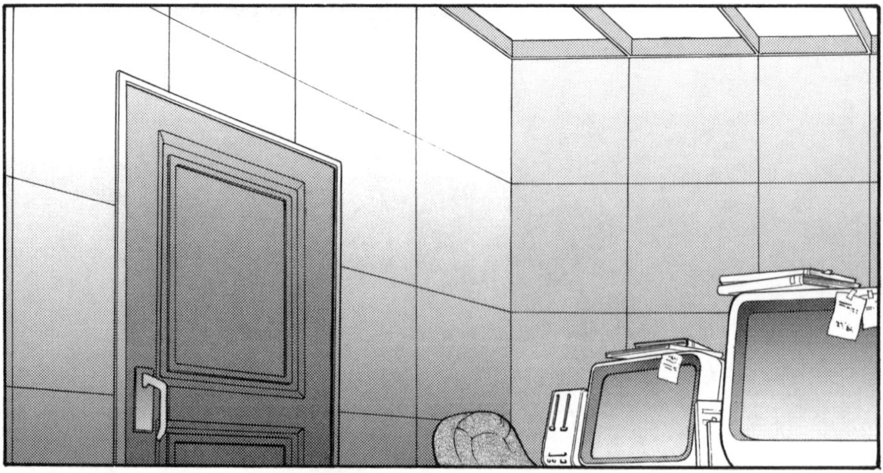

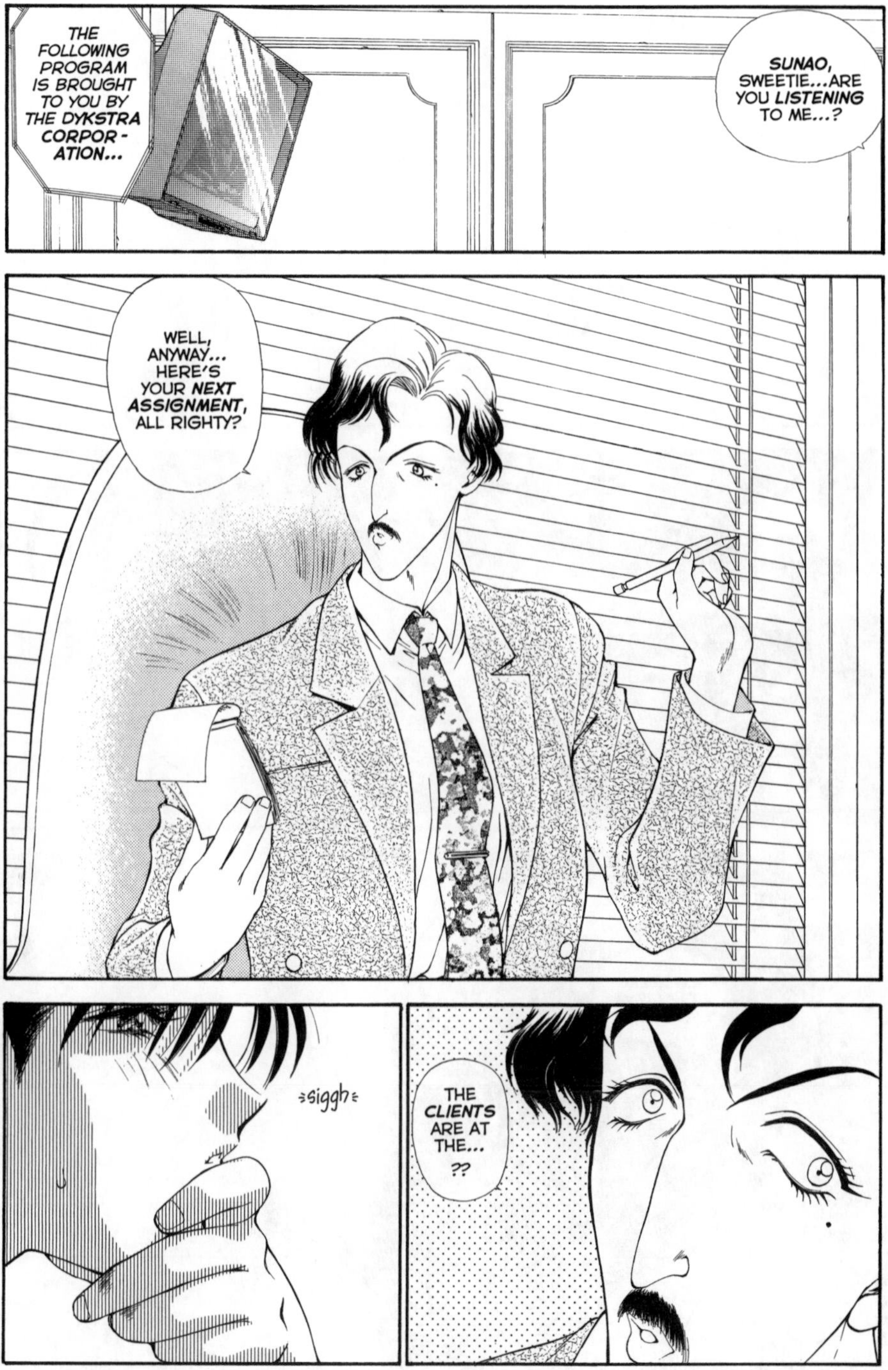
THE FOLLOWING PROGRAM IS BROUGHT TO YOU BY THE DYKSTRA CORPOR-ATION...
SUNAO, SWEETIE...ARE YOU LISTENING TO ME...?
WELL, ANYWAY... HERE'S YOUR NEXT ASSIGNMENT, ALL RIGHTY?
sigggh
THE CLIENTS ARE AT THE...
??

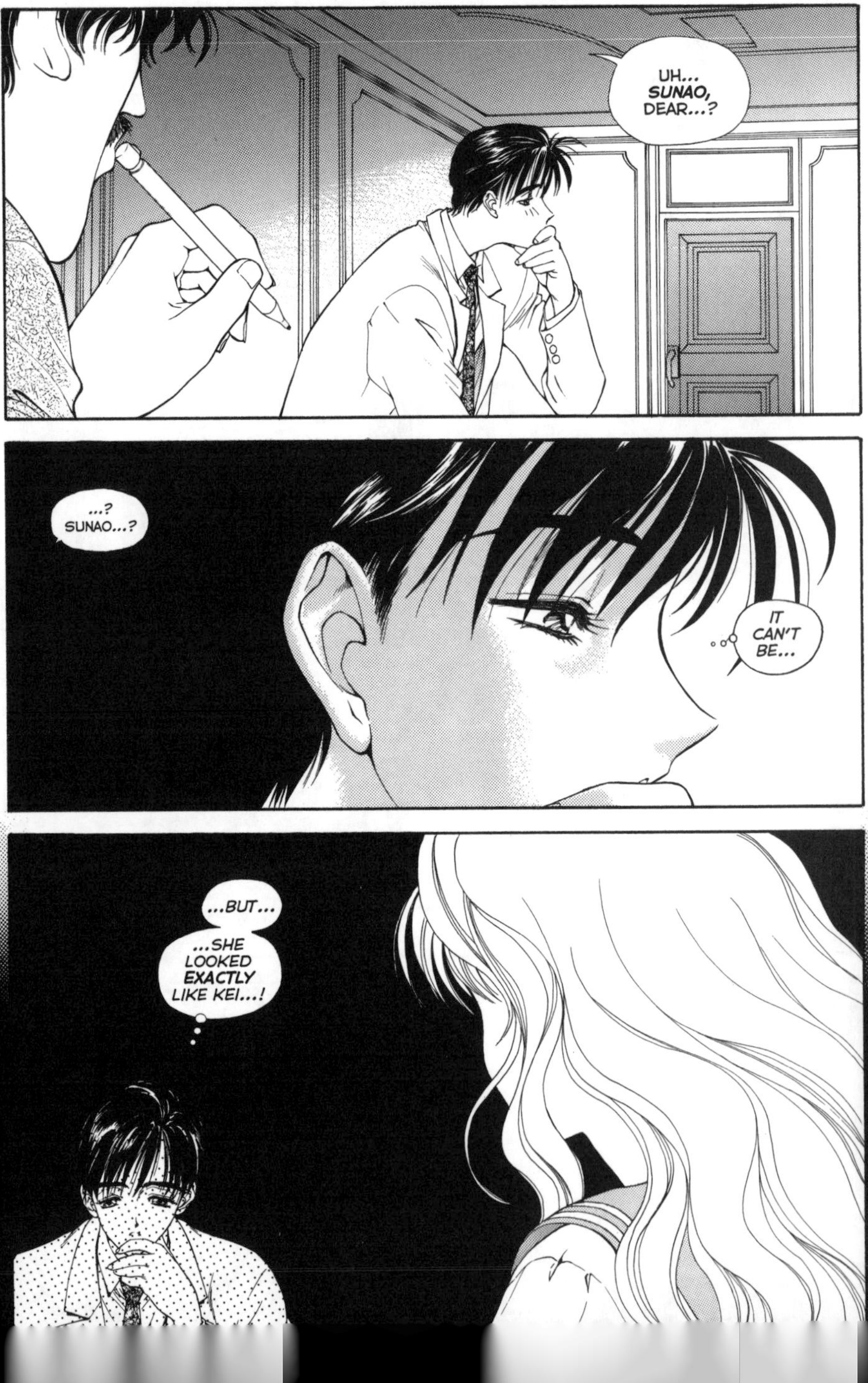
UH... SUNAO, DEAR...?
...? SUNAO...?
IT CAN'T BE...
...BUT...
...SHE LOOKED EXACTLY LIKE KEI...!

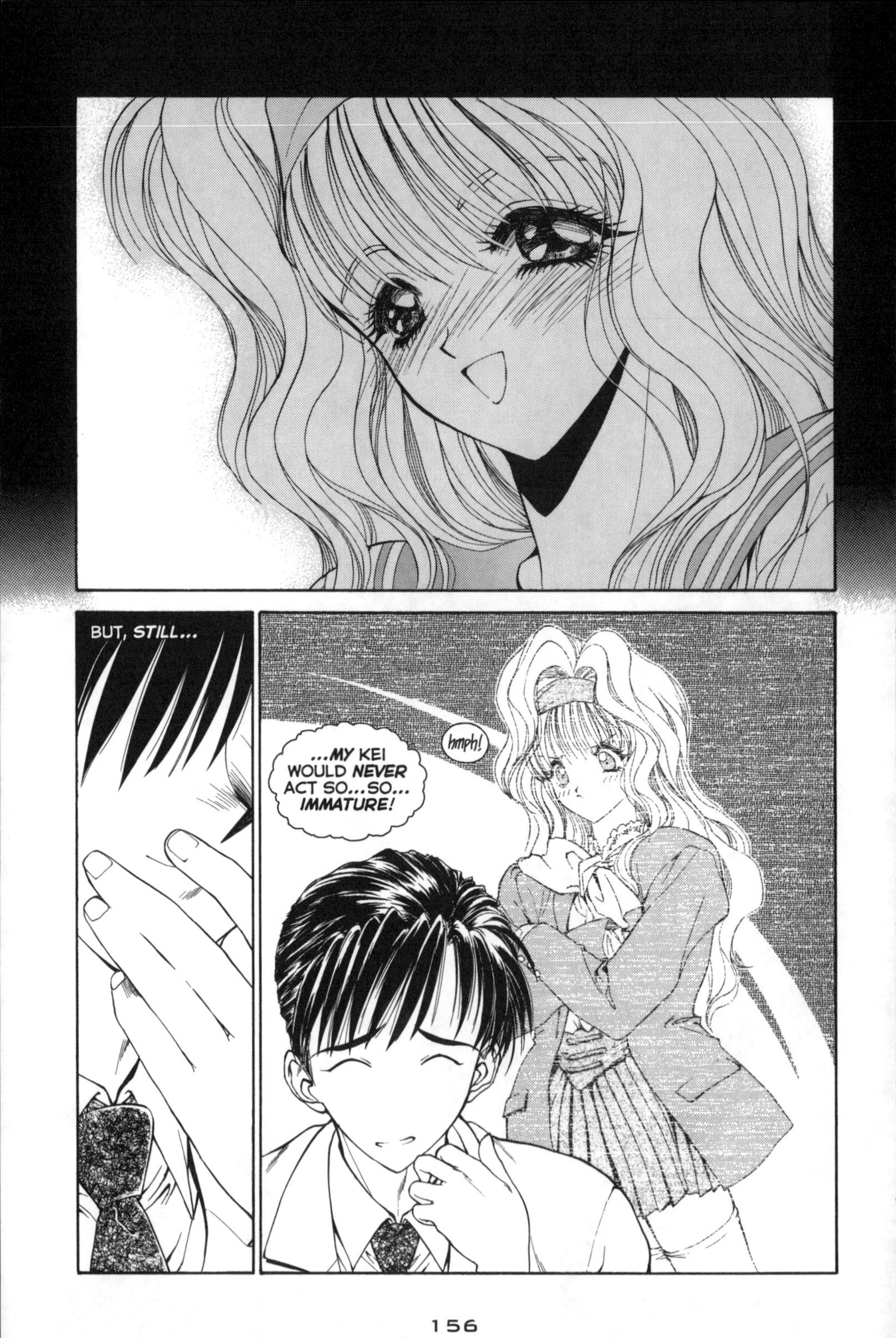
BUT, STILL...
...MY KEI WOULD NEVER ACT SO...SO... IMMATURE!
hmph!

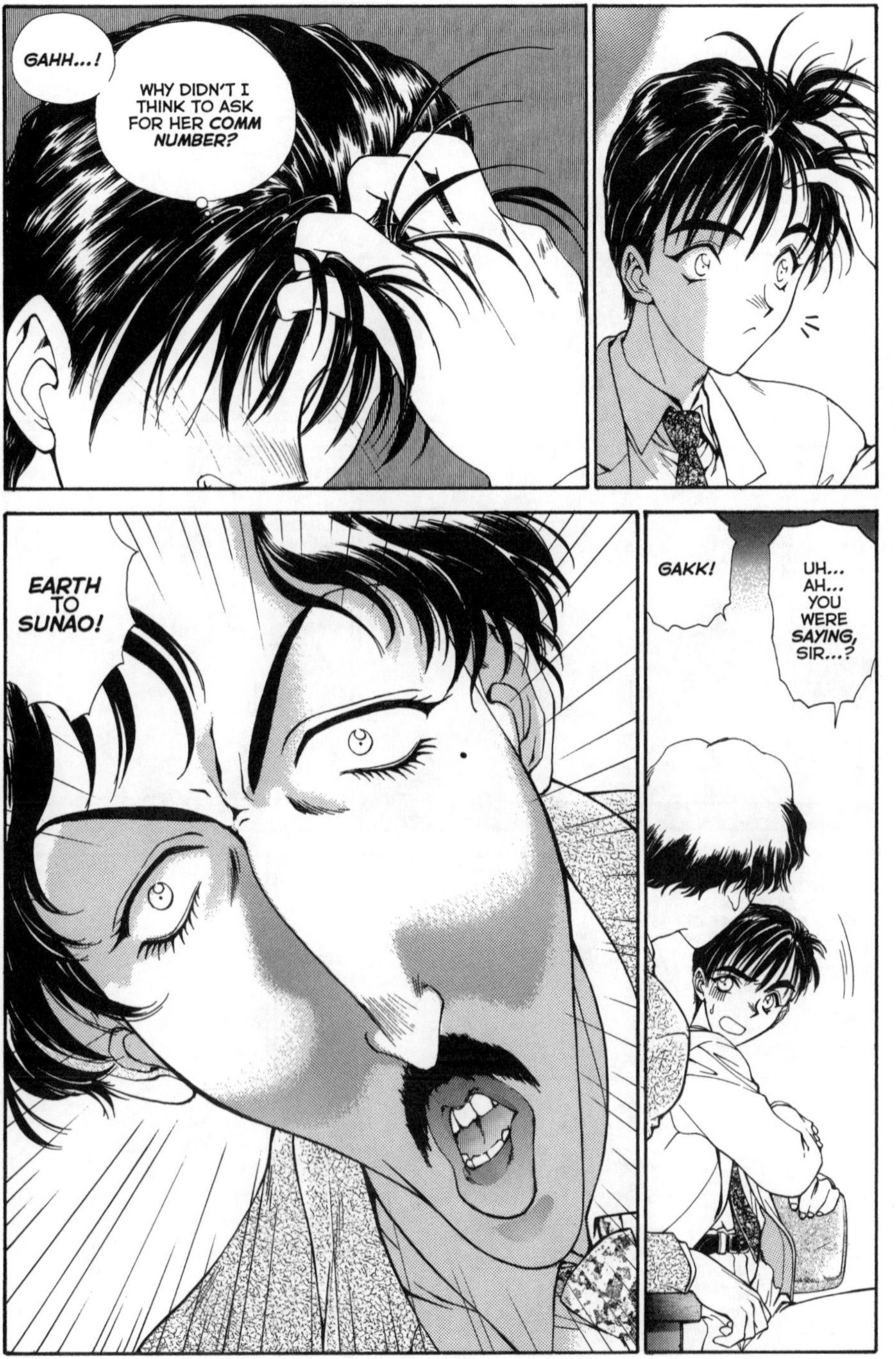
GAHH...!
WHY DIDN'T I THINK TO ASK FOR HER COMM NUMBER?
EARTH TO SUNAO!
GAKK!
UH... AH... YOU WERE SAYING, SIR...?

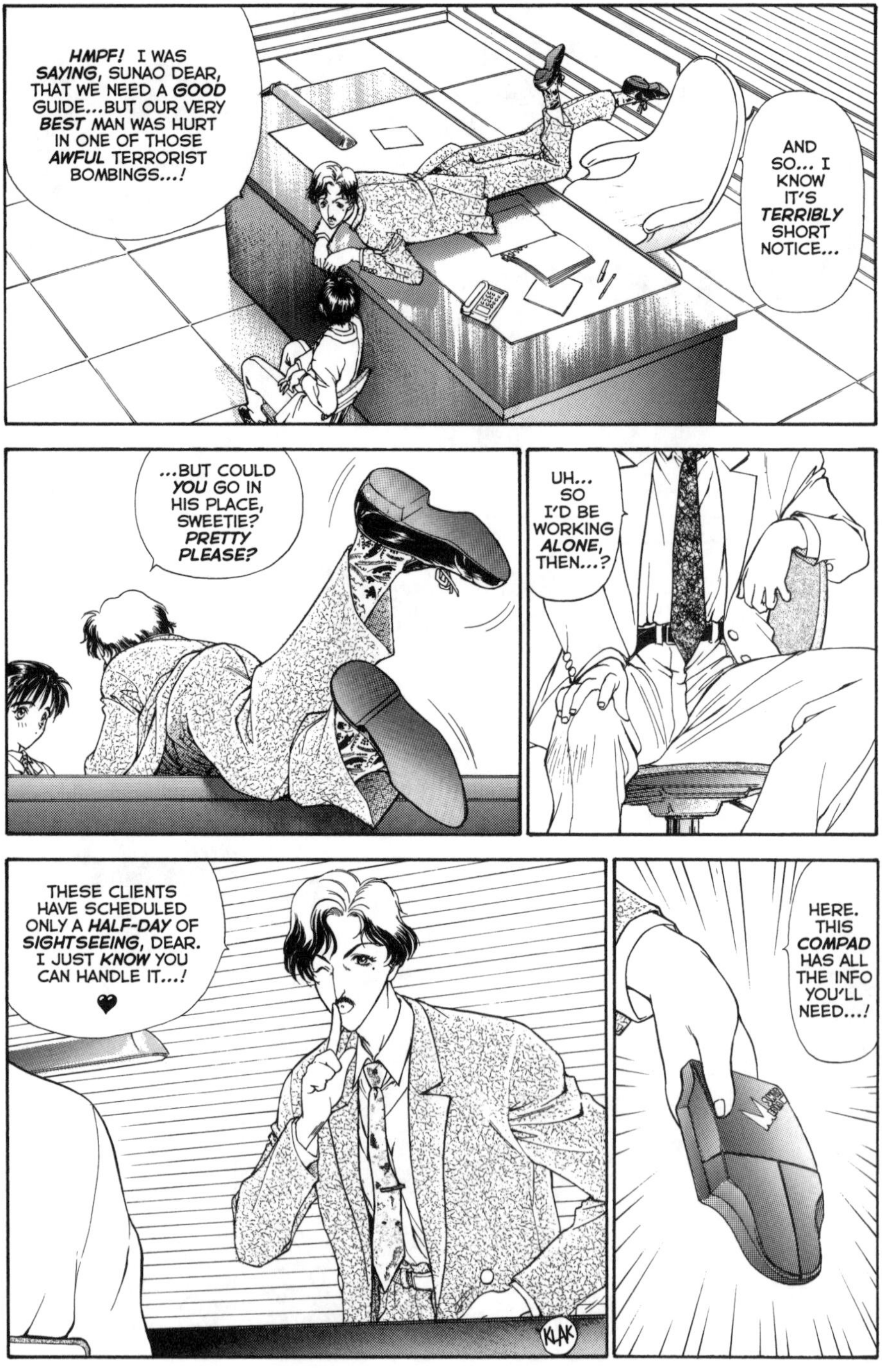
HMPF! I WAS SAYING, SUNAO DEAR, THAT WE NEED A GOOD GUIDE...BUT OUR VERY BEST MAN WAS HURT IN ONE OF THOSE AWFUL TERRORIST BOMBINGS...!
AND SO... I KNOW IT'S TERRIBLY SHORT NOTICE...
...BUT COULD YOU GO IN HIS PLACE, SWEETIE? PRETTY PLEASE?
UH... SO I'D BE WORKING ALONE, THEN...?
THESE CLIENTS HAVE SCHEDULED ONLY A HALF-DAY OF SIGHTSEEING, DEAR. I JUST KNOW YOU CAN HANDLE IT...! ♥
KLAK
HERE. THIS COMPAD HAS ALL THE INFO YOU'LL NEED...!

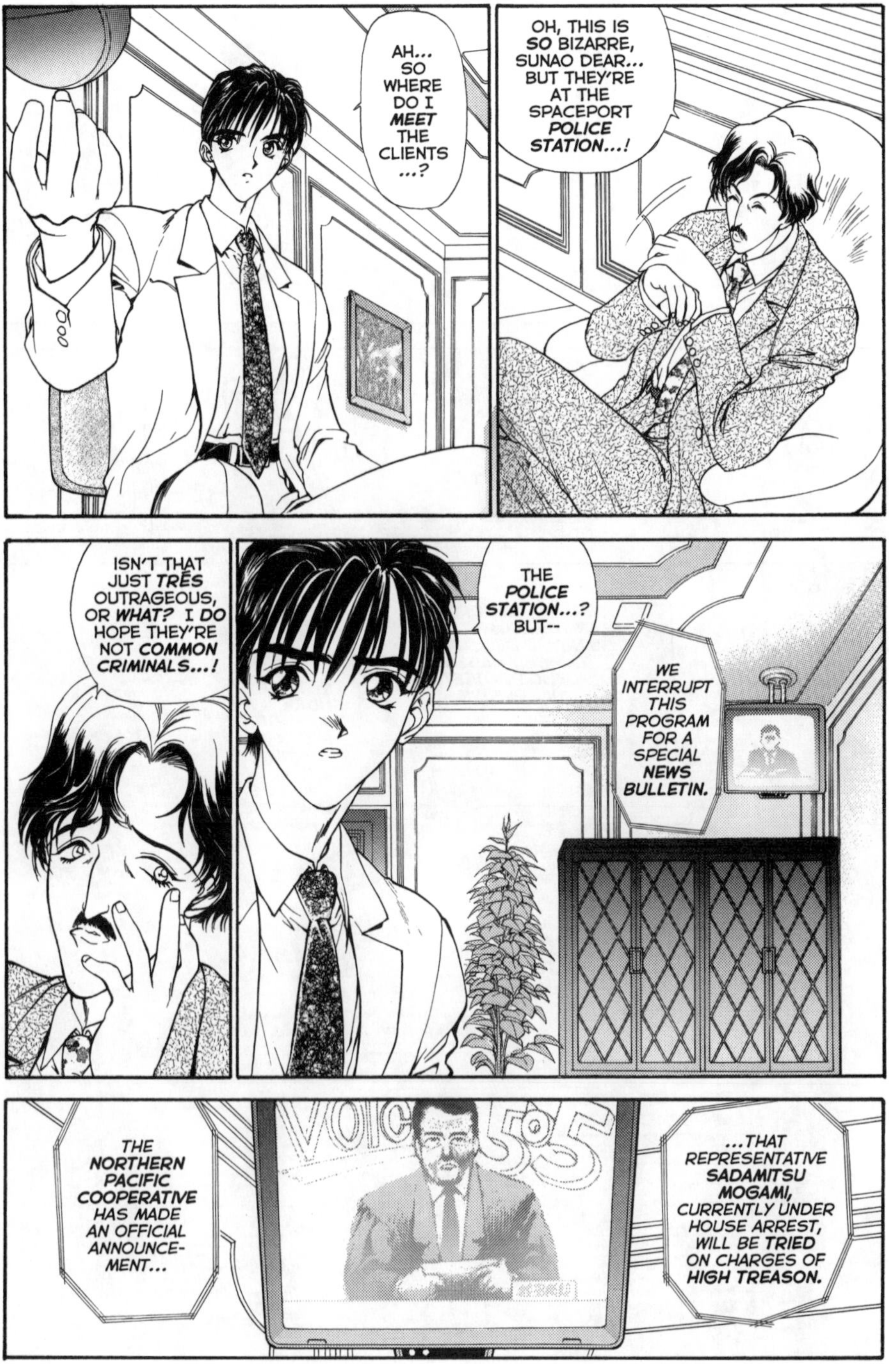
AH... SO WHERE DO I MEET THE CLIENTS ...?
OH, THIS IS SO BIZARRE, SUNAO DEAR... BUT THEY'RE AT THE SPACEPORT POLICE STATION...!
ISN'T THAT JUST TRÈS OUTRAGEOUS, OR WHAT? I DO HOPE THEY'RE NOT COMMON CRIMINALS...!
THE POLICE STATION...? BUT--
WE INTERRUPT THIS PROGRAM FOR A SPECIAL NEWS BULLETIN.
THE NORTHERN PACIFIC COOPERATIVE HAS MADE AN OFFICIAL ANNOUNCE-MENT...
...THAT REPRESENTATIVE SADAMITSU MOGAMI, CURRENTLY UNDER HOUSE ARREST, WILL BE TRIED ON CHARGES OF HIGH TREASON.

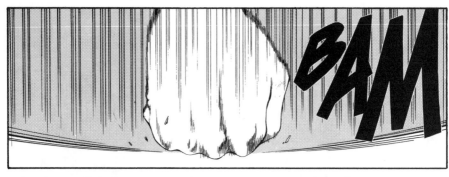

TERRAN AUTHORITIES FEAR THE COOPERATIVE'S SURPRISE DECISION WILL TRIGGER MASSIVE PUBLIC PROTESTS AND RIOTING.

THE NEWS SENT SHOCKWAVES THROUGH THE STOCK AND CURRENCY EXCHANGE MARKETS, WHICH WERE...

WHY...?
WH... WHAT'S WRONG, SUNAO DEAR...?
R-REALLY ...YOU NEEDN'T GET SO UPSET... THE CLIENTS ARE WITH THE U.N., SO THEY PROBABLY WON'T BE RIOTING... ha, ha ...
ER... THAT WAS A JOKE, YOU KNOW...!
SIR!
WHEN IS MY VISA BACK TO EARTH GOING TO BE APPROVED?
EEK!

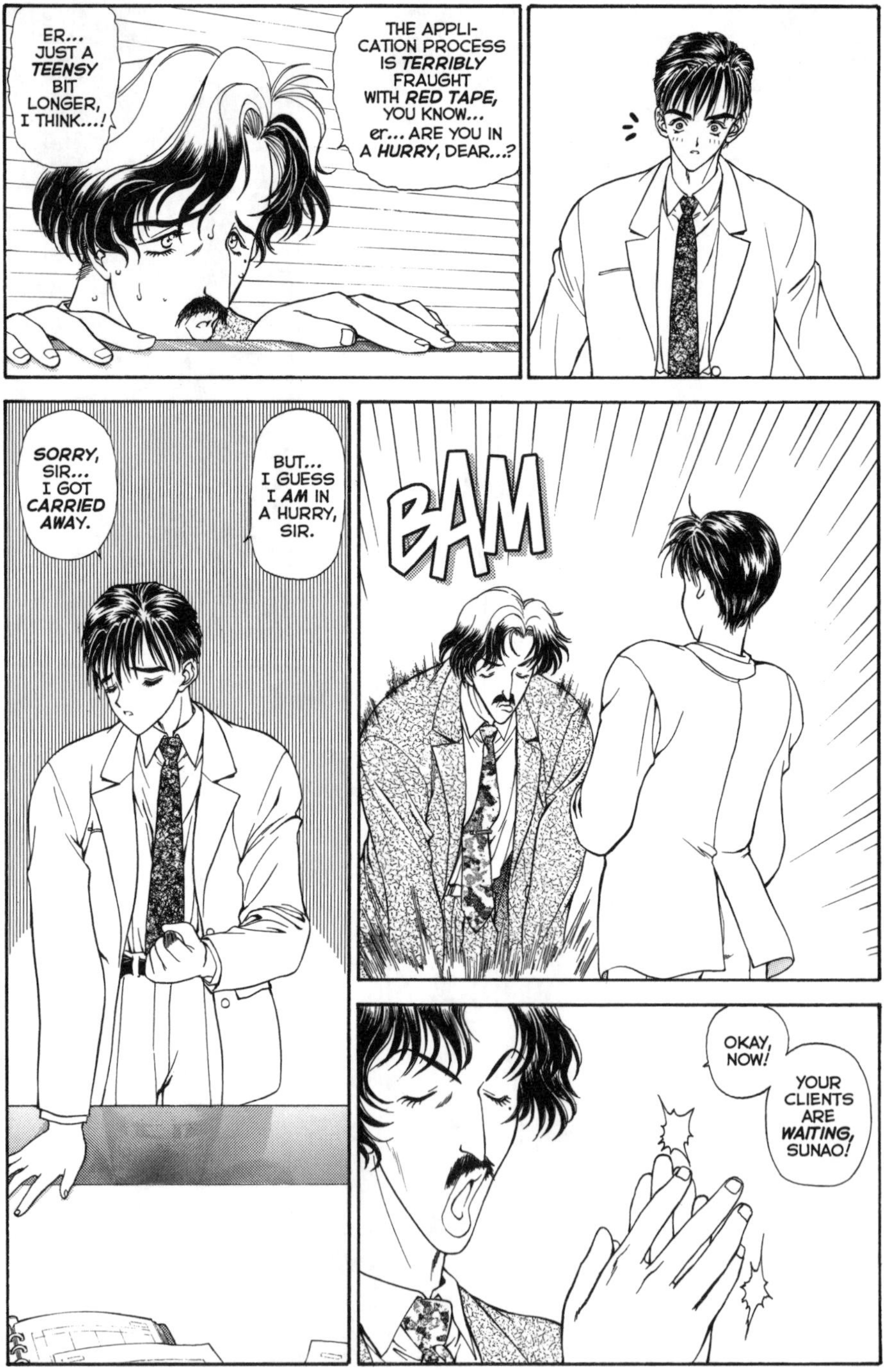

ER... JUST A TEENSY BIT LONGER, I THINK...!
THE APPLICATION PROCESS IS TERRIBLY FRAUGHT WITH RED TAPE, YOU KNOW... er... ARE YOU IN A HURRY, DEAR...?
SORRY, SIR... I GOT CARRIED AWAY.
BUT... I GUESS I AM IN A HURRY, SIR.
BAM
OKAY, NOW!
YOUR CLIENTS ARE WAITING, SUNAO!

UH... YES, SIR! I'M ON IT, SIR!
SLAM
PHEWWWW!
GOODNESS ME, DEAR BOY...
...WHAT-EVER WAS THAT ALL ABOUT...?

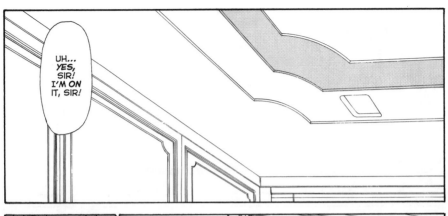

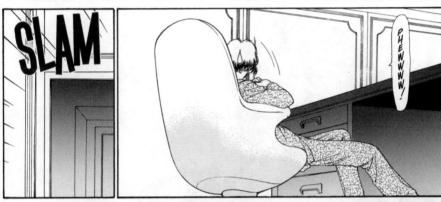

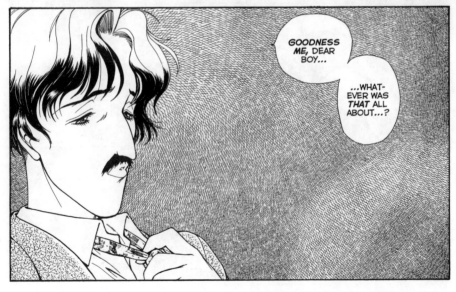

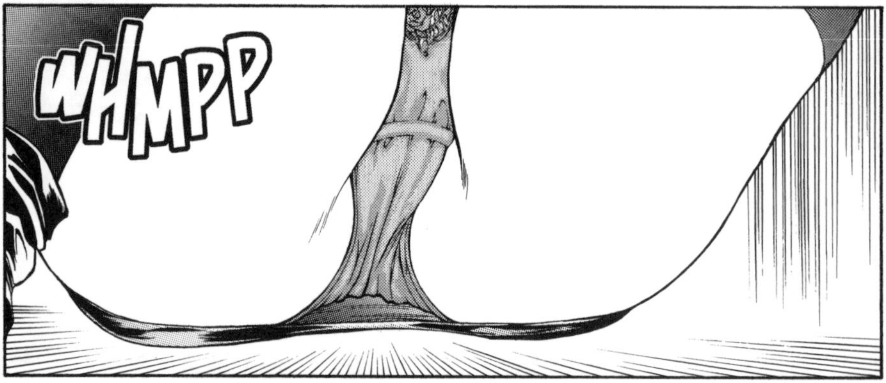
WHMPP

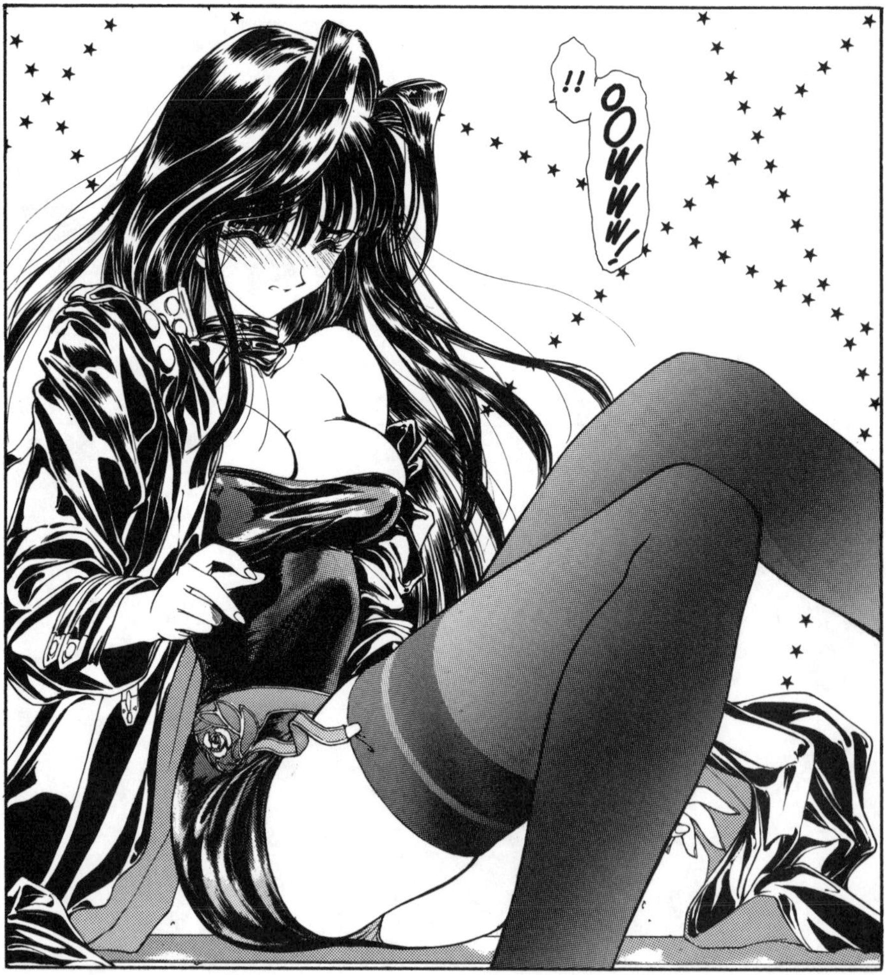
!!
OOWWW!

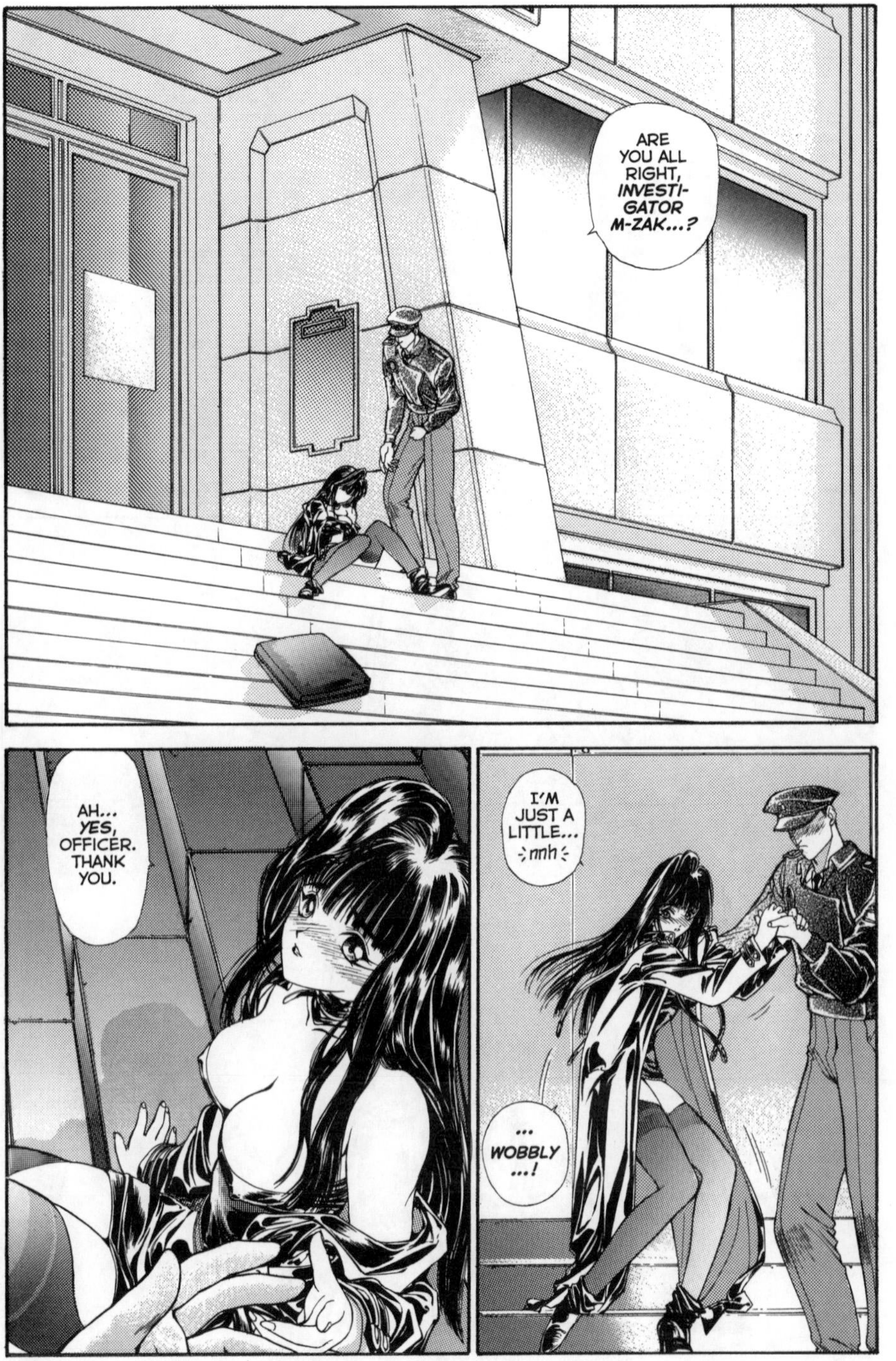
ARE YOU ALL RIGHT, *INVESTI-GATOR M-ZAK...?*
AH... *YES,* OFFICER. THANK YOU.
I'M JUST A LITTLE... mnh
... *WOBBLY* ...!

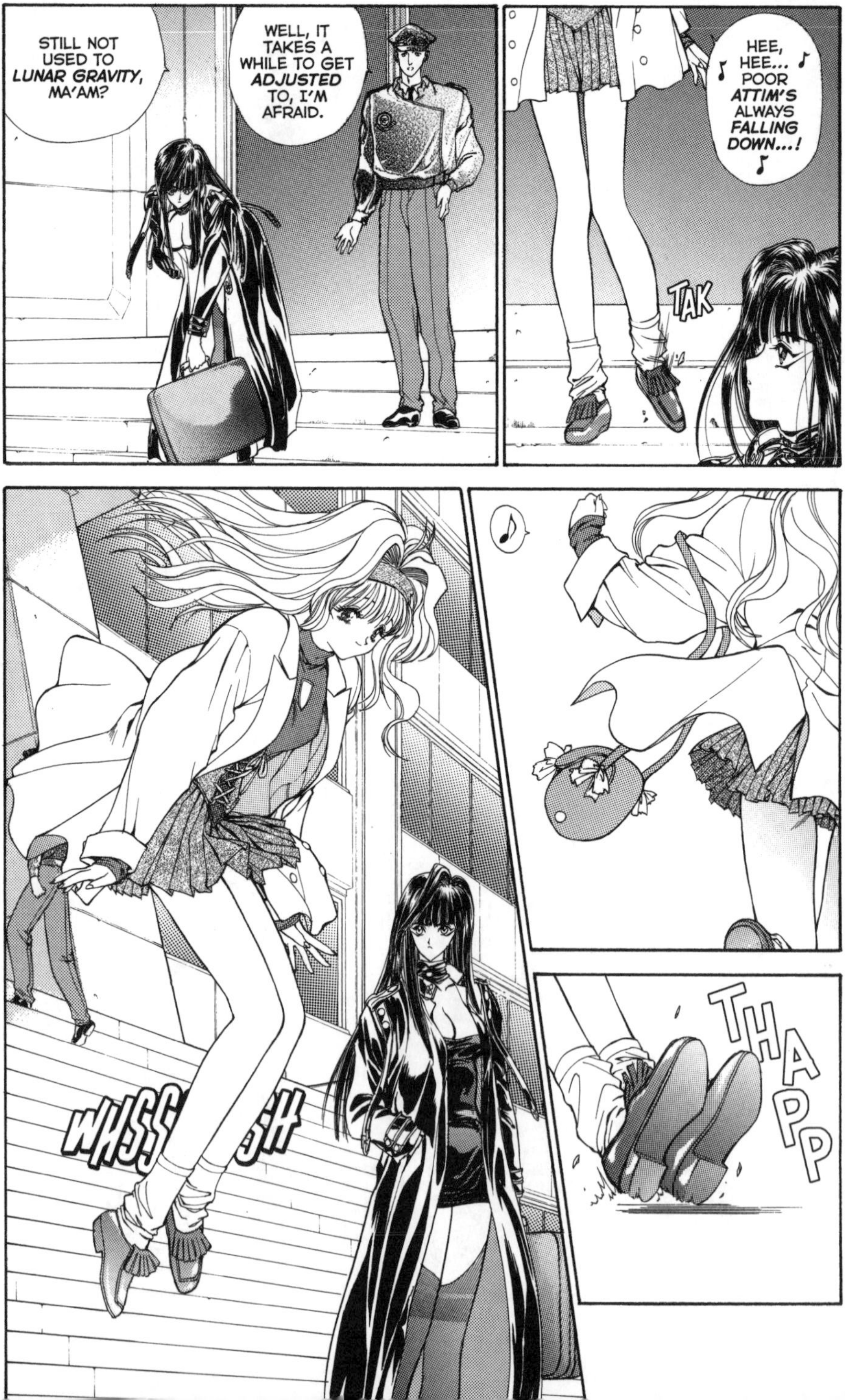
STILL NOT USED TO LUNAR GRAVITY, MA'AM?
WELL, IT TAKES A WHILE TO GET ADJUSTED TO, I'M AFRAID.
HEE, HEE... ♪ POOR ATTIM'S ALWAYS FALLING DOWN...! ♪
TAK
♪
THAPP

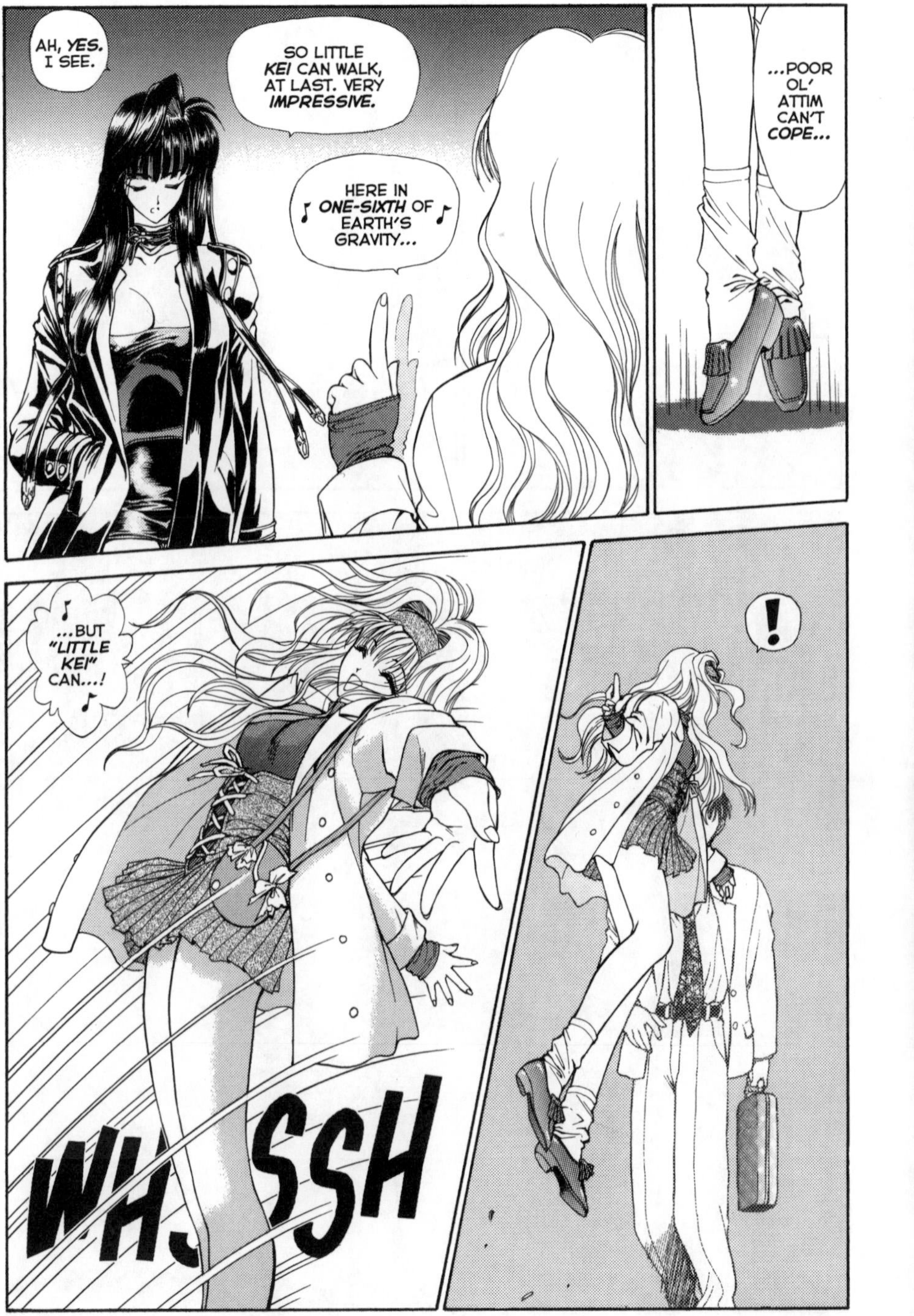
AH, YES. I SEE.
SO LITTLE KEI CAN WALK, AT LAST. VERY IMPRESSIVE.
HERE IN ONE-SIXTH OF EARTH'S GRAVITY...
...POOR OL' ATTIM CAN'T COPE...
...BUT "LITTLE KEI" CAN...!
!
WHSSH

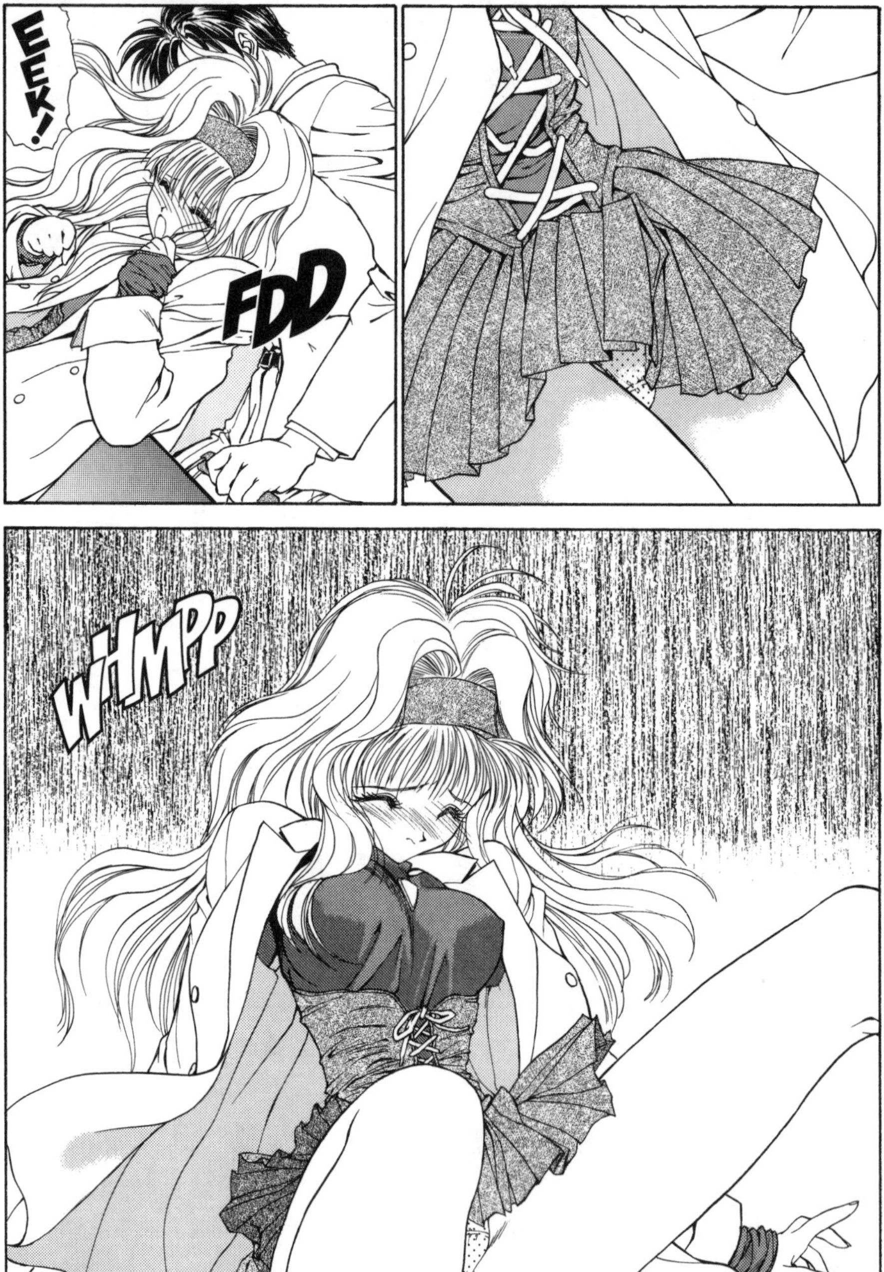
EEEK!
FDD
WHMPP

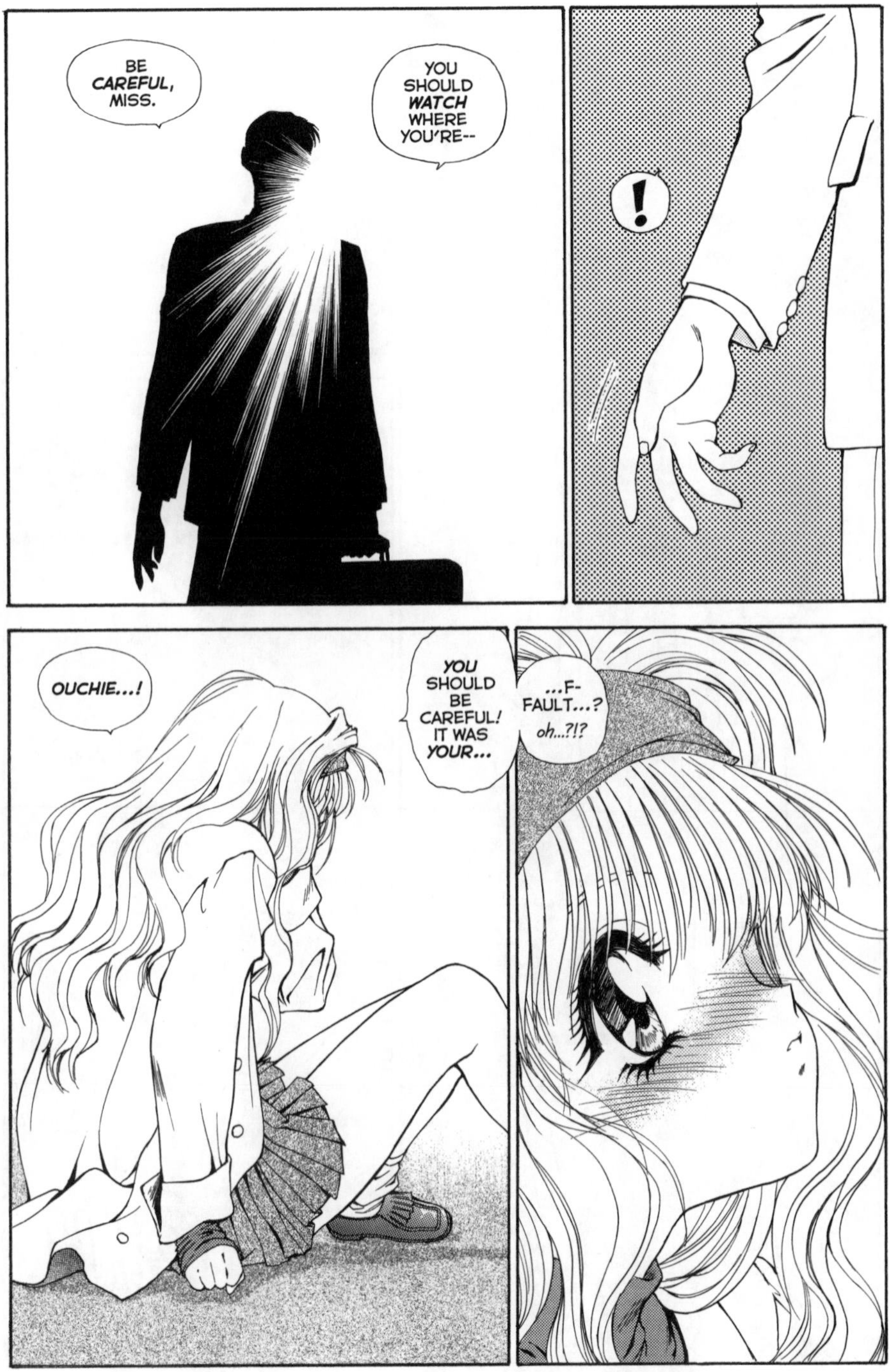
BE CAREFUL, MISS.
YOU SHOULD WATCH WHERE YOU'RE--
!
OUCHIE...!
YOU SHOULD BE CAREFUL! IT WAS YOUR...
...F-FAULT...?
oh...?!?

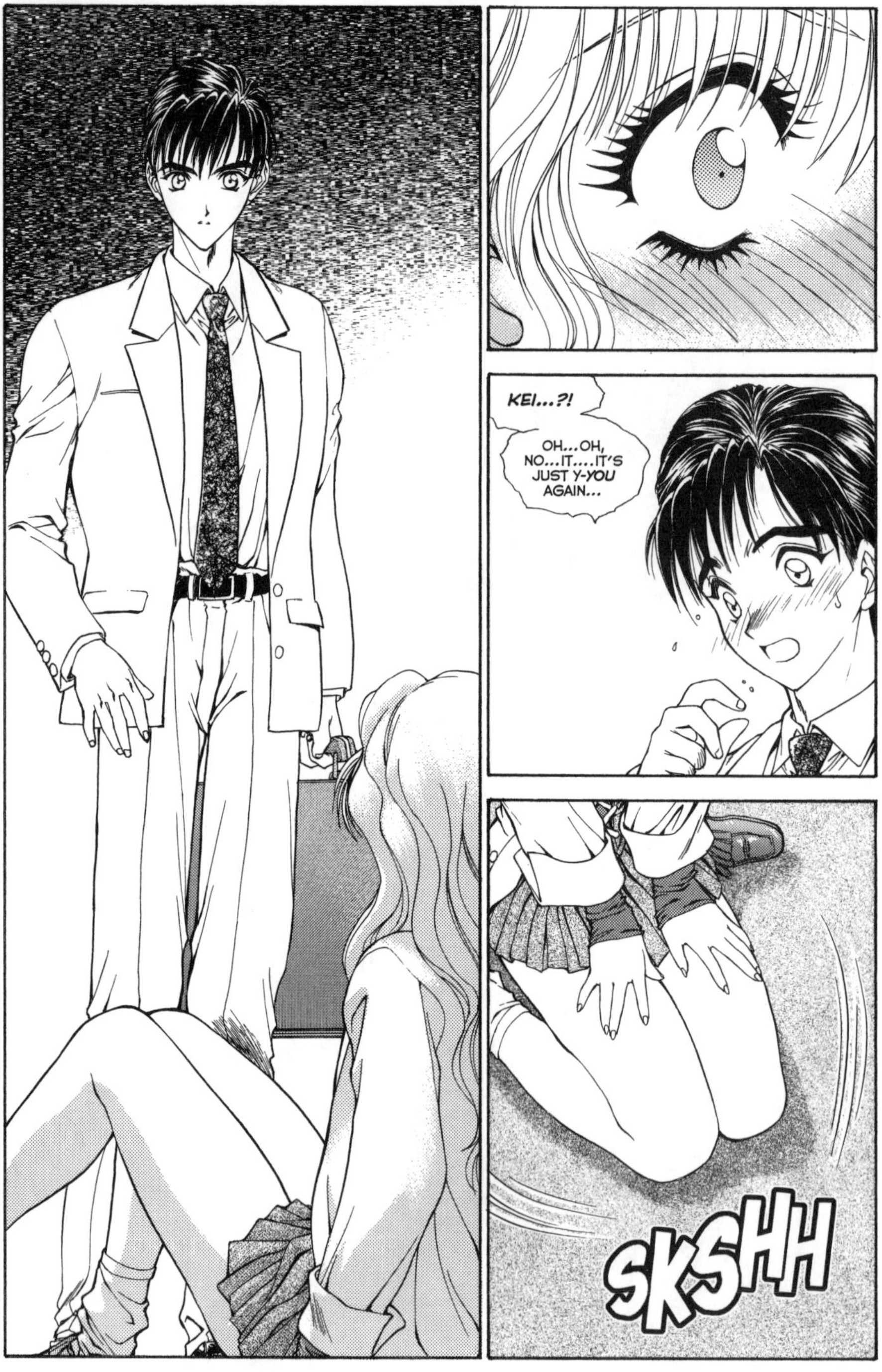
KEI...?!
OH...OH, NO...IT....IT'S JUST Y-YOU AGAIN...
SKSHH

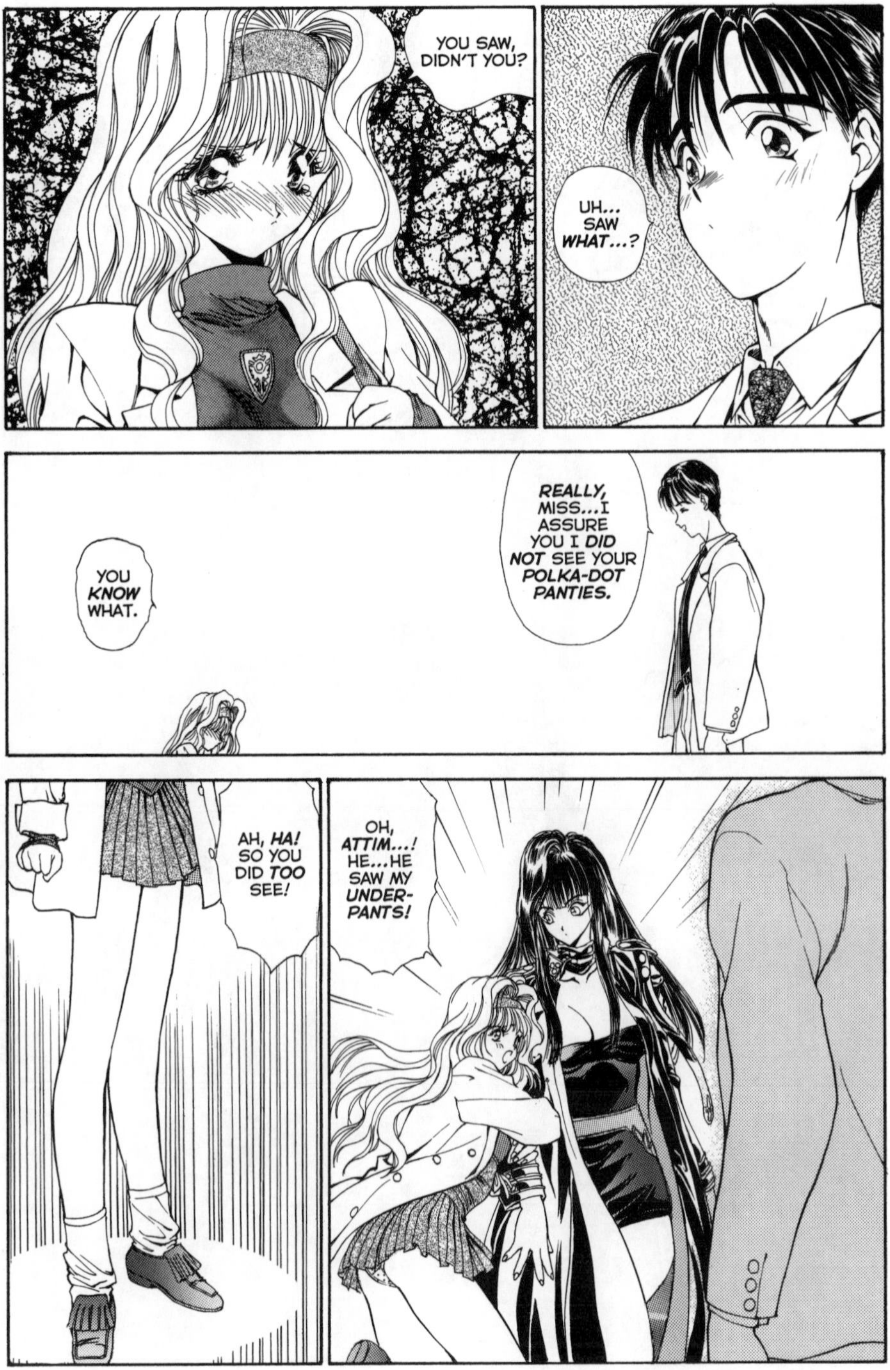
YOU SAW, DIDN'T YOU?
UH... SAW WHAT...?
YOU KNOW WHAT.
REALLY, MISS...I ASSURE YOU I DID NOT SEE YOUR POLKA-DOT PANTIES.
AH, HA! SO YOU DID TOO SEE!
OH, ATTIM...! HE...HE SAW MY UNDER-PANTS!

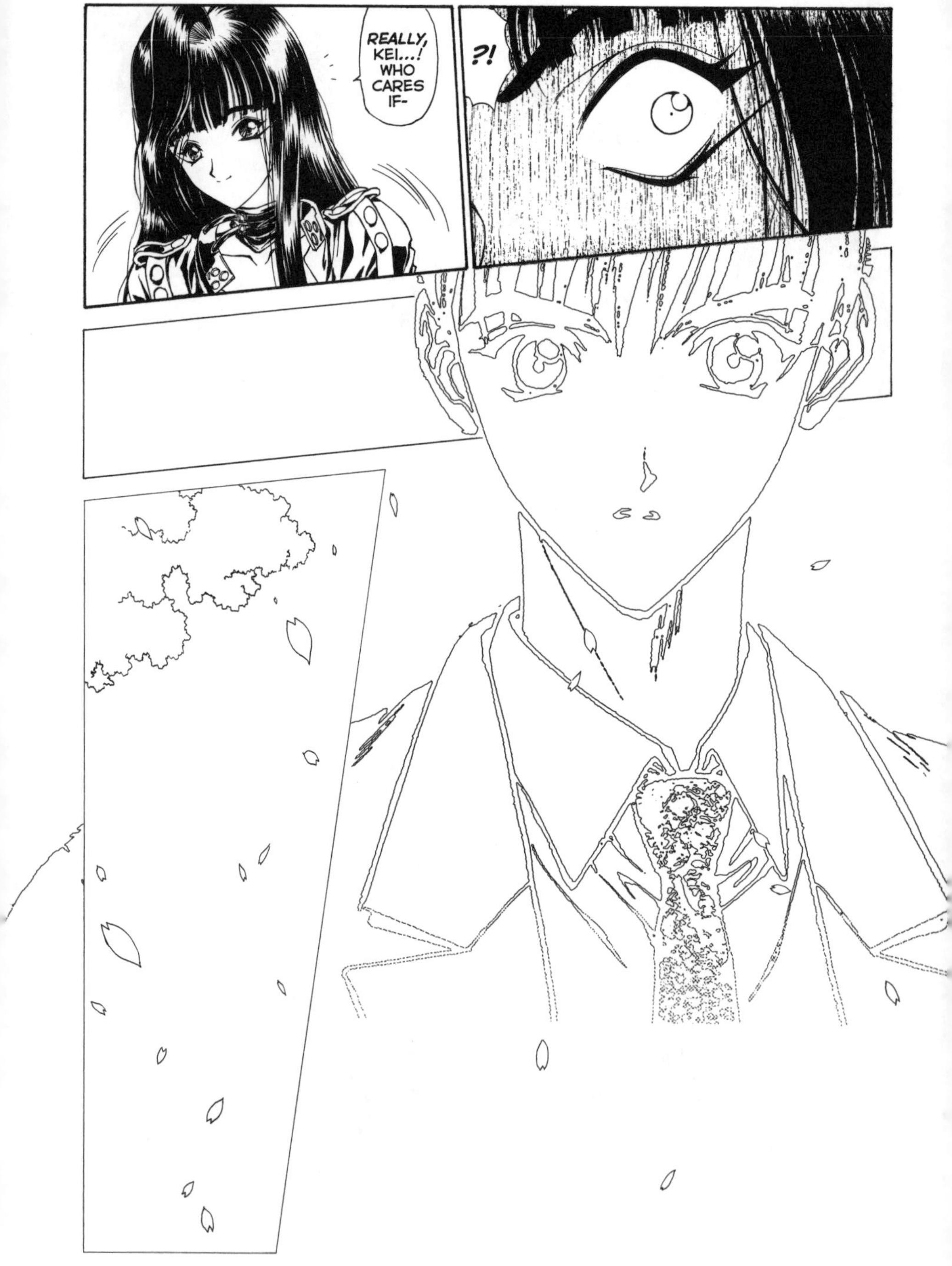
?!
REALLY, KEI...! WHO CARES IF-

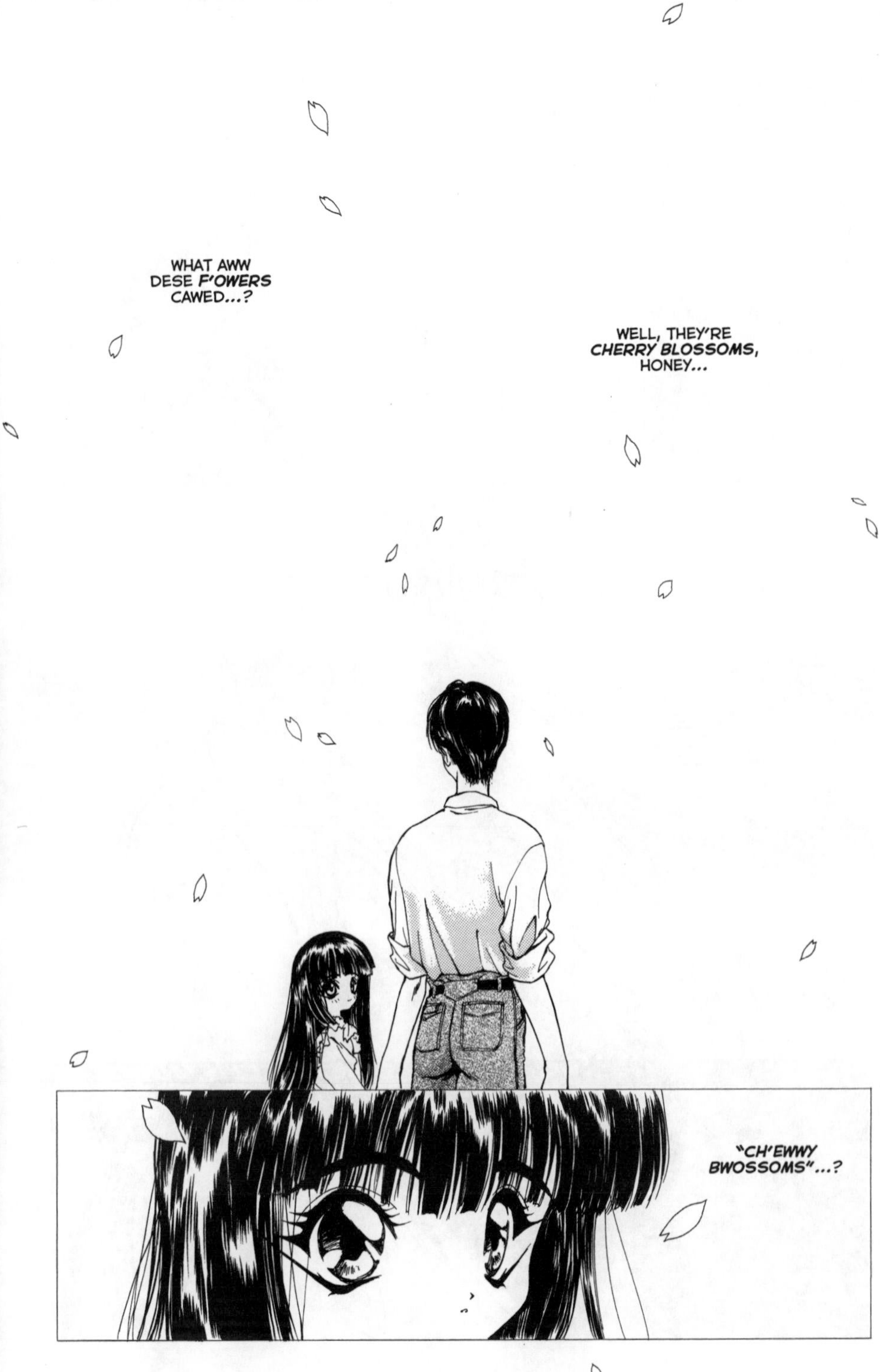
WHAT AWW DESE F'OWERS CAWED...?
WELL, THEY'RE CHERRY BLOSSOMS, HONEY...
"CH'EWWY BWOSSOMS"...?

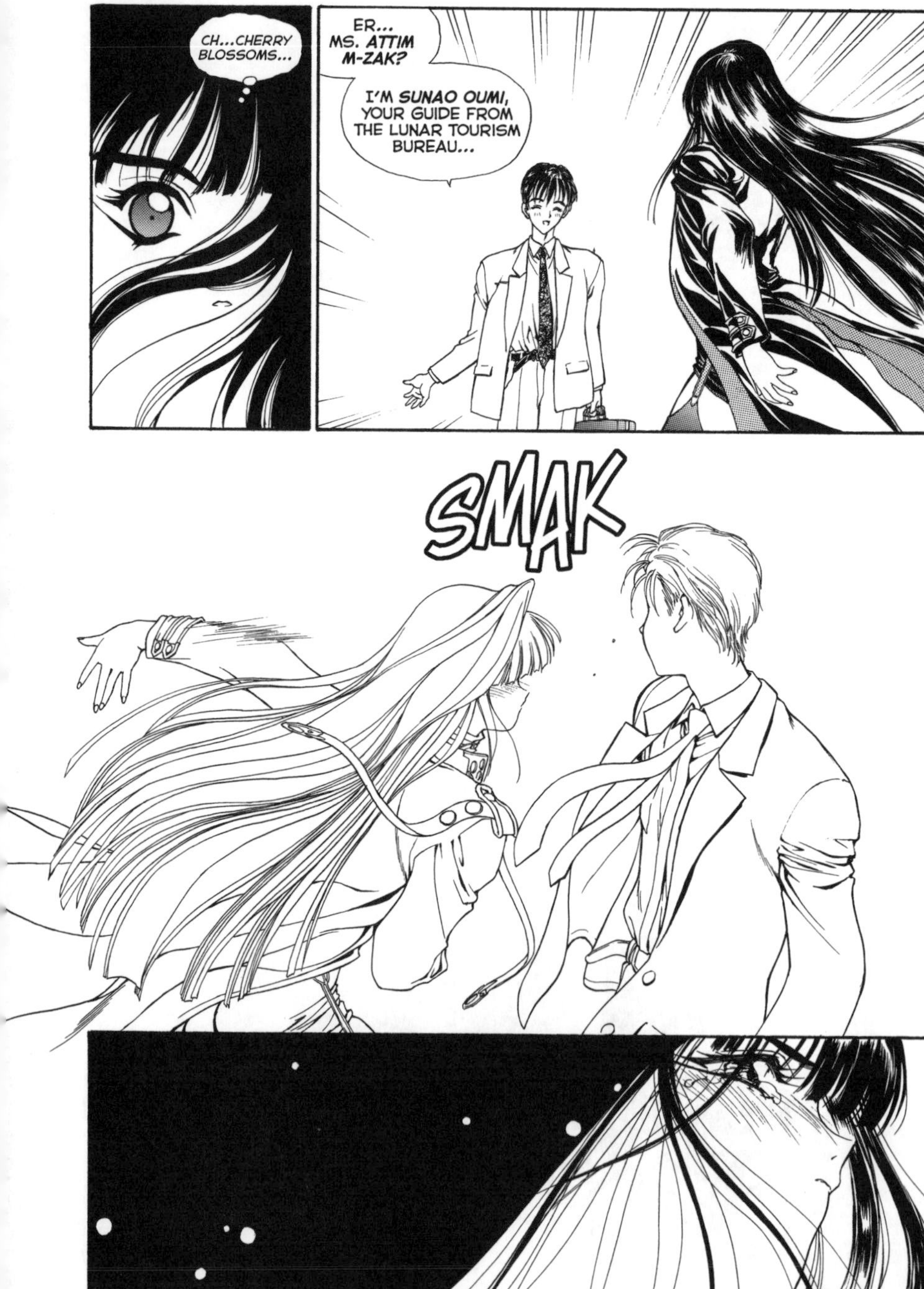
CH...CHERRY BLOSSOMS...
ER... MS. ATTIM M-ZAK?
I'M SUNAO OUMI, YOUR GUIDE FROM THE LUNAR TOURISM BUREAU...
SMAK

Act 5

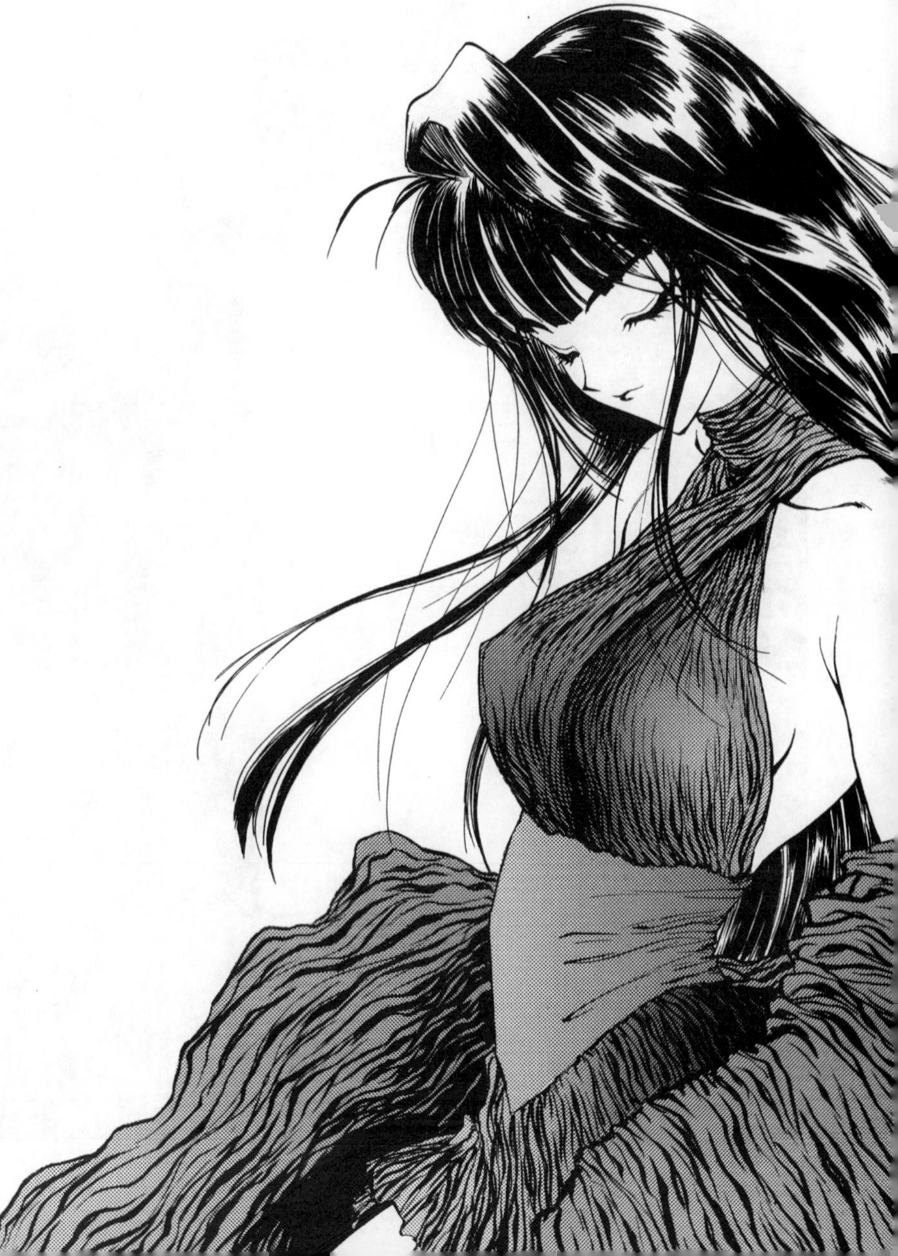

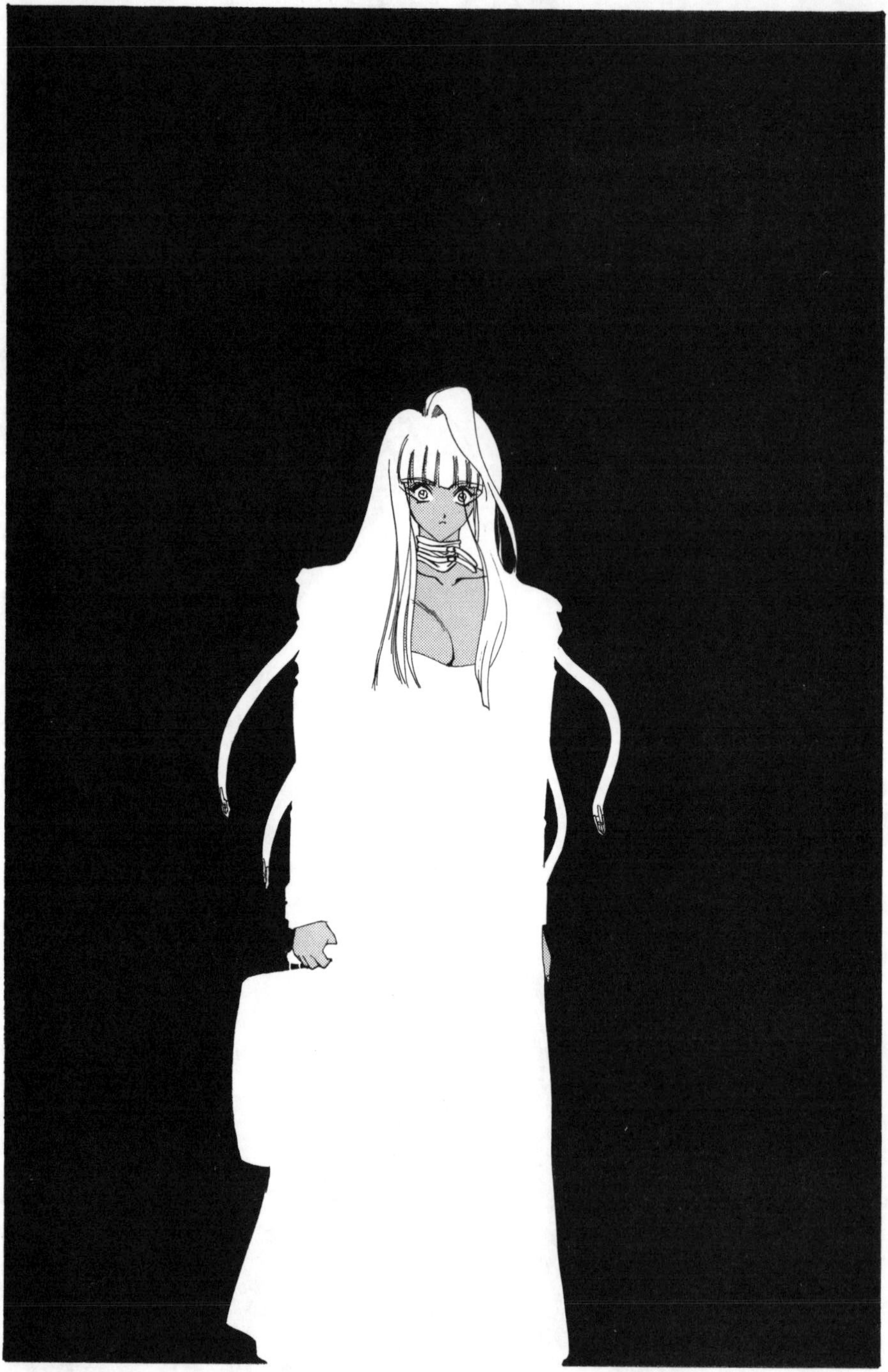

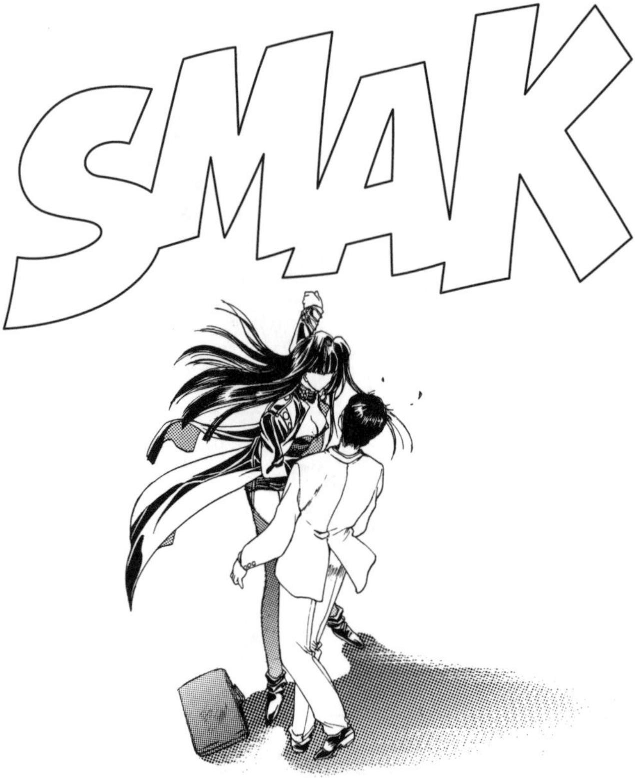
SMAK
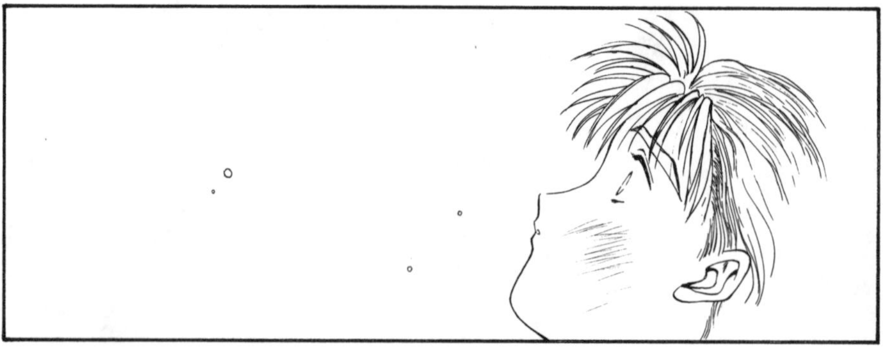

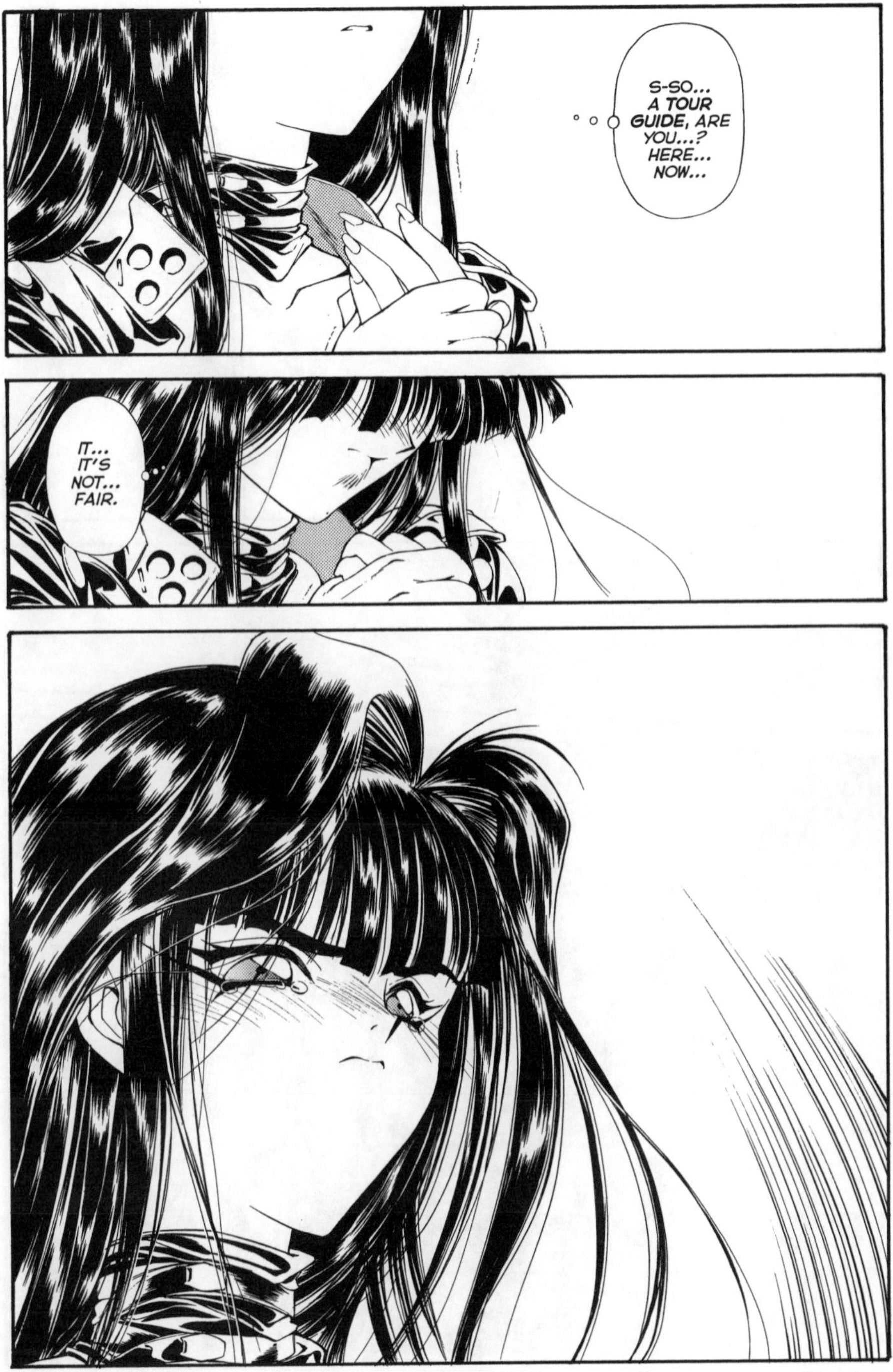
S-SO... A TOUR GUIDE, ARE YOU...? HERE... NOW...
IT... IT'S NOT... FAIR.

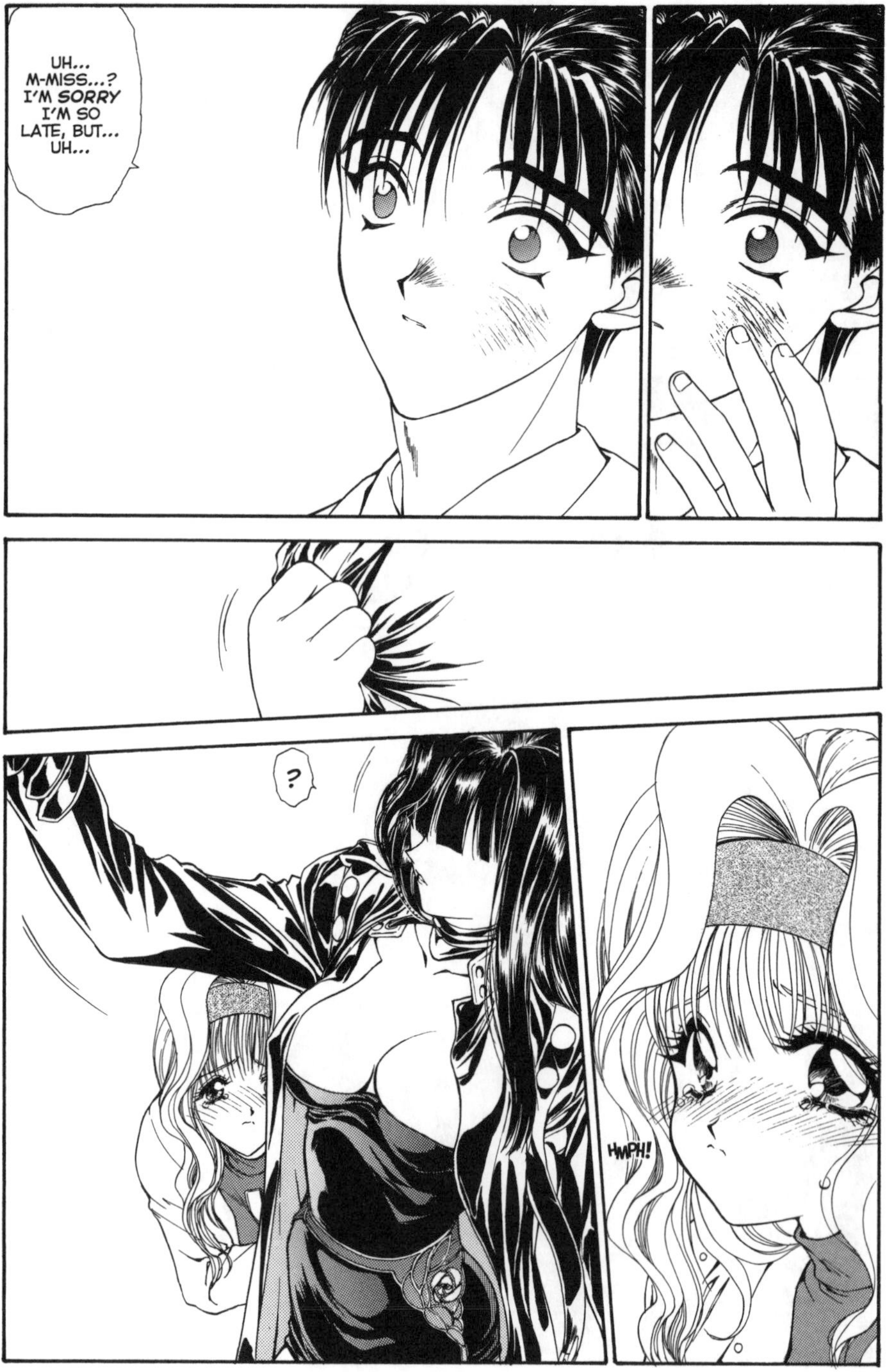
UH... M-MISS...? I'M *SORRY* I'M SO LATE, BUT... UH...
?
HMPH!

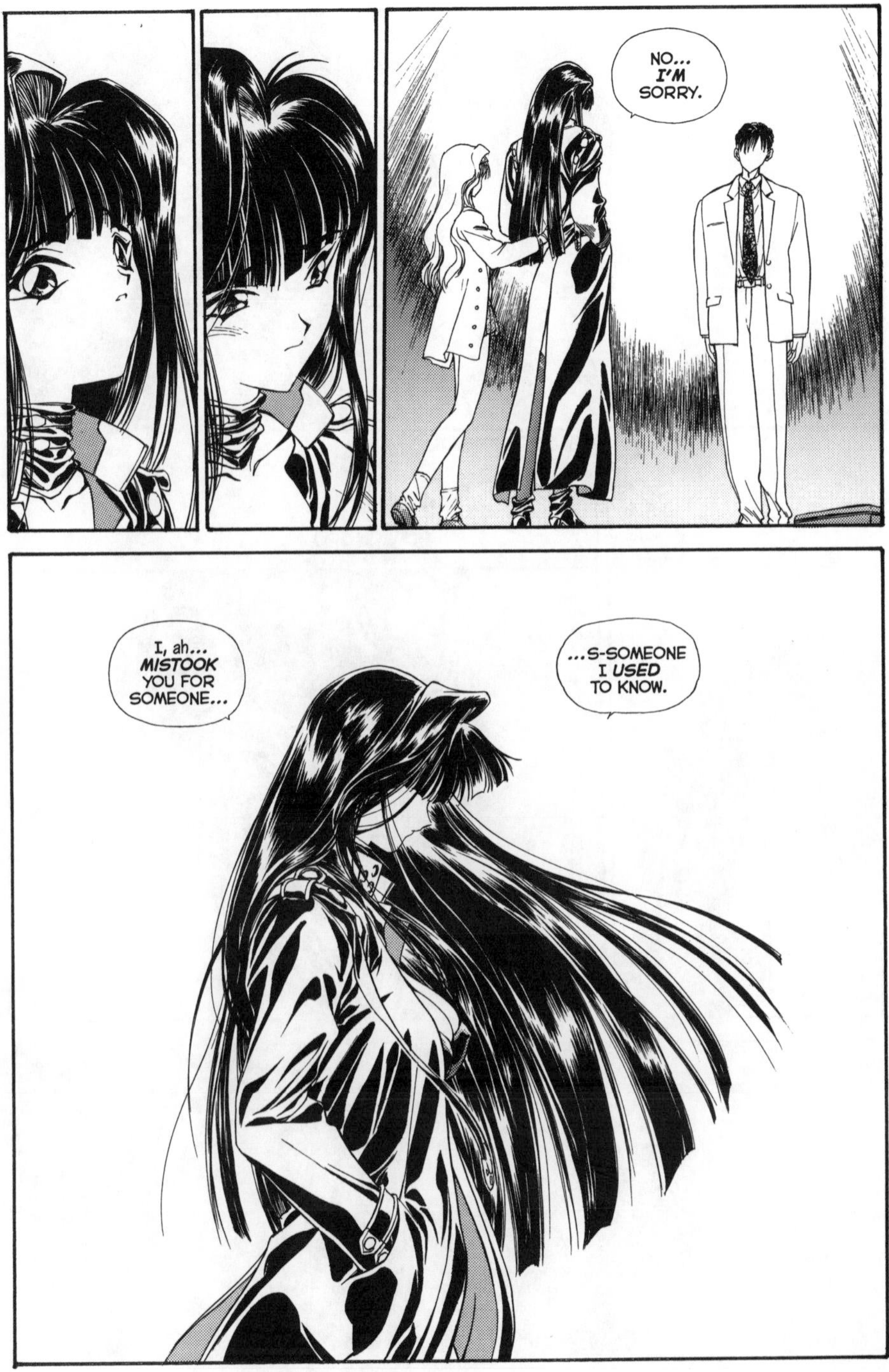
NO... I'M SORRY.
I, ah... MISTOOK YOU FOR SOMEONE...
...S-SOMEONE I USED TO KNOW.

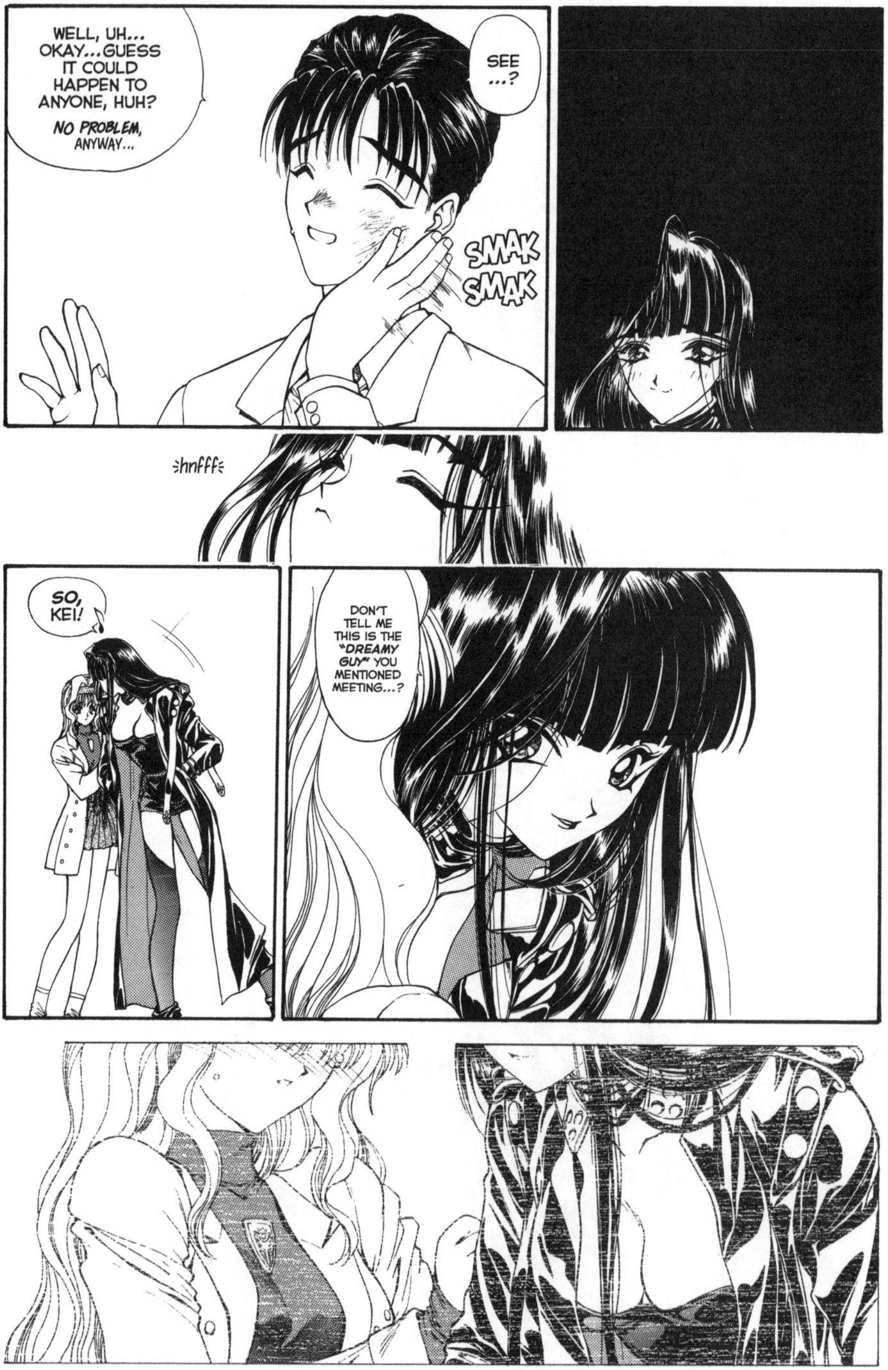
WELL, UH... OKAY...GUESS IT COULD HAPPEN TO ANYONE, HUH? NO PROBLEM, ANYWAY...
SEE ...?
SMAK SMAK
hnfff
SO, KEI!
DON'T TELL ME THIS IS THE "DREAMY GUY" YOU MENTIONED MEETING...?

UH, PARDON ME, MISS...? ARE YOU HURT...?
?
OH, THOSE TEARS OF HERS? NO, THE GIRL'S JUST, WELL... EMOTIONAL. GIVE HER SOME TASTY FOOD, AND SHE'LL BE GOOD AS NEW! RIGHT, KEI?
SO, I KNOW IT'S A BIT EARLY, BUT WHY DON'T WE HAVE DINNER NOW, HMM?
KEI WOULD BE SO APPRECIATIVE! ♥
UM...
CERTAINLY, MISS! I'LL JUST REARRANGE A FEW THINGS, HERE...
YOU PREFER CHINESE CUISINE, I BELIEVE... AH, HERE WE ARE.
ER...WE'VE ARRANGED A RESERVATION AT THE PANDA INN, AND IT CAN BE MOVED UP, BUT...
...IT'S A RATHER... um... HIGH-CLASS PLACE, SO, YOU KNOW... IF YOU'LL EXCUSE MY SAYING SO...

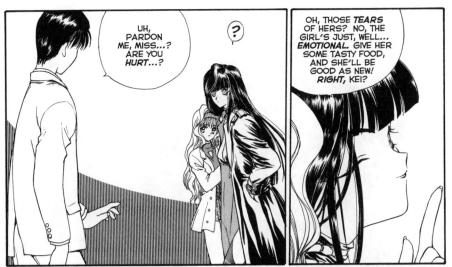

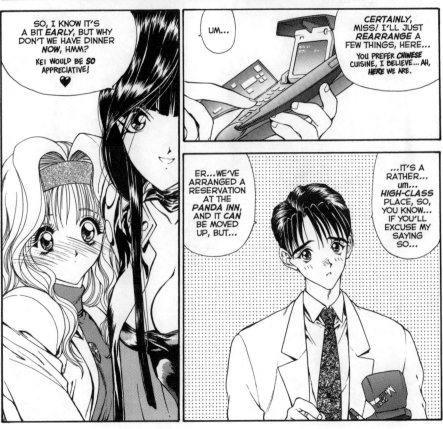

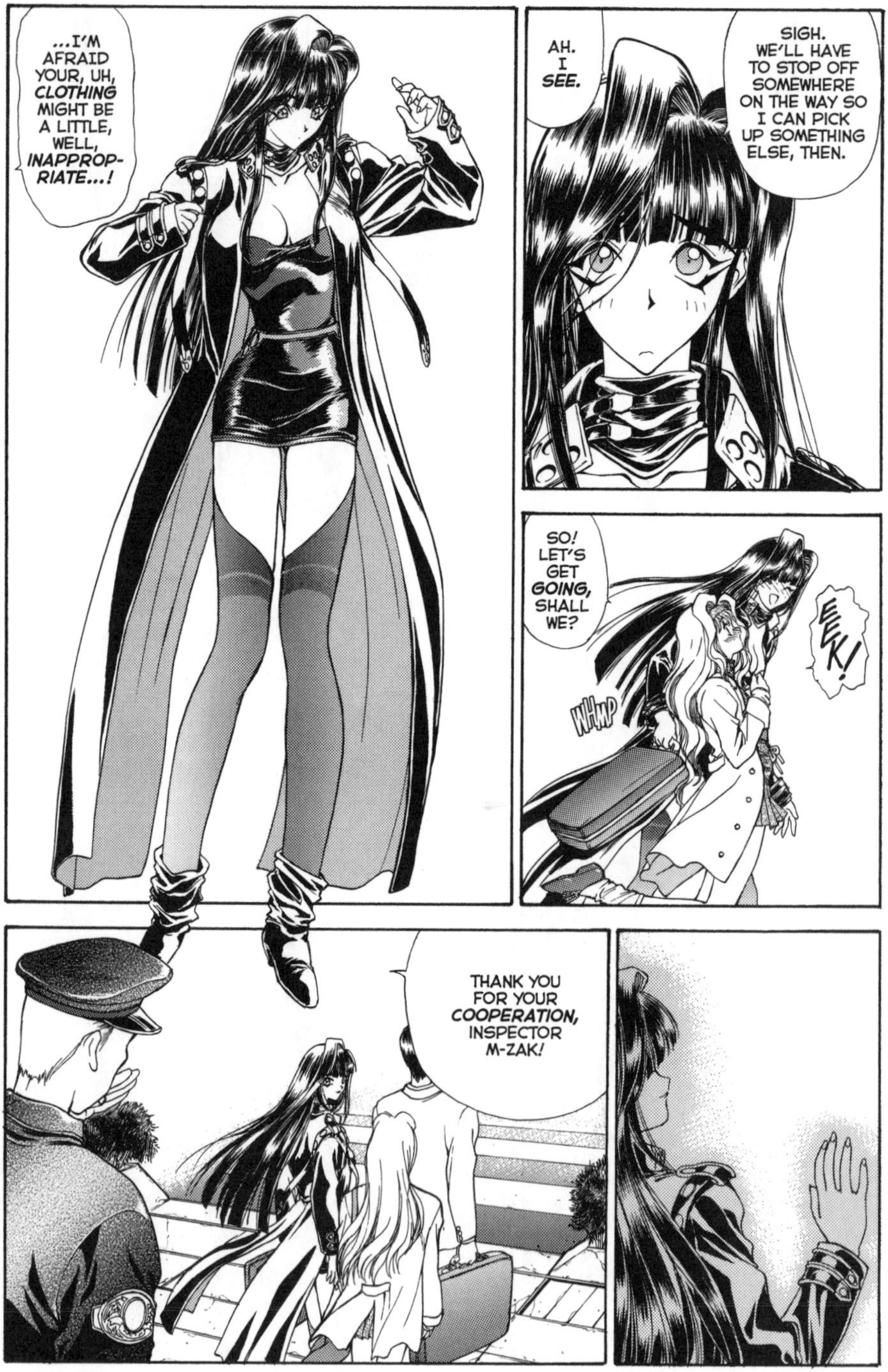
...I'M AFRAID YOUR, UH, CLOTHING MIGHT BE A LITTLE, WELL, INAPPROPRIATE...!
AH. I SEE.
SIGH. WE'LL HAVE TO STOP OFF SOMEWHERE ON THE WAY SO I CAN PICK UP SOMETHING ELSE, THEN.
SO! LET'S GET GOING, SHALL WE?
EEK!
WHMP
THANK YOU FOR YOUR COOPERATION, INSPECTOR M-ZAK!

WELL...IS OUR *U.N.* INVESTI-GATOR GONE?

YES, SIR!

AND QUITE A *LOOKER* SHE WAS, TOO, *SIR!*

YES...WELL, ONCE YOU'RE MAKING AUGMENTATIONS, WHY STOP WITH THE *INTERNALS,* YES? HMM. ONE OF THE *U.N.'S* FEW *FULLY AUGMENTED* INVESTIGATORS. INTERESTING.

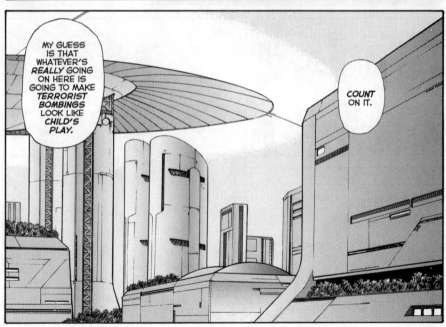

MY GUESS IS THAT WHATEVER'S *REALLY* GOING ON HERE IS GOING TO MAKE *TERRORIST BOMBINGS* LOOK LIKE *CHILD'S PLAY.*

COUNT ON IT.

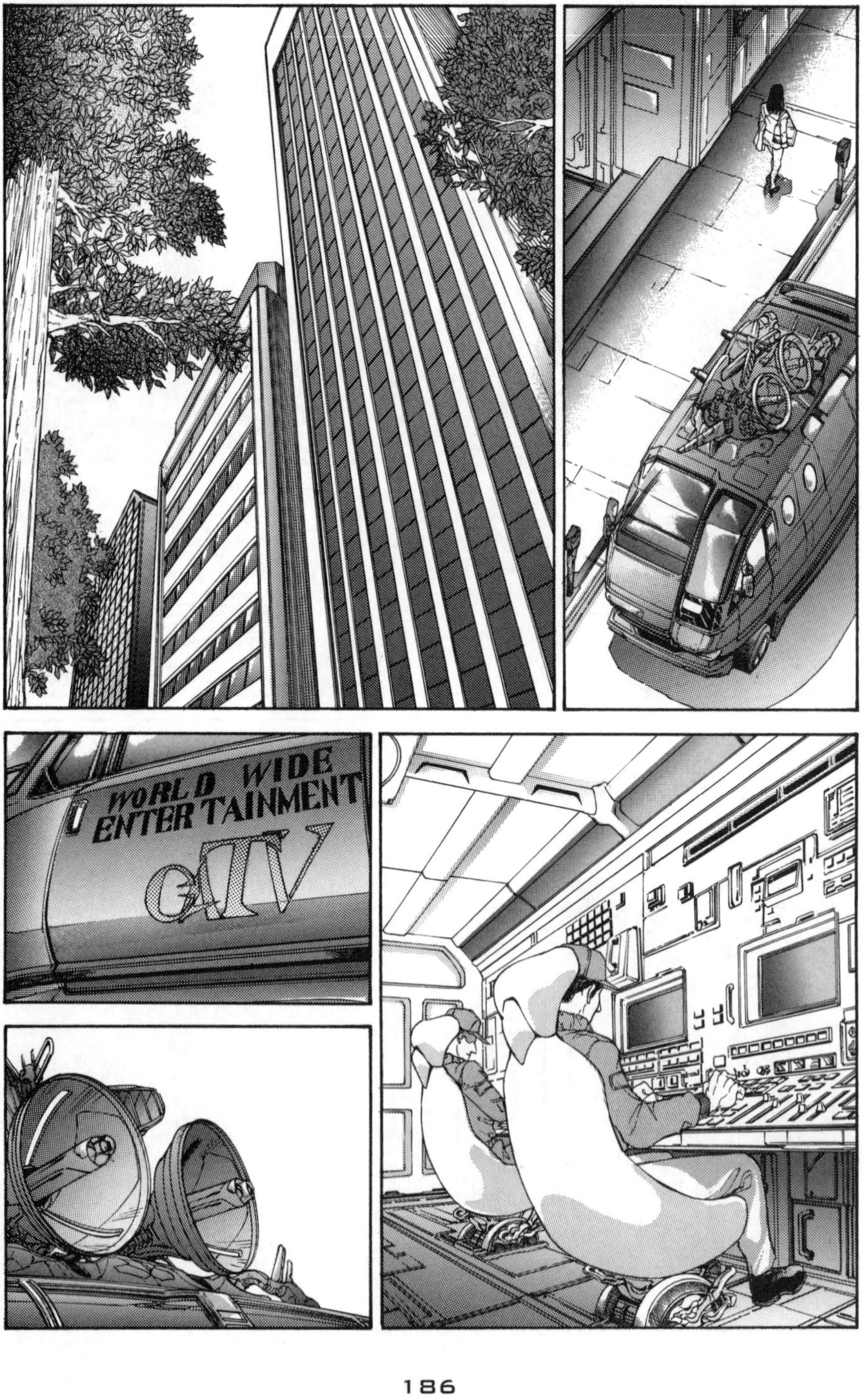
WORLD WIDE
ENTERTAINMENT

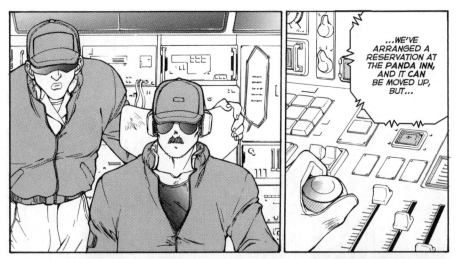

...WE'VE ARRANGED A RESERVATION AT THE *PANDA INN*, AND IT CAN BE MOVED UP, BUT...

THEY'RE HEADED TO THE *PANDA INN*--THAT'S IN HORTON PLAZA! *MOVE IT!*

SHOULD WE NOTIFY *RIX HAYWARD*, SIR...?

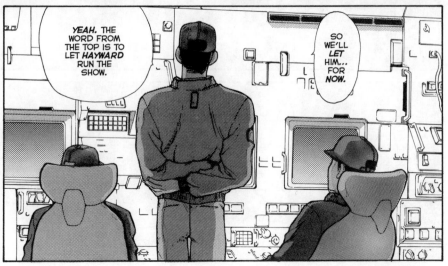

YEAH. THE WORD FROM THE TOP IS TO LET *HAYWARD* RUN THE SHOW.

SO WE'LL *LET HIM...* FOR *NOW.*

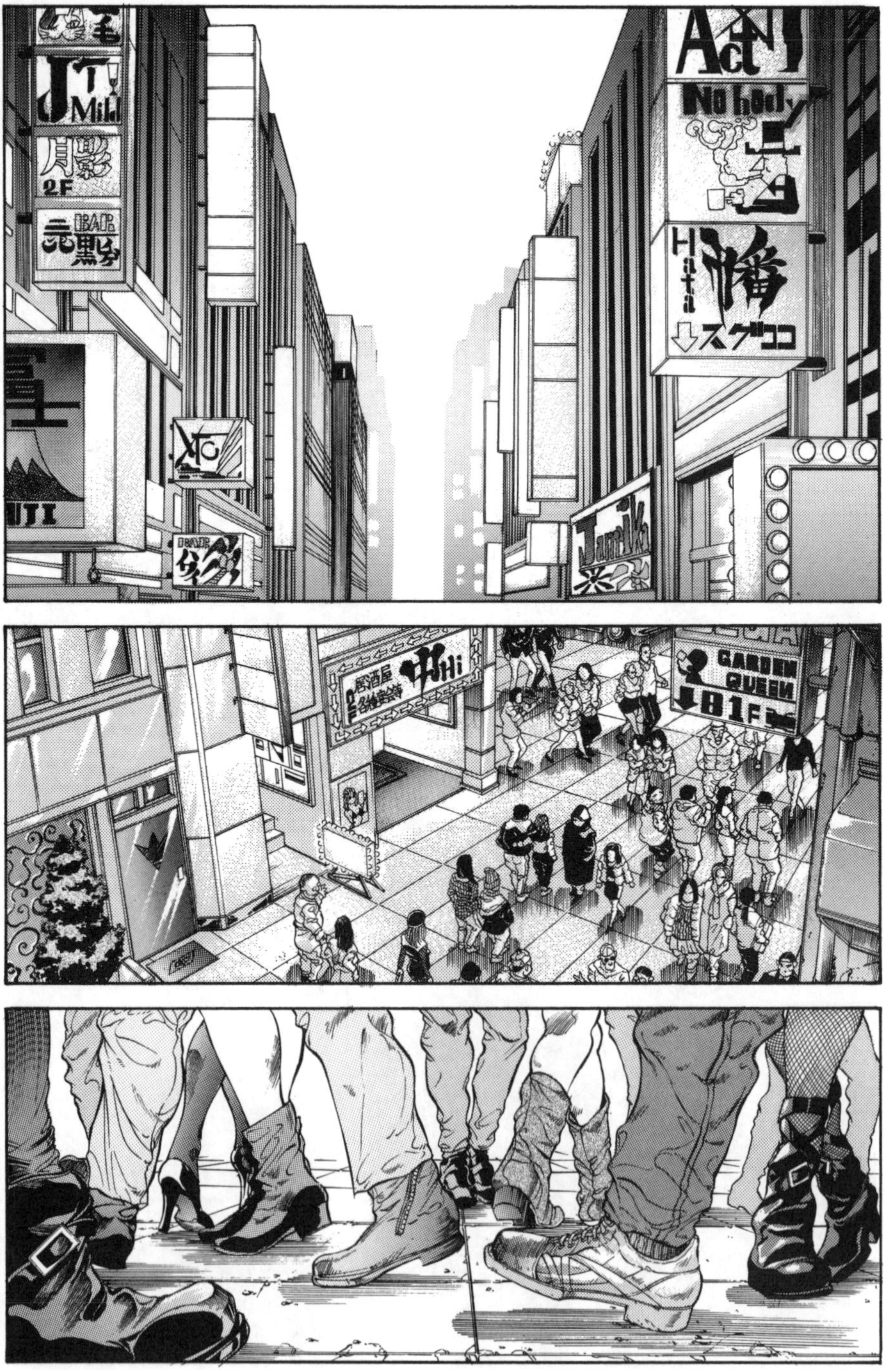
月影
2F
Act
No body
スグココ
GARDEN
QUEEN
B1F

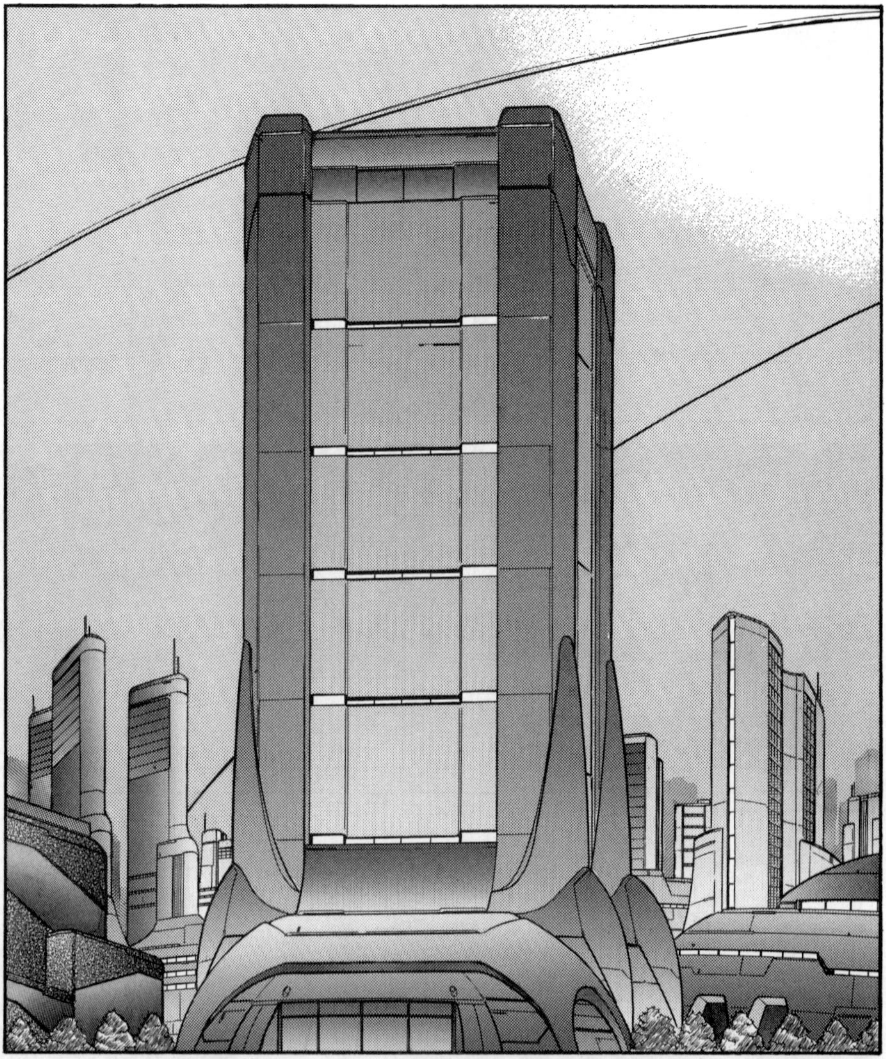

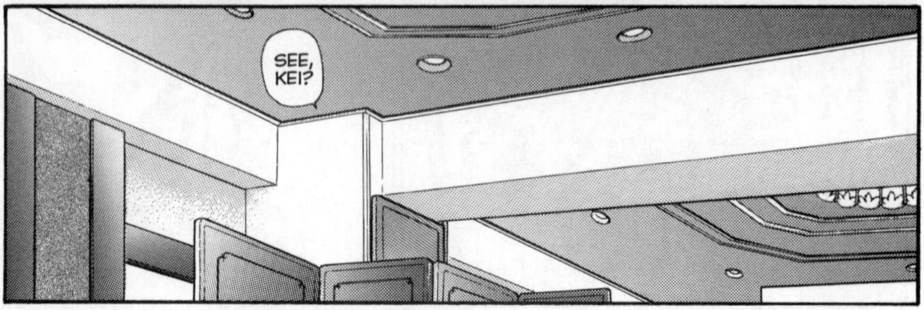
SEE, KEI?

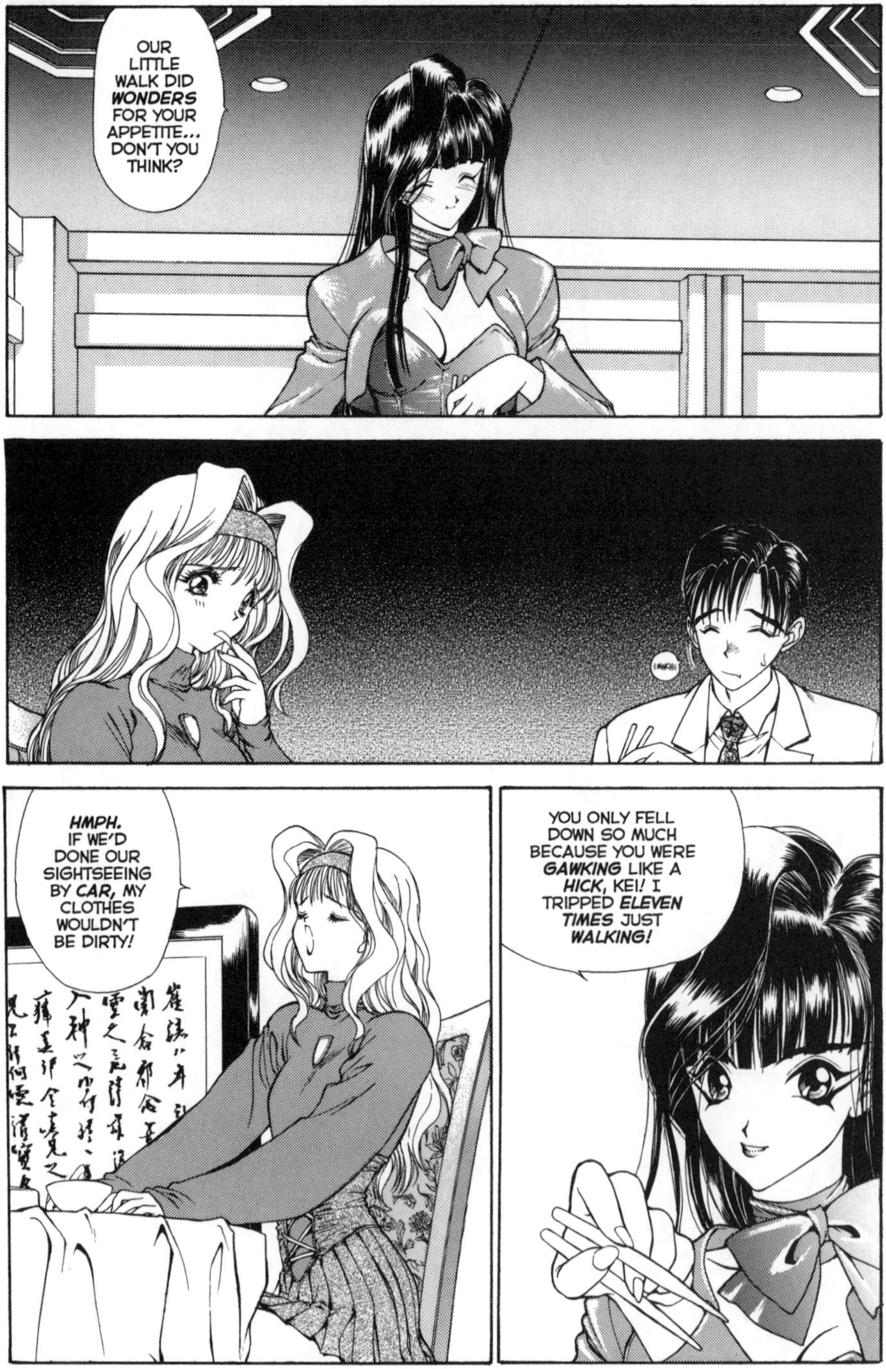
OUR LITTLE WALK DID *WONDERS* FOR YOUR APPETITE... DON'T YOU THINK?
HMPH. IF WE'D DONE OUR SIGHTSEEING BY *CAR,* MY CLOTHES WOULDN'T BE DIRTY!
YOU ONLY FELL DOWN SO MUCH BECAUSE YOU WERE *GAWKING* LIKE A *HICK,* KEI! I TRIPPED *ELEVEN TIMES* JUST *WALKING!*

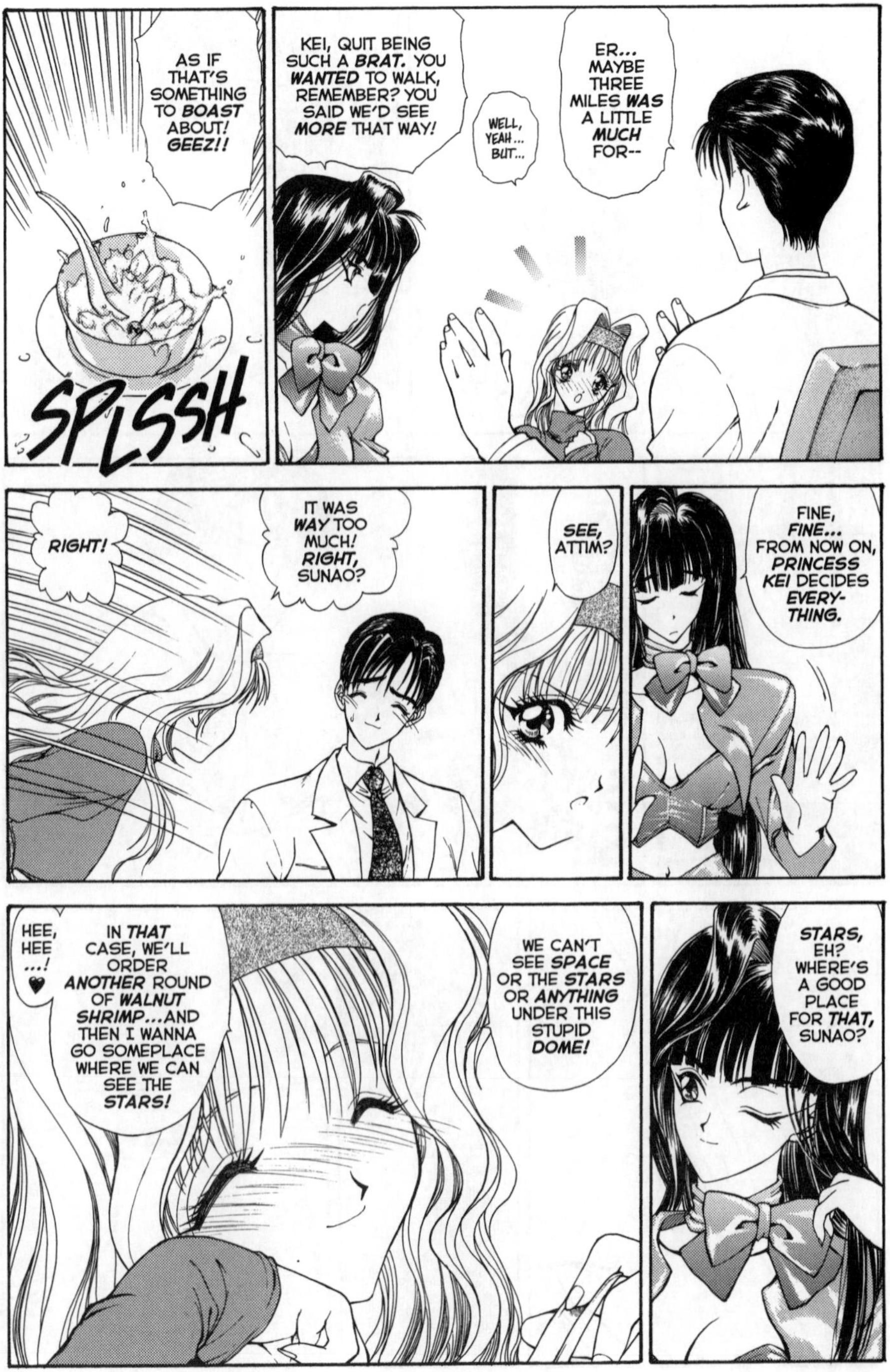
AS IF THAT'S SOMETHING TO BOAST ABOUT! GEEZ!!
SPLSSH
KEI, QUIT BEING SUCH A BRAT. YOU WANTED TO WALK, REMEMBER? YOU SAID WE'D SEE MORE THAT WAY!
WELL, YEAH... BUT...
ER... MAYBE THREE MILES WAS A LITTLE MUCH FOR--
RIGHT!
IT WAS WAY TOO MUCH! RIGHT, SUNAO?
SEE, ATTIM?
FINE, FINE... FROM NOW ON, PRINCESS KEI DECIDES EVERYTHING.
HEE, HEE ...! ♥
IN THAT CASE, WE'LL ORDER ANOTHER ROUND OF WALNUT SHRIMP... AND THEN I WANNA GO SOMEPLACE WHERE WE CAN SEE THE STARS!
WE CAN'T SEE SPACE OR THE STARS OR ANYTHING UNDER THIS STUPID DOME!
STARS, EH? WHERE'S A GOOD PLACE FOR THAT, SUNAO?

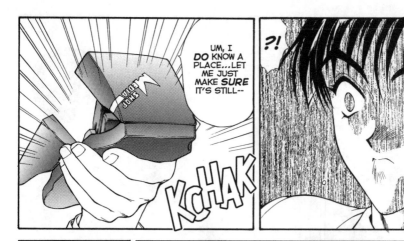

UM, I *DO* KNOW A PLACE...LET ME JUST MAKE *SURE* IT'S STILL--

?!

KCHAK

MY... MY SMART- CARD... IT'S GONE!

BR EEP

SHKK SHKK

OH, MAN... I JUST GOT IT *REPLACED*, TOO! WHERE THE HECK...?

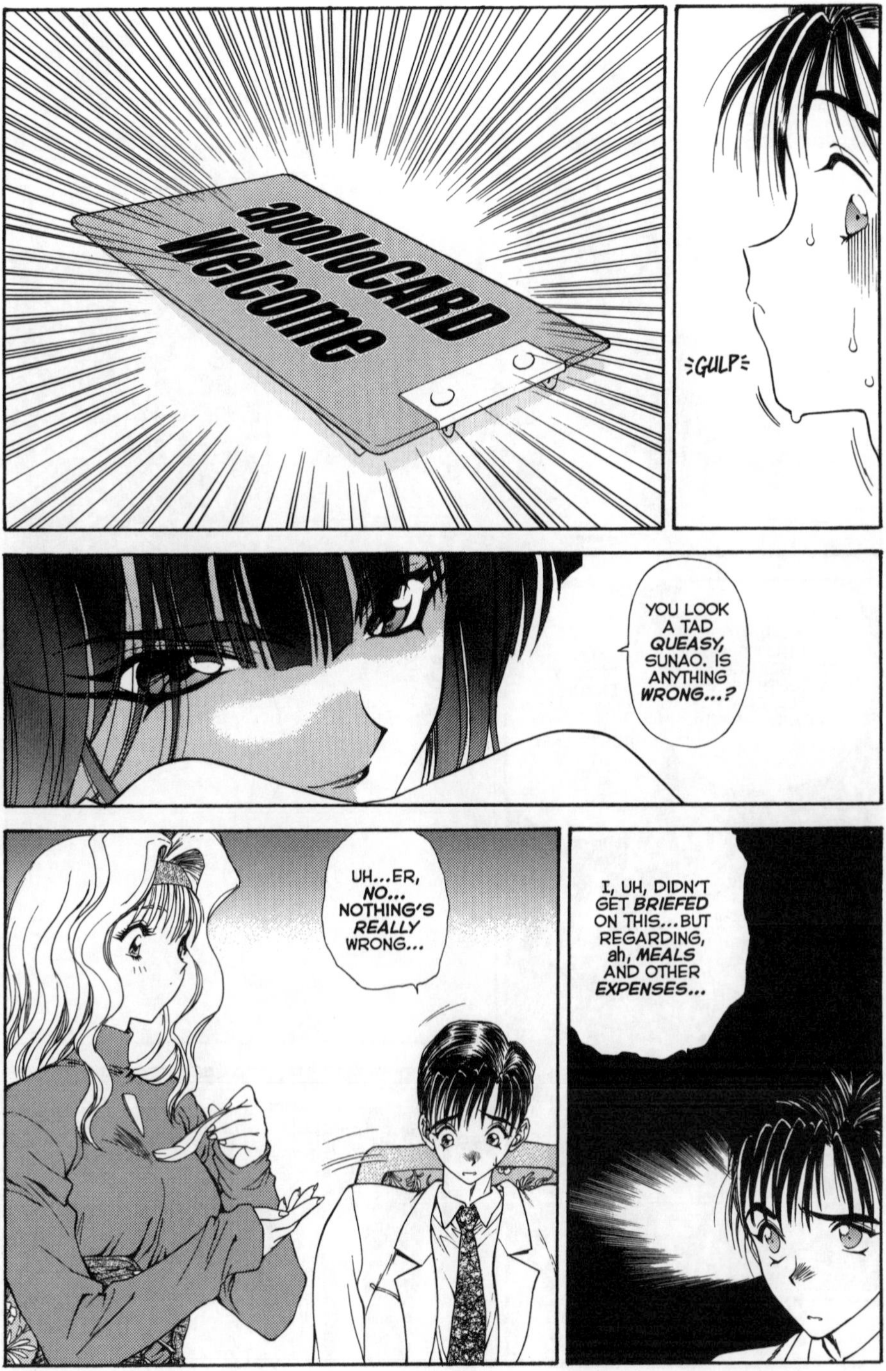
apolloCARD
Welcome
GULP
YOU LOOK A TAD QUEASY, SUNAO. IS ANYTHING WRONG...?
UH...ER, NO... NOTHING'S REALLY WRONG...
I, UH, DIDN'T GET BRIEFED ON THIS...BUT REGARDING, ah, MEALS AND OTHER EXPENSES...

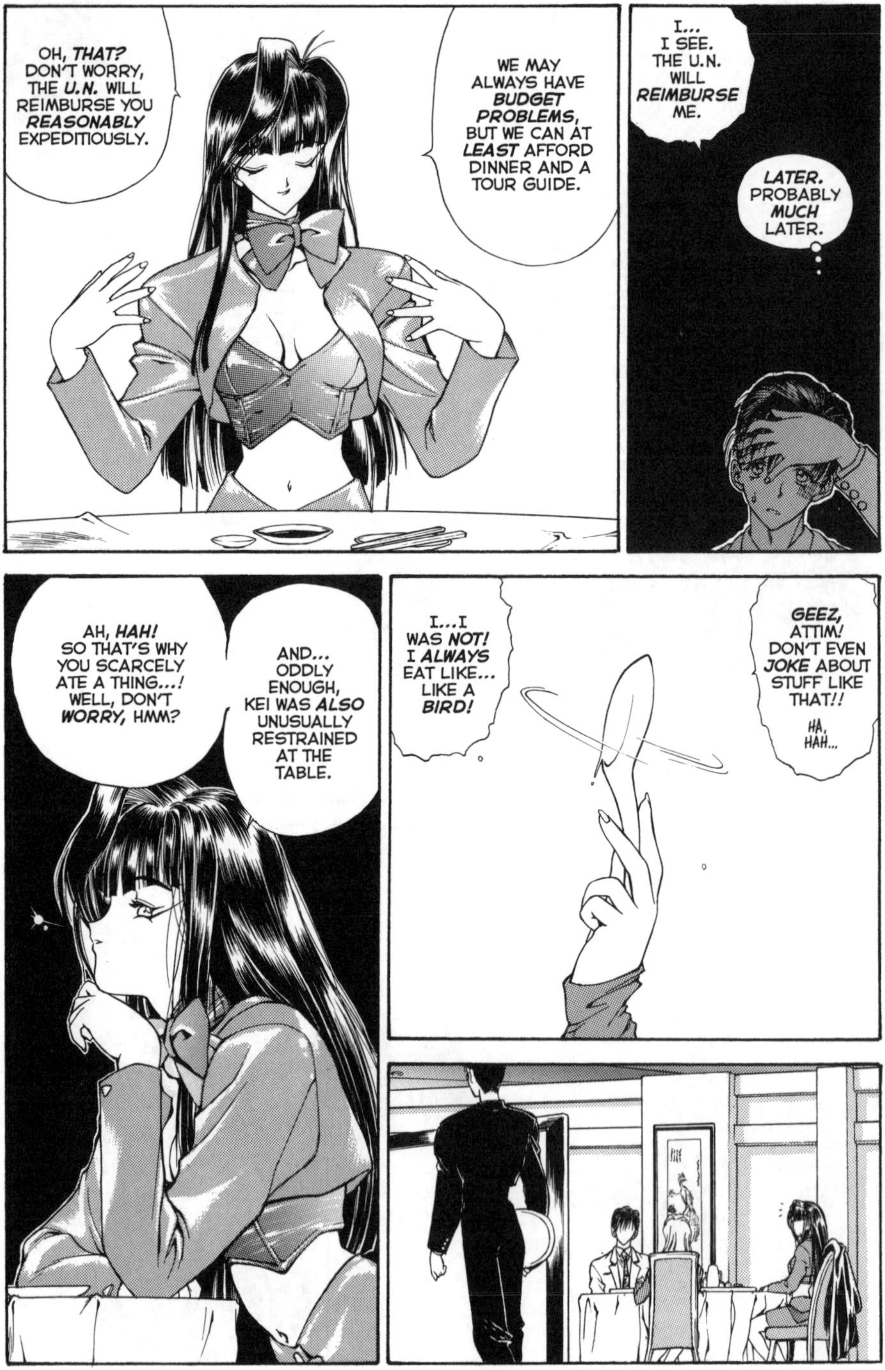
OH, THAT? DON'T WORRY, THE U.N. WILL REIMBURSE YOU REASONABLY EXPEDITIOUSLY.
WE MAY ALWAYS HAVE BUDGET PROBLEMS, BUT WE CAN AT LEAST AFFORD DINNER AND A TOUR GUIDE.
I... I SEE. THE U.N. WILL REIMBURSE ME.
LATER. PROBABLY MUCH LATER.
AH, HAH! SO THAT'S WHY YOU SCARCELY ATE A THING...! WELL, DON'T WORRY, HMM?
AND... ODDLY ENOUGH, KEI WAS ALSO UNUSUALLY RESTRAINED AT THE TABLE.
I...I WAS NOT! I ALWAYS EAT LIKE... LIKE A BIRD!
GEEZ, ATTIM! DON'T EVEN JOKE ABOUT STUFF LIKE THAT!!
HA, HAH...

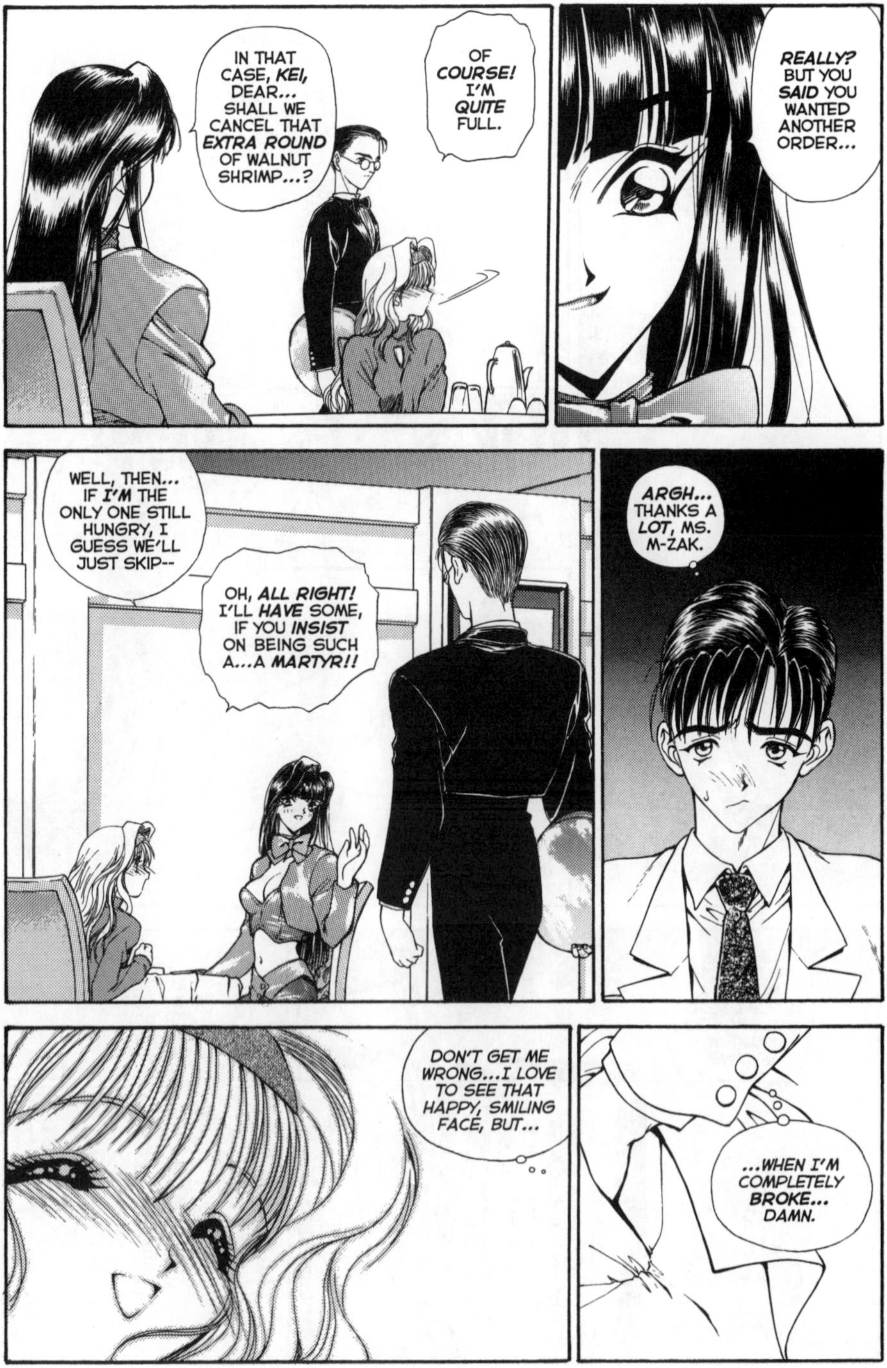
IN THAT CASE, *KEI,* DEAR... SHALL WE CANCEL THAT *EXTRA ROUND* OF WALNUT SHRIMP...?
OF *COURSE!* I'M *QUITE* FULL.
REALLY? BUT YOU *SAID* YOU WANTED ANOTHER ORDER...
WELL, THEN... IF *I'M* THE ONLY ONE STILL HUNGRY, I GUESS WE'LL JUST SKIP--
OH, *ALL RIGHT!* I'LL *HAVE* SOME, IF YOU *INSIST* ON BEING SUCH A...A *MARTYR!!*
ARGH... THANKS A *LOT,* MS. M-ZAK.
DON'T GET ME WRONG...I LOVE TO SEE THAT HAPPY, SMILING FACE, BUT...
*...WHEN I'M COMPLETELY **BROKE**... DAMN.*

NOPE... NOT IN MY POCKET, EITHER.

NOW WHAT? CLIMB OUT THE BATHROOM WINDOW?

I CAN'T HIT UP MY CLIENTS FOR A LOAN... CAN I...?

....! ....!

WAIT A SEC!

MAYBE THEY'LL BILL IT TO THE TOUR COMPANY ...?

UH...CAN YOU EXCUSE ME FOR A SEC? I NEED TO...UH...GO MAKE A *PHONE CALL.*

YOU CAN CALL FROM *HERE* WITH THAT COMPAD... CAN'T YOU?

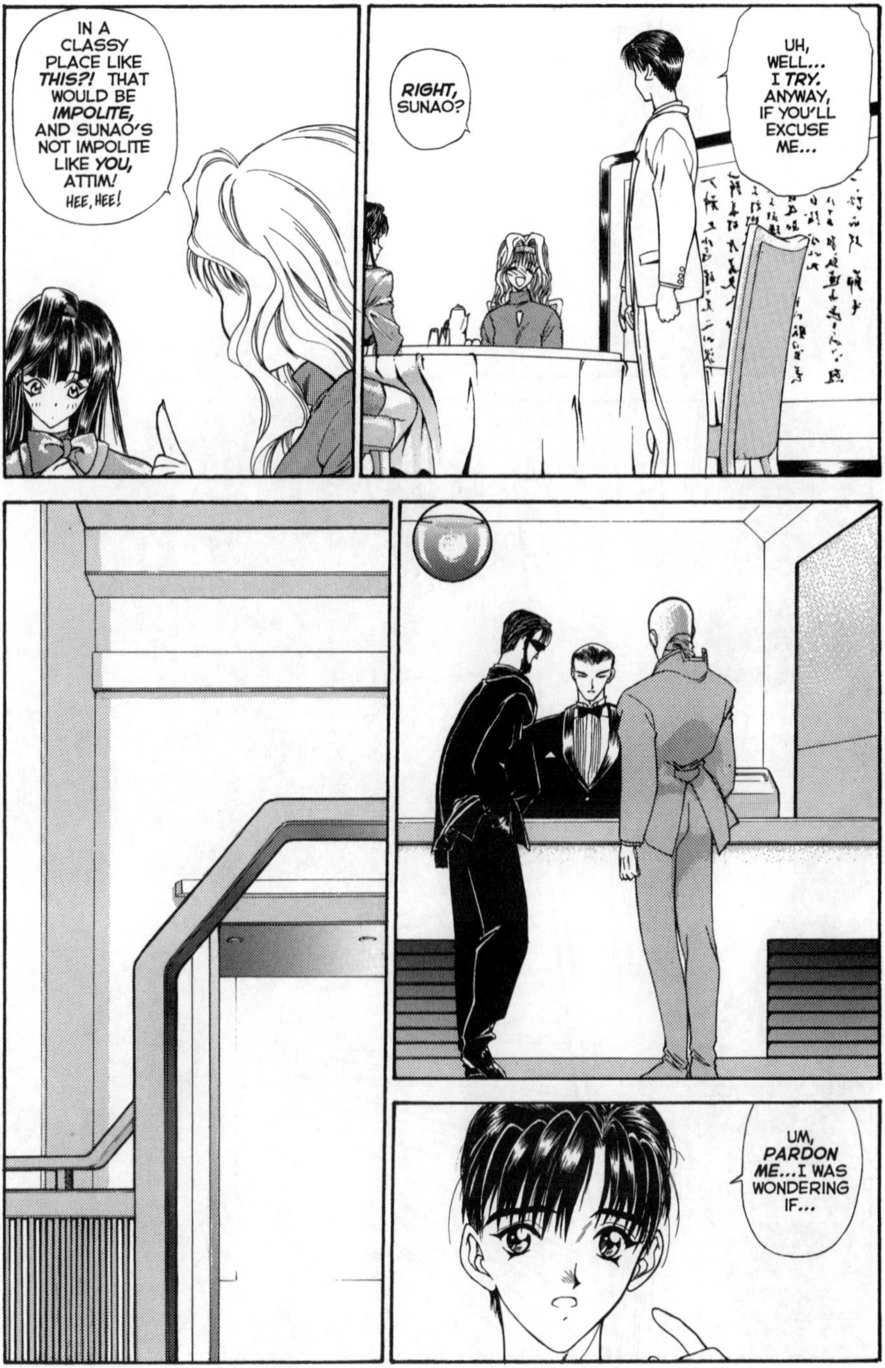
IN A CLASSY PLACE LIKE THIS?! THAT WOULD BE IMPOLITE, AND SUNAO'S NOT IMPOLITE LIKE YOU, ATTIM! HEE, HEE!
RIGHT, SUNAO?
UH, WELL... I TRY. ANYWAY, IF YOU'LL EXCUSE ME...
UM, PARDON ME...I WAS WONDERING IF...

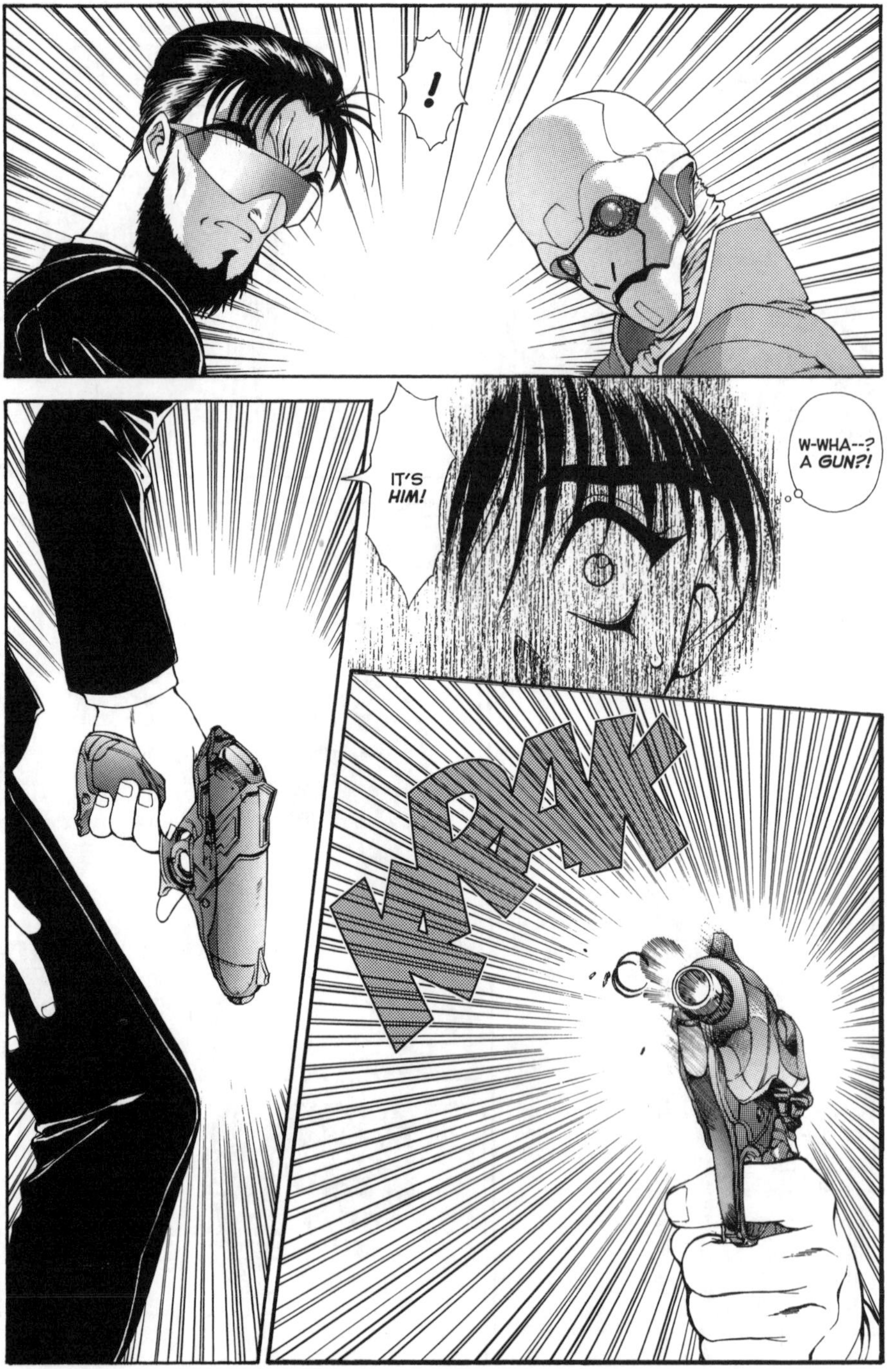
!
IT'S HIM!
W-WHA--? A GUN?!
KRAAK

ACT 6

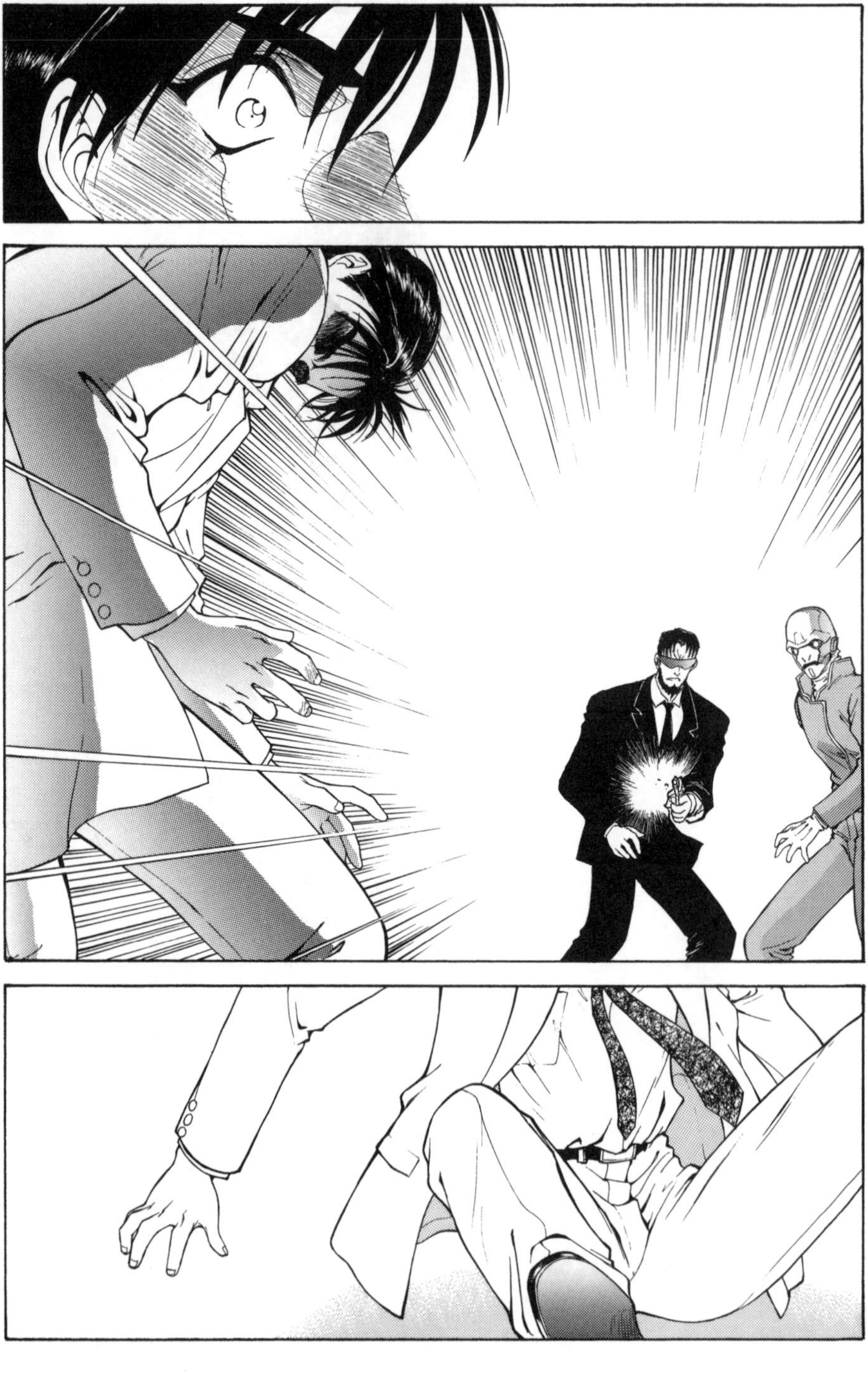

HAHH
HOLY CRAP!
HAHH
GUESS I BETTER GIVE UP ON THE IDEA OF ASKING THEM TO BILL ME...
ULP

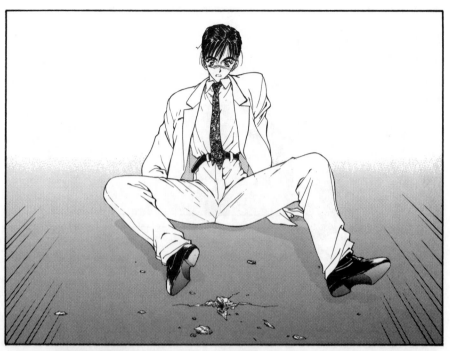

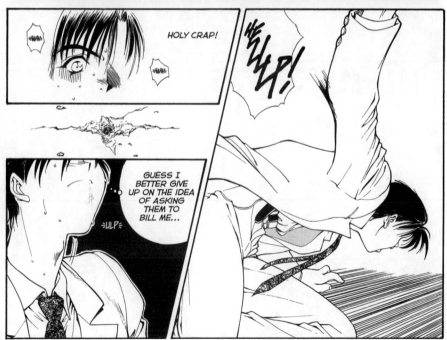

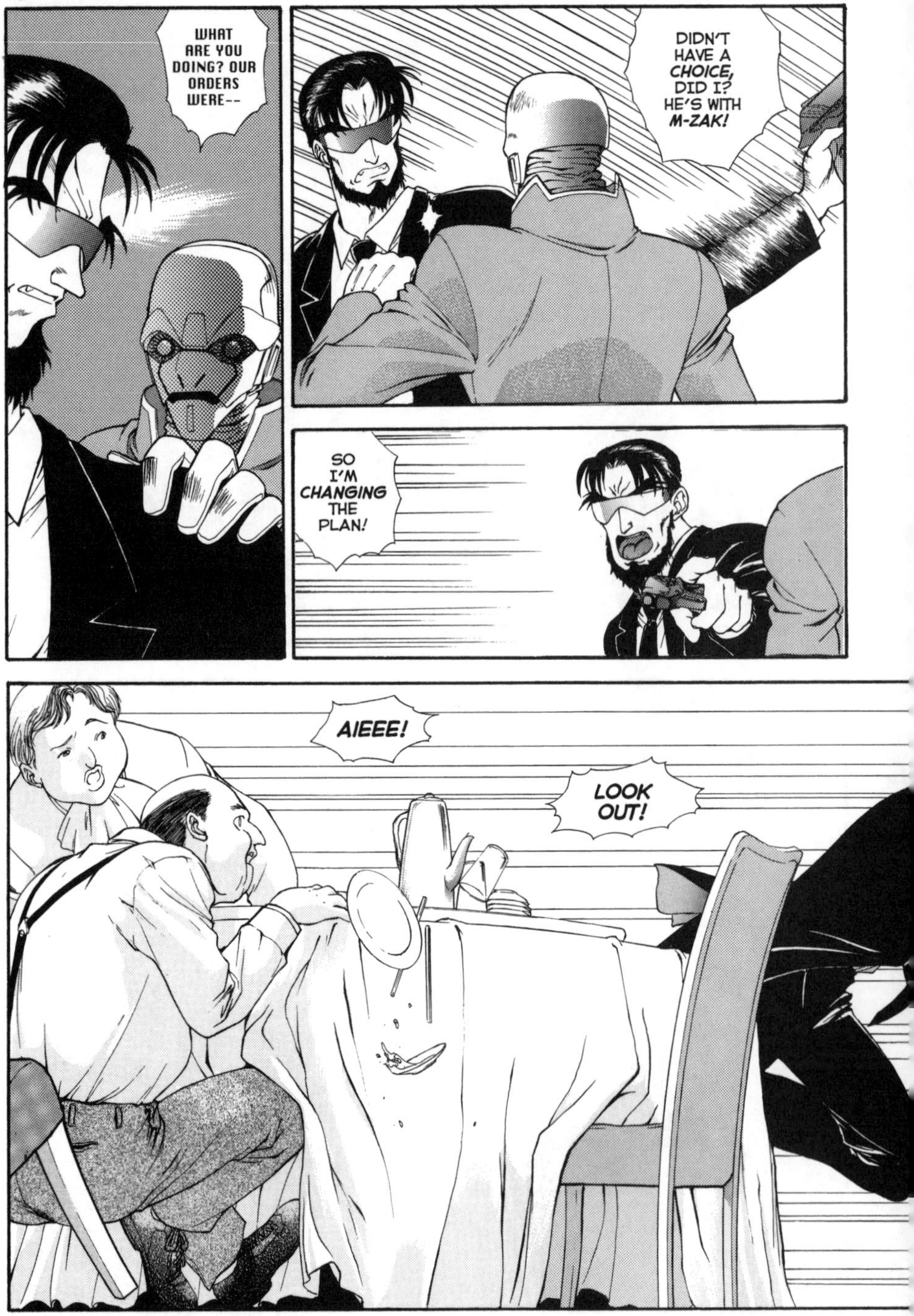
WHAT ARE YOU DOING? OUR ORDERS WERE--
DIDN'T HAVE A CHOICE, DID I? HE'S WITH M-ZAK!
SO I'M CHANGING THE PLAN!
AIEEE!
LOOK OUT!

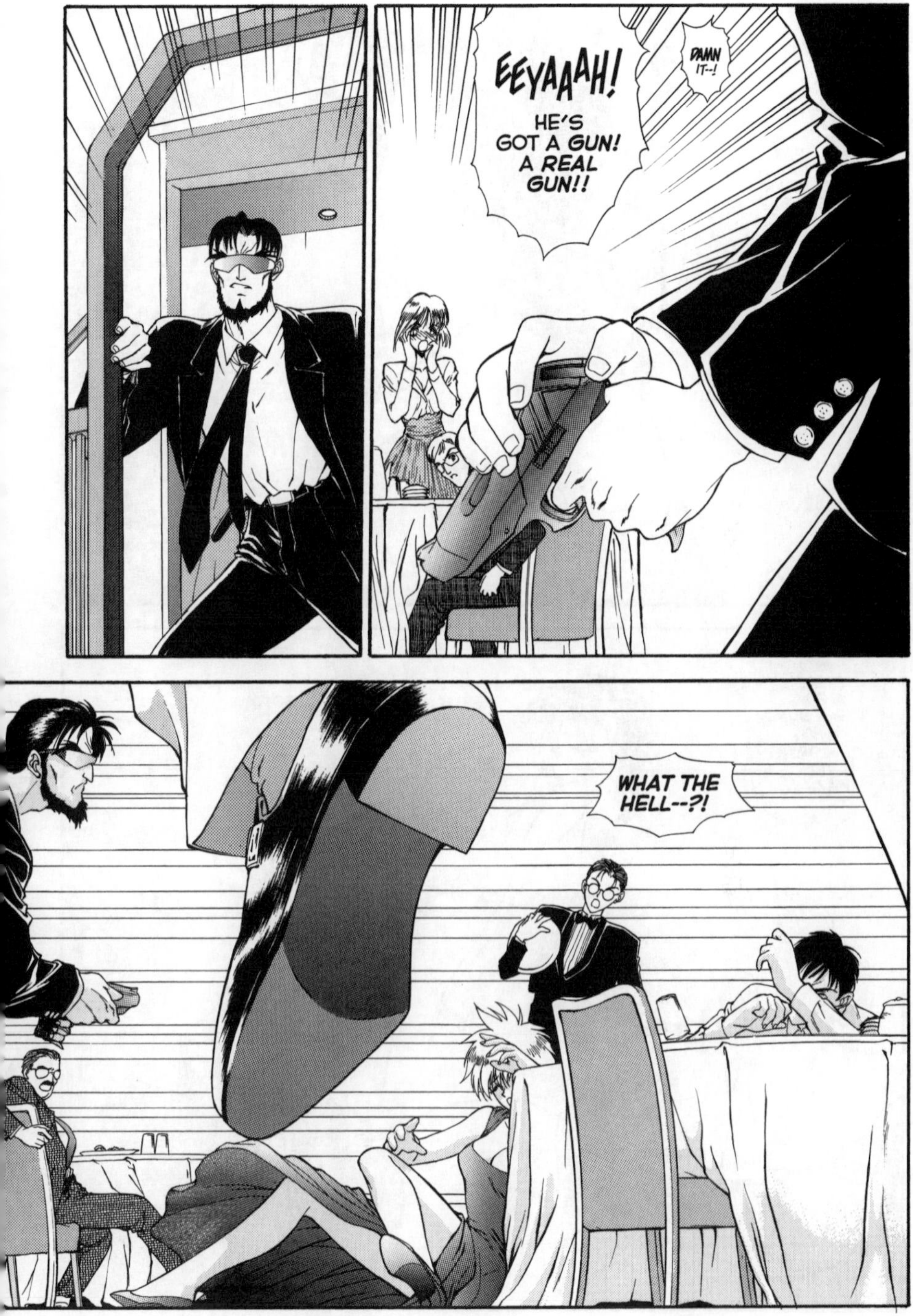
EEYAAAH!
HE'S GOT A GUN! A REAL GUN!!
DAMN IT--!
WHAT THE HELL--?!

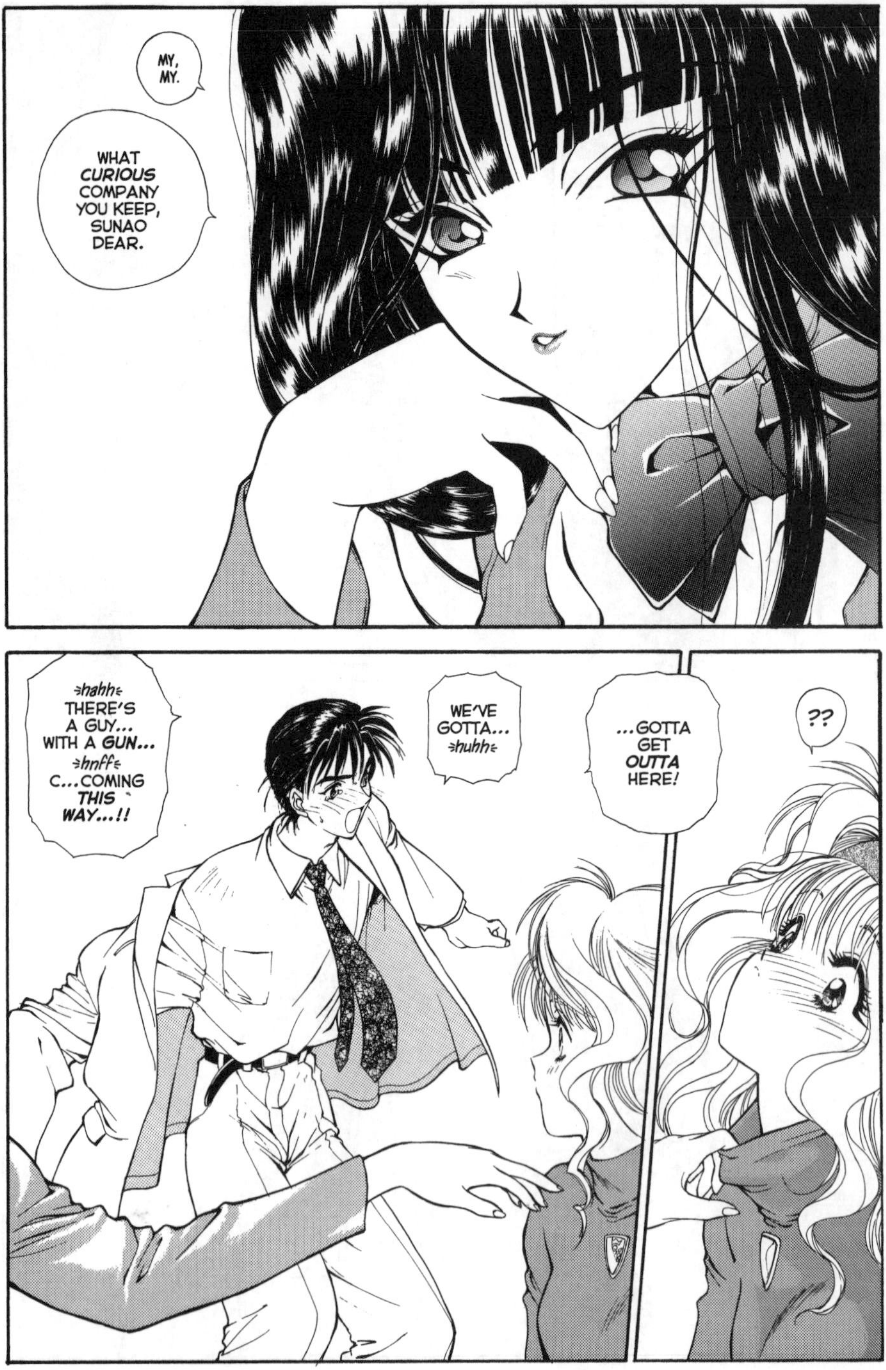
MY, MY.
WHAT CURIOUS COMPANY YOU KEEP, SUNAO DEAR.
hahh THERE'S A GUY... WITH A GUN... hnff C...COMING THIS WAY...!!
WE'VE GOTTA... huhh
...GOTTA GET OUTTA HERE!
??

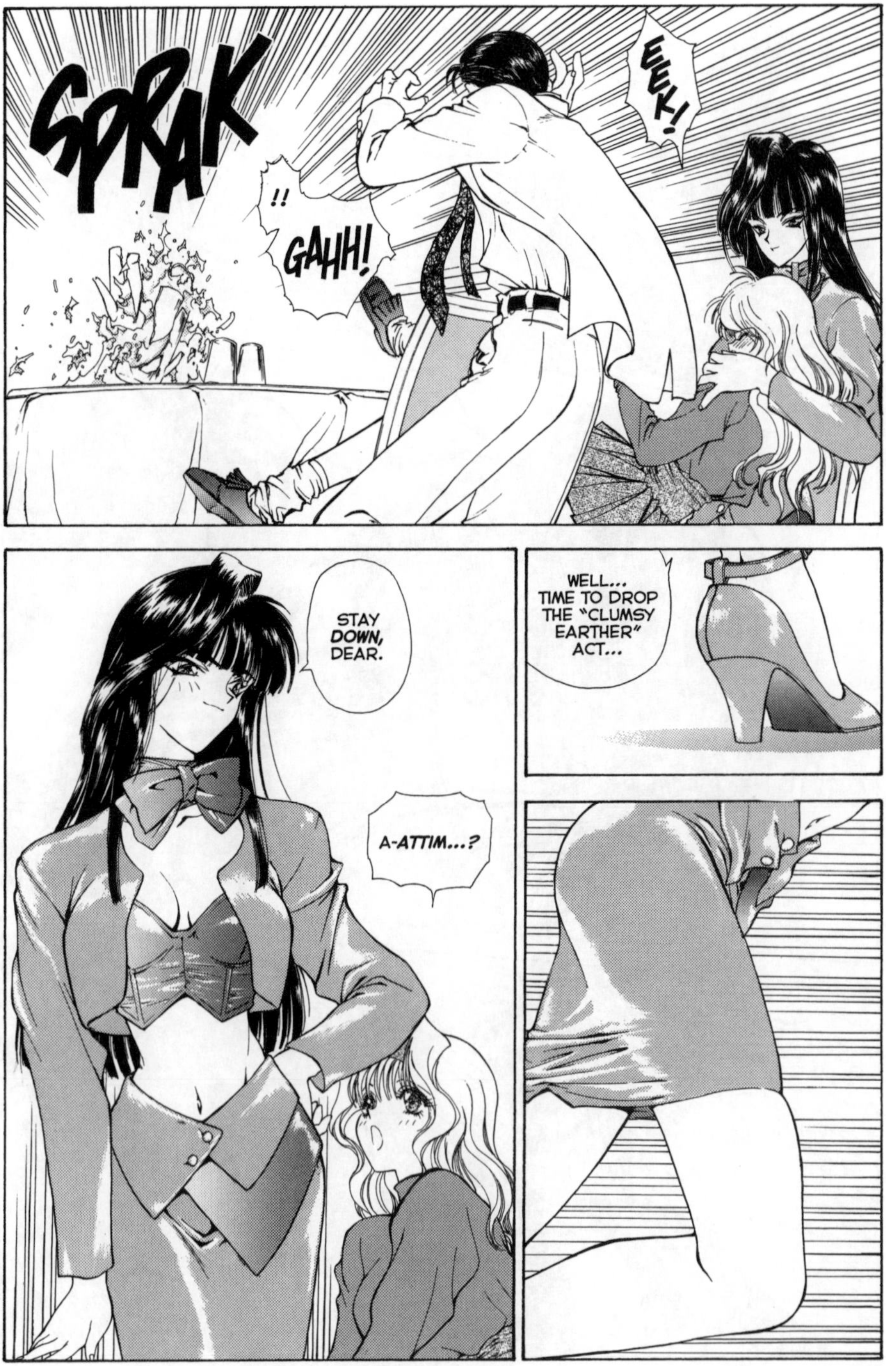
SPRAK
!!
GAHH!
EEK!
STAY DOWN, DEAR.
A-ATTIM...?
WELL... TIME TO DROP THE "CLUMSY EARTHER" ACT...

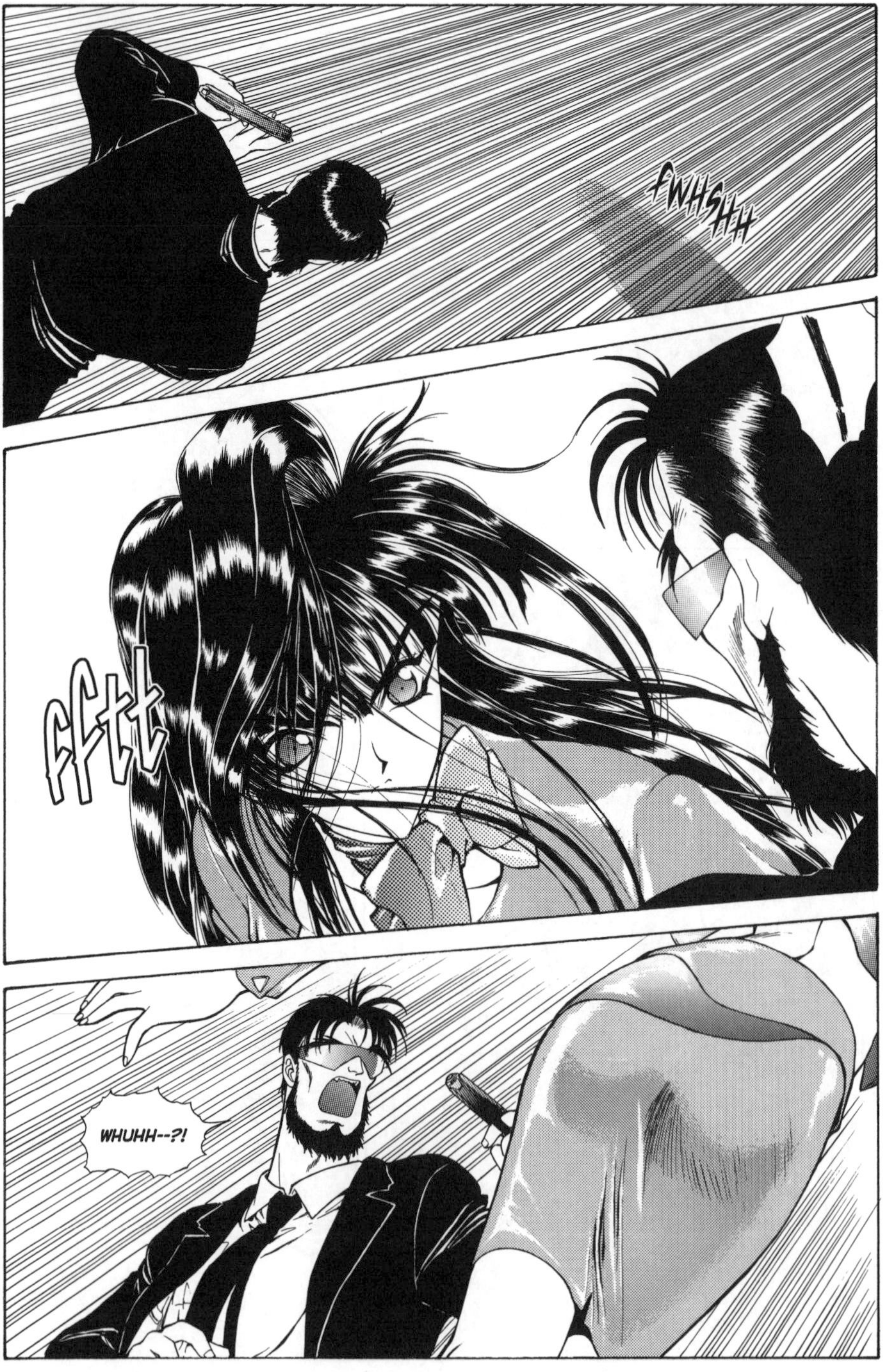
FWHSHH
FFTT
WHUHH--?!

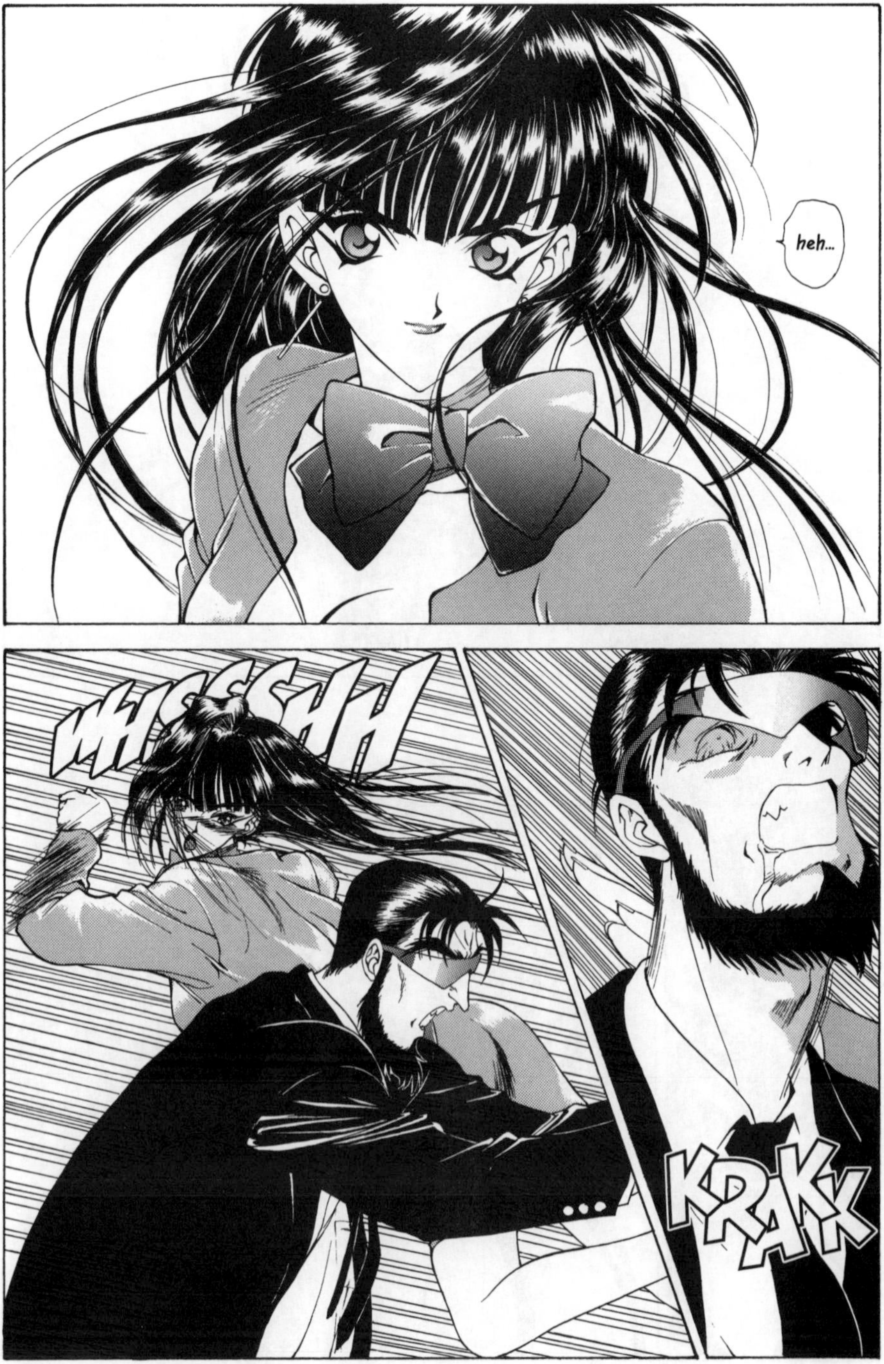
heh...
WHISSHH
KRAKK

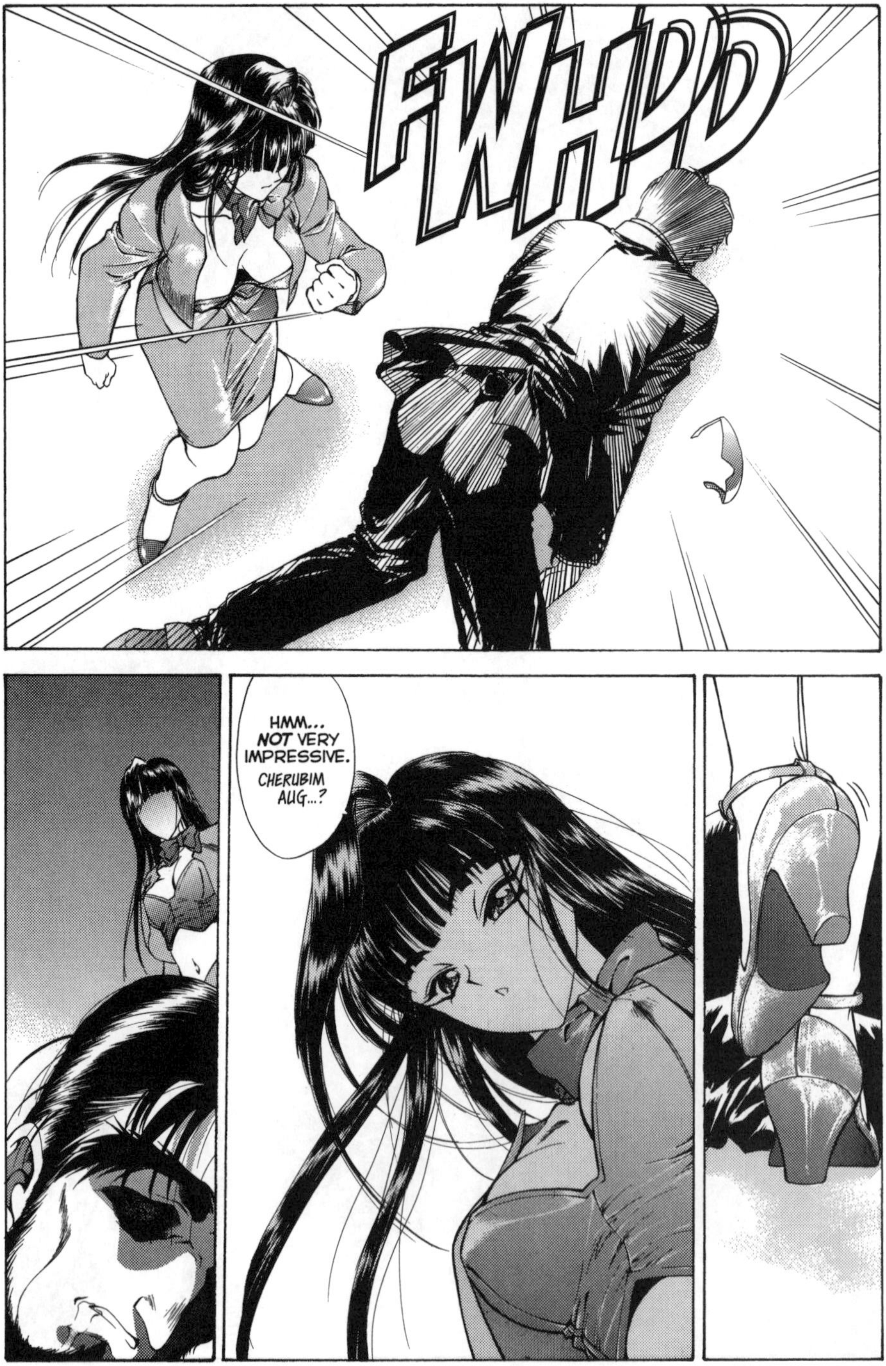
FWHDD
HMM... NOT VERY IMPRESSIVE.
CHERUBIM AUG...?

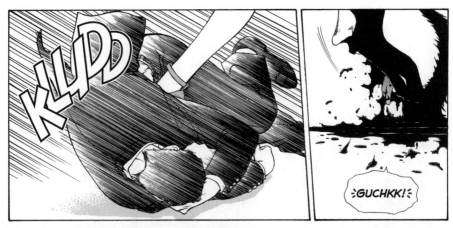

:GUCHKK!:

WHAT THE HELL HAPPENED...?

DID YOU SEE THAT?

THE POLICE! SOMEBODY CALL THE DAMN POLICE!

WHO... WHO WAS THAT...?

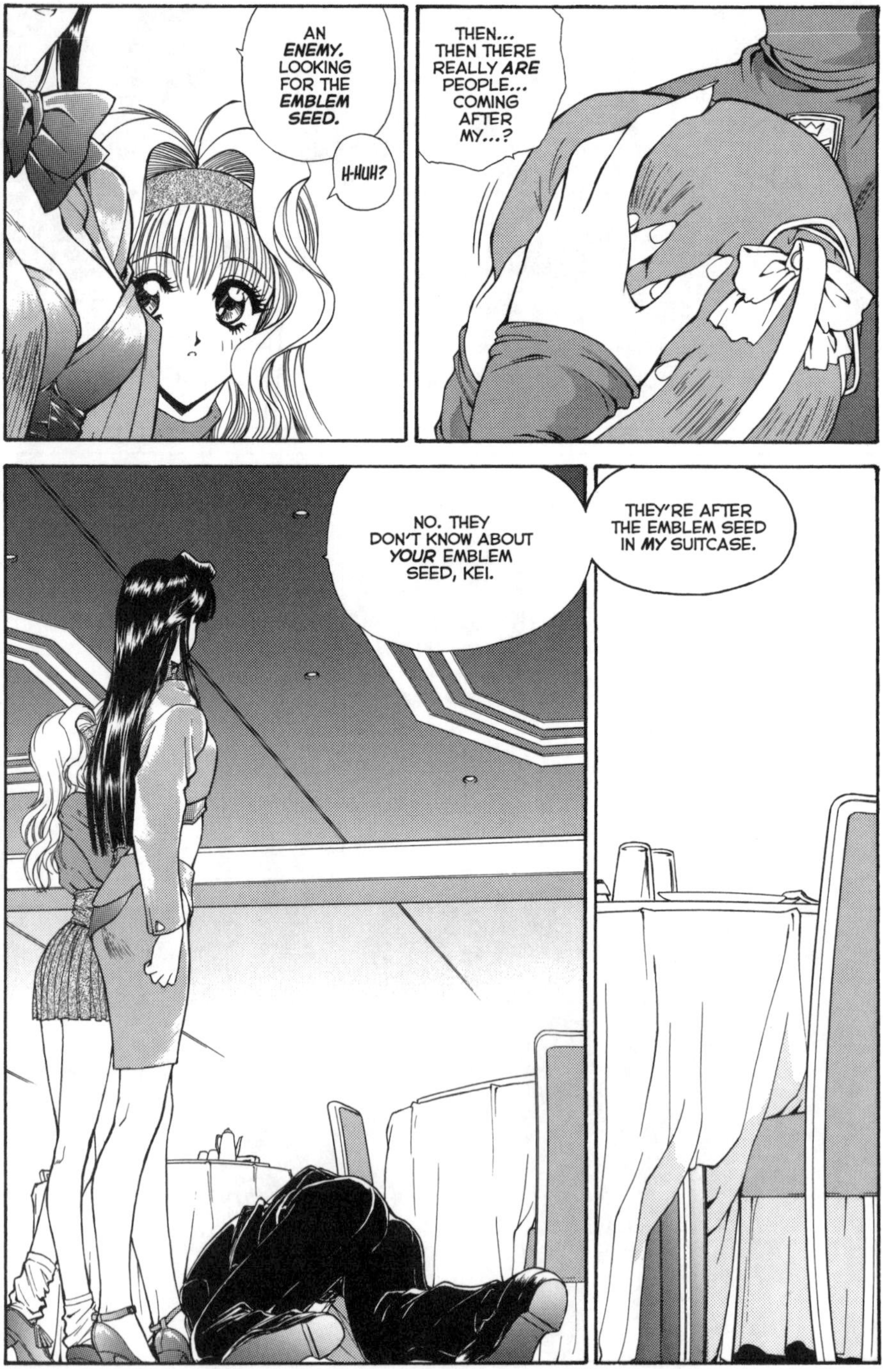
AN ENEMY. LOOKING FOR THE EMBLEM SEED.
H-HUH?
THEN... THEN THERE REALLY ARE PEOPLE... COMING AFTER MY...?
NO. THEY DON'T KNOW ABOUT YOUR EMBLEM SEED, KEI.
THEY'RE AFTER THE EMBLEM SEED IN MY SUITCASE.

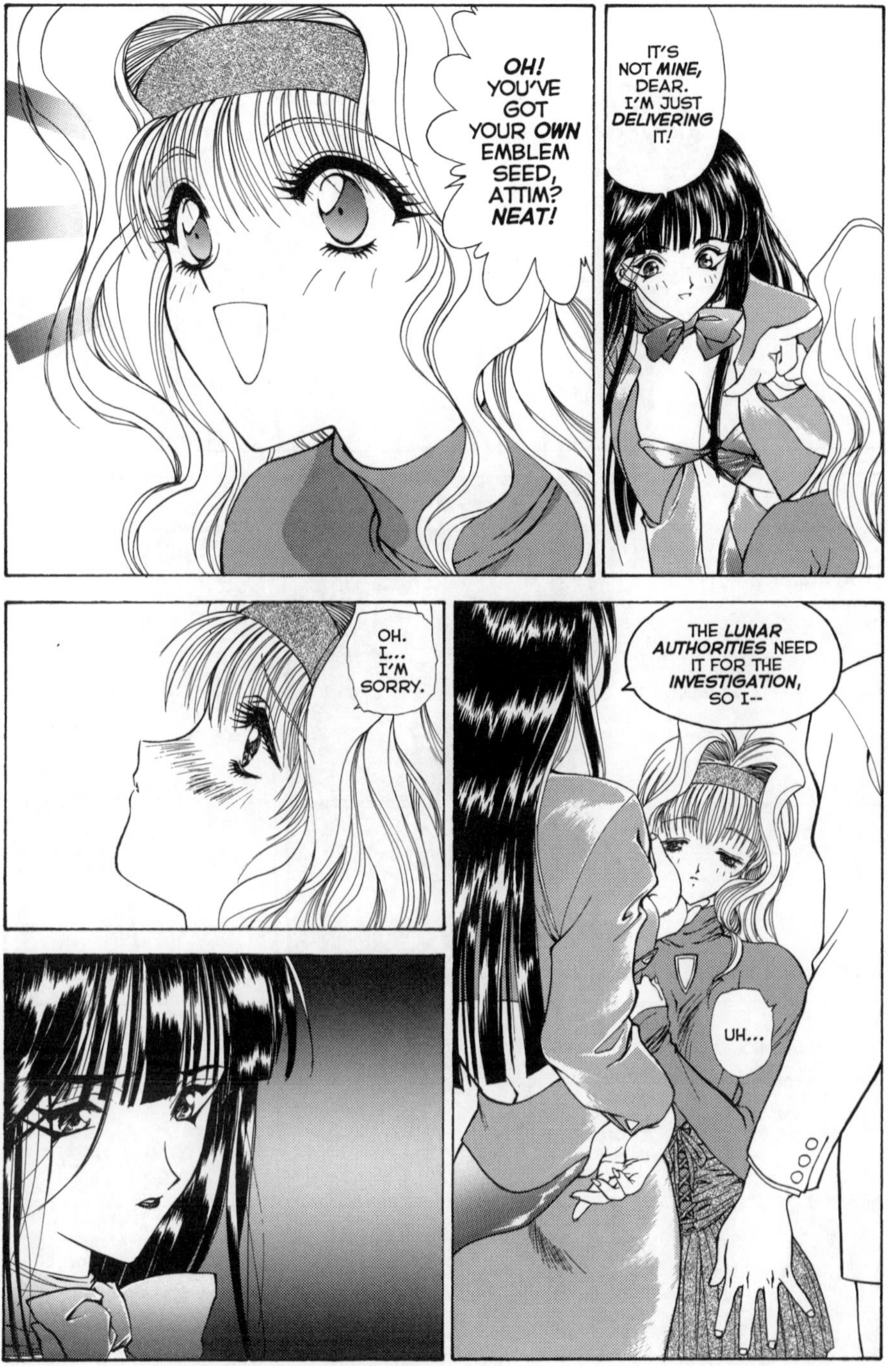
OH! YOU'VE GOT YOUR OWN EMBLEM SEED, ATTIM? NEAT!
IT'S NOT MINE, DEAR. I'M JUST DELIVERING IT!
OH. I... I'M SORRY.
THE LUNAR AUTHORITIES NEED IT FOR THE INVESTIGATION, SO I--
UH...

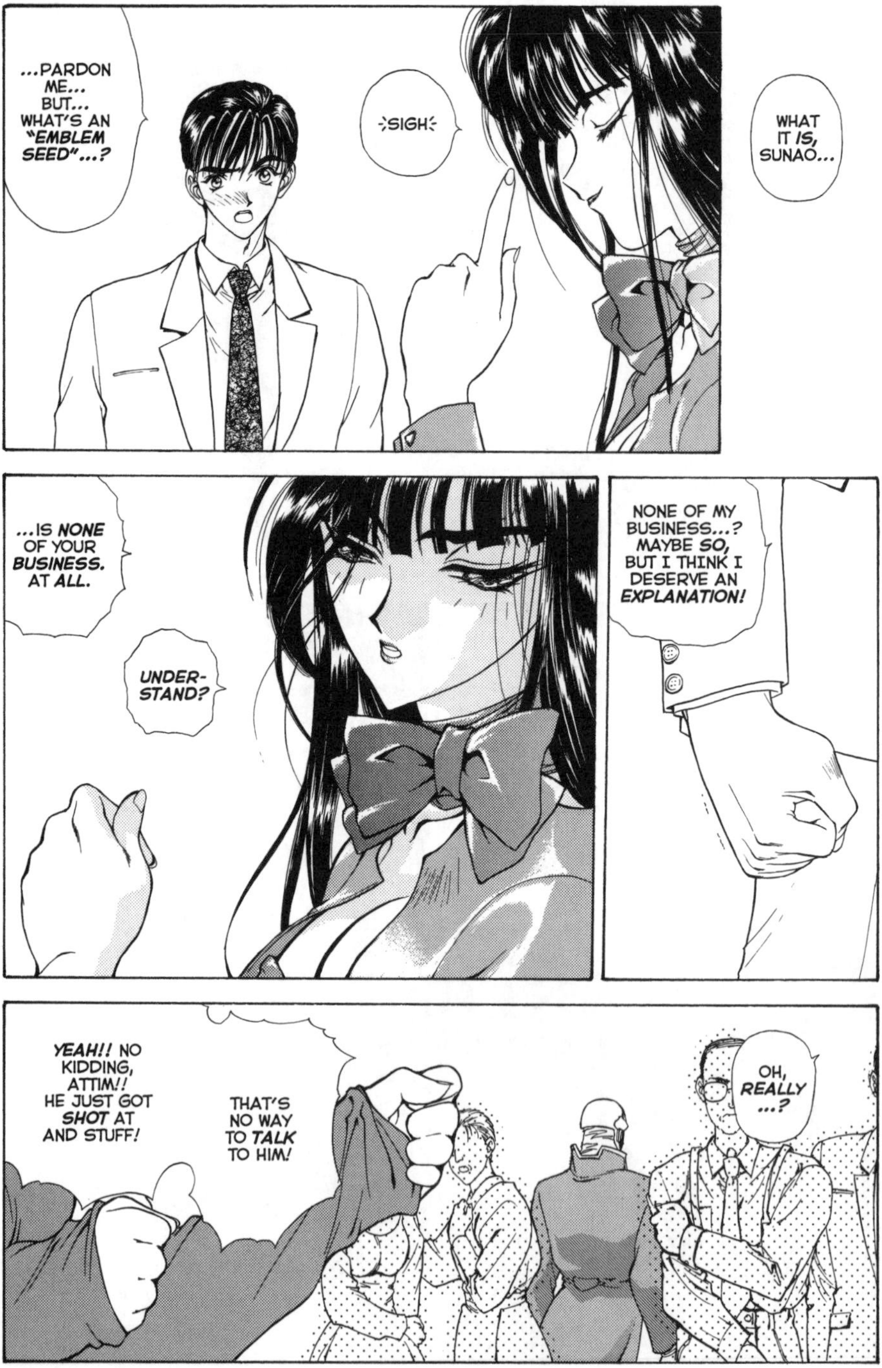
...PARDON ME... BUT... WHAT'S AN "EMBLEM SEED"...?
-SIGH-
WHAT IT IS, SUNAO...
...IS NONE OF YOUR BUSINESS. AT ALL.
UNDERSTAND?
NONE OF MY BUSINESS...? MAYBE SO, BUT I THINK I DESERVE AN EXPLANATION!
YEAH!! NO KIDDING, ATTIM!! HE JUST GOT SHOT AT AND STUFF!
THAT'S NO WAY TO TALK TO HIM!
OH, REALLY ...?

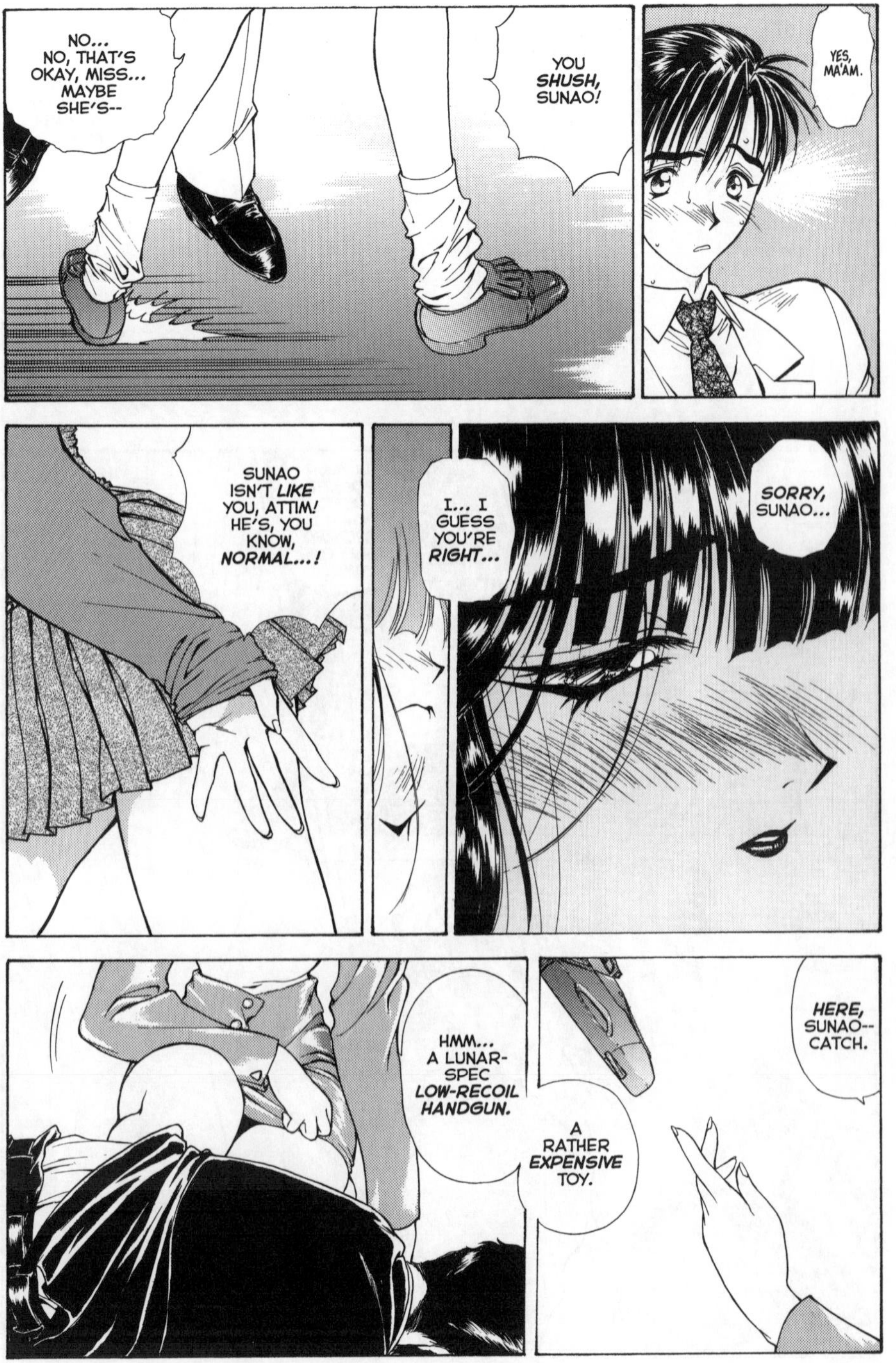
NO... NO, THAT'S OKAY, MISS... MAYBE SHE'S--
YOU SHUSH, SUNAO!
YES, MA'AM.
SUNAO ISN'T LIKE YOU, ATTIM! HE'S, YOU KNOW, NORMAL...!
I... I GUESS YOU'RE RIGHT...
SORRY, SUNAO...
HMM... A LUNAR-SPEC LOW-RECOIL HANDGUN.
A RATHER EXPENSIVE TOY.
HERE, SUNAO-- CATCH.

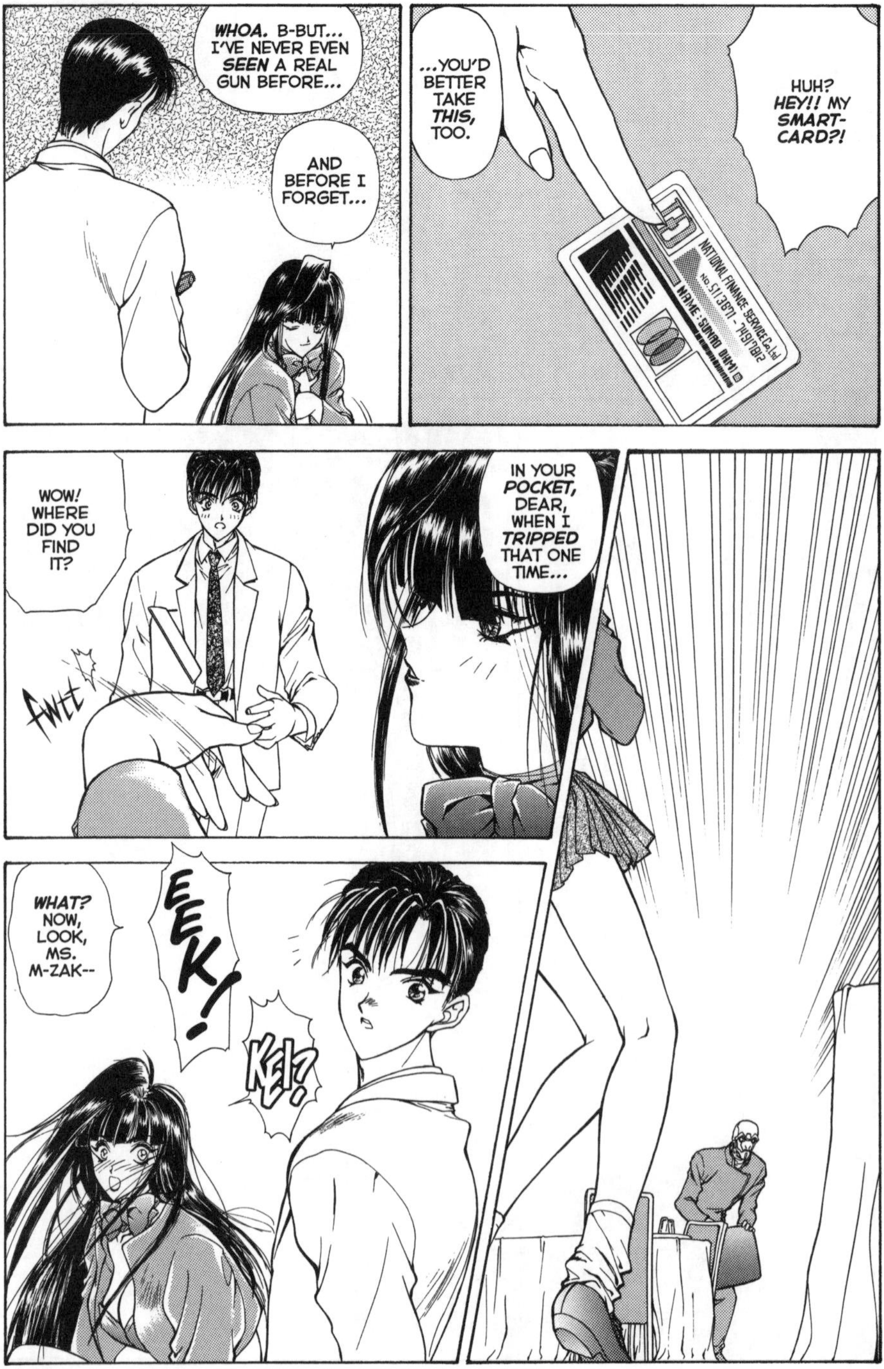
WHOA. B-BUT... I'VE NEVER EVEN SEEN A REAL GUN BEFORE...
AND BEFORE I FORGET...
...YOU'D BETTER TAKE THIS, TOO.
NATIONAL FINANCE SERVICE Co.,Ltd
HUH? HEY!! MY SMART-CARD?!
WOW! WHERE DID YOU FIND IT?
FWIT
IN YOUR POCKET, DEAR, WHEN I TRIPPED THAT ONE TIME...
WHAT? NOW, LOOK, MS. M-ZAK--
EEK!
KEI?!

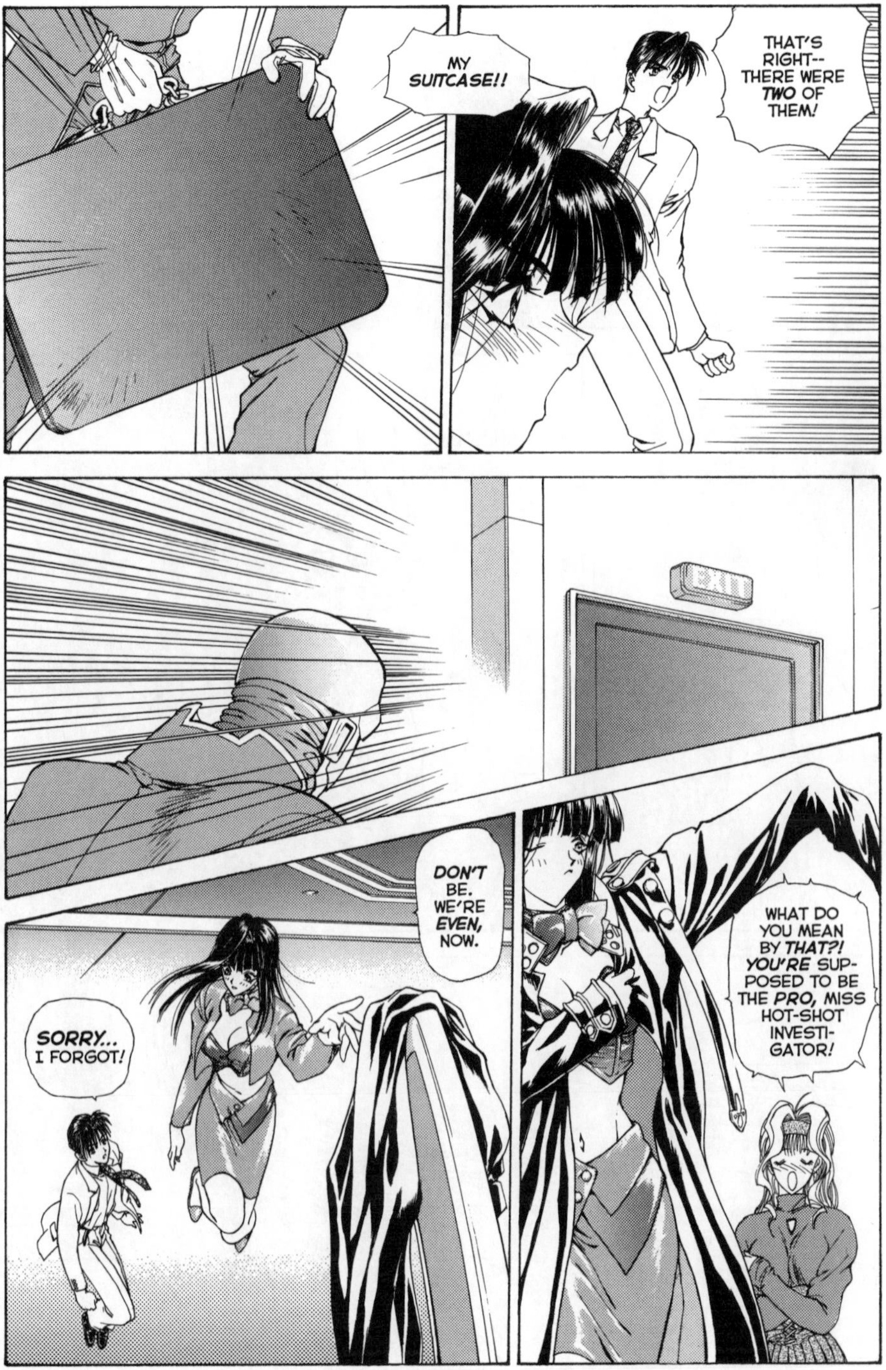
MY SUITCASE!!
THAT'S RIGHT--THERE WERE TWO OF THEM!
EXIT
SORRY... I FORGOT!
DON'T BE. WE'RE EVEN, NOW.
WHAT DO YOU MEAN BY THAT?! YOU'RE SUPPOSED TO BE THE PRO, MISS HOT-SHOT INVESTIGATOR!

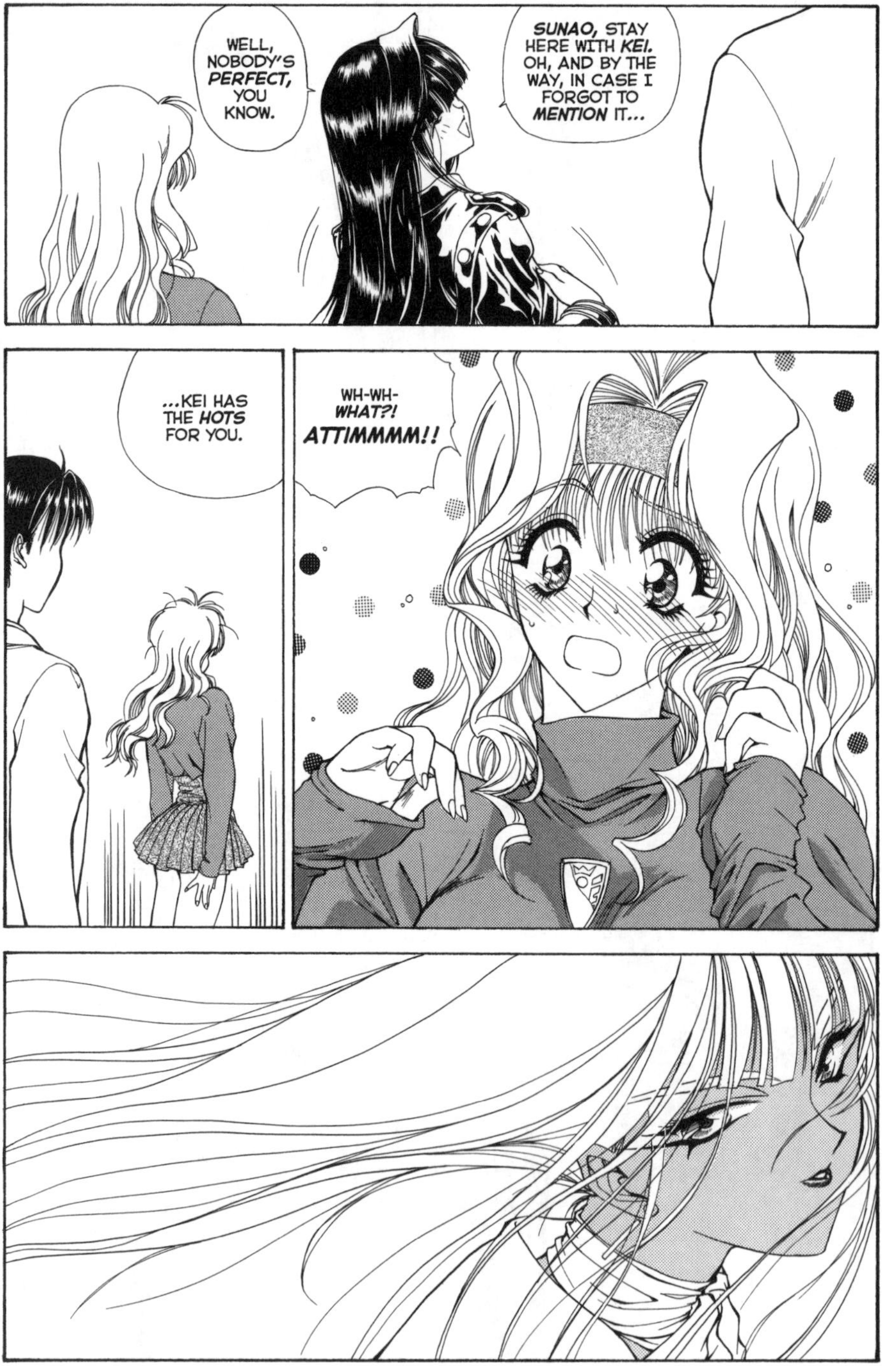
WELL, NOBODY'S PERFECT, YOU KNOW.
SUNAO, STAY HERE WITH KEI. OH, AND BY THE WAY, IN CASE I FORGOT TO MENTION IT...
...KEI HAS THE HOTS FOR YOU.
WH-WH-WHAT?! ATTIMMMM!!

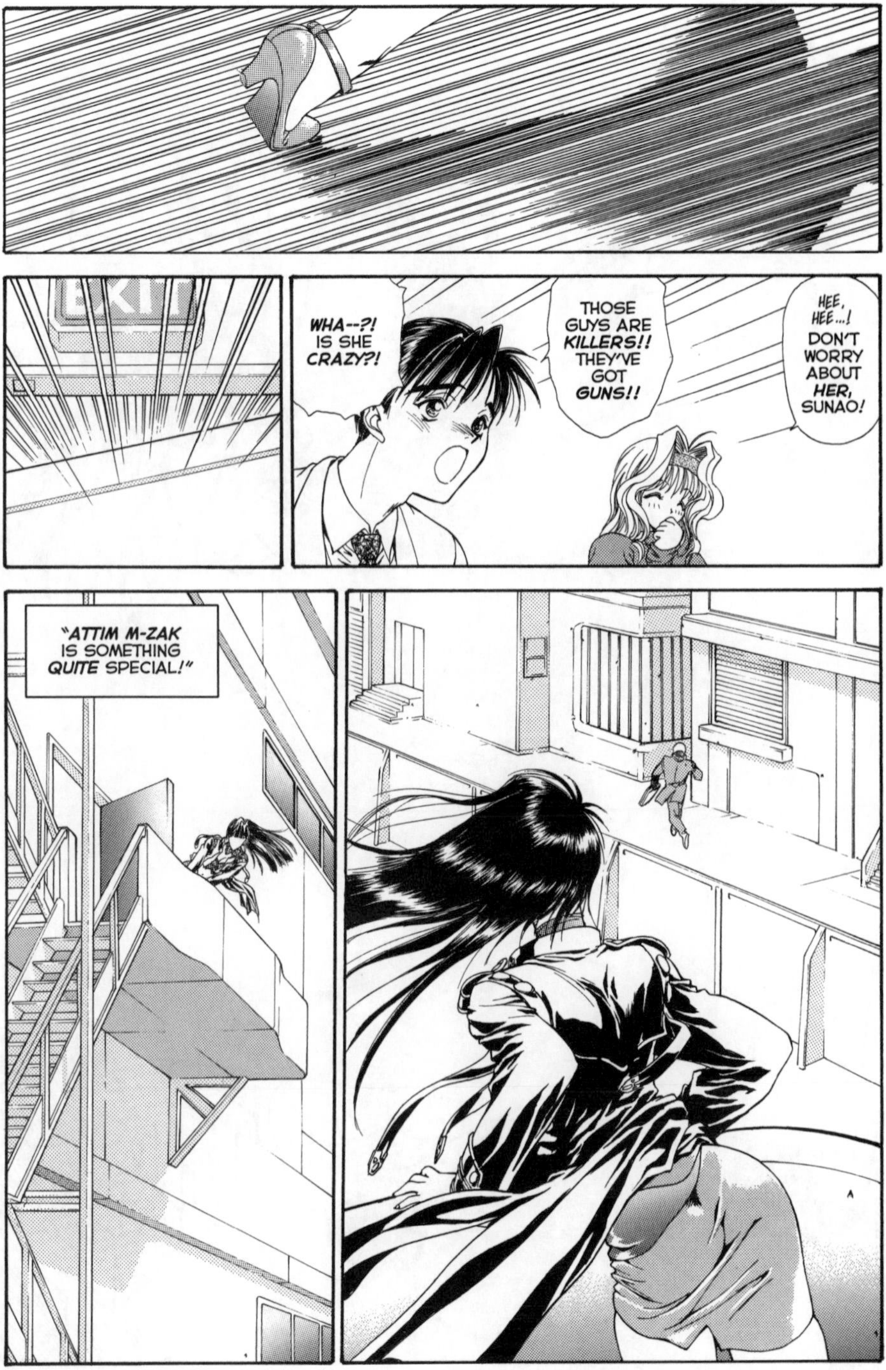

WHA--?! IS SHE CRAZY?!
THOSE GUYS ARE KILLERS!! THEY'VE GOT GUNS!!
HEE, HEE...! DON'T WORRY ABOUT HER, SUNAO!
"ATTIM M-ZAK IS SOMETHING QUITE SPECIAL!"

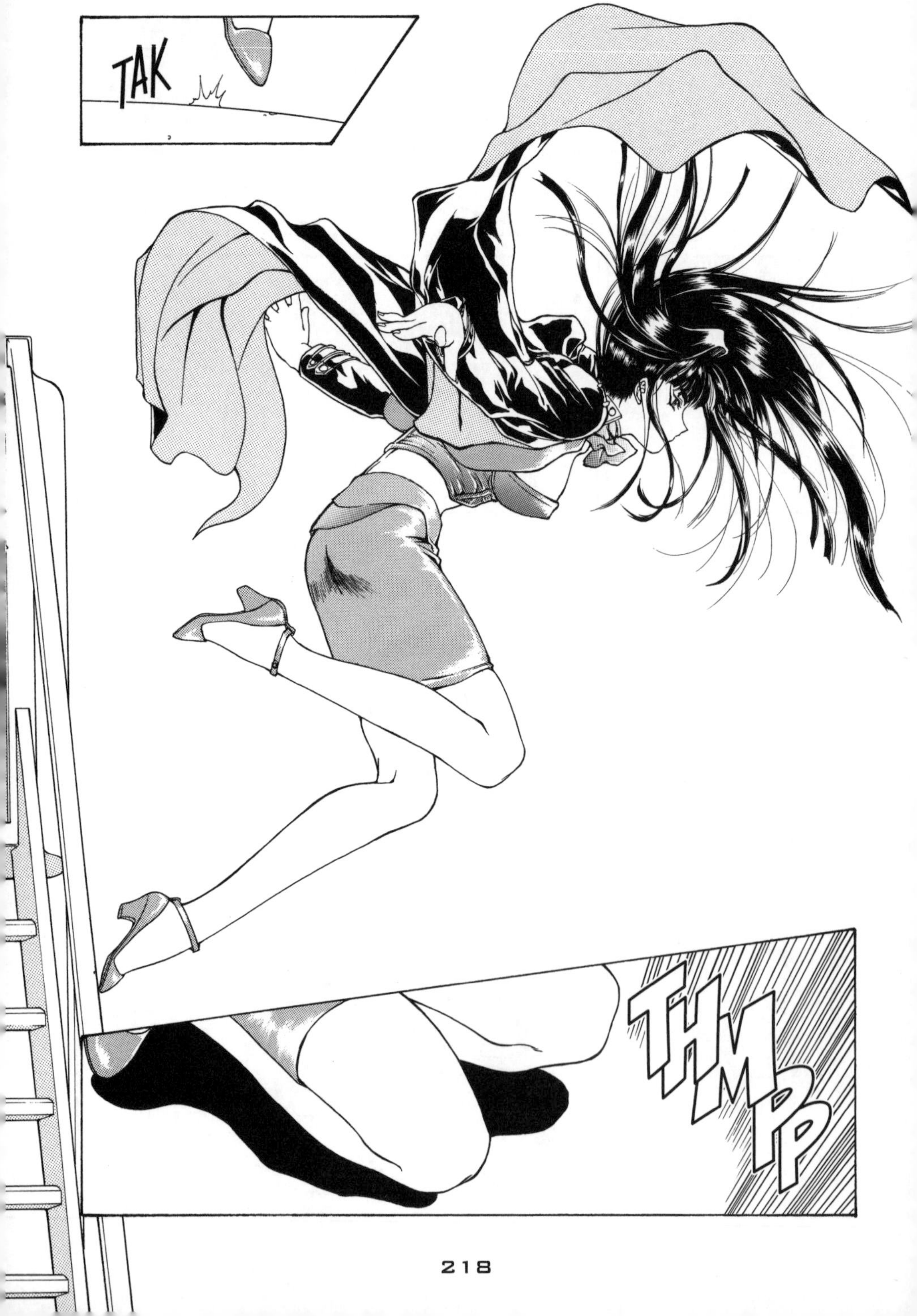
TAK
THMPP

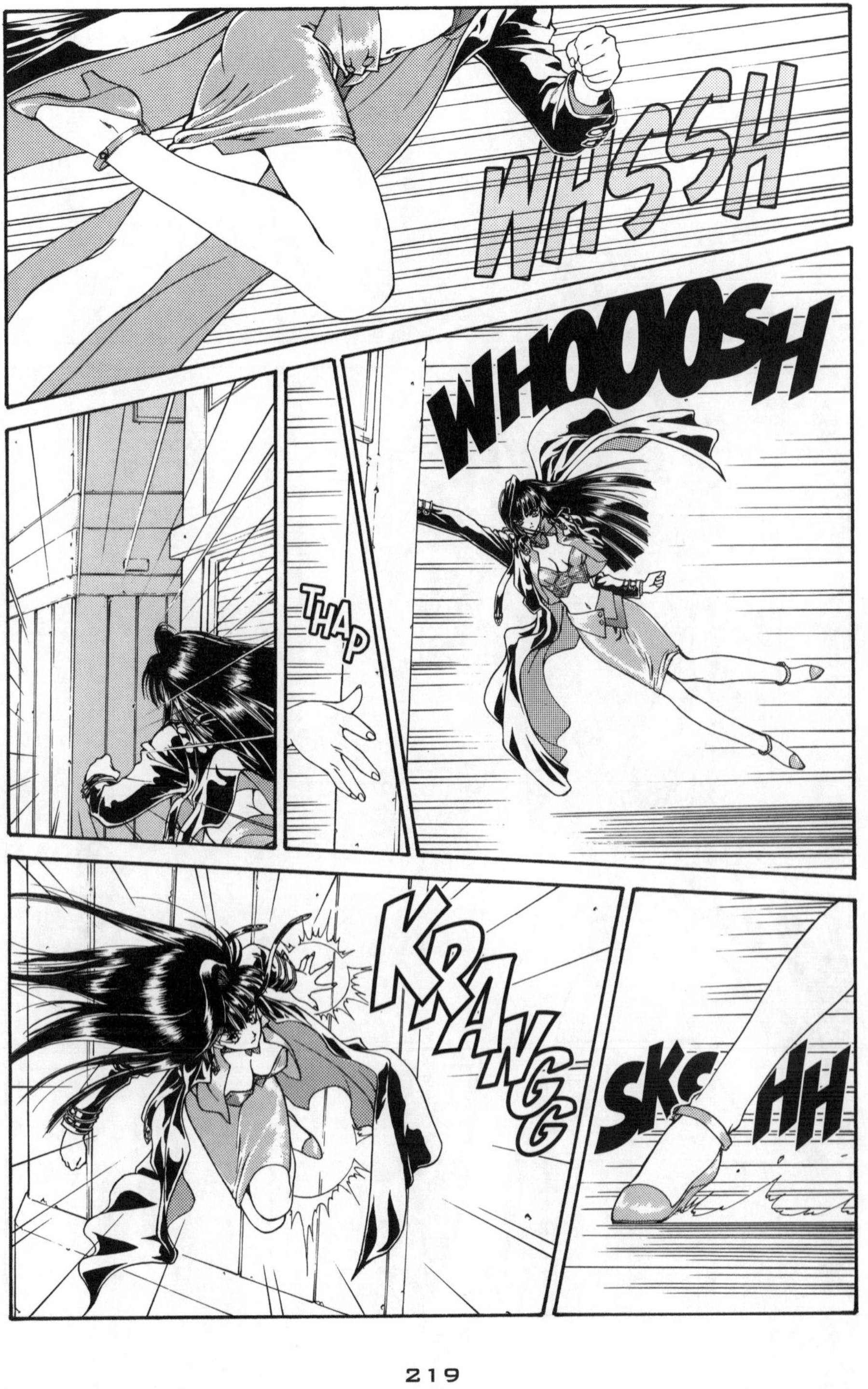
WHSSH
THAP
WHOOOSH
KRANGG
SKSHH

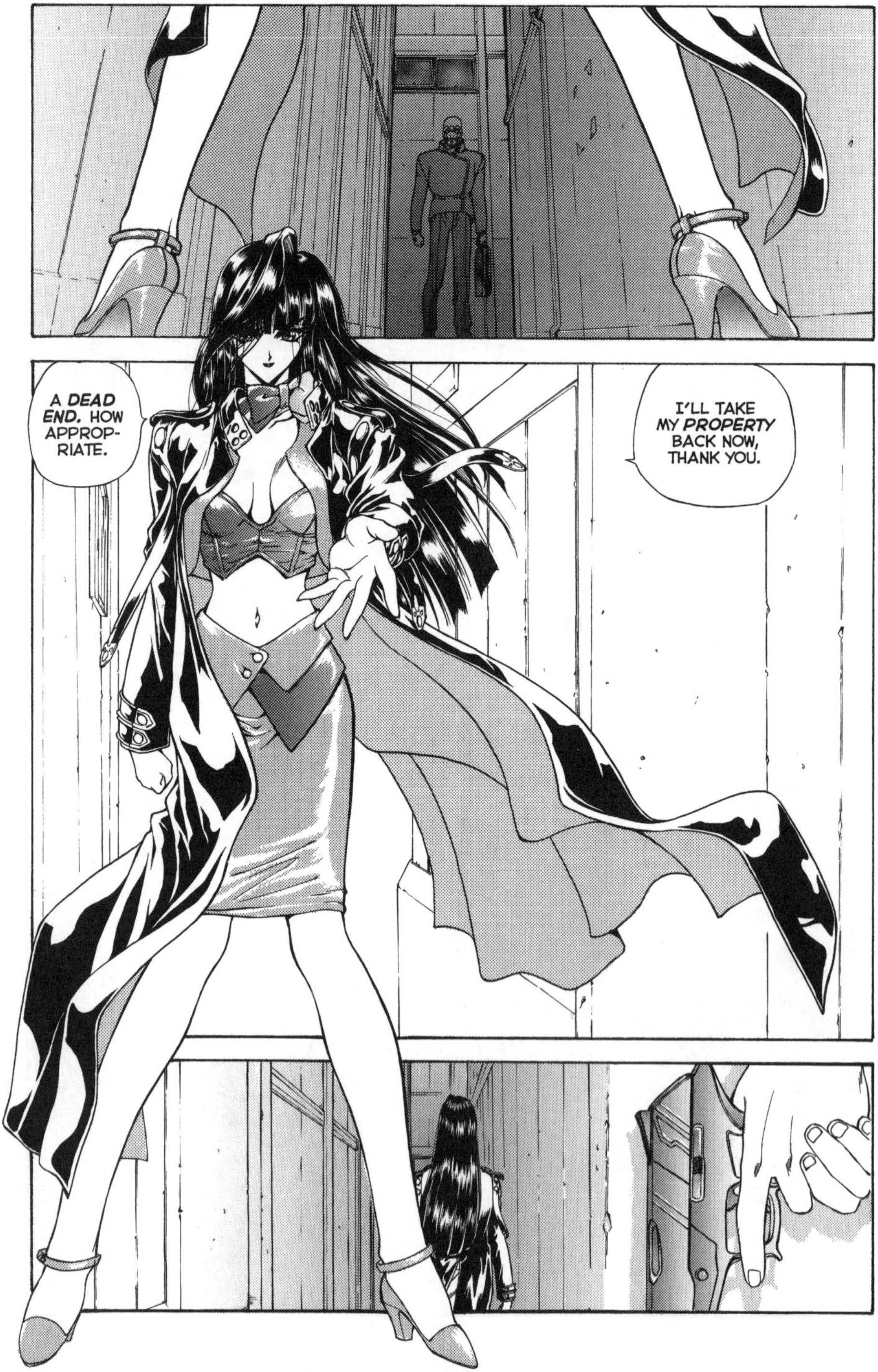
A DEAD END. HOW APPROPRIATE.
I'LL TAKE MY PROPERTY BACK NOW, THANK YOU.

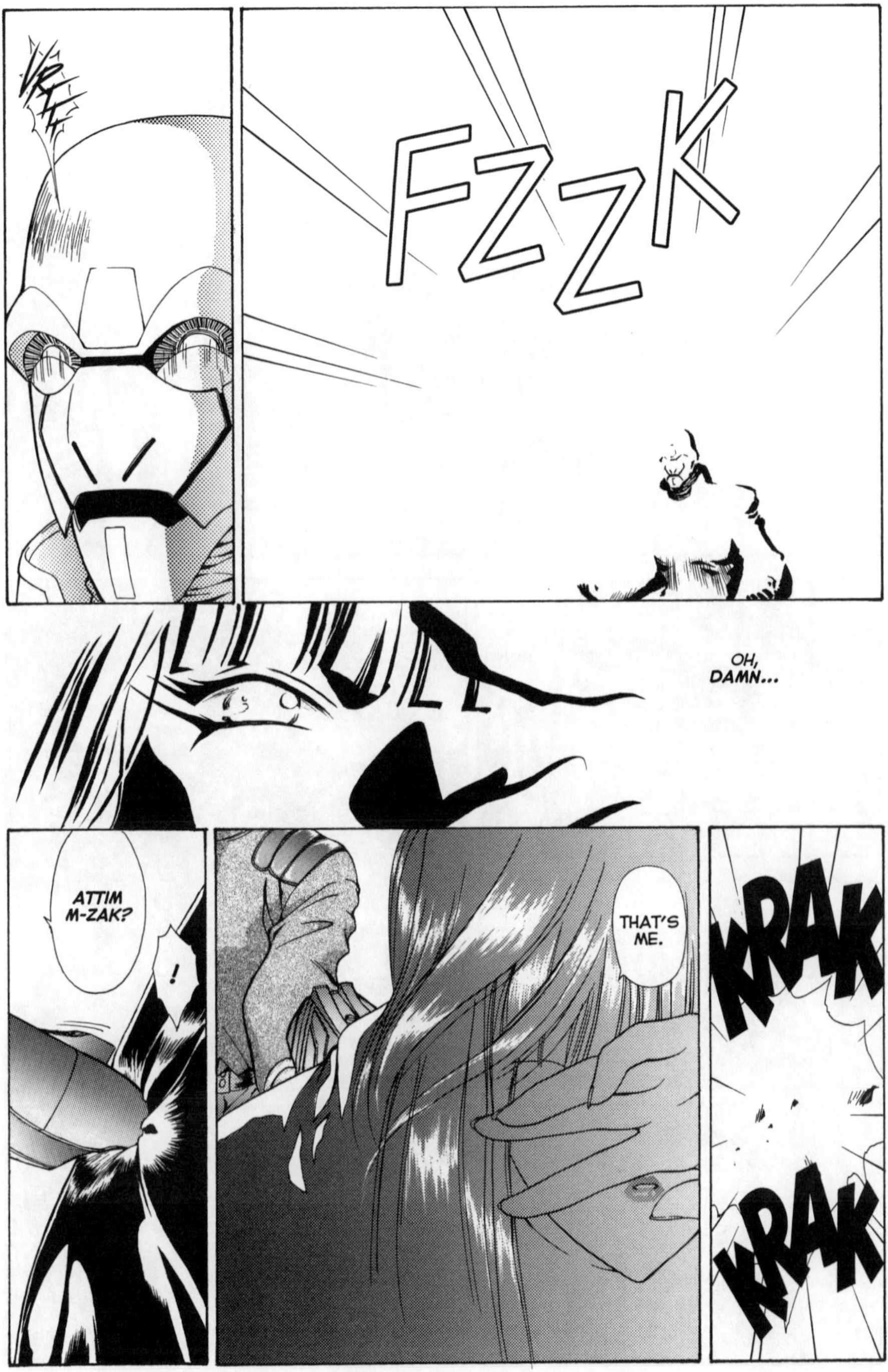
FZZK
OH, DAMN...
ATTIM M-ZAK?
!
THAT'S ME.
KRAK
KRAK

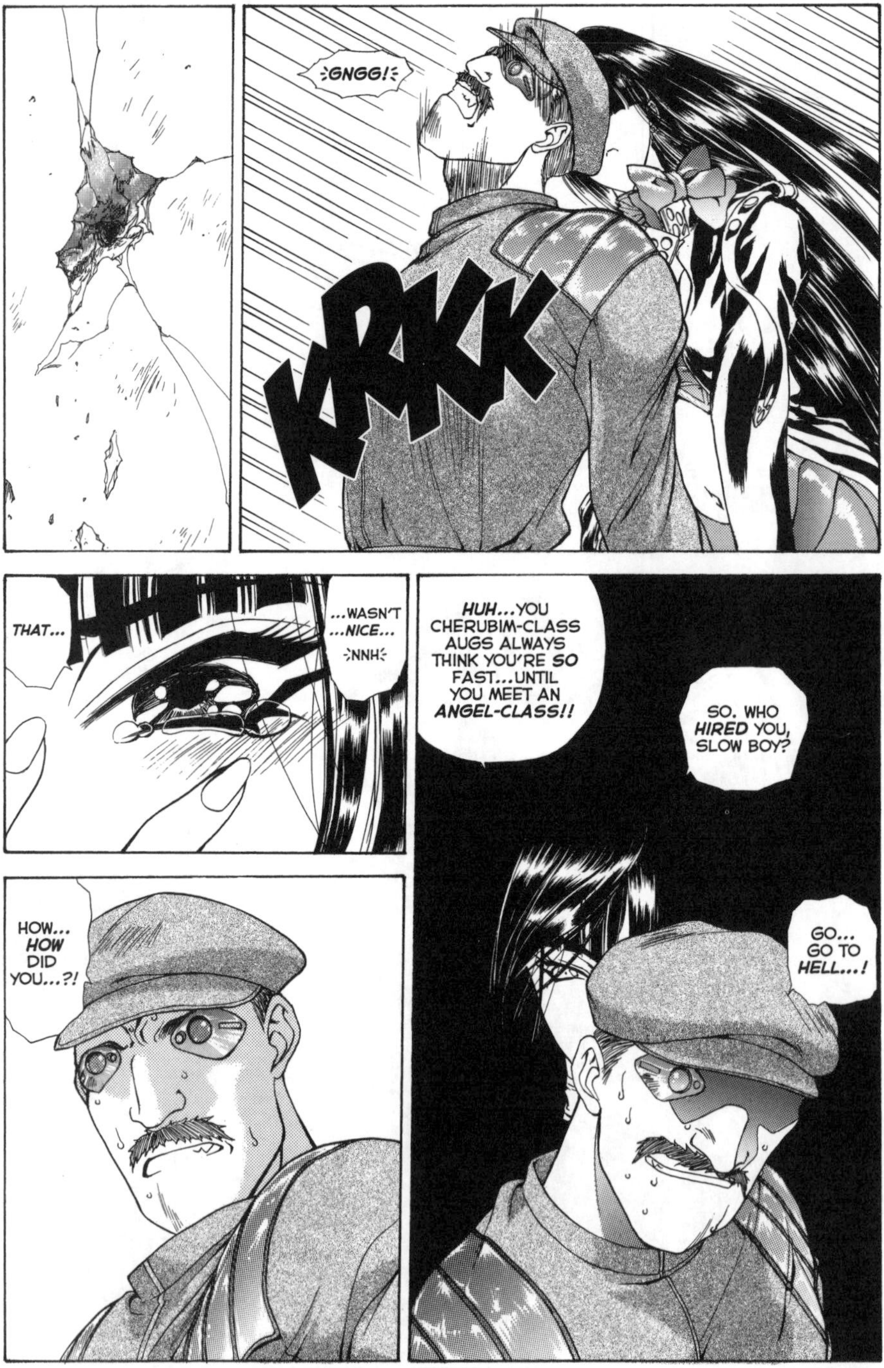
GNGG!
KRKK
THAT...
...WASN'T ...NICE...
NNH
HOW... HOW DID YOU...?!
HUH...YOU CHERUBIM-CLASS AUGS ALWAYS THINK YOU'RE SO FAST...UNTIL YOU MEET AN ANGEL-CLASS!!
SO. WHO HIRED YOU, SLOW BOY?
GO... GO TO HELL...!

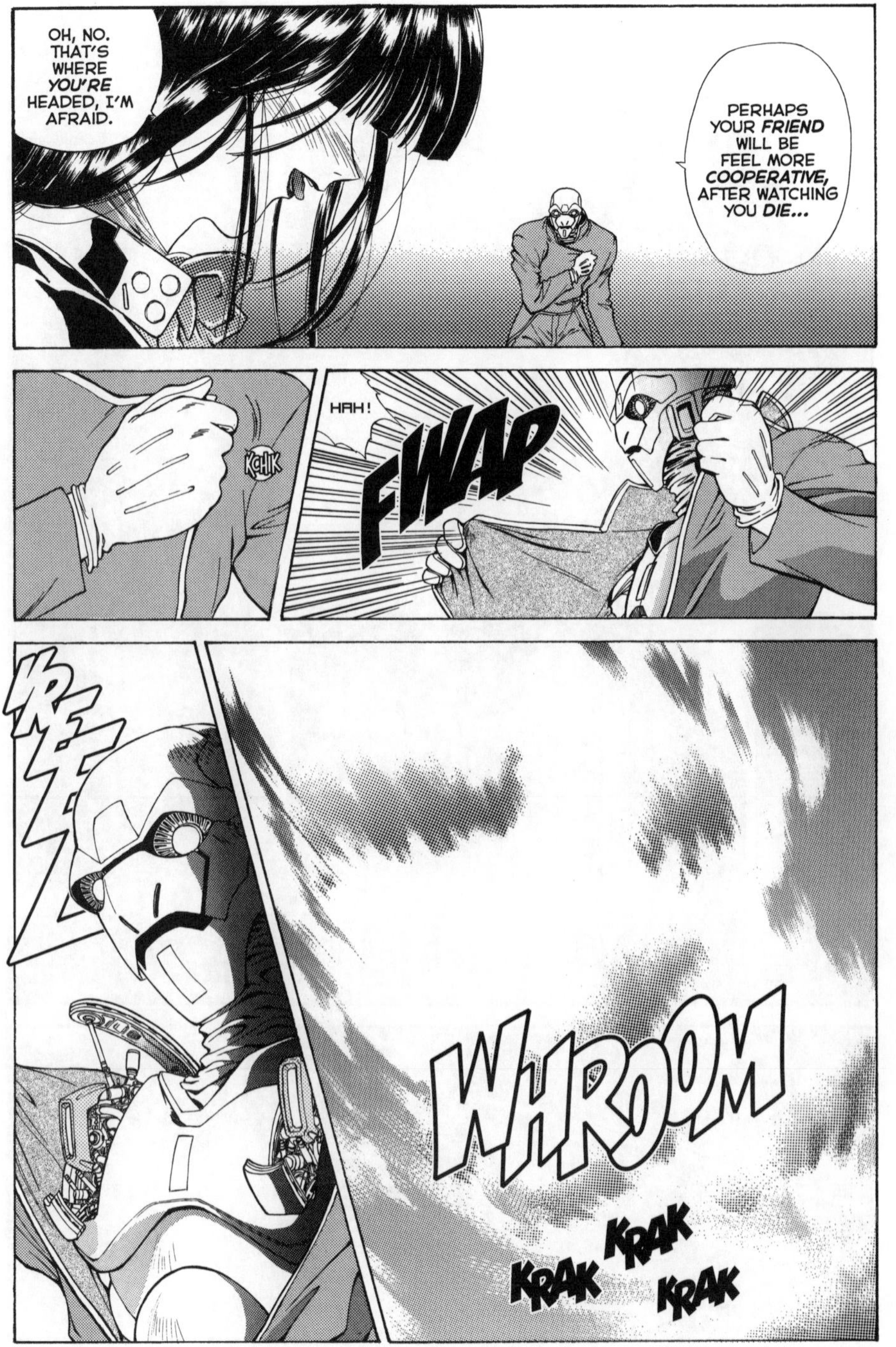
OH, NO. THAT'S WHERE YOU'RE HEADED, I'M AFRAID.
PERHAPS YOUR FRIEND WILL BE FEEL MORE COOPERATIVE, AFTER WATCHING YOU DIE...
KCHIK
HAH!
FWAP
WHROOM
KRAK
KRAK
KRAK

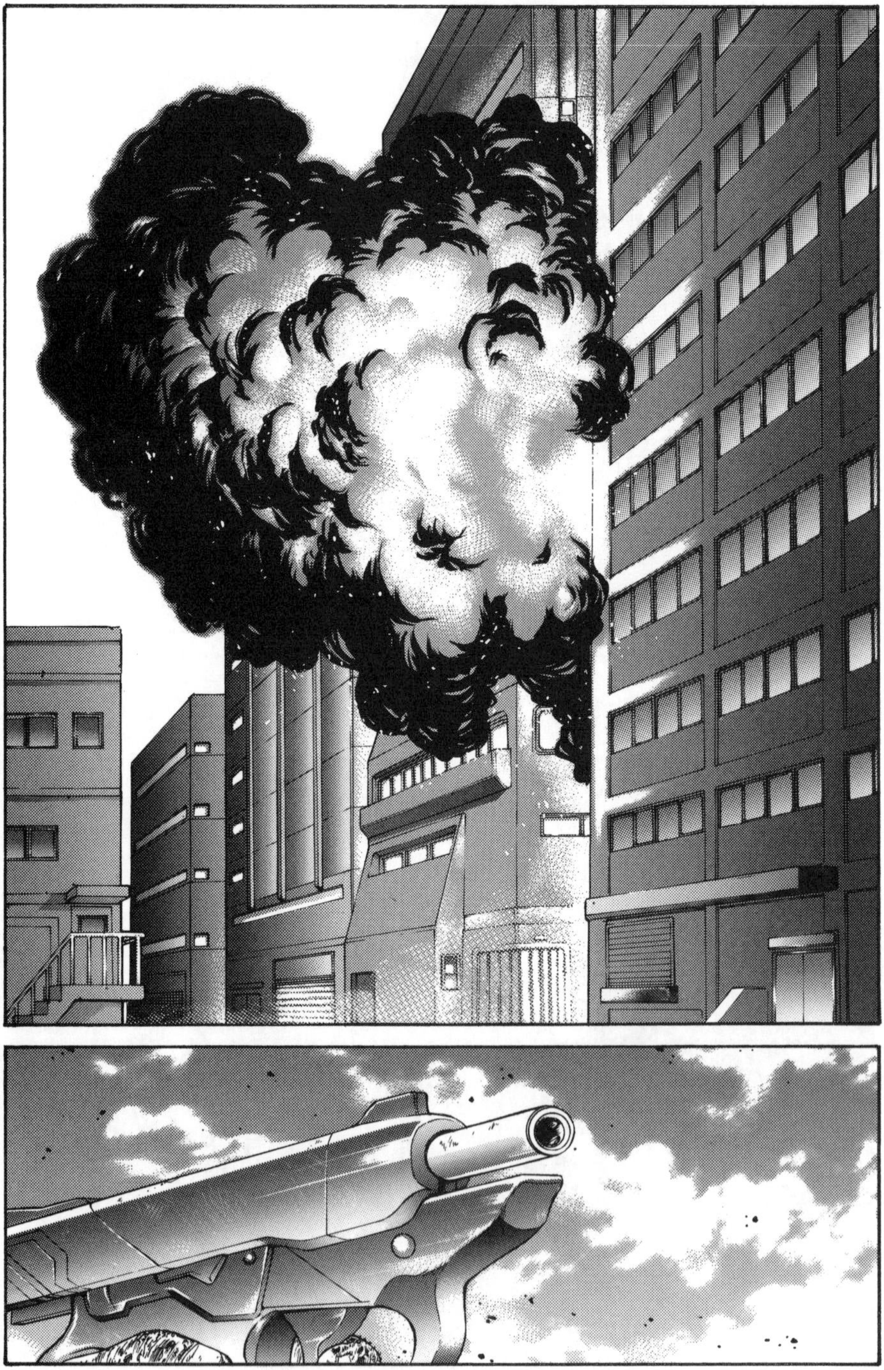

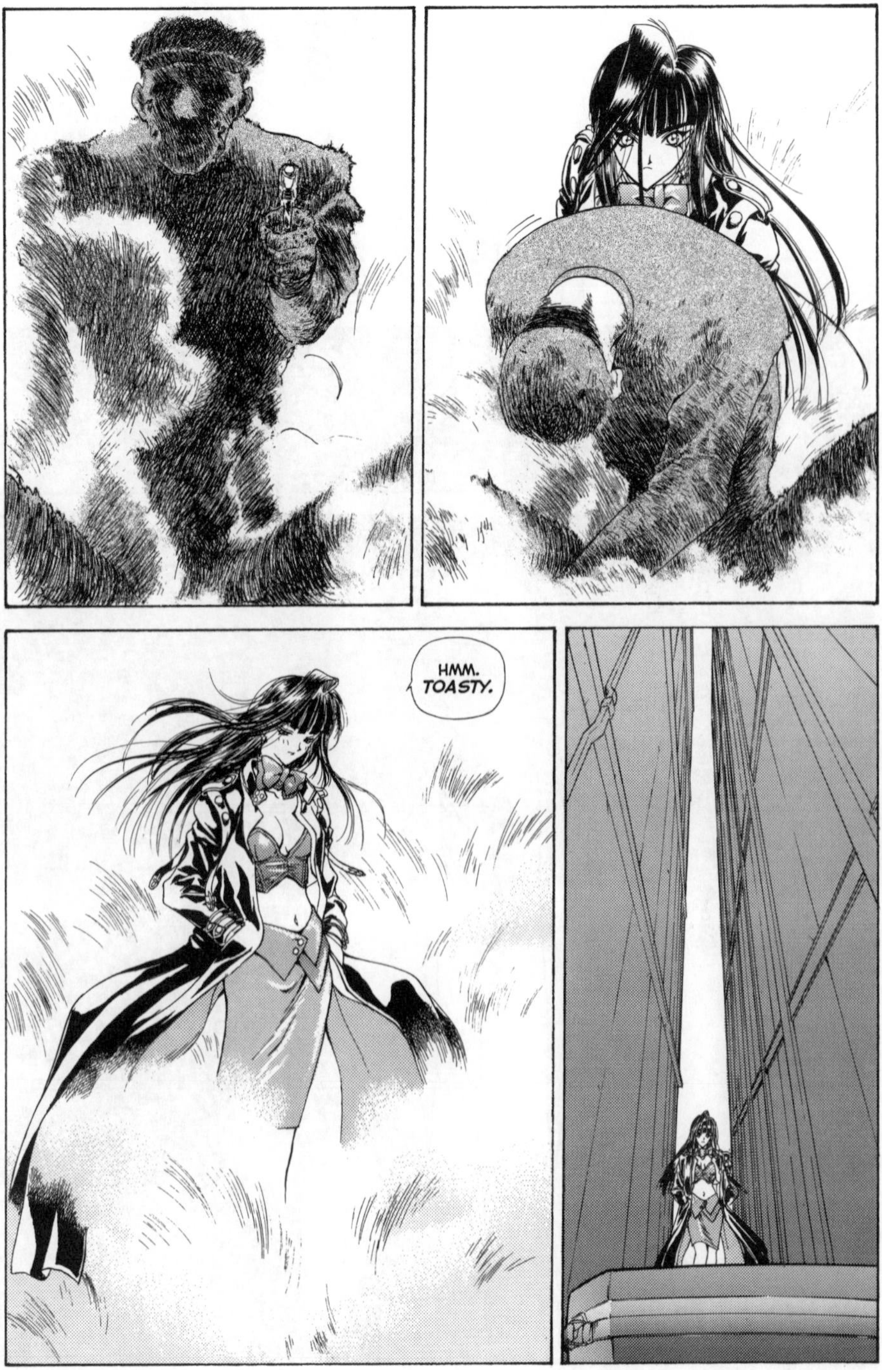
HMM.
TOASTY.

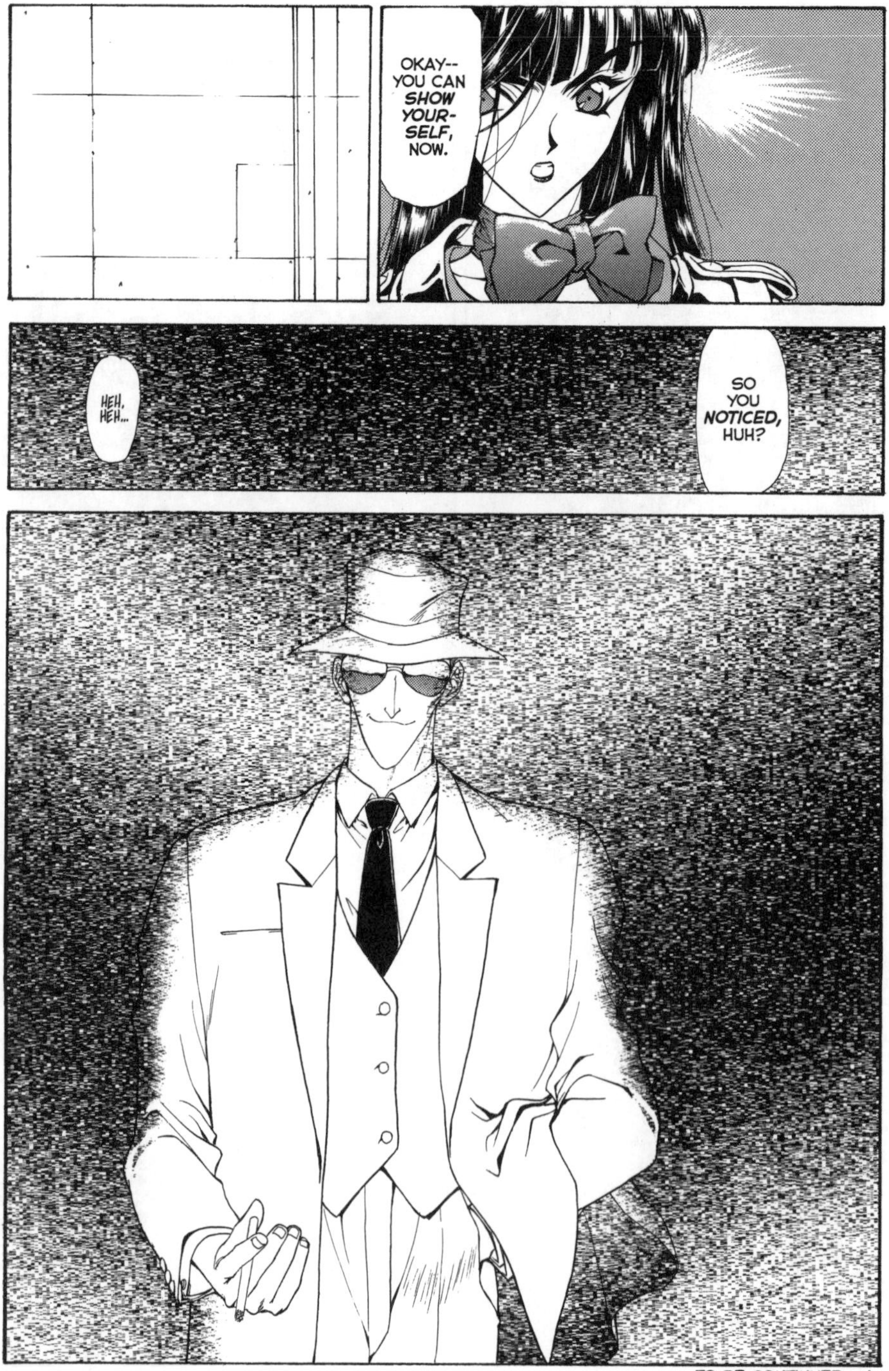
OKAY-- YOU CAN **SHOW** **YOUR-SELF**, NOW.
HEH, HEH...
SO YOU **NOTICED**, HUH?

TO BE CONTINUED...!

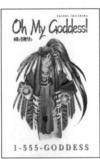

Gunsmith Cats

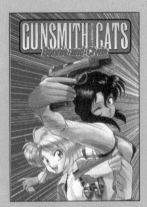